Theory of Class Actions

Theory of Class Actions

by

Craig Jones

THEORY OF CLASS ACTIONS
© Irwin Law Inc., 2003

Published in 2003 by
Irwin Law Inc.
347 Bay St.
Suite 501
Toronto, ON
M5H 2R7
ISBN: 1-55221-080-4

National Library of Canada Cataloguing in Publication Data
Jones, Craig E. (Craig Elton), 1965-
    Theory of class actions : optimal aggregation in mass tort litigation / Craig Jones.

Includes index.
ISBN 1-55221-080-4

    1. Class actions (Civil procedure).   2. Torts.   I. Title.

K2243.J65 2002   346.03   C2002-904747-1

The publisher acknowledges the financial support of the Government of Canada through the Book Publishing Industry Development Program (BPIDP) for our publishing activities.

Printed and bound in Canada
1   2   3   4   5   07   06   05   04   03

For S.M.W.
who made me think . . .

Summary Table of Contents

Table of Contents

Part III
National Classes In Canada

Foreword

Mass torts, and the use of the class action to adjudicate them, confront common and civil law systems with some of the most pressing questions of public policy and institutional structure. In this book, Craig Jones develops a general theory that explains and justifies aggregate resolution of claims arising from a mass tort event. He then applies the theory, showing that a broader reliance on class action coheres with the legal norms and practice of Canada. His analysis, findings, and proposals will advance thinking on mass tort class actions worldwide.

The book breaks new ground both in substance and methodology. Jones comprehensively integrates perspectives from tort and procedure, which marks a fruitful departure from the conventional "proceduralist" focus. He resolutely employs the functional approach: this is the scientific method of specifying and defending the social objectives that the law should pursue, designing models of rules and systems to achieve these goals, and testing for the best among competing designs by evaluating their relative empirical effects on relevant behavior and on the interests of individuals and institutions.

If I may take the liberty of quick characterisation, Jones's theory posits that the means of production dictates the means of justice. In particular, the means of mass-producing primary goods — products and services — requires use of the same collective means to provide the secondary goods — tort deterrence and compensation. This thesis is not deterministic or essentialist, but rather strictly a hypothesis of rational choice. Individuals seeking maximum well-being in a world of scarce resources and accident risk, logically and as revealed by overwhelming evidence of their actual choices, prefer that the law adjudicate mass torts by collective means: in practical terms, by class action.

The reason is that resolving mass tort claims on a disaggregated basis not only would jeopardise the secondary goods of tort deterrence and compensation, but also by distorting incentives and costs, would devalue the primary goods of products and services. Production of both types of goods demands collective action because, in essence, the whole is greater than the sum of its parts. This point goes well beyond the joint interest in securing scale economies by fabricating and marketing products and services from standardised designs, and the class action analog, by adjudicating mass tort claims based on common questions of liability and damages. Indeed, the major, generally overlooked solidarity of interest relates to raising the quality of these goods. The higher and more concentrated the aggregate return for a producer — the firm providing products and services; the lawyer providing tort deterrence and compensation — the higher and more concentrated the producer's aggregate investment in better quality as well as in greater quantity. In Jones's model, individuals benefit from more useful and safer products and services (and given risk aversion, from more effective tort insurance) when the law promotes class action than when it allows — let alone encourages — any degree of separate action. Jones fully and lucidly elaborates the basic ideas and implications — theoretical as well as practical.

The reader should not discount these innovative insights as too remote from the thinking of real world lawmakers. It is apparent in the United States, for instance, that the more or less intuited understanding of the collectivity of interest in mass production goods animated judicial adaptation of tort law in the direction of collectivisation. The trend is evident from the advent of the Industrial Revolution and, as Holmes observed, the rise of systematic, generalised "injuries to person or property by railroads, factories, and the like."[1] These conditions prompted courts, as Holmes explained and supported,[2] to replace costly and personalised negligence rules with the more aggregative and probabilistic norms and processes of strict liability either indirectly by adopting external, risk-proportioned and presumptive standards for negligence or outright by adopting "strict" standards for extra-hazardous activities. In eliminating the privity of contract limitation on negligence claims that greatly enhanced the effective scope of joint and several liability, Cardozo relied on the necessities of mass production that lodge with manufacturers nearly exclusive expertise and opportunity to discover and prevent product risks.[3] Recognition of these necessities, especially after Traynor's comprehensive account,[4] propelled acceptance of strict products liability in the late twentieth century. Increasingly, awareness of the reciprocal relationship between mass production of products and services and of tort deterrence and compensation is prompting courts to determine causation and, more generally, liability and damages on explicit, scientifically reliable estimates of the probabilities.[5]

This book achieves a new intellectual plateau in our understanding of the nexus between the systems of production and justice. It reorients and advances the agenda for research and the terms of debate on mass tort class actions.

David Rosenberg

Harvard Law School
August, 2002

---

1. O.W. Holmes, "The Path of the Law" (1897), 10 Harv. L. Rev. 457 at 467, reprinted at (1997), 110 Harv. L. Rev. 992 at 999.

2. See David Rosenberg, *The Hidden Holmes: His Theory of Torts in History* (Cambridge, MA: Harvard University Press, 1995).

3. See *MacPherson* v. *Buick*, 217 N.Y. 382; 111 N.E. 1050 (1916).

4. See *Escola* v. *Coca-Cola Bottling Co. of Fresno*, 24 Cal.2d 453; 150 P.2d 436 (1944) (concurring).

5. See e.g. *Sindell* v. *Abbott Laboratories*, 163 Cal. Rptr. 132, 26 Cal.3d 588, 607 P.2d 924 (1980); *Fairchild* v. *Glenhaven Funeral Services* [2002] UKHL 22.

Author's Note

This book began as my master's thesis at Harvard Law School. My original proposal was quite modest; I hoped to pick my way through the various problems encountered by the "national", or "interprovincial", class action. As my work progressed, it became apparent that many of the questions with which I was struggling spoke more fundamentally to the way we approach the aggregation of claims generally. Increasing familiarity with the work done on class action theory in the United States led me to develop – as much for my own benefit as anything – the rational framework for class action system design I set out here.

It is therefore too late to deny that the ambition of this work is to provide a comprehensive theoretical basis for the class action, examining the idea of the class action from its conceptual underpinnings to its practical implementation. It is my hope that judges, litigators and academics in Canada and elsewhere might find it useful, if not as a guide then at least as a starting point for discussion in some of the more contentious areas of the field of complex litigation.

I was profoundly fortunate to have as my thesis supervisor David Rosenberg, whose work on mass tort theory over the past three decades forms the foundation for much of the analysis in this book. Professor Rosenberg's international reputation is such that he certainly didn't need to show such extraordinary patience as my project grew to nearly three times its initially expected length. I am honoured that he has agreed to provide the Foreword to this work.

My friend and colleague John Kleefeld reviewed my précis and from that point forward constantly passed along cases, snippets and ideas; this work has benefited greatly from our frequent conversations. Jamie Cassels introduced me to the problems of aggregation and probabilistic causation and has been a mentor and great friend since then.

I am also indebted to the partners, associates and staff of Bull, Housser & Tupper, my professional family since 1996, and to my friends and colleagues both in legal practice and academia, in particular Joe Arvay, John Dives, Howard Ehrlich, Tom Berger, Robin Elliot, Greg Lewis, Elliott Myers, Wes Pue, Talha Syed, and Dan Webster. Each contributed in some way to the eventual production of this book. Ward Branch and David Klein, two of Canada's most experienced class action counsel, have been generous with their time and candid with their thoughts. Ryan Dalziel assisted me in turning the original paper into this book's present format, and provided thoughtful suggestions and feedback on the content. Jeff Miller at Irwin Law showed enthusiasm for this book since the earliest days, and his support has sped the project along.

Apart from the very direct assistance of Professor Rosenberg, at Harvard I benefited from classes with the redoubtable Charles Fried, Detlev Vagts, Alan

Dershowitz, the late Stephen Jay Gould, and Harvey Cox. Steven Shavell graciously allowed me to sit in on his lectures, which clarified the economic analyses of tort law. Gail Hupper and Nancy Pinn of the Graduate Program went out of their way to support my work.

My parents, cheerfully (if ruthlessly) rational, questioning and exacting, struggled through early manuscripts, proofreading and offering immensely helpful suggestions for organisation and style. My brother Adam has set a standard of academic writing that is a continual source of inspiration and awe.

Above all, I am grateful to my wife Amanda, who walked the dogs, paid the mortgage, sold her convertible and drove a rusty mustard-yellow 1980 Volvo so I could afford to go off for my year at Harvard. I will need a lifetime to properly thank her.

A Note on Uniform Citation

While the Canadian and American rules for legal citation are similar, there are some differences. This book, while developed in the course of my studies in the United States, is designed principally for a Canadian readership, and therefore where citation practice diverges between the two countries, I have chosen the Canadian citation guidelines set out in the *Canadian Guide to Legal Citation* (3d ed.) (Toronto: Carswell, 1992) over the American authority, *The Bluebook: A Uniform System of Citation* (15th ed.) (Cambridge, MA: Harvard Law Review Association, 1991). In the Canadian guide, American case citations follow the U.S. norms, with minor variations. More obvious differences are in the citations to journal articles and texts.

I hope that this decision will not make the text less accessible for American readers.

Craig Jones   June 2002

CHAPTER ONE

——

Introduction

Our law of torts comes from the old days of isolated, ungeneralized wrongs, assaults, slanders, and the like, where the damages might be taken to lie where they fell by legal judgment. But the torts with which our courts are kept busy to-day are mainly the incidents of certain well known businesses. They are injuries to person or property by railroads, factories, and the like. The liability for them is estimated, and sooner or later goes into the price paid by the public.

— *Oliver Wendell Holmes, Jr.*[1]

A. OVERVIEW

It is now over a century since Holmes's recognition of the economic reality of mass tort cases, and twenty years since both the Supreme Court of Canada and the Ontario Law Reform Commission offered unambiguous endorsements of legislative reform to permit class proceedings. A decade ago, Ontario's *Class Proceedings Act* came into force and lawsuits for the "non-isolated, generalized wrongs" contemplated by Justice Holmes began in earnest.

The dire scenarios predicted by the class action's most strident critics have not come to pass. Indeed, a student of developments in the field of mass tort litigation will be struck by the progress made in Canada compared with that in the United States in the last two decades. Canadian courts have been able to avoid some of the worst aspects of the American experience while designing a mass tort resolution system that, at least at this early stage, appears in many ways more robust and effective than its southern neighbour's, even as differences in sub-

---

1.   Oliver Wendell Holmes, "The Path of the Law" (1897) 10 Harv. L. Rev. 457 at 467. Holmes originally delivered the paper as a lecture on January 8, 1897, at the dedication of a new hall at the Boston University School of Law.

stantive and procedural law and a smaller and less wealthy plaintiffs' bar have so far made such suits less frequent in this country.

While the U.S. courts have remained deeply uncertain whether class actions are *ever* preferable to individual actions in catastrophic tort claims, Canadian courts have embraced the idea of such actions, overseeing scores of mass tort aggregate resolutions including a complex $1.5 billion compensation scheme for victims of tainted blood. Where the American federal system is often paralysed by choice-of-law and due process concerns in interstate class litigation, in Canada several decisions have certified — and in some cases resolved — nation-wide classes, controversially brushing aside the seemingly intractable theoretical and constitutional problems involved. In what might be seen as a further thumbing of the nose at U.S. judicial conservatism, the Supreme Court of Canada has authorized courts in provinces without class proceedings legislation to design *ad hoc* aggregative procedures for representative plaintiffs before them, reversing a position it had taken as recently as 1983 and flying in the face of the basic assumption underlying class actions since the U.S. Federal Rules were changed in 1966: that class actions were entirely dependent on statute. With *Western Canada Shopping Centres Inc.* v. *Dutton*,[2] the class action has been recognized as a device of virtually unquestioned social utility.

But some problems persist, and others may be worsening or only now becoming apparent. The single, national class (never clearly defended on a principled basis) is threatened, just as – and in part *because* – more provinces are adopting class proceedings statutes. As class actions increase in number, "settlement classes" become more common, with their attendant problems of agency and claims value depression. The plaintiffs' bar is becoming more entrepreneurial and aggressive, and could begin to chafe against the judicial oversight necessary to avoid agency problems. Important questions are coming to the fore: exactly what are we trying to achieve through class actions? What is the best way of doing it?

There has been little original debate or discussion over class action system design since the Ontario Law Reform Commission undertook the first and only truly comprehensive review in 1982 (as we shall see, law reform bodies in several other provinces have subsequently issued less substantial, though still useful, analyses). In the interim, a considerable amount of work on questions of mass tort policy has been produced in the United States – particularly from scholars applying functionalist analyses – yet these efforts have passed with little notice from the Canadian judiciary and academics. As a result, recent Canadian class action decisions, while often courageous and at times inspired, often lack a cohesive theoretical framework or social vision for aggregate litigation in the country. This is a pity, as the Canadian class action environment might be in many ways more accommodating of policy-driven experimentation and reform than the American has been.

---

2.   2001 SCC 46.

The issues upon which I focus here – the economic analysis of aggregation, the necessity of the national class, the misapplication of deterrence principles, and so on – have never received the treatment they deserve in the Canadian literature. It is my frank ambition to provide here, if not a comprehensive theoretical explanation of the class action, then at least a set of observations, proposals and positions that might serve as a basis for further deliberation and dialogue on the subject. In short, I wish to re-engage public and private law scholars and practitioners in the theoretical conversation that has been muted, if not entirely absent, since 1982.

B.   THEORETICAL FRAMEWORK OF CLASS ACTION SYSTEM DESIGN

The analysis that follows generates some basic principles of effective class litigation against which the Canadian litigation models might be judged. I set them out here in brief:

First, an aggregate litigation system should promote the objectives of negligence law; that is, it should assist in the reduction of the overall cost of mass accidents. This can best be achieved in a system that values deterrence highly, and in particular more highly than it does compensation.

Second, the effects of spreading litigation costs through claims aggregation must be clearly understood. Aggregation increases the internalization of harm by the defendant in three main ways:

a)   Claims that otherwise cannot be economically pursued (for both financial reasons and those based on non-pecuniary utility or "psychological factors") can be advanced in the aggregate;

b)   The "settlement depression effect" due to inequalities in plaintiffs' and defendants' litigation investment incentives in mass cases are ameliorated, facilitating fuller, more accurate settlements; and

c)   Aggregation permits optimal litigation investment that increases the *chances* that claims will, on average, be successful, and therefore the expected value of all claims is raised closer to the optimal level.

As a result, in order to maximise deterrence, an aggregate litigation system should (1) promote maximum claims aggregation; (2) promote accuracy in settlements and awards; and (3) provide optimal litigation investment incentives for plaintiffs' counsel.

A system designed to fulfill the criteria above will have certain characteristics: it will permit national classes, and indeed prefer them to several smaller actions in the case of torts with interprovincial impact; it will avoid subclasses except for the resolution of non-common issues; it will favour mandatory classes most, opt-out classes somewhat less highly, and opt-in actions least of all; it will not permit class settlements made in the absence of the threat of full class litigation; it will disdain "scrip" or "in-kind" settlements and will otherwise closely supervise settlements in order to avoid "structural collusion"; and finally, it will provide counsel fee structures which are sufficiently predictable and sufficiently generous to maximise litigation investment.

C. STRUCTURE

The purpose of my book is to review class litigation in Canada as it relates to the most useful goal of negligence law – the reduction of the costs of accidents.

Part I sets out the support for the theoretical framework I have described above. Building on the work of economic analysts of law, I take as my starting point that the class action's central function is to provide an economy of scale that approaches the one that a mass tort defendant enjoys as a matter of course. In doing so, I demonstrate that the class proceeding has benefits that extend far beyond the aggregation of numerous low value claims. In fact, by giving plaintiffs an economy of litigation scale that approaches that of defendants in mass tort cases, the class action lawsuit promotes optimal litigation investment and optimal settlement regardless of individual claims' value, thus ensuring that the wrongdoer internalizes more of the costs of the harm it has caused.

This is particularly important because, of the three stated goals of Canadian class actions – access to justice, judicial economy and behaviour modification – the last is most usefully explored, both with reference to the goals of negligence law generally, and mass tort litigation in particular. My analysis examines two elements of behaviour modification: first, the goal of "general" deterrence, long recognized to be one of the main functions of tort law, but – especially in mass tort cases – systematically undervalued; and second, the modification of the resolution of actual disputes, principally the role of aggregation in providing incentives to reach the appropriate settlement amount. I suggest that these two elements form the basis of a realizable "behaviour modification," which contributes most significantly to the minimization of accident costs through reduction of the sum of the costs of precautions, unavoided harm, and litigation expenses.

I then examine what I argue is a secondary function of claims aggregation: compensation or "optimal tort insurance." Here I also confront some familiar objections to claims aggregation that purport to be based on principles of "fairness" or "justice," comparing individual preferences ex ante (pre-accident) and ex post (post-accident) to demonstrate that aggregation is more "fair" (in the sense of maximising welfare across the full range of possible outcomes) than a system which sacrifices efficiency in the interest of an individual claimant's "day in court." I suggest that concerns over fairness are frequently overstated, are argued in a framework developed for individualized litigation, and are simply unhelpful anachronisms when applied as rigid rules in class proceedings. At the close of Part I, I reach some tentative conclusions regarding optimal mass tort system design.[3]

Part II describes the development of class action litigation in the U.S. and Canada, with particular attention to the divergence of Canadian practice from the American. I argue that the reason for the differences is a fundamentally different view of the class action as a tool for dealing with mass tort, and a willingness in this country to use robust aggregative strategies in a wider variety of cases, in fact wherever the ends of the litigation will be thereby advanced. Where there is confusion and uncertainty in the application of class actions, it is because these ends are not fully understood nor rationally articulated. At the close of Part III I give examples of situations in which misapplication of aggregation theory (and in particular a misunderstanding of the deterrent effects of aggregation) may be leading to inadequate consideration of when class proceedings are "preferable" to individual actions or alternative compensation mechanisms; the sufficiency of settlement amount; and under what circumstances "settlement classes" (simultaneous certification and settlement) are appropriate.

In Parts III and IV, I discuss some further shortcomings of the present system that seem to arise from an insufficient appreciation of mass tort theory, and I suggest approaches that might reduce some of the barriers erected (often unwittingly) to optimal aggregation. Part III is concerned with the possibility of the Canadian system's retreat from the idea of truly "national" classes. Part IV considers possible directions for more fundamental reform, including mandatory classification and several models for dealing comprehensively with "futures" claims – those dealing with harm that is not yet manifest at the time the action is prosecuted. Also in Part IV, I discuss ways in which the Canadian systems of public and private insurance might exploit the class action to provide optimal compensation for the victims of tortious harm through aggregation *across* claims, rather than simply *within* them.

Of particular interest to me in Part IV are those provisions of Canadian class proceedings statutes that have not yet been explored. For instance, each jurisdiction permits the calculation of an aggregate award without proof of individual causation in any particular case; and all allow the courts discretion to distribute the money, not only to the class members, but also to any entity or fund that the court deems would be for the class members' benefit. Tantalizingly, some of the legislation appears to permit certification without notice under certain circumstances, suggesting that mandatory certification may be possible. On this point, I note that the Canadian constitutional system does not offer any of the impediments experienced in the United States: there is no constitutional right to a jury

---

3. When I speak of "system design" here I am referring to all the consciously manipulable factors that affect the outcome of mass tort cases. This includes the statutory and common law framework (substantive and procedural) as well as the discretionary decisions made by individuals – mainly but not exclusively judges – within that system.

trial, and no civil "property" or "due process" guarantee that might be interpreted so as to preserve a "right" to the "day in court."

D. SOME PARTICULAR PROBLEMS AND APPROACHES

The main objective of this work is to demonstrate that a full appreciation of the goals and potential of claims aggregation could have important implications for Canadian class action system design. Deterrence and compensation effects, for instance, mandate that the class be as large as the economic "footprint" of the wrong; because that "footprint" often (if not usually) extends interprovincially, then so ought the plaintiffs' class. With reference to important decisions from other federal jurisdictions (the U.S. and Australia), I recommend several means for achieving the certification of national classes or the consolidation of multiple overlapping provincial claims. Optimal aggregation requires that single, national classes be constituted on an opt-out basis, a feature not explicitly permitted by Canadian class action legislation and becoming more difficult as more provinces adopt restrictive "opt-in only" regimes for non-resident class members.

The same principles lead to the conclusion that so-called "settlement-only" class actions should be viewed with suspicion, and no settlement ought to be approved by the Court unless the defendant faces the appropriate risk of litigating the fully-aggregated claims. To this end I suggest that courts insist that the "comprehensive plan" required by statute as a condition of certification include a timeline for litigation in settlement class actions that will be adhered to if the settlement is rejected. I describe how optimal tort deterrence and optimal compensation affect system design with respect to so-called "futures" or "immature" mass tort claims, particularly within the Canadian system of extensive social insurance coverage, and I explore ways in which the social safety net can assist in aggregation *across* claims. Finally, I argue that it is only when the class action's role in "behaviour modification" is given sufficient weight that the main discretionary device available to courts in managing the effectiveness of the deterrence – class counsel fee approval – can be properly assessed.

PART I

—

Optimal Aggregation of Mass Tort Claims

CHAPTER TWO

—

The Purpose and Function of Aggregation

A. INTRODUCTION

A class proceeding[1] is a lawsuit brought by one or more individuals (the "class representatives") on behalf of a group of persons similarly situated ("the class") to assert a common claim against the same defendant or group of defendants.[2]

Rather than seek to provide an exhaustive description of "mass torts," I will instead try to identify some characteristics of the type of claim that I discuss in this book. The term primarily indicates a situation where a central decision-making process by the defendant(s) creates decentralized harm in the community. This might arise as a result of single mass accidents, but will more often concern cases of defective or harmful products, toxic exposure, or perhaps misrepresentations in the advertising or securities settings. Mass tort claims are often marked by substantial diversity in the value of individual claims within the class (including "futures" or "risk-based" claims in toxic exposure cases), and indeed a mass tort class may include claims that are relatively small (for instance the cost of

---

1. Canadian class actions statutes (with the exception of Saskatchewan's) prefer the term "class proceeding" to "class action," so as to emphasize that claims may be aggregated whether they are commenced as lawsuits or applications. Throughout this book I use the terms "class action" and "class proceeding" interchangeably.
2. Here, as throughout this work, I deal only with plaintiffs' class actions.

medical monitoring against future harm) and very large (catastrophic injury or death).[3]

Of course aggregate claims need not be framed exclusively in tort. I do not here discuss aggregate litigation arising from breach of contract as a discrete category. However, to the extent that the policy goals of such claims also require the internalisation by the wrongdoer of the harms arising from the breach, most of the analysis herein applies equally to such claims.

At the time of this writing, three Canadian jurisdictions have decided cases under comprehensive class action statutes: Quebec[4], Ontario[5] and British Columbia.[6] Of these three, Quebec's law is the oldest, originating in 1978, but the class proceeding remained under-utilized[7] until Ontario followed in 1992 and B.C. in 1995. Very recently, Saskatchewan[8] and Newfoundland[9] have passed similar legislation, and Manitoba and Alberta appear poised to introduce their own based on the recommendations of their respective law reform advisory bodies, joining other Commonwealth jurisdictions with formal class action regimes.[10] The various statutes have many features to facilitate recovery by plaintiff groups. For instance, they allow for the participation of subclasses and

---

3. In this I adopt the broad definition proposed in David L. Shapiro, "Class Actions: The Class As Party and Client" (1998) 73 Notre Dame L. Rev. 913 at 921.

4. The Quebec law is found in *Code de Procédure Civile* 1978 c.8, Book IX and the *Code civil du Québec* 1991 c.64 ss. 2848, 2897 & 2908. Unless otherwise specified, all references herein are to the *Code de Procédure Civile* ("*Quebec Act*"; section references denoted by: "Quebec art. __"; reference to the *Code civil* will be cited as "Civil Code s. __").

5. *Class Proceedings Act 1992*, S.O. 1992, c. 6 (*Ontario Act*; section references denoted by: "Ontario s. __").

6. *Class Proceedings Act*, R.S.B.C. 1996, c. 50 (*B.C. Act*; section references denoted by: "B.C. s. __").

7. In fact the filings of class actions in Quebec by 1987 represented only .04% of civil claims, 1/25th of the anticipated number: W.A. Bogart, "Questioning Litigation's Role – Courts and Class Actions in Canada" (1987) 62 Ind. L.J. 665 at 689-90. Ward Branch reports only 233 applications for certification in Quebec between 1984 and 1998, or an average of just over one per month: Ward Branch, *Class Actions in Canada* (Toronto: Canada Law Book, looseleaf) §4.1950.

8. *Class Actions Act*, S.S. 2001 c. C-12.01 (came into force January 1, 2002) (section references denoted by "Saskatchewan s. __").

9. *Class Actions Act*, S.N. 2001 c. C-18.1 (came into force April 1, 2002).

10. See for instance Part IVA of the *Federal Court of Australia Act 1976* (the representative proceedings provisions date from 1991 amendments); in England reform has taken the shape of the Group Litigation Order (GLO) rules, enacted as *Civil Procedure Rules 1998* (U.K.) Rules 19.10-19.15, Practice Direction 19B – Group Litigation. The GLO rules came into force in 2000.

even individuals with divergent interests or issues,[11] as well as for the introduction of statistical evidence otherwise barred.[12] A province might provide financial assistance to plaintiffs,[13] or otherwise modify the law of costs to reduce risk to plaintiffs.[14] A common feature of class actions is the extension of limitation periods so that potential class members' claims are not prejudiced between filing and certification.[15]

The fact that, prior to 2002, only three provinces had in force class action statutes demonstrates that this type of litigation was not universally welcomed. The reasons for this reluctance will be explored throughout this book, but the concern most often cited reflects a fear of the "Americanization" of what was perhaps viewed as a more civilized litigative environment than that found south of the border.[16] Particularly in Canada, where defendants usually enjoy the protection of being able to recover part of their costs if they prevail, there has been a serious concern that legislation must be drafted and applied in such a way as to continue to discourage frivolous suits. To do otherwise, defence counsel fear,

---

11. Ontario ss. 6, 25; B.C. ss. 6, 27, 28; Quebec arts. 1022, 1037.

12. Ontario s. 23; B.C. s. 30.

13. Ontario *Law Society Act*, R.S.O. 1990, c. L.8, s. 59.1.

14. B.C. s. 37. Although there is no statutory presumption against costs in Quebec or Ontario, courts in the latter province at least have been reluctant to award them if the proceedings have been "reasonably pursued": Michael A. Eizenga, Michael J. Peerless & Charles M. Wright, *Class Actions Law and Practice* (Toronto, Butterworths, 1999) at §12.4-12.5. There is some suggestion that this may be changing: *Pearson* v. *Inco Ltd.* 2002 Ont. Sup. C.J. LEXIS 104 (Ont. Sup. Ct. J.) (award of costs against the plaintiff in three pre-certification motions apparently without applying rules that differed from ordinary individual actions).

15. Ontario s. 28; B.C. s. 39. There is a difference, however, in what happens should a class proceeding fail certification. In Ontario, the limitation period resumes on final denial of certification. In British Columbia, the Courts have interpreted virtually identical provisions to *retroactively* resume the running of the limitation period. Thus in B.C., plaintiffs who would, in absence of a class proceeding wish to proceed individually, must file their myriad suits while awaiting certification. For discussion see Eizenga et al. *ibid.* at §§6.1-6.7.

16. See for instance Derek J. Mullan, Q.C. and Neo J. Tuytel, "The British Columbia Class Proceedings Act: Will It Open the Floodgates?" (1996) 14 Can. J. Ins. L. 30; P. Iacano, "Class actions and Products Liability in Ontario: What Will Happen?" (1991-92) 13 C.I.L.R. 99. The litigiousness of Americans might be considerably overstated: when adjusted for population, American court filings are in the same general range as those in Ontario, Australia, England, and Denmark. See Marc Galanter, "Reading the Landscape of Disputes: What We Know and Don't Know (and Think We Know) About Our Allegedly Contentious and Litigious Society" (1983) 31 UCLA L. Rev. 4 at 55. Marc Galanter "Real World Torts: An Antidote to Anecdote" (1996) 55 Md. L. Rev. 1093 at 1104-06.

may lead to a climate of "artificial" or "nuisance" settlements and an increasingly litigious business environment.[17]

No aspect of class actions in the U.S. has led to as much controversy, vacillation and hand-wringing as the suitability of the aggregate device for handling mass catastrophic tort claims. It is interesting to observe, then, that Canadian class proceedings statutes appear to have been actually drafted with such actions in mind. Consider the description provided by the Ontario Court of Appeal in the recent decision of *Carom* v. *Bre-X*:

> Disasters spawn litigation. Trains collide or derail, planes crash, ships sink, lakes and rivers become polluted, chemical factories explode, ordinary people eat, drink, wear or use unhealthy or defective products. People — sometimes hundreds, even thousands — are injured or killed by these events. When the crisis subsides, some of the victims turn to the courts for redress and compensation.
>
> One of the modern mechanisms for dealing with the litigation fallout from major disasters is the class action...[18]

The Canadian statutes were drafted to avoid some of the shortcomings of the American approach, and the courts have interpreted them generously. As a result, there is considerable potential to employ Canadian class actions in creative and innovative ways to achieve global resolutions of mass tort claims, something the U.S. appellate courts and Congress alike have fairly consistently refused to do.[19]

---

17.   The Alberta Law Reform Commission's *Report on Class Action Legislation* (Final Report #85, 2000) [*Alberta Report*] lists and discusses eight popularly-held objections to class actions at pp. 55-63. Most are based on issues raised in Deborah R. Hensler et al., *Class Action Dilemmas: Pursuing Public Goals for Private Gain*, (Santa Monica, CA: RAND Institute for Civil Justice, March 1999). Hensler's book, incidentally, provides one of the most comprehensive overviews of class action policy in the United States.

18.   *Carom et al.* v. *Bre-X Minerals Ltd. et al.* (1999), 44 O.R. (3d) 173 (S.C.J.). See also the Manitoba Law Reform Commission, *Class Proceedings* (Report #100) (Winnipeg: Manitoba Publications Branch, January 1999) [*Manitoba Report*], which synopsised at pp. 17-18 types of litigation that can benefit from claim aggregation:

> Class actions are useful in tort cases for mass disaster claims (claims arising from single incident mass accidents, such as train derailments and environmental disasters) and for creeping disaster claims (claims for bodily injury arising from consumer products, such as tobacco and asbestos, or medical products, such as intra-uterine devices, breast implants, contaminated blood, jaw implants, silver mercury fillings and heart pacemakers). Other uses include "claims of group defamation, nuisance, the principle in *Rylands* v. *Fletcher* (1868), L.R. 3 H.L. 330, various statutory torts, damages claims for breach of *Charter* rights, claims arising from illegal strikes, negligent house construction, and negligent misstatement."

19.   See the discussion on development of class action suits in Part II, below.

An appreciation of how the Canadian legislative regime conforms to the best goals of aggregate litigation can provide insights into the development of the jurisprudence that may otherwise be overlooked.

Regrettably, there has been precious little written on the *theory* of the class action in Canada, where writing in the field tends instead to be doctrinal and descriptive.[20] That work, however helpful to the practitioner, is of less assistance to the student of system design theory. Fortunately, we may benefit from the extraordinary outpouring in the field of tort policy and class actions the United States. To that end, my discussion in this book builds upon the work of Guido Calabresi, Richard Posner, A. Mitchell Polinsky, Louis Kaplow and Steven Shavell.[21] Much of the theory I present here is also derived from the "function-

---

20. The principal texts and the overwhelming majority of articles on class actions in Canada are written by and for practitioners, including those I rely upon here. Leading texts written by litigators include: Branch, above note 7; Eizenga, Wright & Peerless, above note 14; Dean F. Edgell, *Product Liability Law in Canada* (Toronto: Butterworths, 2000). For examples of articles see Ward K. Branch, "Chaos or Consistency? The National Class Action Dilemma" (Branch McMaster January 24-25, 2002) www.branmac.com (accessed February 15, 2002), Ward K. Branch and John C. Kleefeld, "Settling a Class Action (or How to Wrestle an Octopus)", presented to the Canadian Institute Conference on Litigating Toxic Torts and Other Mass Wrong (Toronto: December 4-5, 2000); Rosenberg, below note 22; Mullan & Tuytel above note 16; R. Bruce Smith, "Class Actions and Financial Institutions" (1998) 17 Nat'l Banking L. Rev. 35; Michael J. Peerless & Michael A. Eizenga, "Class Actions in Breast Implant Litigation" (1996) 16 Health L. Can. 78; John A. Campion and Victoria A. Stewart, "Class Actions: Procedure and Strategy" (1997) 19 Advocates' Q. 20; David A. Crerar, "The Restitutionary Class Action: Canadian Class Proceedings Legislation as a Vehicle for the Restitution of Unlawfully Demanded Payments, Ultra Vires Taxes, and Other Unjust Enrichments" (1998) 56 U.T. Fac. L. Rev. 47; Rodney L. Hayley, "'Monsters of Complexity and Cost'? Class Action Certifications in British Columbia" (1996) 14 Can. J. Ins. L. 91. I do not here list the wealth of materials presented at numerous continuing legal education seminars throughout the country.

21. Guido Calabresi, "Some Thoughts on Risk Distribution and the Law of Torts" (1961) 70 Yale L.J. 499; Guido Calbresi, *The Costs of Accidents: A Legal and Economic Analysis* (New Haven: Yale University Press, 1970); A. Mitchell Polinsky, *An Introduction to Law and Economics* (2d.) (Boston: Little Brown, 1989); Richard A. Posner, *Economic Analysis of Law* (5th) (Boston: Little, Brown, 1998); Steven Shavell, *Economic Analysis of Accident Law* (London: Harvard University Press, 1987) [Shavell, *Economic Analysis*]; Steven Shavell, "The Level of Litigation: Private Versus Social Optimality of Suit and of Settlement," (1999) 19 Int'l Rev. L. & Econ. 99; Louis Kaplow & Steven Shavell, "Fairness vs. Welfare" (2001) 114 Harv. L. Rev. 961 ["Fairness vs. Welfare"].

alist" models of mass tort litigation developed in a series of articles by American scholars, and particularly those by Harvard professor David Rosenberg.[22]

These authors challenge the system designer of mass tort actions to think in ways that are, at least initially, difficult. They rely heavily on economic models to make predictions of system behaviour; they tend to emphasize policies justified through a focus on ex ante, rather than ex post preferences, and they require that we analyse problems of large-scale wrongs, negligence and so on *probabilistically*, rather than anecdotally. Probabilistic analysis is a much younger discipline than the law of tort,[23] but underlies the theories of substantive mass tort law (whether based on negligence or strict liability) and the various aggregative strategies available to deal with it.

B.   THE PURPOSES OF CLAIMS AGGREGATION

It is repeatedly said that class proceedings legislation is designed to be solely procedural, and not substantive,[24] a characterisation that, at least in so simplistic

---

22.   David Rosenberg, "A "Public Law" Vision of the Tort System" (1984) 97 Harvard L. Rev. 849; David Rosenberg, "Class Actions for Mass Torts: Doing Individual Justice by Collective Means" (1987) 62 Ind. L.J. 561 [Rosenberg, "Doing Individual Justice"]; David Rosenberg, "Of End Games and Openings in Mass Tort Cases: Lessons from a Special Master" (1989) 69 B.U. L. Rev. 695 [Rosenberg, "End Games"]; David Rosenberg, "Individual Justice and Collectivizing Risk-Based Claims in Mass-Exposure Cases (1996) 71 N.Y.U. L. Rev. 210 [Rosenberg, "Risk-Based Claims"]; David Rosenberg, "Mandatory-Litigation Class Action: The Only Option for Mass Tort Cases" (2001) 115 Harvard L. Rev. 831 [Rosenberg, "The Only Option"].

23.   For a history of probabilistic analysis, see Peter L. Bernstein, *Against the Gods: The Remarkable Story of Risk* (New York: Wiley, 1996) Bernstein traces the theory of probability, the root of all the modern principles of insurance, investment and risk tolerance – and by implication substantive notions of objective reasonableness – to no earlier than 1654, a remarkably short time ago. That our legal system has yet to fully accept it is perhaps some testament to the extent to which probabilistic thinking runs against the natural grain of human thought.

24.   *Ontario New Home Warranty Program* v. *Chevron Chemical Co.* (1999), 46 O.R. (3d) 130 at 143 (S.C.J.) (*ONHWP*):

. . . there is no jurisdiction conferred by the *Class Proceedings Act* to supplement or derogate from the substantive rights of the parties. It is a procedural statute and as such, neither its inherent objects nor its explicit provisions can be given effect in a manner which affects the substantive rights of either plaintiffs or defendants.

See also *Chadha* v. *Bayer Inc.* (2001), 54 O.R. (3d) 520 at 542 (Div.Ct.).

a form, is not without controversy.[25] Even assuming such Acts to be procedural, though, it does not necessarily follow that the system designer should ignore the substantive effect of aggregation on the outcomes of litigation. Indeed, although generally phrased in procedural terms, the principal purpose of aggregate actions remains to influence who can sue whom for what, and most importantly, how successfully.

The next question that automatically will follow is, "to what end?" In other words, what social ambitions are we trying to fulfill with mass litigation system design? The obvious answer is that class action suits for negligence should be designed to complement and further the goal of negligence law itself, which I here defend as the minimisation of overall accident costs.

C. NEGLIGENCE LAW SHOULD REDUCE ACCIDENT COSTS

In order to analyse class action system design in a prescriptive way – i.e. in a way that might allow us to jettison the unnecessary, emphasize the important and add that which is needed — I must take a moment to explain some standards of preference that I here assume.

First, the reader will become aware that my analysis generally focuses on negligence principles, rather than strict liability.[26] Whether negligence will continue to be the rule for products liability appears to be an open question at common

---

25. The substantive / procedural question is revisited in the course of the discussion of the "national class", below Part III.

26. Strict liability applies where a plaintiff can show injury resulting from the condition of the defendant's "unreasonably dangerous" product, used in a foreseeable way in the condition in which it left the defendant's custody. The idea was described by Laskin J. (dissenting in part) in *Rivtow Marine Limited* v. *Washington Iron Works* (1973), 40 D.L.R. (3d) 530 at 551-552 (S.C.C.), as follows:

> That liability rests upon a conviction that manufacturers should bear the risk of injury to consumers or users of their products when such products are carelessly manufactured because manufacturers create the risk in the carrying on of their enterprises, and they will be more likely to safeguard the members of the public to whom their products are marketed if they must stand behind them as safe products to consume or use. They are better able to insure against such risks, and the costs of insurance, as a business expense, can be spread with less pain among the buying public than would be the case if an injured consumer or user was saddled with the entire loss that befalls him.

> There is an ongoing debate about whether the American cause of action in "strict liability" applies, or ought to apply, in Canada: See for instance Giovanna Roccamo, "Medical Implants and other Health Care Products: Theories of Liability and Modern Trends" (1994) 16 Advocates Q. 421.

law.[27] For our purposes, very little turns on the issue, as under either regime the goal is to shift the cost of harm to the wrongdoer.[28]

Calabresi's familiar assertion that the primary goal of modern negligence law is to minimise the overall costs attributed to accidents[29] underlies nearly all relevant economic analysis, as it seeks to quantify the "risk-utility" approach enshrined in the so-called "Learned Hand" formula generally accepted by Canadian courts in the products liability context.[30] I accept the term "accident costs" to be the sum of the cost of precautions taken to avoid accidents, the cost of harm which is – any precautions notwithstanding – suffered, and the cost involved in the litigation of resulting accident claims.[31]

---

27. *ter Neuzen* v. *Korn*, [1995] 3 S.C.R. 674 at 682 per Sopinka J. ("the applicability of strict liability in tort is best left for another day."). Strict liability has been introduced through legislation in New Brunswick, Saskatchewan and Quebec, as well as in the U.S., the U.K., Australia, and the European Community: *Consumer Product Warranty and Liability Act*, S.N.B. 1978, c. C-18.1, s. 27; *Consumer Protection Act*, S.S. 1996, c. C-30.1 s. 64; *Consumer Protection Act*, R.S.Q. 1980, c P-40.1, s. 47; *Civil Code*, S.Q. 1991, c. 64, ss.1468, 1469; *Uniform Commercial Code*, U.C.C. s.2-318 (U.S.); *Consumer Protection Act*, 1987, c.43 (U.K.); *Trade Practices Act*, 1974, as amended (Australia); European Communities Directive 85/374/EEC (Europe).

28. Indeed, there may be little to choose between strict liability for "unreasonably dangerous" products and the requirement under negligence law that manufacturers take what precautions are "reasonable" to avoid foreseeable injury, especially with the recent requirement that, where products are "inherently dangerous", special care is required on the part of the manufacturer. See *Buchan* v. *Ortho Pharmaceuticals (Canada) Ltd.* (1984), 8 D.L.R. (4th) 373 (Ont. H.C.J.) at 386, aff'd (1986), 54 O.R. (2d) 92 (C.A.) and *Shandloff* v. *City Dairy Ltd.*, [1936] O.R. 579 (C.A.) at 590; and *Heimler* v. *Calvert Caterers Ltd.* (1975), 8 O.R. (2d) 1 (C.A.).) A thorough consideration of strict liability vs. negligence rules is found in Shavell, *Economic Analysis*, above note 21

29. Calabresi, *The Costs of Accidents* above note 21 at 24-33. Calabresi actually identified a second primary goal of negligence law: "justice," which he admits has an "elusiveness" that "justifies delaying discussion of it." *Ibid.* at 26. I share this ambivalence, and discuss the independent weight, if any, of "justice" or "fairness" at various points as they appear inclined to restrain various aspects of optimal system design.

30. Lewis N. Klar, *Tort Law* (2d) (Toronto: Carswell, 1996) at 277, citing *McEvoy* v. *Ford Motor Co.*, [1989] B.C.J. No. 1639 (S.C.); *Rentway Canada Ltd.* v. *Laidlaw Transport Ltd.* (1989), 49 C.C.L.T. 150 (Ont. H.C.), aff'd (unreported January 13, 1994) Doc. C.A. 16/90, C. 9877 (C.A.).

31. Please note that this is distinct from the goal of reducing only the harm to victims from accidents. Calabresi's analysis, and those of all who have applied law and economics analysis to negligence law since, introduced the costs of precautions

16

In a sense, this assumption is in itself a conclusion, because it requires that we reject, or at least disregard, some of the other functions occasionally attributed to tort law, to the extent that they are unrelated to reducing accident costs. For instance, Justice Linden in his book *Tort Law* lists, aside from the components of the goal of reducing accident costs (i.e. compensation and deterrence) several purported "functions" of tort law. It is, he suggests, "an educator";[32] an "ombudsman";[33] a provider of "psychological comfort to the injured" and a regime established, at least in part, to "kee[p] the peace."[34] It is also frequently suggested that tort law advances the interests of "fairness," with that term defined in various ways.[35]

Justice Linden rejects professor Ernest Weinrib's strikingly romantic suggestion that "goals have nothing to do with tort law" which, "just like love" "has no ulterior end,"[36] an idea which if it were accepted might justify turning system design questions over to poets rather than lawyers, economists and politicians.[37] My assertion here is that, to the extent that negligence law does *not* reduce the costs of accidents (i.e. is not in some way related to compensation, deterrence, or social costs), it has little independent value as an educator, ombudsman, or psychological comfort.[38]

---

into the equation because it was – and is here – assumed that there is an acceptable level of accident associated with legal activities; whether there are exceptions to this rule is an interesting question beyond the scope of this book. It will be expected that there will be something of an equilibrium established between the level of activity that society desires and for which they will tolerate a certain level of risk (called "reasonable risk") that precaution should not be permitted to depress further.

32. Allen M. Linden, *Canadian Tort Law* (7th ed.) (Toronto, Butterworths, 2001) at 14.
33. *Ibid.*at 22.
34. *Ibid.*at 17.
35. Jules Coleman & Arthur Ripstein, "Mischief and Misfortune" (1995) 41 McGill L.J. 91 at 94 (describing "the claim that each person should bear the costs of her activities" as "the principle of fairness").
36. Linden, above note 32 at 2-3, citing Ernest Weinrib, "Understanding Tort Law" (1989), 23 Val. L.J. 485 at 526.
37. I mention only Weinrib's formalism because he is determined to defend its application even to negligence law (see for example Ernest J. Weinrib, "Legal Formalism: On the Immanent Rationality of Law" (1988) 97 Yale L.J. 949). I do not deny Weinrib's assertion that negligence analysis bears many features of the self-regarding logic of legal formalism; whether such characteristics are "immanent" cause or self-justificatory effect does not matter to my analysis here, provided that the reader accepts my contention that any application of formalism which *undermines* the role of tort law in reducing accident costs must be rejected, unless it is supported on other pragmatic or functional grounds.
38. Klar for instance is ambivalent over whether tort law is an effective deterrent, but

Similarly, arguments that tort law "teaches a moral lesson"[39] or is "a rein-forcer of values"[40] teeter between irrelevance and tautology when applied to non-intentional torts.[41] Such effects may or may not be present by serendipity, but they play no role in system design as I here envisage it; once again, my analysis assumes that there should be no compromise of the functional goal for such ethereal or purely deontological ends.[42]

In studying the effect of aggregation upon tort claims in this book, I emphasize the main components of Calabresi's analysis, as expressed by Rosenberg: examining the theory of class litigation from the "functional" standpoint of "minimizing the costs of accidents, most importantly by achieving appropriate levels of deterrence and compensation consistent with the efficient administration of justice."[43]

---

seems nonetheless enthusiastic regarding its role as "educator", in showing us "how things *should be done*" [emphasis Klar's]: Klar above note 30 at 14-17. But what good is being shown if no behaviour is adjusted as a result?

Similarly, Klar (*ibid.* at 17) agrees with Linden that tort actions against government play an "ombudsman's" role, but presumably this role too is only meaningful if it is reflected in behaviour modification (i.e. as a restraint on government behaviour) or if it results in compensation (although admittedly this compensation can be otherwise than through the civil judicial process).

I will discuss in more detail later the idea of the psychological comfort possibly provided by one's "day in court." I should however note at this point that overall I view such objections with considerable scepticism. I have yet to meet any victim of negligence who has expressed any great pleasure in the process of seeking redress through the courts, although, as I will describe in Chapter Four, there may be *some* independent value for victims in "being heard" by persons in authority.

39. Linden, above note 32 at 14, citing Glanville Williams, "Aims of the Law of Tort", [1951] Current Legal Problems 137 at 149.

40. Linden, *ibid.* at 14.

41. The purpose of negligence law is to regulate the level of care taken in the course of socially-useful activities through adjustments to the standard of care, and accepts that some harm will be suffered even if appropriate care is taken. The law of intentional tort, on the other hand, is a method of enforcing absolute or near-absolute prohibitions on certain anti-social behaviour.

42. See generally Kaplow & Shavell, "Fairness vs. Welfare" above note 21. This is not to say that perceptions of "fairness" or "justice" do not have demonstrable value independent of other effects. To the extent that they can be shown to do so, they must be accommodated in the analysis. This is discussed more extensively later.

43. Rosenberg, "Risk-Based Claims", above note 22 at 214.

D. BASIC FUNCTIONAL PRINCIPLES OF AGGREGATE LITIGATION

(1) Economic Analysis and Its Assumptions

It is of considerable assistance (and not a little relevance) that the mass tort "era" has coincided with the emergence of the field now known as "law and economics," the advocates of which attempt to apply econometric models of expected behaviour to various legal regimes in order to improve system design.

The analysis of law using economic principles is often controversial, particularly to the extent to which it has tended to value "wealth maximisation" as the central social goal, or to which its advocates otherwise purport to offer a normative framework for social decision-making.[44] However, the economic analysis of *mass* tort litigation need not become mired in political or philosophical debate. Economic analysis of the effect of claims aggregation on such things as deterrence and settlement requires no assumptions rooted in morality, politics, economic principles or general welfare beyond those introduced by the substantive

---

44. See, e.g., Ronald M. Dworkin, "Is Wealth a Value?" (1980) 9 J. Legal Stud. 191 at 219-20 (rejecting the normative and descriptive claims of "economic analysis of law"); Anthony T. Kronman, "Wealth Maximization as a Normative Principle" (1980) 9 J. Legal Stud. 227 at 242 (describing Posner's theory of wealth maximisation as "a bad principle as well as incoherent one"); Arthur Allen Leff, "Economic Analysis of Law: Some Realism About Nominalism" (1974) 60 VA. L. Rev. 451 at 459 (criticising American legal nominalism because it substitutes definitions for both normative and empirical propositions); Gary Minda, "Toward a More "Just" Economics of Justice — A Review Essay" (1989) 10 Cardozo L. Rev. 1855 at 1876 (criticizing Posner's theory of law and economics because it fails to recognize "human dimension of moral and political philosophy"); Robin West, "Authority, Autonomy, and Choice: The Role of Consent in the Moral and Political Visions of Franz Kafka and Richard Posner" (1985) 99 Harv. L. Rev. 384 at 391 (concluding that Posner's identification of consent as moral justification of wealth maximisation rests on an "inadequate picture of human nature"). See also Robin Paul Malloy, "Invisible Hand or Sleight of Hand? Adam Smith, Richard Posner, and the Philosophy of Law and Economics" (1988) 36 U. Kan. L. Rev. 209; Frank I. Michelman, "Some Uses and Abuses of Economics in Law" (1979) 46 U. Chi. L. Rev. 307. The controversy is well described in Kaplow & Shavell, "Fairness vs. Welfare" above note 21 at 996 n. 68. For a recent Canadian discussion of the "law and economics" school, see Avner Levin, "Quantum Physics in Private Law" (2001) 14 Can. J.L. & Juris. 249 at 253. Levin reiterates the common criticism of Posner's emphasis on wealth-maximisation as a social goal ("Posner actually views the maximization of wealth as the purpose of all human activity"), though it would seem that Posner has long retreated from such an extreme position, if indeed he ever held it.

law of tort. We can study the effect of aggregation of claims simply to see whether and how the social choices made by tort law – about what kind of behaviour is "wrong" and should be discouraged, and what level of compensation is appropriate for victims – are affected by hearing numerous similar claims at the same time. In doing so, it is not necessary to determine whether the substantive rules of tort liability in themselves are moral, just or right.

In fact, any general objections that might be raised with respect to the application of economic analysis to aggregate litigation must be tempered by the pragmatic observation that economic principles are, historically and unavoidably, the *raison d'àtre* of the class action.[45] It therefore stands to reason that certain economic effects of aggregation must be confronted if the promise of the class action lawsuit is to be more fully realised, or even more clearly defined.

Nevertheless, it would be a mistake to completely ignore the interaction between substantive and procedural rules in the system's design. Arguably, the inefficiencies I describe in the "traditional," individualistic tort regime as it applies to mass torts represent social choices. For instance, the extent to which manufacturers bear only a fraction of the risk of their product's harm might be seen as a social preference to transfer the manufacturer's risk to consumers (and through public and private insurance to the population generally) in order to provide greater incentives for economic activity and perhaps for product innovation, all to the general social welfare. Presumably, the inequality of wealth that this generates among *groups* (to the extent, for instance, that harmed consumers tend to be comparatively poor and injuring corporations tend to be comparatively wealthy) might be offset through the much more efficient taxation system.[46]

If this is so, then aggregation of claims, to the extent that it forces more of the product's harm to be internalised by its manufacturer, may be in the end compensated for by an adjustment in substantive law; by, for instance, relaxing the standard of care or the necessity for warning. While providing for such a possibility,[47] I am nevertheless building my analysis from the central assumption that there is nothing in numerosity of claims *itself* that should determine the recovery afforded by the law of tort; there is no reason why a plaintiff should be awarded less only because there are many others who have been injured in the same way by the same defendant. Similarly, there is no social good served by relaxing the deterrent effect on a wrongdoer because his wrong has many victims. As Hay

---

45. When one speaks, for instance, of "efficiencies" "judicial economy" and "general deterrence," one is employing an economic or functionalist analysis of law.

46. See generally Louis Kaplow & Steven Shavell, "Why the Legal System is Less Efficient that the Income Tax in Redistributing Income" (1994) 23 J. Legal Stud. 667.

47. I also assume here that there is no independent value to social hypocrisy; that is to say, that there is nothing to be gained in having a tort system that systematically favours mass tort defendants over plaintiffs in ways contrary to its stated objectives.

and Rosenberg put it, "the outcome of litigation should not depend on how dispersed the plaintiffs are."[48]

My main interest is to examine the function of various aspects of claims aggregation and how they serve to advance or frustrate the goals for which negligence law is designed. There are times, though, that system design for mass tort aggregation raises objections that claim to be based on subjective social choices independent of a more efficacious pursuit of otherwise valid tort principles. This is so, for instance, when ideas of "fairness" are raised, either with respect to defendants and their "reasonable expectations" or a citizen's "autonomous rights" apart from the aggregate of claimants similarly situated. My insistence that advocates of independent principles should at least bear some burden to support their application from a functionalist perspective will lead me to dismiss objections based on morality "in the air," or assertions of fairness that are unsupported by – or worse, contrary to – the interests of functional utility.

When the two assumptions that I make here regarding the purposes of tort law (to minimise the costs of accidents) and tort procedure (to facilitate that goal) are combined with respect to mass torts, and filtered through the pragmatic observation that mass tort actions almost always feature firms in the role of defendant, we might summarise the role of mass tort litigation as a method of controlling "the systematic risks of business activity,"[49] be that activity the making of statements in a prospectus, the design and manufacture of a product, or the release of toxins into the environment.

One final word on the economic models that I use throughout this part (especially to those readers not familiar with econometrics): they should not be taken literally. That is, when consequences of decisions are graphed, the representation necessarily ignores a host of complicating factors; they are, inevitably, pictures of what will occur "all things being equal," which of course they never are.[50] However, such comparisons are very useful to show the *tendencies* of response to particular procedures and rules, and that is the way I intend them to be interpreted here.

(2) Mass-Produced Wrongs and Structural Asymmetry

When we speak of mass torts, we are speaking of a situation where diffuse harm results from a decision or series of decisions made centrally, almost always in the course of conducting business or providing government services. Most often,

---

48. Bruce Hay & David Rosenberg, "'Sweetheart' and 'Blackmail' Settlements in Class Actions: Reality and Remedy" (2000) 75 Notre Dame L. Rev. 1377 at 1388.

49. David Rosenberg, "The Path Not Taken" (1997) 110 Harv. L. Rev. 1044.

50. Space here does not permit me to discuss each of these assumptions individually; most will, I believe, be apparent, but anyone with a keen interest in the subject would be well advised to review one of the excellent texts on the subject, for instance those by Polinsky, Posner or Shavell, all above note 21.

these decisions involve the design and manufacture of a mass-market product, but mass torts also arise from decisions as to the design of processes or systems; thus (in the U.S. at least) racial discrimination can be a mass tort when it arises from a large employer's central policies;[51] dangerous working conditions might similarly become the subject of mass tort claims, as could decisions with respect to medical treatment, to the extent that the wrong is centralized and the harm diffuse.[52] Some torts that are inherently individual, like sexual assault, can be mass torts when, for instance, an allegation of supervisory failure or vicarious liability is made. In each case there is a decision by a central entity, the effects of which radiate out and cause or contribute to the harm of others.

In the "traditional" or individualistic legal regime, a tort action may be viewed as connecting the tortfeasor on one hand and its victim on the other. In a mass tort, by comparison, the tortfeasor lies at the hub of the actions which might be seen to radiate from the decisions made at the centre. Viewed in this way, it is not difficult to see how the economy of scale in a dispute resolution process will naturally favour the defendant, who can reuse the work product involved in the defence of issues common to all the claims. Not so the numerous plaintiffs, who must begin anew with each new case, even on the common issues.[53] This

---

51. In Canada, discrimination has not been recognized as a tort, and such cases would usually proceed under the various human rights Acts, which have their own rules regarding aggregated and representative actions. However, it is possible for discrimination claims to proceed as actions for "unjust enrichment"; thus far, Canadian courts appear unwilling to consider class actions appropriate for such claims on grounds of preferability: *Franklin* v. *University of Toronto* (2001), 56 O.R. (3d) 698 (Sup. Ct. J.) (denying certification in claims of alleged systemic discrimination of female employees of university, but allowing case to proceed individually).

52. A notorious example would be the central decisions made with respect to the screening of the blood supply in many countries (including Canada, for blood borne diseases during the 1980s); less obvious examples might be standard practices negligently adopted by hospitals or, on a larger scale, by medical self-regulatory bodies.

53. This imbalance has existed from the very beginning of mass tort law. Recall that the plaintiff in *Donoghue* v. *Stevenson*, filing her appeal *in forma pauperis*, was up against a relatively well-off manufacturer of consumer goods, who faced the prospect of numerous similar claims for negligence in bottling his ginger beer and who fought this first "test case" all the way to the House of Lords: See William McBride, "The Story of the Snail in the Bottle Case" in Peter Burns ed., *Donoghue* v. *Stevenson and the Modern Law of Negligence: The Paisley Papers* (Vancouver: Continuing Legal Education Society of B.C., 1991) at 25. Obviously, the litigative power of Mr. Stevenson's sole proprietorship is in turn dwarfed by that of modern consumer-goods firms.
Another central feature of numerosity of tort claims can also be traced to Ms.

dichotomy is at the heart of mass tort – the defendant has mass-produced the wrong; the plaintiffs suffer the harm and bear the costs individually. This "structural asymmetry"[54] – it has been called a systemic bias in favour of defendants[55] – carries through from the manufacture of the product to the final resolution of the dispute, with the result that the plaintiffs are placed at a considerable disadvantage.[56]

It is not difficult to foresee the results of structural asymmetry in the individual litigation of mass tort claims. Mass tort defendants will tend to overspend on litigation in individual suits because their economy of scale permits them to invest in each initial claim an amount far greater than the claim is worth;[57] this strategy makes success more likely in the early suits, compounding the advantage in the aggregate.[58] Faced with such unequal litigative power, suits are dis-

---

Donoghue's experience; the first party to file the claim faces the additional indignity of knowing that there are numerous others who will "free ride" upon it by taking advantage of the legal work product (including perhaps the decision itself) and – to the extent that it becomes part of the public record – the discovery information paid for by the trailblazer in prosecuting their own claims.

54. "Developments – The Paths of Civil Litigation" (2000) 113 Harv. L. Rev. 1752 ["Developments"] at 1834.

55. David Rosenberg, "Mass Tort Class Actions – What the Defendants Have and Plaintiffs Don't" (2000) 37 Harv. J. Legis. 393 [Rosenberg, "What the Defendants Have"].

56. *Blue Cross & Blue Shield of N.J., Inc.* v. *Philip Morris, Inc.* 133 F. Supp. 2d 162 at 177 (E.Dist. N.Y. 2001) per Weinstein J. ("Standard case-by-case adjudication of mass tort claims not only may deny litigation efficiencies to plaintiffs, but may afford large litigation advantages to defendants.")

57. R.J. Reynolds general counsel J. Michael Jordan described such a strategy to his fellow tobacco industry lawyers in 1988: "[t]he aggressive posture we have taken regarding depositions and discovery in general continues to make these cases extremely burdensome and expensive for plaintiffs' lawyers . . . . To paraphrase General Patton, the way we won these cases was not by spending all of [R.J. Reynolds'] money, but by making the other son of a bitch spend all his." Quoted in *Haines* v. *Liggett Group, Inc.*, 814 F. Supp. 414 at 421 (D.N.J. 1993).

58. *Ibid.* For a fuller discussion of this phenomenon, see Sally Moeller, "Class Auctions: Market Models for Attorney's Fees in Class Action Litigation" (2000) 113 Harv. L. Rev. 1827 at 1833. Moeller outlines the problem of overinvestment thus:

Commentators customarily explain heavy spending by defendants on litigation as an attempt to overwhelm and intimidate individual plaintiffs or as a consequence of risk aversion with regard to the precedential impact of the judgment in an individual suit. Such motives aside, the most compelling reason for defendants to spend more than individual plaintiffs is that the full amount of their expected risk exceeds the individual claim.

couraged or settled for too little, and confidentiality agreements exacted by defendants at the time of settlement may preclude "free riders" from taking full advantage of the work that has been done before,[59] while the defendant is free to do so.

Practically speaking, the marketplace will attempt to compensate for this inequality through a variety of aggregative strategies employed by the plaintiffs' bar to achieve some kind of economy of scale. Lawyers will begin to specialise in suits regarding a particular defendant, product, or event, allowing fixed costs (expert reports, legal and factual research, etc.) to be spread across the lawyer's "inventory" of similarly-situated plaintiffs. Thus the emergence in the U.S. during the 1990s of "asbestos lawyers," "tobacco lawyers," and so on.[60] Moreover, lawyers and firms will enter into (more or less formal) cooperative agreements, which may run the gamut from co-counsel arrangements to "clearinghouse" systems whereby legal or factual information regarding a mass tort is pooled and accessed at a much reduced fee.[61]

These alternative methods of claims aggregation, however, suffer from serious structural setbacks that allow them only marginal advantages over unconnected individual claims. Unless the cooperation among plaintiffs can reach the level of cooperation within the defendant firm, the fundamental structural advantage to the defendant remains. Moreover, the existence "in the wings" of non-cooperating plaintiffs may lead to "free riding" on initial claims,[62] further discouraging meaningful economies of scale by discouraging cooperation among

---

59. Such "secret settlements" prevent disclosure of the nature of the claim, the information obtained during discovery, and the terms of settlement . See *Seattle Times Co.* v. *Rhinehart*, 104 S. Ct. 2199 (1984); David Rosenberg, "The Dusting of America: A Story of Asbestos — Carnage, Cover-up, and Litigation" (Book Review) (1986) 99 Harv. L. Rev. 1693 at 1701.

60. John C. Coffee, Jr., "Class Wars: The Dilemma of the Mass Tort Class Action" (1995) 95 Colum. L. Rev. 1343 [Coffee, "Class Wars"] at 1358-59.

61. See generally Howard M. Erichson, "Informal Aggregation: Procedural and Ethical Implications of Coordination among Counsel in Related Lawsuits" (2000) 50 Duke L.J. 381; See also Eizenga et al. above note 14 at §2.5 (describing the Australian experience with group litigation strategies). For a criticism of the "litigation network" approach, see John C. Coffee, "Rescuing the Private Attorney General: Why the Model of the Lawyer as Bounty Hunter is Not Working" (1983) 42 MD. L. Rev. 215 at 239-41, nn. 56-57.

62. "Free riding" is possible because a litigation in the ordinary course generates a significant amount of publicly available information regarding the common issues. Factual information gained through discovery or trial, legal research and arguments all represent expensive investments by plaintiff's counsel, and each may be obtained for only token cost by a "free rider" who wishes to exploit the investor's work product, provided that the case proceeds to hearing or trial.

plaintiffs. Rosenberg and Fried explain the inefficiencies of informal cooperation in a forthcoming article:

> The tort system is increasingly characterized by large-scale, corporately structured organizations comprised of plaintiffs' lawyers, specialists in claim-finding and investigation, and allied experts in an array of disciplines that exploit scale economies by preparing multiple business-related claims en masse. Although these organizations compete for market share and financial backing, they may share information and align litigation strategy to some degree. Yet, collective action problems persist to prevent cost-effective information investment in maximizing aggregate net recovery of tort damages and hence aggregate deterrence benefit from tort litigation. In particular, the combination of high costs of organizing and monitoring collaboration compounded by agency problems and strong incentives for free-riding converge to preclude plaintiffs' attorneys from efficiently achieving the maximum scale economies required for deterrence purposes.[63]

For these reasons, mass tort theorists increasingly accept that a fundamental – some say the *only* fundamental – reason for aggregating litigation is to redress the imbalance between mass tort defendants and plaintiffs, to "level the playing field" so that plaintiffs can enjoy the economies of scale that defendants have always exploited, and thereby increase their recovery.[64]

Assuming for the moment that aggregation of claims into a single "global action" advances the policy objectives of tort law (and in particular the related objectives of compensation and deterrence) in a mass tort setting, the decisions remain to be made regarding the most effective way to combine them.

Certainly, governments can and have enacted particular legislation to deal with some widespread injuries; this generally takes the form of an insurance scheme (formal or informal) for the victims coupled with a mechanism by which to recoup the costs of the insurance from the perceived wrongdoers. Workers' compensation laws can be viewed in this context,[65] but are not necessarily related to *mass* torts; perhaps more focused examples would be the Black Lung[66] and

---

63. Charles Fried & David Rosenberg, "Making Tort Law: What Should be Done and who Should Do It" (forthcoming 2002: unpublished manuscript on file with the author) at 74.

64. See Hay & Rosenberg, above note 48 at 1383 (arguing that the elimination of wasteful redundancy is a goal secondary to increasing plaintiff recovery through exploitation of economies of scale).

    Redressing this imbalance has also been viewed as an aspect of the goal of "behaviour modification" as distinct from general deterrence (see discussion of *Chace* v. *Crane Canada*, below Chapter Three.).

65. Most schemes involve a mandatory (and generally exclusive) insurance plan to benefit injured workers, while assessing premiums from employers based on the nature of their industry its aggregate injury record, and their individual claims history.

66. See *Black Lung Benefits Act of 1972*, 30 U.S.C. §§901 *et seq.*, discussed in *Usery* v. *Turner Elkhorn Mining Co.*, 428 U.S. 1, 15 (1976).

Childhood Vaccination[67] statutes in the United States or the tobacco-related health care costs recovery schemes of British Columbia[68] and Newfoundland.[69] Extreme and fundamental changes to tort law are also not unknown; the American *Drug Dealer's Liability Act* has been adopted in 14 U.S. jurisdictions,[70] and assigns civil liability to drug dealers for all drug-related harm within the area deemed to be their "market," bypassing requirements for any showing of causation.

Other devices available to plaintiffs are voluntary joinder and test cases; the former, however, is impractical for classes over an easily manageable size, and the latter are plagued by problems of application (i.e. issue estoppel and *res judicata*). Equitable aggregation, long accepted in Anglo-American jurisprudence, is another option, described (in the context of interprovincial classes) in detail in Part III below.

Such devices, though, are generally limited to particular types of harm and lack the fluid responsiveness of the tort litigation "marketplace." Moreover, mass tort judgments – or more often settlements – are more meticulously drafted, often over a period of years, by the very stakeholders in the dispute; it can be expected

---

67. *National Childhood Vaccination Injury Act of 1986*, Pub. L. No. 99-660, tit. III, s. 301, 100 Stat. 3755, 3756 (1986) (codified at 42 U.S.C. 300aa (1986)).

68. *Tobacco Damages and Health Care Costs Recovery Act*, S.B.C. 2000, Chap. 30.

69. *Tobacco Health Care Costs Recovery Act*, S. Nfld. & Lab. 2001, c. T-4.2.

70. Arkansas: *Drug Dealer Liability Act*, 1995 Ark. Acts No. 896 (codified at Ark. Code Ann. " 16-124-101 to -112 (Michie Supp. 1997)); California: *Drug Dealer Liability Act*, 1996 Cal. Legis. Serv. 3792 (West) (codified at Cal. Health & Safety Code " 11700 to 11717 (West Supp. 1998)); Colorado: Colo. Rev. Stat. 13-21-801 to 813; Georgia: *Drug Dealer Liability Act*, 1997 Ga. Laws 387 (codified at O.C.G.A. ' 51-1-46 (Supp. 1998)); Hawaii: *Drug Dealer Liability Act*, 1995 Haw. Sess. Laws ch. 203 (codified at Haw. Rev. Stat. Ann. ' 663D (Mich. Supp. 1997)); Illinois: *Drug Dealer Liability Act*, 1995 Ill. Leg. Serv. 89-293 (West) (codified at 740 ILL. COMP. STAT. ANN. 57/1-25 (West Supp. 1997)); Indiana: *Drug Dealer Liability Act*, 1997 Ind. Acts 2924 (codified at Ind. Code Ann. ' 34-1-70 (Michie Supp. 1998) (repealed by 1998 Ind. Acts. 8 (effective July 1, 1998)); Louisiana: *Louisiana Drug Dealer Liability Act*, 1997 La. Sess. Law Serv. 719 (West) (codified at La. Rev. Stat. Ann. " 9:2800.61-.76 (West Supp. 1998)); Michigan: *Drug Dealer Liability Act*, 1994 Mich. Legis. Serv. 27 (West) (codified at Mich. Comp. Laws Ann. " 691.1601-.1619 (West Supp. 1998)); Oklahoma: *Drug Dealer Liability Act*, 1994 Okla. Sess. Law Serv. ch. 179 (West) (codified at Okla. Stat. Ann. tit. 63, " 2-421 to -435 (West 1997)); South Carolina: S. Carolina Stat. 44-54-10 to 140; South Dakota: *South Dakota Codified Laws* Sec. 34-20 C-1 et seq.; Utah: *Drug Dealer's Liability Act*, 1997 Utah Laws 1991 (codified at Utah Code Ann. " 58-37e-1 to -14 (Supp. 1998)); U.S. Virgin Islands: 19 V.I.C. 641 to 658.

that they will be substantially more nuanced than legislation arrived at through political compromise, and indeed experience has borne this out.[71]

It is not surprising, then, that the most successful aggregative tool adopted in fault-based liability jurisdictions – the class action lawsuit – was designed sufficiently loosely to provide a broad segment of society (potential plaintiffs and their lawyers) with some measure of regulatory power, as well as to provide otherwise marginal plaintiffs (i.e. those whose cases might not economically merit individual adjudication) with appropriate compensation. Nevertheless, present system design is suboptimal to the extent that it limits its ambitions to these objectives alone.

(3) The Functions of Class Litigation

(a) Stated Goals

In the United States at the time of the adoption of Rule 23 of the *Federal Rules of Civil Procedure*,[72] little thought went into the question of the class action's role in society beyond a rather simple ambition to provide a mechanism of benefit to individuals who were otherwise without recourse to the courts.[73] Despite the experience of almost forty years of class actions, it is still not unusual to find modern scholars discussing the purposes of aggregate litigation in essentially these terms. In a comprehensive article on developments in civil litigation, for instance, the *Harvard Law Review* in 2000 discussed the "two important functions" of "the modern class action":

> . . . first, it provides individuals with injuries insufficient to justify the cost of a lawsuit an economically feasible avenue of redress; second, it helps relieve the burden on court dockets . . . arising from mass torts . . .[74]

Only somewhat later does the Harvard article discuss deterrence, and it does so only as an aspect of "procedural fairness," focusing again on "widespread, but

---

71. See generally Peter Schuck, "Mass Torts: An Institutional Evolutionist Perspective" (1995) 80 Cornell L. Rev. 941 [Schuck, "Institutional Evolutionist Perspective"] at 985-987. A Canadian example of a comprehensive settlement establishing a *de facto* administrative scheme can be seen in that arising from the tainted blood litigation in Quebec, Ontario and British Columbia. The terms of the settlement and the reasons for approval are described in the decisions of Smith J. in *Endean* v. *Canadian Red Cross Society* (1999), [2000] 1 W.W.R. 688, 68 B.C.L.R. (3d) 350 (S.C.), the decision of Winkler J. in *Parsons* v. *Canadian Red Cross Society*, [1999] O.J. No. 3572 (S.C.J.), and the decision of Morneau J. in *Honhon c. Canada (Procureur général)*, [1999] J.Q. no 4370 (S.C.).

72. See Chapter 6.

73. See generally Arthur A. Miller, "Of Frankenstein Monsters and Shining Knights: Myth, Reality, and the 'Class Action Problem'" (1979) 92 Harv. L. Rev. 664.

74. "Developments" above note 54 at 1806-1807.

individually minimal harm."[75] This pervasive emphasis on the class action's deterrent effect on numerous low value claims, has taken deep root in Canada,[76] where the goal of access to justice is described as overarching.[77]

Despite the significant differences between the U.S. and Canadian statutes, courts often rely on U.S. literature to divine the latter's purposes, as did the Supreme Court of Canada in *Western Canada Shopping Centres Inc.* v. *Dutton*,[78] where the role of deterrence was minimised by listing it third behind purely procedural ambitions, and emphasizing deterrence principally with respect to such numerous low value claims:

> 27 Class actions offer three important advantages over a multiplicity of individual suits. First, by aggregating similar individual actions, class actions serve judicial economy by avoiding unnecessary duplication in fact-finding and legal analysis. The efficiencies thus generated free judicial resources that can be directed at resolving other conflicts, and can also reduce the costs of litigation both for plaintiffs (who can share litigation costs) and for defendants (who need litigate the disputed issue only once, rather than numerous times)[.]

> 28 Second, by allowing fixed litigation costs to be divided over a large number of plaintiffs, class actions improve access to justice by making economical the prosecution of claims that would otherwise be too costly to prosecute individually. Without class actions, the doors of justice remain closed to some plaintiffs, however strong their legal claims. Sharing costs ensures that injuries are not left unremedied[.]

> 29 Third, class actions serve efficiency and justice by ensuring that actual and potential wrongdoers do not ignore their obligations to the public. *Without class actions, those who cause widespread but individually minimal harm might not take into account the full costs of their conduct, because for any one plaintiff the expense of bringing suit would far exceed the likely recovery. Cost-sharing decreases the expense of pursuing legal recourse and accordingly deters potential defendants who might otherwise assume that minor wrongs would not result in litigation[.]*[citations omitted] [emphassis added][79]

This is not to suggest that the Supreme Court is unaware of the basic economic principles of negligence law, which hold that optimal deterrence will be achieved when the full costs of harm are "internalised" by the wrongdoer.[80] Yet,

---

75. *Ibid.*, 1809-10.
76. See for instance Edgell above note 20 at 179 (describing the "reason" for class proceedings as related to claims that are "uneconomic to pursue" and "not [individually] viable".).
77. See for instance Ontario Law Reform Commission, *Report on Class Actions, 3 vols.* (Toronto: Ministry of the Attorney General, 1982) [*Ontario Report (1982)*] at 139 ("effective access to justice is a precondition to the exercise of all other legal rights.")
78. 2001 SCC 46 (*Dutton*).
79. *Ibid.*at paras 27-29. See also *Hollick* v. *Toronto (City)*, 2001 SCC 68 at para. 15.
80. Indeed in *Hollick ibid.* at para. 15, another class action certification case decided in 2001, the Court recognised that deterrence required that "actual and potential

throughout Anglo-Canadian jurisprudence and commentary (and indeed through much of the American), the goal of deterrence is referred to generally with respect to individually non-viable claims.[81] In cases involving both individually viable and non-viable claims, deterrence is regarded as something of a serendipitous side-effect of class litigation; not without value, but subservient to procedural ambitions. The Ontario Law Reform Commission, for instance, discussed deterrence as an "essentially inevitable, albeit important byproduct of class actions [involving a diversity of claims values]."[82]

The mistake is conceptually fundamental and surprisingly widespread, and central to the analysis throughout this book. Insufficient consideration of the true impact of aggregation on deterrence means that the class action device risks being undervalued when assessing it against individualistic alternatives for claims that *are* individually viable. This blindness to the full extent of the class action's deterrent effect leads to systemic inefficiencies in class action system design.[83]

This is a very important point so I must emphasize it here. *The idea that the deterrence advantage of aggregation is lost where some or all of the claims are viable individually is misconceived,* and the fact that so many authoritative sources consider it a truism must lead to the suspicion that deterrence is being systematically undervalued by both courts and legislatures when weighing whether the class action is appropriate, especially when considering cases involving higher-value claims.

(b) Compensation and Deterrence

Many of my arguments with respect to aggregative legislation rely on an assumption that deterrence is, from a public policy perspective, a more important

---

wrongdoers modify their behaviour to take full account of the harm they are causing, or might cause, to the public."

81. Lord Woolf spoke of providing "access to justice where large numbers of people have been affected by another's conduct, but individual loss is so small that it makes an individual action economically unviable": Lord Woolf, *Access to Justice* (Final Report, 1996) [*Woolf Report*] at para. 2. In the report that provided the foundation for Ontario's present legislation, deterrence was featured a little more forcefully, with the Act serving to provide a "sharper sense of obligation to the public by those whose actions affect large numbers of people.": *Report of the Attorney General's Advisory Committee on Class Actions Reform* (Toronto: Attorney General of Ontario, 1990) [*Ontario Report (1990)*].

82. *Ontario Report (1982)* above note 76 at 145-146.

83. I stress again that by "system design" I mean the legislative framework in combination with particular judicial and party decisions made with respect to certification, settlement, and counsel fees. In other words, given the latitude afforded the courts by the various Acts, and given the latitude afforded parties in negotiation and strategy, "system design" can vary considerably from one case to the next.

objective than compensation in furthering the goals of class litigation. Because this might at first appear to be counterintuitive (or at least debatable[84]), I will spend considerable time in this chapter justifying this emphasis.

If we begin with the three identified "benefits" or "advantages" of class proceedings, "access to justice," "judicial economy," and "behaviour modification," a rational interrelationship can be discerned. To begin with, one can consider the first two, access and economy, as methods of facilitating the application by an aggrieved party to the court for redress. As such one might reduce them to a single goal, that of facilitating "efficient compensation."[85] We might consider (for now) compensation as one way of reducing overall accident costs, and thus a valid function of tort law.

Behaviour modification too can be viewed rather malleably. It can consist, for instance, of "general deterrence" (modifying the ex ante behaviour of defendants – and plaintiffs – to prevent the accident from ever happening); it might also be viewed in terms of "specific deterrence" (preventing the same defendant – or plaintiff – from acting negligently in the future). Each of these serves the goal of reducing overall accident costs, and both are therefore valid functions of negligence law.

However, there is another aspect of behaviour modification that I will mention now and discuss in more detail throughout this book: the goal of modifying the behaviour of the parties ex post – after the accident has occurred – not with

---

84. Commentators and judges too often consider compensation of paramount importance, but offer no analysis in support of the position: William W. Schwartzer, "Settlements of Mass Tort Class Actions" (1995) 80 Cornell L. Rev. 837 at 837 (referring to the primary objective of the tort system as "to compensate injured parties in fair and rational ways"); Richard M. Posner, "A Theory of Negligence" (1972) 1 J. Legal Stud. 29 at 30 (describing the orthodox view of scholars that "the dominant purpose of civil liability for accidents is to compensate the victim"); Warren A. Seavey, "Book Review" (1931) 45 Harv. L. Rev. 209 at 211-212 (Tort liability . . . exists chiefly to compensate an individual, as nearly as may be, for loss caused by the defendant's conduct, either by making the financial position of the plaintiff as good as it was before, or would have been if the defendant had not acted, by giving him balm for his wounded pride or damaged body or by doing both.").

85. The reader might think I am taking a liberty when I interpolate the goal of "access to justice" into that of "compensation". There may be more benefit in "access to justice" than simply receiving money to offset losses. It might be argued, for instance, that one's "day in court" is of value in itself, in that it offers an opportunity to be vindicated (the "day in court ideal" will be discussed in greater detail later). Also, tort scholars sometimes discuss the value of the court process in avoiding "self-help"; i.e., preventing people from taking justice into their own hands. I do not consider the "self-help" concern particularly relevant to negligence as distinct from intentional torts, and it is not discussed in any detail here.

a view to directly preventing them from causing future accidents, but rather with a view to resolving their existing dispute in a way that will further the valid functions of tort law. To take settlement negotiations as an example, such negotiations will only be successful if the amount received by the plaintiff is, probabilistically, close to that to which he is entitled. If he settles for too little, there is insufficient deterrence and undercompensation; if the defendant pays too much, there is overdeterrence and — possibly — overcompensation.[86] It might be suggested, then, that this aspect of behaviour modification — modifying the behaviour of parties during the litigation process — is a component of *both* compensation and deterrence, and therefore might be employed to further the valid functions of tort law. The speed with which a resolution is reached is also important, as reducing litigation expense is one way of further reducing the overall costs of accidents. We might also view some aspects of the goal of "judicial economy" as similarly bifurcated – it arguably advances both compensation and deterrence, but has an independent value to the extent that it tends to reduce litigation costs incurred by society.

Compensation and deterrence are not conceptually co-dependent; that is, one can have a system to redress negligence that advances deterrence without providing compensation (a regulatory or criminal scheme, for instance), or one could have a system that compensates without deterring (for instance, through governmental or private first-person insurance). To the extent that the two can be divorced conceptually,[87] can we express a preference for one over the other?

It might be immediately apparent that effective deterrence has certain obvious structural advantages to effective compensation. If the goal of negligence law is to minimise the overall harm to society caused by accidents (and I assume throughout this analysis that this is indeed the goal), then avoiding the accident to begin with has an indisputable advantage over *any* method which relies on a process of ex post assessment of damages, and subsequent transfer of wealth

---

86. I say "possibly" because it is also possible that the plaintiffs' *net* recovery after litigation costs are paid may still represent incomplete restitution for harms suffered.

87. Some scholars discuss the idea of "corrective justice," the idea that there is innate benefit in the transference from the injurer to the injured that transcends both compensation and deterrence, but happily accomplishes both: see for instance Richard A. Posner, "The Concept of Corrective Justice in Recent Theories of Tort Law" (1981) 10 J. Legal Stud. 187 at 198. While I do not reject the possibility that there may be utility above and beyond compensation and deterrence, it seems better to consider this a question of the value assigned to the "taste for notions of fairness" described by Kaplow & Shavell in "Fairness vs. Welfare" above note 21 at 1350-55. The propositions in this book rest in large part on a rejection of the Aristotelian notion of "corrective justice" as superior to (or even necessarily distinct from) a system designed around economic principles, or as Posner puts it *ibid.* at 206, "whether corrective justice imposes duties regardless of cost."

from one party to another in amelioration.[88] To look at it another way, the common law has long accepted a definition of compensation as *restitutio ad integrum*; the idea that the victim should be put in the position that she would have been in had the accident not occurred. An admirable ambition, but a practical impossibility when the only method available is the transfer of financial wealth. Taking a broader view, one might say that *only* deterrence fulfills the idea of *restitutio*; only if the accident is avoided will the victim be truly in that same position.

On the scale of society as an aggregate of individuals, each of whom might become tortfeasor or tort victim, we might foresee a situation in which an equilibrium of "optimal tort deterrence" is attained. That is, a situation in which very few are negligent because it will cost more to compensate the victim than to take appropriate precautions. In such a case, the only "unknowables" are the extent of the duties among individuals and the related question of the standard of care, which together determine the social tolerance for accidents.[89] In this paradigm, the only purpose of the court system would be, through the minimum number of cases necessary, to define and track the standard of care.[90] Thus accurate deter-

---

88. Yet obviously, deterrence, like compensation, has a price; its price is expressed mostly in the cost of precautions designed to avoid the accidents, and the opportunity cost of lessened risky activity as well. These expenses will be discussed further as we look at the economics of aggregation; for now it should be kept in mind that favouring deterrence over compensation essentially involves forcing the person engaging in risky behaviour to "internalise" the cost of avoiding the accident, rather than forcing the victim and society to absorb the expenses. "Reasonable" precautions will by definition be cheaper than ex post compensation for the harm caused.

89. As callous as it might be to articulate, negligence law anticipates that virtually every activity carries both risks and rewards; it is only *undesirable* (i.e. "unreasonable") risks that the common law of tort seeks to discourage. "Our society is not," as Calabresi noted, "committed to preserving life at any cost.": *The Costs of Accidents*, above note 21 at 17. Viewed this way, tort liability is a method of manipulating the degree of care taken to achieve the socially optimal level of risk.

90. Posner describes a "capital stock of precedents" as arising from those cases in which the value estimates of the defendant and plaintiff diverge. If the legal uncertainty is great, more litigation will ensue. Writes Posner in *Economic Analysis of Law* (above note 21 at 589):

> But since litigation generates precedents, the surge in litigation will lead to a reduction in legal uncertainty, causing the amount of litigation to fall in the next period. Eventually, with few new precedents being produced, legal uncertainty will rise as the old precedents depreciate (because they are less informative in a changed environment), and this uncertainty will evoke a new burst of litigation and hence an increased output of precedents. Thus, even though there is no market for precedents as such, the production of precedents will rise when their

rence reduces not only harm to the victim, but also social costs associated with recovery for such harm.

Of course, in the realm of mass tort, citizens are *not* equally likely to become victims or tortfeasors; the nature of mass torts means that the majority stand to be victims of tort rather than beneficiaries of the tort. To the extent that this is true,[91] a society of risk-averse potential victims might be said to prefer deterrence even more than they would in the standard economic model of risk-neutrality.

So we reach the conclusion that, between accurate compensation and accurate deterrence, deterrence is, overall, to be preferred, in part because only it properly "compensates," but also because it best fulfills the goal of reduction of overall accident costs. This leads to the further conclusion that the most effective form of compensation will be the one that most effectively deters, because, again, effective deterrence fulfills the truest goals of compensation *ad integrum*, when viewed on a macro scale. This argument might appear at first somewhat circular, but it is not, if we start from the assumption that accidents and their costs represent a social ill that must be minimised.

(c) The Role of Compensation

While deterrence is a form of "perfect compensation," compensation alone in a negligence system can never provide similarly perfect deterrence. There will always be a level of precaution above which a defendant will not spend, because it is not in its financial interest to do so. Setting aside, for the moment, the transaction costs involved in recovering the compensation from the wrongdoer, we might ask, "what is the level of compensation that would provide the appropriate level of deterrence?" Phrased this way, it might be helpful to view for the time being the compensation as a "fine"; our question is then, "how much should the defendant have to pay to achieve the optimum level of deterrence?" The answer, at least in a system relying on negligence, is that the defendant should pay the full costs – individual or social – resulting from his behaviour that failed to meet the appropriate standard of care.[92]

---

social value rises as a consequence of increased legal uncertainty and fall as that value falls.

91. It might be argued that in an age where the majority of potential tort victims own shares of corporations (directly, or indirectly through pension or mutual funds), the division between tortfeasor and victim is less clear today than it was even a few decades ago. This may have the result, econometrically at least, of making society less risk-averse, even if it is not likely to make individuals less so. I am unaware of any published work analysing this question, and so raise it here only as an aside.

92. There is another dimension to the reduction of accident costs through deterrence, and that is the level of the risky activity, which may be reduced as liability is internalised. Activity level is generally not considered in the determination of "reasonableness" in tort law, apparently for policy reasons. This is accepted to be a "defect in the negligence rule" and one reason that economic analysts of law frequently

Therefore it might be said that, in our present tort system, where the bulk of the "fine" imposed is in the form of compensation paid to the plaintiff, it is seen as desirable that the plaintiff be compensated, to the extent possible, for the entire amount of his loss. Does the individualistic tort system accomplish this?

It would appear not. The fearsome transaction costs involved in litigation, not to mention the time and energy a plaintiff must devote to a private suit, are a strong disincentive to the victim to pursue compensation. As a result, as a practical matter, only a small number of aggrieved parties actually use the tort system to recover any damages at all.[93] Instead, most potential tort victims either purchase first party insurance policies or participate in a social welfare system based on premiums exacted through taxation to see them through accidents or injuries. In other words, the tortfeasor is frequently able to externalize the costs of his wrongdoing, to spread those costs among his victims and over society generally. To the extent that these costs are higher than the cost of avoiding them would have been, public and corporate taxation rates incorporating such tort insurance premiums will also be above what is socially optimal.[94]

In fact, the civil legal system as it has evolved has shown itself to be a remarkably *in*efficient way of compensating tort victims. Compared to first person insurance, which costs around twenty cents per dollar of recovery, tort systems generally cost a dollar or more when all expenses (plaintiff's, defendant's and society's) are factored in.[95] Moreover, because the "premiums" of "tort insur-

---

favour a strict liability model: see for instance Shavell, *Economic Analysis of Accident Law*, above note 21 at 21-32.

93. Claiming rates vary sharply depending on the type of incident; in the U.S., it would appear that at least half of persons injured in motor vehicle accidents make at least an informal attempt to collect from another party, while the overall rate of pursued tort grievances is 3.8%: Richard E. Miller & Austin Sarat, "Grievances, Claims, and Disputes: Assessing the Adversary Culture" (1981) 15 L. & Soc'y Rev. 525 at 544-5. See also Michael J. Saks, "Do We Really Know Anything About the Behavior of the Tort Litigation System – and Why Not?" (1992) 140 Pa. L. Rev. 1147 at 1286 ("So little compensation is achieved through the tort system that only as an act of hyperbole can it be said to be part of an injury compensation system.") The possibility that Canadian rates are lower still due to the higher degree of social insurance is supported by recent data on the pursuit rate of medical malpractice claims in U.S. States, which suggests that those with insurance are less likely to sue (as are the poor and elderly, though likely for different reasons): E.J. Thomas, D.M. Studdert, H.R. Burstin, E.J. Orav, T. Zeena, E.J. Williams, K.M. Howard, P.C. Weiler, T.A. Brennan, "Incidence and types of adverse events and negligent care in Utah and Colorado" (2000) 38 Medical Care 261.

94. Rosenberg, "What the Defendants Have" above note 55 at 408 n. 37.

95. Shavell, *Economic Analysis of Accident Law* above note 21 at 263 (suggesting the $1 figure for tort compensation). Consider a fictitious personal injury claim where the damages are $100. The plaintiff's attorney might take $30 as his contingent fee.

ance" are built into the prices of consumer goods as well as into public taxation, poorer consumers end up "subsidising" richer ones (who, due to their higher income, will have relatively larger damages if an accident occurs).[96]

But even this misses the central insight of economists who have studied accident law: because tort damages will always exceed the costs of reasonable precautions, as long as legitimate negligence claims are, for whatever reason, not being brought, a disproportionate and unnecessary amount of society's wealth is being spent compensating for harm compared to that required to avoid it.[97]

So when designing tort law focusing ostensibly on compensation principles, we might consider that the rules governing compensation are not self-justified; their objectives in fact serve the main purpose of the tort action – the beneficial modification of social behaviour and the elimination of undesirable risks. This point bears repeating because it is an integral part of this analysis: the purpose of tort law is to compel, through market forces, potential defendants to internalise something approaching the true costs of their negligence, thus providing an incentive to exercise an appropriate degree of care.

With respect to negligence, then, the general rule must be that compensation awarded in the form of damages must reflect as closely as possible the true mag-

---

Assume that the defendant's spending is roughly the same, and expenditures by the government (court costs etc.) is $10, and you have $70 spent to compensate the plaintiff, who receives the same $70 after her lawyer's fee is deducted. In fact this may be low. Although figures in Canada are not readily available, studies done in the United States indicate that, in non-automobile tort litigation, plaintiffs receive on average 43% of the total spent on litigation: James S. Kakalik & Nicholas M. Pace, *Costs and Compensation Paid in Tort Litigation* (Washington, D.C.: Rand, 1986) at 74.

96. See Richard L. Abel, "A Critique of American Tort Law" (1981) 8 Brit. J.L. & Soc'y 199 at 202-06; George L. Priest "A Theory of the Consumer Product Warranty" (1981) 90 Yale L.J. 1297 at 1350-51. A similar point has been made about many rules of contract law: William Bishop, "The Contract-Tort Boundary and the Economics of Insurance" (1983) 12 J. Legal Stud. 241 at 258.

97. Steven Shavell uses the following simple table to illustrate the idea of "optimal deterrence': imagine that taking various levels of precautions will decrease the chance of an accident occurring that will cause harm of 100 (you can think of these units as dollars, though they are not necessarily). In Shavell's scenario, moderate precautions will reduce the accident probability from 15% (without precautions) to 10%. Exercising a high level of precautions will reduce them further to 8%, but will cost twice as much. Therefore:

Precautions	Cost of Care	Accident Probability	Harm	Total costs
None	0	15%	15	15
Moderate	3	10%	10	13
High	6	8%	8	14

Shavell, *Economic Analysis of Accident Law*, above note 21 at 7.

nitude of the harm caused by the defendant's unreasonable failure to take precautions.[98] This does not mean that the appropriate precautions are *always* measured by tallying dollars: sometimes, a harmful activity may be seen as having some overriding social utility, in which case the general public can reasonably be expected to accept some risk of loss in exchange for the benefits derived.[99] Similarly, a desire to constrain the recklessness of individuals can lead to rules in which recovery is reduced (or liability negated outright) if the plaintiff voluntarily assumed the risk, or was himself negligent.[100]

Viewed this way, compensation is the measure of unreasonable harm, and assigning it to the defendant is simply a way of furthering the main goal of deterrence. Indeed, the fact that the traditional, individualistic products liability or other mass tort cases often involve claims for punitive or aggravated damages may be indicative, from a purely economic view, of the tort system's fundamental failure to deter negligent decisions on the part of mass-producers. In a system of efficient litigation of valid tort claims, such awards would no longer be required, at least not in order to assuage the courts' suspicions that the claims before them represent only a fraction of the harm actually caused by the defendant and other tortfeasors.

---

98.   I make the point repeatedly here that deterrence tends to be undervalued as a goal in class litigation. This is not, however, universally the case. Discussing objections that class action judgments are prohibitively large, the *Alberta Report* offers a succinct riposte above note 17 at 59:

> [I]n our view, to limit access to justice on the grounds that it will impose costs on wrongdoers is not the appropriate social policy. The measure of the wrong is the loss caused by the wrongful conduct.

99.   But such policy considerations are generally reflected in substantive rules of tort designed to protect the freedom to pursue certain activities. Hence exemptions from negligence liability for governmental policy decisions, the common law's tolerance for industrial pollution or nuisance that is not, in the court's view, "unreasonable", or international accords capping liability for losses suffered in air disasters.

100.   It is apt to note, as have several scholars and judges, that all notions of "reasonableness" in tort – for instance those found as elements of the standard of care, foreseeability, reliance, failure to warn, strict liability, contributory negligence, and so on – are themselves the product of a "virtual aggregation"; i.e. that the imposition of objective standards inherently relies upon an average view of the standards of the similarly-situated population: see for instance Rosenberg, "Risk-Based Claims" above note 22 at 248-52; Thomas E. Willging, "Mass Tort Problems and Proposals: A Report to the Mass Torts Working Group," (Federal Judicial Center 1999, available at http://www.fjc.gov/public/pdf.nsf/lookup/MassTApC.pdf) at 41. It may be, therefore, that aggregation will allow these factors to be considered in an actual aggregate population, rather than in the fictional thought experiments centred on the behaviour of Clapham Omnibus passengers.

(d) A Larger View of Deterrence

I have proposed that if one accepts the truism that litigation is far worse at providing compensation than is insurance, then the court process must be seen principally as a method of encouraging defendant investment in care – i.e. as a deterrent. It follows that, while the somewhat distinct goal of "conservation of judicial resources," is certainly worthy,[101] it too serves the final end of deterrence through minimising social cost (and thus shifting a higher percentage of the cost of harm on to the defendant) as well as facilitating recovery (and thus also shifting a higher percentage of the social cost onto the defendant).[102] In contrast to these two aims of "access to courts" (for compensation) and "judicial economy" (reduction of social harm), which most efficiently serve, as I have said, as indirect methods of behaviour modification, only this third goal, deterrence, is directly connected to the overall end – the overall reduction of accident costs.

Yet we must draw a distinction here between the true, robust, role of deterrence that I have described, and the much more modest role proposed by most advocates of class litigation. As we have seen, when commentators focus on the role of deterrence in mass tort litigation, they tend to regard only the effect of aggregating multiple, low-value claims, i.e. claims that could not economically be brought individually. The analysis here suggests that the proper role for class litigation in promoting social objectives requires examination of ways in which aggregation furthers deterrence regardless of the independent viability of the individual claims. This point is important, because it provides answers to frequently-stated objections to the idea of collective litigation of high-value claims.

So, to restate this idea by way of introduction to the ensuing analysis: my conclusion will be that mass tort policy generally – and deterrence in particular — benefits from the procedural aggregation of claims to the greatest practicable extent. But I stress that the impact of aggregation upon deterrence goes well beyond that generally attributed to it; in other words, aggregation will tend to optimise deterrence not only in situations of numerous low-value claims, but even where many claims are sufficiently valuable to be brought individually. The next chapter is largely devoted to explaining why this is so.

---

101. Although, as we shall see, conservation of judicial resources in a class action system may be unrealistic as an independent goal given that many aggregated claims would not have been pursued individually.

102. If there is confusion about the role of litigation costs in the simple deterrence model sketched out in footnote 97 above, it might assist for now to simply consider it part of the "harm" suffered, listed in the final column.

CHAPTER THREE

—

Deterrence and Behaviour Modification

A. INTRODUCTION

The purpose of this chapter is to review the ways in which the aggregation of claims into a class action affects the outcome of litigation. My objective is to review some of the generally-accepted benefits derived from class actions, such as enhanced per-claim recovery and deterrence of otherwise un-actionable wrongs, and also to demonstrate some of the less apparent ways in which aggregation of claims provides market effects that beneficially modify the behaviour of potential mass tortfeasors.

As the discussion proceeds, I will also introduce some public law implications of class action system design, such as the sometimes controversial vision of the class counsel as "private prosecutor," serving the public's interest in deterrence of wrongdoing.

B. AGGREGATION, COMPENSATION AND DETERRENCE

In the examples that follow throughout this book, I use the term "defendant" to describe the potential mass-producer of a tort, whether or not the tort has yet occurred (i.e. whether we are considering ex ante – from the viewpoint of deterrence incentives – or ex post – after the damage has arisen and litigation is underway or threatened).

(1) Aggregation and Compensation

Consider a situation where a tortfeasor harms three remote people through a centralized decision. Each of the three suffers $500 damages. Assume it will cost $300 (for each plaintiff and the defendant) to litigate the action, so each of the claims is independently viable. The defendant, though, exploiting its economy of scale, spends only $300 to defend all the actions.[1]

You could view this example in the aggregate, as the defendant would: the defendant's damages exposure is $1500; its litigation costs are $300, so the total it stands to lose is $1800. The plaintiffs stand to receive $1500 less their own litigation costs of $900, for a net recovery of $600, or $200 each.[2]

In such circumstances it is not difficult to see the immediate impact that aggregation will have on compensation. If the three claims are combined, and if litigation costs remain fixed, then the plaintiffs stand to recover $1200 ($1500 minus $300 litigation costs), or $400 each. This is the immediate effect of aggregation on compensation and is simply the result of the elimination of redundant costs.[3]

But notice that, so far, there is no enhanced *deterrent* effect from the aggregation; in either case, the defendant "internalises" something approaching the full cost of harm: $1500 plus its own expenses. If any of the three claims is *not* independently viable (i.e. it costs more for the plaintiff to litigate than could be recovered), then optimal deterrence might be lost if the claims were pursued individually.[4]

So we can tell that there is an immediate *compensation* benefit to aggregation regardless of whether the claims are individually viable. However, in this simple example, there is no increase in *deterrence* unless some of the claims would not have been brought as individual actions. This simple calculation is the source of the general belief that aggregation of numerous individually-viable claims does nothing to enhance the deterrence effect; that deterrence, in other words, relies on the inclusion of claims that would not otherwise be pursued.

---

1. Assuming for simplicity's sake that there are no non-common issues; the example will hold to some degree if there is any "issue overlap" at all.
2. For simplicity's sake I am assuming no "loser pays" cost-shifting rules apply.
3. David Rosenberg, "Mass Tort Class Actions – What the Defendants Have and Plaintiffs Don't" (2000) 37 Harv. J. Legis. 393 [Rosenberg, "What the Defendants Have"] at 398.
4. Consider for instance if two of the three claims were worth only $250 each, and the other $500, and litigation costs remained fixed at $300. The two low-value claims would not be pursued; the defendant, having caused $1000 worth of damages, would face only $500 in claims and a total of $800 in overall exposure.

(2) Non-Pecuniary Utility and Information Deficits

The above example is an oversimplification, because it makes the familiar econometric error of equating "utility" or "welfare" of an individual with that person's "wealth." That is to say, it is a model of what risk-neutral "wealth maximizers" will do given perfect information and infinite rationality.

In fact, the decision whether to sue is often based on a number of not easily quantifiable non-monetary factors. Very few people, as every lawyer knows, are drawn to the litigation process. Many, many more are inclined to avoid it, because they are pessimistic about the outcome, concerned over the stress of the process, possess a general aversion to lawyers and courts, or even have an inclination to travel abroad – all considerations that might weigh against their expected gain or recovery from litigation.

Therefore, to the extent that any individual plaintiffs consider other aspects of "utility" – the value of their time, stress, the value of "moving on," and so on, it is likely that their (technically viable) claims will not be pursued, unless the expected recovery is sufficient to overcome their reluctance. Some plaintiffs, for instance, would not bother litigating for $100 expected recovery; others might not go to court even if the recovery were much higher. The important point is that whatever the value of an individual's reluctance to litigate, this amount accrues to the defendant as, in effect, a bonus; it will reduce its precautions, not with regard to the harm it causes, but rather with regard only to the recovery that persons will make the effort to extract from it.

In an aggregated claim, all of an individual's extraneous "utility costs" that are associated with the personal conduct of litigation are removed (except for a single representative plaintiff perhaps) as the claims are turned over to an experienced and risk-neutral "manager" – the class counsel. Class actions can provide redress, in other words, where individuals would not seek help themselves, even though they could. It might be argued that there is no pressing reason to help people who do not seek help, and perhaps would not individually accept the help even if it were offered. To accept such an argument is to ignore the deterrence effect; it allows the defendant to externalise potentially vast aggregate harm simply because it is not in any individual's interest to take it to task.

There is a further problem that can prevent the pursuit of valid claims: information deficit. In many cases, persons who have suffered harm may not know it; typical examples might be securities fraud, telephone or bank overcharges, or where a person has been unknowingly exposed to a toxic substance that has increased the risk of a particular disease, but where the disease is either not manifest or is not attributed by the victim to the exposure.

To this extent, aggregation of individually viable claims *does* have an immediate impact on deterrence, and deterrence increases with the universality of the aggregation. That is, a mandatory class would provide optimal deterrence; voluntary joinder, or "opting in" would tend to provide less, and standard "opt out" classes would be somewhere in between.

(3) The Role of the Cost-Spreading of Litigation Investment

The compensation advantages that accrue to mass tort victims as a result of aggregation are the result of cost-spreading of litigation expenses among the members of the class. Initial deterrence effects are noted when claims which are either unviable individually or are viable but not adequately pursued due to non-pecuniary interests of the plaintiffs, are brought on a class-wide basis by class counsel acting as investor in and manager of the claims. This class-wide spreading of litigation costs, though, has an important secondary effect that is not generally acknowledged: the greater the aggregation, the larger may be the global amount at stake. In other words, the whole of an aggregate claim will be worth considerably more than the sum of its parts.

The conceptual mistake comes from our initial assumption of the harm as fixed and equal to the expected recovery. In the real world, of course, this is not the case: litigation investment is not an all–or–nothing enterprise. Participants recognize that their chances of prevailing in a lawsuit increase with the amount of investment in the litigation,[5] and so an investor in the litigation (defendant or

---

5.   While many would wish it otherwise, it is an easy point to demonstrate in the abstract. One might require only a few hundred dollars to file a lawsuit in the superior court of any province. If that is all a plaintiff invests in the litigation, he will certainly lose (assuming that the other side shows up), and so has a zero percent chance of recovery, even if he has a valid claim for $100,000.

At the other end of the scale, even a limitless commitment of resources far in excess of the possible recovery would not guarantee 100% success in all but the rarest instance. Yet it is easy to suppose that there will be many, many investment decisions falling within those extremes that will increase the plaintiff's chance of realizing his $100,000, and thus raising the expected value of the claim in absolute terms. One example would be an investment in airline tickets and extra lawyers' fees so that discovery might be conducted in another town; another obvious example is investment in expert reports, which can substantially improve a case's chance of success. In our example, an investment of $10,000 might yield a 50% chance of recovery, increasing the "expected value" of the claim to $50,000.

Judge Posner provides perhaps the kindest explanation of why increased litigation investment increases chances of victory at trial when he suggests that expenditures "increase the probability of a correct decision by giving the tribunal more information": Richard A. Posner, *Economic Analysis of Law* (5th) (Boston: Little, Brown, 1998) at 620-621. Other writers also stress investment as an aid to "accuracy," while a more cynical view might be that without optimum plaintiff investment, massive defendant investment would tend to increase *in*accuracy of result. See generally Louis Kaplow, "The Value of Accuracy in Adjudication: An Economic Analysis" (1994) 3 J. Legal Stud. 307.

plaintiff) can be expected to invest up to the point of diminishing returns.[6] But because, like other forms of speculation, litigation return is probabilistic (i.e. expressed as a certain "chance" of recovering a given amount of damages), the calculation of "optimal" investment will depend on the amount expected – the more at stake, the greater the incentive to invest to the optimal point, after which returns will be expected to diminish. In a classable claim (a claim with common issues), each additional plaintiff in the aggregate group adds to the gross amount of damages at stake, and increases incentive for optimal investment.

So we could easily foresee a situation where the chances of success in litigation go from perhaps 10% without any significant investment to, say, 80% with optimal investment (that is, investment to the point of diminishing expected returns).

Viewed in economic terms, then, a $100,000 individual claim has a value of between $10,000 and $80,000 to the investor, based on straightforward probability of return. In such an instance, an incentive exists for that investor (either a plaintiff or a lawyer) to consider the optimal level of investment to maximise return.

In an aggregated action, after the initial break-even point, it is self-evident that potential recovery will increase in a linear fashion at a higher rate than expenses. Every shared cost is spread among the plaintiff class, and the cost-per-claim diminishes as the plaintiff class grows. Following this reasoning, the larger the class, the lower the per-claim investment required to ensure a high probability of success and the more likely that the optimum investment point will be reached. In this way, the cost-spreading effect, in addition to making it cheaper to pursue each claim (and as increasing individual plaintiff recovery), actually makes all of the claims more likely to succeed.

This means that the true value of the claim (when viewed in terms of its probability of success) is increased *in its entirety*. If a group of 100 claims is potentially worth $100,000 but does not allow optimum investment in litigation, then the probabilistic value of the aggregated claims might be only 40% of that amount ($40,000) given the uncertainty of the outcome. However, in doubling the class to 200 members we might increase the probability of success to 60% ($120,000) through extra investment in litigation for which an incentive now exists. Even if this advantage is gained through a wholesale doubling of litigation investment, it is still obviously worthwhile, and to the extent that deterrent effect is governed by making the defendant pay the highest proportion of the harm it has unlawfully caused, the purposes of deterrence are enhanced. Per-claim recovery is also in this scenario increased, from $400 to $600 (less per-claim litigation expenses that, in this example, remain constant).

It is important to note that this effect, like all other plaintiff advantages realised by cost-spreading, is fully realised only when the plaintiff group encom-

---

6.   That is, up to the point at which an additional input of investment will yield an equal or lesser amount in expected return.

passes all possible litigants on the common issues; the more potential claimants omitted (yet with respect to whose claims the defendant can aggregate costs), the less likely that optimal litigation investment will be attained. Rosenberg observes that "[t]he [potential defendant] makes the optimal investment in precautions only if plaintiffs not only threaten enforcement of all claims, but also aggregate universally to motivate the optimal litigation investment."[7]

However, at this juncture agency problems can arise between the litigation investor (lawyer) and the members of the class. Assuming that the investor has unlimited opportunity to carry a "portfolio" of separate class claims, he can attempt to maximise investment without regard to the gross return in any particular case. This is because, while an incentive exists to invest optimally to maximise return, *this is not necessarily the same as the optimum level necessary to maximise global recovery* (and thus deterrence).

If, for instance, the $10,000 expected return can be secured with a $500 investment in filing fees alone (if, for instance, one in ten defendants will settle immediately for the full amount, or every defendant can be expected to settle for 10% of the amount), that may constitute a superior investment to paying $30,000 for the 80% chance of success, as the yield in percentage terms is much higher in the first instance. This would certainly be the wiser strategy if the investor had an unlimited number of similar investment opportunities as the averaging effect would virtually guarantee substantial return. However, it would also mean either that those nine out of ten meritorious cases that do *not* immediately settle will not be pursued, or that every case will settle immediately but for the minimal amount. In either case, the defendant is forced to pay only 10% of the harm it has caused, and there is no incentive for the plaintiff investor to pursue a higher amount.[8]

This is an important point that should not be glossed over: in some cases, there exists an incentive for investors in plaintiff litigation to spend considerably less than the optimal amount in pursuing their cases. If the strategy as described above is successful, and the investor is content with the high return on investment even though only one in ten of his cases succeeds, then (again assuming that the other 9 had merit) the deterrent effect upon defendants will be reduced to 10% of its optimum level.

---

7.   David Rosenberg, "Mandatory-Litigation Class Action: The Only Option for Mass Tort Cases" (2001) 115 Harvard L. Rev. 831 [Rosenberg, "The Only Option"] at 664 n. 43.

8.   It might be argued that a "loser pays" fee-shifting arrangement offsets this problem, but in fact it could do so partially at best. Until the point where the investor could be 100% assured of recovering every dollar (or unit of utility) spent in litigation (a practical impossibility), the prospect of recovering fees cannot in itself provide incentive to invest optimally.

(4) Class Counsel as Private Prosecutor

In a class action suit pursued to advance deterrence, the plaintiffs' attorney is acting in the capacity of private prosecutor, exercising the public's right to appropriate deterrence of wrongdoing.[9] It can be expected that entrepreneurial lawyers will be more vigorous in the prosecution of the public's interest than would be regulatory agencies set up as an alternative to the tort system, though some have proposed the latter as preferable.[10] There is no necessary conflict of interest to the extent that he might also be seeking to vindicate the rights of the class members; they share with the public a desire to see the wrongdoer held liable for the appropriate amount – the maximum recovery to which they are entitled at law. The important difference is with respect to the counsel's motivation. As an agent for the class, counsel's fees must be carefully monitored to ensure that they do not inappropriately affect the members' compensation. However, from a deterrent point of view, there is no immediately apparent social interest in restricting the percentage of recovery kept by class counsel; in fact, the more the lawyer is able to keep, the more likely optimal litigation investment will be made and optimal deterrence achieved.[11]

It should be apparent by now that designing the "investor incentives" in the form of plaintiffs' counsel fee structure can be one of the most important policy

---

9.   See generally Owen M. Fiss, "The Political Theory of the Class Action" (1996) 53 Wash. & Lee L. Rev. 21.

10. See Peter Huber, "Safety and the Second Best: The Hazards of Public Risk Management in the Courts" (1985) 85 Colum. L. Rev. 277 at 330. I do not here compare the relative benefits of class actions vis-à-vis administrative regimes to reduce systematic business risk-taking, but I share with Rosenberg doubt of the efficacy of such bureaucracies: David Rosenberg "Class Actions for Mass Torts: Doing Individual Justice by Collective Means" (1987) 62 Ind. L.J. 561 at 579. Of Huber's proposals, Rosenberg writes: "Contrary to the strong but unexplained faith some commentators have expressed in the administrative solution . . . the merits of such a solution are far from unambiguous. The history of regulatory laxity, timidity, and even co-optation in regard to certain large-scale risks does not generate optimism."

It is worrisome, then, that Canadian courts have viewed the existence of oversight and prosecutorial agencies as negating the need for class actions as a positive deterrent, at least with respect to anti-trust cases: see for instance *Price* v. *Panasonic Canada Inc.*, [2002] O.J. No. 2362 (Sup. Ct. J.) at para. 49-50. Yet it has never been a principle of tort law that its deterrent functions are irrelevant if the behaviour complained of is also criminal. It is submitted that only in cases where prosecution has actually occurred, and the resulting penalties are deemed an adequate deterrent, should the regulatory effects of class actions be discounted.

11. Providing there are sufficient safeguards in place to guard against suits filed for their nuisance value alone. This topic is discussed in greater detail later in this part.

decisions made by legislatures or courts. Too little incentive, and neither the social interest in deterrence nor the class interest in compensation will be satisfied. On the other hand, lawyers' fees which seem to take disproportionately from the class recovery appear objectionable *per se*. But should it be so?

Consider the case where proposed counsel fees would consume all or virtually all of the proposed recovery. Courts and commentators have expressed a visceral opposition to such a proposal, even when the claims at issue are so small as to be individually untenable.[12] In such a case, the reaction indicates that deterrence is being considerably undervalued, and the role of plaintiffs' counsel in exercising the public rights is being ignored. As distressing as it may seem, such an arrangement might be the only way of pursuing the wrongdoer, and courts ought to be alive to this possibility.

There is no doubt that some aspects of public disapproval of high fee recoveries are based upon the negative perceptions of lawyers as enriching themselves excessively from the misery of others. But if one considers that the lawyers' gains in such a case would otherwise remain with the wrongdoer, the moral issue becomes more ambiguous. *Someone* is going to gain financial benefit from the injuring activity. Should it be the injurer who benefits (and who will therefore benefit from continued negligence as well), or should it be the one who (albeit for purely selfish reasons) punishes the injurer and makes recurrence of the negligence less likely?[13]

C. BEHAVIOUR MODIFICATION EX POST: AGGREGATION AND SETTLEMENT

(1) The Economics of Settlement Incentives

It is occasionally recognised that the ability of the class action to facilitate equitable settlements of mass claims is another way in which the procedure con-

---

12. See Victor E. Schwartz, Mark A. Behrens & Leah Lorber, "Federal Courts Should Decide Interstate Class Actions: A Call for Federal Class Action Diversity Jurisdiction Reform" (2000) 37 Harv. J. Legis. 483 at 494-95 (criticising apparently empty "in kind" or "cy pres" settlements which nonetheless provided class counsel with large fees).

13. This is not to say that abusive arrangements are impossible. Schwartz *et al.* refer to a case where holders of escrow accounts received refunds from the Bank of Boston of up to $8.76 each, yet some had counsel fees of $144.25 deducted from their accounts as part of a settlement: *Ibid.* at 494, citing anecdotal reports surrounding the resolution of *Kamilewicz* v. *Bank of Boston Corp.* 92 F.3d 506 (7th Cir. 1996). Nevertheless, to extrapolate such apparently bizarre results to a general argument that lawyers' fees should not, as a matter of principle, consume most or all of an award (as Schwartz *et al.* do) seems unwarranted if deterrence is valued as an objective of mass tort litigation.

tributes to "behaviour modification." In *Chace* v. *Crane Canada*, Mackenzie J. noted that:

> There have already been at least two decided cases, one in the B.C. Provincial Court, Small Claims division, and one in this court, referred to in the affidavit of Dean Schmode, in which the plaintiffs were successful in proving negligence. Crane has not accepted these decisions as having any general application and there is no reason to conclude that Crane would treat further cases any differently. There is also the problem of limitation periods running against individual claimants while a test case is being litigated.

> Crane asserts that it is prepared to settle individual claims and has settled such claims in the past. However, it is apparent that its settlement posture includes a denial of negligence which gives it a substantial advantage in negotiations because of the high relative cost of proof on that issue. A class proceeding would deal effectively with that imbalance.[14]

This statement is a rare explicit recourse to what we might call "ex post behaviour modification": the realisation that the inequality between plaintiff and defendant in individual actions will systematically depress the settlement values of individual claims, and thus of the aggregate of all claims' total value, and that class actions can correct this. The balance of this section is dedicated to explaining this concern.

As a practical matter, the overwhelming majority of aggregate suits, like individual ones, will never go to trial but instead will settle. Indeed, aside from the uncertainty of a trial's outcome[15] (and thus different opinions regarding the true value of any claim), both plaintiff and defendant have a strong incentive – in the form of their own litigation costs – to avoid trial.[16]

The standard model of litigation settlement holds that the defendant's "maximum offer" will be the expected judgment amount plus litigation costs. The plaintiff's "minimum demand" will be the judgment *minus* litigation costs. In ordinary circumstances, the parties will settle on average at the mean point between the maximum offer and minimum demand.[17]

We might graph the settlement relationship in simple terms by assuming that the expected value of any individual claim is $300 (i.e. a certain claim for that amount, or a 50% probability of recovering $600, etc.). We might suppose that

---

14. *Chace* v. *Crane Canada* (1996), 26 B.C.L.R. (3d) 339 (S.C.) at para. 24.

15. And disregarding variables such as unequal bargaining power, differential risk-aversion, and so on.

16. Again, "loser pays" costs-shifting arrangements do not affect this incentive, though they may increase or reduce it in certain circumstances, principally to the extent that information regarding the value of the claim is imperfect.

17. See generally Steven Shavell, "Suit, Settlement, and Trial: A Theoretical Analysis under Alternative Methods for the Allocation of Legal Costs" (1982) 11 J. Legal Stud. 55. The implications of this model in aggregate systems were observed in David Rosenberg, *Mass Torts and Complex Litigation Seminar (Materials)*, Harvard Law School (Unpublished, 2002, on file with the author).

defendant's litigation costs and plaintiff's are identical at $200 for a single claim. The standard formula for settlement would indicate that a plaintiff's minimum position (the amount below which it would be uneconomical to settle, in Fig. 1 called his "Bargaining Position") will be the probable recovery minus litigation costs, or for a single claim, $100. The defendant's threshold bargaining position (above which he has no incentive to go) will be the probable recovery plus litigation costs, or $500. All else being equal, the claim will settle for the "correct" amount for deterrence purposes, $300.

As is clear from Figure 1 below, as the individual claims multiply, the defendant spreads the costs of litigation over the number of claims, and its per-claim costs go down, causing a corresponding decline in his per-claim exposure.[18] With the largest number of claims, the defendant has no incentive to settle for an amount higher than the plaintiff's probable recovery. One could imagine this as represented by the calculation that, as the number of claims reaches infinity, the defendant's per-claim litigation expenses approach zero. At this theoretical point, settlement will occur at $200, halfway between the value of the claim ($300) and the plaintiff's expected net gain after paying fixed litigation costs of $200 per claim ($100).

Because plaintiffs' litigation costs (and thus their bargaining positions) remain fixed regardless of the number of actions undertaken, the average per-claim settlement will decrease from $300 to $160 as the claims increase from one to ten.

If we consider that maximum deterrence will be achieved only if the costs to the defendant approximate the probable value of the claim (and thus the harm), then the result of aggregation in this scenario is that incentive for deterrence goes from 100% of optimal to less than 54% of optimal. *The defendant is rewarded simply because its wrongdoing has harmed more people.*

Now, consider what will occur if the claims are aggregated into one, and both the defendant *and the plaintiff* can take advantages of the scale economy (Fig. 2). In such a case, the threshold bargaining position of the plaintiffs *improves* with every claim, offsetting the advantage of scale already enjoyed by the defendant. In this case, we arrive at a per-claim settlement amount that is identical to the probable value of the claim.

Optimal deterrence will be achieved in these circumstances regardless of the size of the class (although obviously increases in class size sharply affect each

---

18. For the sake of simplicity, these examples make the assumption that the economy of scale is perfect, i.e. that ten claims cost the same to litigate as one. In actual fact there would be varying amounts of increase, from a small amount if all the claims were identical, to a larger amount if the issues were different. Introduction of this variable into the graphs will make no analytical difference to the trends in the outcome, providing that it costs *some* amount less to prosecute or defend a second, third or fourth claim.

Fig. 1 Settlement Outcomes in Multiple Individual Claims

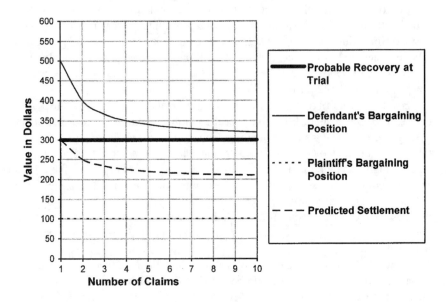

Fig. 2 Settlement Outcomes in Aggregated Claims

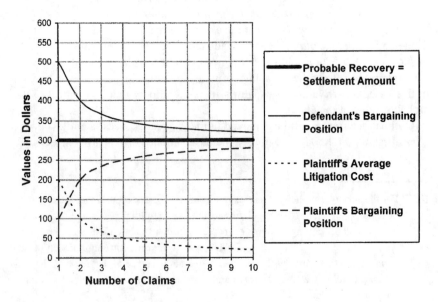

plaintiff's net recovery – as a percentage of the gross – after litigation costs are deducted).

All analysis until now assumes that there is a unity of plaintiff and investor; i.e. that the lawsuit is collectively financed by the class. In reality this will almost never be the case,[19] and the class action will generally be financed on a contingency basis by plaintiff's counsel, who is interested in maximising the return on his own litigation investment. It is possible to foresee instances where this interest is not only incongruent with the class members', but may in fact be in direct conflict as the class counsel's interest in a speedy settlement aligns with that of the defendant in reducing its damages. I discuss these agency problems further below.

(2) Behaviourism and Settlement Preferences

Serious criticisms of economic analysis of law have arisen in recent years. Some critics charge that the assumptions made in such analyses – that human beings make rational decisions invariably based on self-interest and adequate information – are demonstrably inadequate approximations of human behaviour. As a result, many economic analysts of law now attempt to incorporate studies of actual human decision-making behaviour into their models.

Because I have been using basic economic models to support the idea of aggregation of claims in mass tort, it is worth a brief look at whether human behaviour related to legal incentives will undermine or support my conclusions.

The point of examining these behavioural phenomena is not to demonstrate further a structural bias against plaintiffs in individual actions, but rather to understand the extent to which they introduce uncertainty and inaccuracy in the litigation process, as they influence plaintiffs to settle for too little, or hold out for too much; in any case, where optimal settlement is frustrated, so will be optimal deterrence.

(a) *Judgment Biases and Settlement*

Much of the impact of behaviourism on legal analysis has to do with individuals' biases when making decisions. That is, the suggestion that there are systematic tendencies throughout populations for individuals to commit errors in predictable ways. Some of these "biases," in particular "hindsight bias," "availability bias," and "overoptimism" suggest that individuals will reach suboptimal decisions when prosecuting their own tort actions. While there does not appear to have been any research on the topic, an inference can be drawn that the effects of these biases are reduced somewhat through aggregation of the individual actions prosecuted by a wealth-maximising counsel unaffected by them.

---

19. With the notable exception of those cases where common insurers pursue the class action through aggregation of subrogated claims.

Hindsight bias refers to the fact that decision-makers tend to assume that a given harm was predictable, based on evidence that it did in fact occur. Thus a plaintiff may believe that an accident or product failure was foreseeable by the defendant simply because that plaintiff was in fact injured, despite statistical evidence to the contrary. Even if this bias has less of an effect upon the judge,[20] in the aggregate more plaintiffs will pursue more claims than they optimally should for purposes of deterrence or judicial economy.[21]

The ability to make unbiased judgments is also affected by the phenomenon of "availability," whereby the frequency with which people are confronted with a particular problem affects judgments respecting causation or foreseeability. For instance, if exposure to a certain drug or product is suspected to increase the risk of a certain disease, and if that disease in fact develops, then the victim's perception as to whether her particular condition was caused by the drug or product will be influenced by the "availability" of such an explanation; in other words, by how often and how recently the purported link between the product and the disease has been reported.[22] An individual in such circumstances is therefore

---

20. The suggestion that a lay plaintiff is more susceptible than a judge to hindsight bias is supported by findings that indicate that judges are less susceptible than jurors: Christine Jolls, Cass R. Sunstein & Richard H. Thaler, "A Behavioral Approach to Law and Economics" in Cass R. Sunstein, ed., *Behavioral Law & Economics* (Cambridge: Cambridge University Press, 2000) at 39, citing Reid Hastie & W. Kip Viscusi, "What Juries Can't Do Well: The Jury's Performance as a Risk Manager" (May 21, 1998) (unpublished manuscript on file with the Stanford Law Review).

21. Occasionally, hindsight bias will not be eased by aggregation, particularly in lawsuits arising out of a company's non-disclosure of material facts to shareholders. In such cases, a withheld fact is more likely to be considered "material" after the fact of a precipitous decline in share value related to it, even if it could not reasonably have been thought so beforehand. Unfortunately, though, this particular phenomenon is not ameliorated through aggregation in claims, and is arguably even exacerbated, in that an ex post observer will attribute "materiality" more readily to an event which affected a larger number of people.

22. This effect can also work in the defendant's favour. In cases where the risks are not generally known, victims who are harmed by a product are *less* likely to attribute their disease to the exposure based on the lack of "availability" of suggested links, or perhaps the more frequent or more recent "availability" of alternative causative explanations. Thus manufacturers of harmful products, through direct advertising or through public relations efforts conducted through industry groups or "think tanks", can realistically expect to influence the conclusions drawn by members of the public with respect to the cause of their harm. This suggests that optimal deterrence is better served by an entrepreneurial plaintiffs' bar acting in a regulatory role. If they have sufficient incentive to do so, self-interested lawyers will busy

poorly placed to assess impartially whether her illness was caused by the product, and may be likely to press for an unrealistic settlement on that basis.[23]

Overoptimism tends to lead people to believe that risks, even risks that they accept in a general sense, do not apply to them in their particular circumstances; thus they tend to be optimistic regarding outcomes. This is less likely to affect firms, who are subject to systematic checks on optimism through structural and legal imperatives that encourage unbiased analyses of possible outcomes. However, individuals may see their odds of winning a court case as better than they actually are.

Behaviourism also offers us some tantalising indications of the extent to which individuals' perception of "fairness" might affect their decisions during litigation. It has been convincingly demonstrated through models like the "ultimatum game" that people are willing to suffer personal loss to avoid the possibility that another might "unjustly" gain.[24] Not surprisingly, individuals' view of

---

themselves researching medical and epidemiological data for more objective estimates of accident and disease patterns with respect to individual products.

23. The aftermath of the terrorist attacks in the United States in 2001 provides some illustration of this. A handful of isolated incidents of anthrax infection received extraordinary levels of coverage in the media. As a result, many Americans began "sterilising" their mail using everything from microwave ovens to household irons, despite the virtual certainty that, statistically speaking, the ordinary use of either device was far more likely to injure them than anything in their mail. Admitting rooms became clogged with people who attributed their sniffles to anthrax, and Hazardous Materials teams were scrambling to deal with thousands of reports of suspicious substances that turned out to be everything from saccharine to guacamole. A poll taken during this period indicated that almost half of Americans were either "very concerned" or "somewhat concerned" that they would become the victims of bioterrorism. This was only one way in which risk-perception became badly skewed in the aftermath of the September 11 attacks. See Jeffery Rosen, "Bad Luck" *The New Republic*, November 5, 2001.

24. In the "Ultimatum Game," two anonymous and isolated players attempt to divide an amount of money. The money (say ten dollars) is given to one person, with the proviso that he must offer a portion of it to the other. If the portion he offers is less than the other has already decided is the least he will accept, he loses all ten dollars. For instance, if the receiver will accept no less than a dollar of the ten and the donor offers only fifty cents, neither party gets any money. In such circumstances, economic predictions would indicate that the receiver would demand no more than the minimal amount, as after all that is better than nothing. Knowing this, the donor would offer an amount close to the minimum amount. In reality, however, the receiver generally demands an average of two dollars, and the donor frequently offers between four and five. In other words, the receiver is willing to lose up to two dollars for no other reason than to punish the donor for not offering more; the donor, probably sensing the likelihood of such "spiteful" behaviour, makes an even

what is "just" tends to be self-interested and self-serving. As a result, individuals may be willing to press their claim further than the economic model would prefer; in fact, experiments show that individuals in the role of injured plaintiff will consistently tend to overestimate the amount of "just" compensation, just as individual defendants will systematically underestimate it. Moreover, concepts of "justice" might lead a party to insist on his "day in court," not because he thinks that his gains will eventually be greater, but simply to cause the defendant greater loss. In fact, the "ultimatum game" suggests that many people might do so even if such "spitefulness" costs them significantly.

These tendencies of some individuals to overlitigate individual claims is implicitly recognised, and systematically discouraged, through the introduction of rules designed to restrict individuals from engaging in litigation for corollary (i.e. non-pecuniary) purposes. For instance, in many jurisdictions, plaintiffs (and, sometimes, defendants) may be sanctioned (generally through an award of court costs or a shifting of lawyer's fees) if they refuse to settle for an amount that is less than they eventually receive as judgment. Often, courts will have mandatory mediation rules to divert as many cases as possible from the judicial process. These programs represent a tacit recognition that a plaintiff's "litigative autonomy," to the extent that it is a "right" at all (discussed below as the "day in court ideal," is a right that must be weighed against society's interest in discouraging unnecessary court costs. Moreover, though, such rules can be seen as an attempt to encourage optimal settlements; that is, settlements that find the "correct" compensation and "correct" deterrent.

In that same vein, it is reasonable to assume that the intervention of a self-interested investor in the claim will reduce or eliminate the tendency to spitefulness in individual class members. Aggregated claims are "depersonalised," and the individual plaintiffs have little or no control over whether the action goes to court. As such, the effect of plaintiff "spitefulness" towards the defendant, to the extent that its exercise would be to the detriment of optimal deterrence, is minimal, and decreases with the size of the class. While it is not immediately apparent that this effect will be markedly more pronounced in an aggregated claim compared to, say, an individual claim pursued on a contingency basis, it is not unreasonable to suspect that in some cases, spiteful or unreasonably overoptimistic plaintiffs in individual litigation could exert pressure on their counsel in a way that would not be possible in an aggregate action.

Not all human tendencies are towards overoptimism or spitefulness; some other characteristics might lead individual plaintiffs to *undervalue* their claims. For instance, behaviourists also recognise the existence of "hyperbolic discounting" as yet another human characteristic that skews the results that economic

---

higher offer to compensate. Remarkably, this phenomenon has been observed in games played even with much larger amounts. See Christine Jolls, Cass R. Sunstein, Richard H. Thaler "A Behavioral Approach to Law and Economics" in Sunstein, ed., above note 20 at 22.

models would otherwise predict. This means that people are likely to discount benefits or losses that are distant in time or spread out over time when compared to benefits or losses that are immediate. Thus plaintiffs are more likely to prefer an immediate settlement for a lower amount, rather than their full due in payments structured over time. Apart from the undesirability of this from the point of view of full compensation (it may be one reason why structured settlements are increasingly common in personal injury cases), this also means that the defendant in such a case is not being confronted with the total cost of the harm caused and thus optimal deterrence is lost.

Another aspect of behaviourism that has been experimentally tested in the context of civil settlements is "context-dependence" in the form of a "contrast effect." This effect leads people to accept a given settlement which is presented along with a clearly inferior settlement. In other words, fewer people will accept a particular offer than if the same offer is accompanied by one which is clearly inferior. This may lead victims of a mass tort to be unduly influenced by other settlements arising from the same claim that may in fact be worth less, just as they may be unrealistically motivated by larger settlements of claims more valuable than their own.[25]

Underlying all these human effects are the problems of information. In an individual action, not just the plaintiff but his attorney will tend to have a suboptimal understanding of the legal strengths and weaknesses of his case, an information deficit that can be corrected only if optimal litigation investment (and therefore optimal legal and factual research and review) is realized.

These phenomena indicate that human beings can be poor, or at least inconsistent, judges of their individual claim's values. They do not prove that a lawyer representing an aggregate of claims would necessarily be better at achieving the full value of the claims, but they certainly suggest that work in this area could prove beneficial to our understanding of individual and group decision-making in litigation.

(b) Risk Aversion

Economic analyses, including those I offer in this book, often assume that individuals will be risk-neutral; that is, that they tend to value gain and loss in equivalent terms. For instance, if a particular risk could lead to either a $1000 gain or a $1000 loss, a perfectly risk-neutral person would take the chance of winning if it was 51%, but would not take it if it was 49%.

Practically speaking, however, human beings frequently behave in a way that indicates they are averse to risk, a characteristic often associated with the phenomenon of diminishing marginal utility.[26] What impact does this have on an

---

25. Mark Kelman, Yuval Rottnstreich & Amos Tversky, "Context-Dependence in Legal Decision Making" (1998) 65 U.Chi. L. Rev. 571.

26. This can be demonstrated by fairly straightforward reasoning. It is generally understood that the utility of wealth increases at a slower rate as one becomes more

analysis of aggregation? Risk aversion suggests that an individual plaintiff is more likely to settle before the point that will achieve either optimal compensation or optimal deterrence. This in turn suggests that ex ante, the rational choice of individuals would be to cover their losses on an insurance or averaging basis rather than receive a bonus upon successful litigation.[27]

In mass torts, even a risk-averse defendant (and most defendants will tend to be less risk-averse than individual plaintiffs[28]) is not as affected as the plaintiff.

---

wealthy. That is, the prospect of gaining (or losing) $1000 is of greater importance to a person who has a net worth of $2000 than for a person who has $10,000. Because individuals tend to dedicate spending first to those purchases which give them the greatest utility (i.e. first to necessities then to luxuries of diminishing utility), a loss of $1000 will deprive a person of more important things than an additional $1000 will allow him to buy. This risk aversion, following this reasoning, is bound to decrease as wealth increases and fewer necessities are at stake.

27.   This argument is not without controversy. Professor Rosenberg's assertion that class members ex ante would give up their rights to a tort "lottery ticket" if they were guaranteed compensation on an insurance basis (Rosenberg, "The Only Option" above note 7 at 870-871) has been criticized by Professor Nagareda on the basis that in fact human beings do in some cases (particularly where the amount risked is small and the amount to be "won" large) prefer the "lottery ticket" approach: Richard Nagareda "Autonomy, Peace and Put Options in the Mass Tort Class Action" (2002) 115 Harv. L. Rev. 749 at 791. However, the support for the proposition offered by Nagareda becomes less convincing as the amount at risk increases: it is not difficult to believe, for instance, that a person will pay $1 for a one-in-ten million chance of winning $1 million. However, it is difficult to conceive of a person making a similar decision in a more plausible tort case (i.e. paying $100,000 for a one in three chance at $200,000). Professor Rosenberg's argument, that human beings regularly express their risk-averse preference through almost universal purchase of first-person insurance, is difficult to counter. As such, "frivolous litigation" (i.e. litigation where the plaintiff is inclined to take undue risks) is unlikely where the plaintiff has already suffered significant loss for which he seeks compensation, and in fact the literature provided by Nagareda suggests that plaintiffs will be "risk-taking" only in cases with low probability of recovery: Chris Guthrie, "Framing Frivolous Litigation: A Psychological Theory" (1998) 67 U. Chi. L. Rev. 163 at 188. These problems, to the extent that they persist, may be ameliorated through rules designed to dismiss frivolous litigation at an early stage of the proceeding and cost-shifting mechanisms that increase the degree of risk. Even if Nagareda's point that plaintiffs are in some cases risk-seeking is taken at face value, it does not lead to his conclusion that this would affect ex ante preferences, as before the harm occurs, behind the "veil of ignorance," the individual does not know whether the harm will be great or small, nor even whether he or she will be tortfeasor or tort victim.

28.   And *a priori* a defendant in a mass tort action is less likely to be risk-averse than

The fact that such a defendant is treating the numerous claims against him in an aggregate sense means that any potential loss will only incrementally affect his total exposure.

The simple act of aggregation, placing the class under the supervision of a self-interested counsel who seeks to maximize return on investment, can ameliorate some of the systematic tendency of individual plaintiffs to abandon suits before optimum settlement is achieved. The class is essentially "corporatized" and those whose personal wealth is at risk (the class members) are isolated from those who are making decisions on a more purely investment-based analysis.[29] This "corporatization" can raise some interesting parallel arguments regarding the role of class members in the "corporation," an aspect which is discussed later in this part.

(3)   The Problem of "Blackmail" Settlements

The Ontario Law Reform Commission's 1982 report addressed the common objection that class actions, by "extorting unjust settlements from defendants," would constitute a form of "legalized blackmail."[30] It was in part this concern that, at the dawn of the class action era in Canada, led the system designers to emphasize rigorous judicial oversight of the entire class process.

The term "strike action" or "strike suit" describes a class proceeding launched on a claim without apparent merit, but in circumstances where a sizeable settlement can be achieved. It has become a rather notorious feature of securities litigation in the U.S., because the suit can have immediate effects on share prices or shareholder and regulatory approvals of corporate initiatives:

> In the United States, the availability of class action procedures combined with a contingency fee structure for plaintiffs' lawyers has led to the creation of an entrepreneurial sector of the legal profession known as the "strike bar." U.S. strike bar lawyers are motivated by sizable contingency fees and relative freedom to direct litigation according to their own interests. Even defendants who have done nothing wrong face Hobson's choice: to pay for a very expensive battle in the courts and eventually risk a potentially exorbitant jury damage award, or settle. Most defen-

---

the plaintiff, as his wealth is almost certainly greater. More than this, though, the corporate form moves decision-makers towards risk-neutrality, as their liability for the consequences (and its impact upon their own welfare) is limited. Add to this the fact that in many instances the case will be defended by an insurer, whose ability to spread losses according to carefully weighed factors makes them naturally less risk-averse in any particular situation. This last point will also hold true if the defendant is self-insuring but carries a diverse "portfolio" of claim-generating activities, as is the case in many large corporations.

29.   This effect will be further enhanced to the extent that the class members (or their counsel) do not face the additional penalty of costs if their action is unsuccessful.

30.   Ontario Law Reform Commission, *Report on Class Actions, 3 vols.* (Toronto: Ministry of the Attorney General, 1982) at 146.

dants eventually swallow their indignation and make the prudent economic choice and, as a result, settlement has become the typical outcome of class action securities litigation in the United States.[31]

The methods of the "strike bar" have been described as follows:

> [A] relatively small number of plaintiffs' attorneys regularly were filing class actions only hours or days after the disclosure of information that precipitated a major move in the price of a corporation's stock. It seemed apparent, even to people sympathetic to claims of open market fraud, that the moving force behind most class actions was not investors aggrieved by the defendants" alleged misrepresentations but plaintiffs' attorneys seeking to earn potentially large contingent fees. The investors in whose names class action [sic] were filed were mere figureheads; their function was to provide these attorneys with "the key to the courthouse." [footnotes omitted][32]

Securities cases provided particularly fertile ground for such actions, because of their potential for interfering with corporate activities (mergers, etc.), but also because their impact on share price could be considerable as well. One commentator concluded that most settlements resulting from securities class actions had no relation to the merits of the cases involved.[33] As a result, federal law in the United States was amended to make "strike suits" less profitable.[34]

But allegations of "blackmail" reach beyond the peculiar economics of securities litigation. Judge Posner, writing for the 7th Circuit Court of Appeals, has suggested that extortionate pressure can be applied in such actions simply

---

31. Steven Sharpe and James Reid, "Aspects of Class Action Securities Litigation in the United States" (1997) 28 Can. Bus. L.J. 348 at 353-4. See also John Avery, "Securities Litigation Reform: The Long and Winding Road to the Private Securities Litigation Reform Act of 1995 " (1996) 51 Bus. Law 335 at 337.

32. Elliott J. Weiss, "Comment: The Impact to Date of the Lead Plaintiff Provisions of the Private Securities Litigation Reform Act " (1997) 39 Ariz. L. Rev. 561 at 561-562.

33. Janet Cooper Alexander, "Do the Merits Matter? A Study of Settlements in Securities Class Actions" (1991) 43 Stan. L. Rev. 497.

34. The *Private Securities Litigation Reform Act of 1995*, Pub. L. No. 104-67, 109 Stat. 737 (1995) (codified as amended in sections of 15 U.S.C.) (requiring a mandatory inquiry by the court at the conclusion of each attempted class action and permitting, *inter alia*, sanctions to be imposed on plaintiffs and lawyers who have brought forward frivolous suits) and the *Securities Litigation Uniform Standards Act of 1998*, Pub. L. No. 105-353, 112 Stat. 3227 (1998) (also to be codified in 15 U.S.C.). See generally: David M. Levine & Adam C. Pritchard, " The Securities Litigation Uniform Standards Act of 1988 : The Sun Sets on California's Blue Sky Laws" (1998) 54 Bus. Law 1 at 1-2; Richard H. Walker, David M. Levine & Adam C. Pritchard, "The New Securities Class Action: Federal Obstacles, State Detours" (1997) 39 Ariz. L. Rev. 641 at 643; and Professor Jill E. Fisch, "Class Action Reform: Lessons from Securities Litigation" (1997) 39 Ariz. L. Rev. 533.

because of the potential size of awards.[35] In other words, a risk-averse defendant will prefer to pay more than the expected aggregate value of the claim (i.e. the potential claim amount multiplied by the probability of recovery), rather than "bet the business on a single flip of the coin."[36]

In truth there is a high degree of uncertainty over the extent to which "blackmail" suits are a problem in mass tort cases, even in the United States where the concern is sometimes said to have reached "Frankenstein monster" proportions.[37] Rosenberg counters Posner's analysis by pointing out that firms are less risk-averse than individuals, and settlement pressure tends to weigh more heavily on the most risk-averse party, almost always the plaintiff:

> First, defendant firms are structured to operate risk-neutrally and have many means of hedging against risk, notably derived from laws limiting liability and affording protection in bankruptcy, opportunities for stockholders to diversify their portfolios, and widespread availability of liability insurance. Second, the "blackmail settlement" pressure from a single, class-wide trial is not systematically directed towards defendants alone, but rather is directed at both sides of the litigation. Risk-averse class members and class counsel are no less likely than a defendant to regard a single class-wide trial with apprehension. In reality, "blackmail settlement" effects in any given case induce both sides to pay a premium for settlement, which nets out to the disadvantage of the most risk-averse.[38]

Moreover, there are three other unique characteristics of U.S. litigation that might lead to suboptimal settlements by defendants (and thus overdeterrence[39]) potentially characterised as "blackmail." First is the unique American reliance

---

35. In Re *Rhone-Poulenc Rorer, Inc.*, 51 F.3d 1293 at 1298 (7th Cir. 1995).

36. Rosenberg, "What the Defendants Have" above note 3 at 429.

37. Samuel Estreicher, "Foreword: Federal Class Actions After 30 Years" (1996) 71 N.Y.U. L. Rev. 1 at 2.

38. Rosenberg, "What the Defendants Have" above note 3 at 430.

39. In fact the problem of overdeterrence may provide a more focused objection to high damage awards than an allegation that such suits constitute "blackmail". For instance, many commentators have speculated that insubstantial claims might achieve large settlements based on questionable evidence. Invariably those advancing this viewpoint to the case of silicon-gel breast implants, a case in which theories of disease causation turned out to be generally unsubstantiated as research progressed: see for example George L. Priest, "Procedural Versus Substantive Controls of Mass Tort Class Actions" (1997) J. Leg. Stud. 521 at 522. Yet the obsession with the anecdotal case of overcompensation of victims ignores the more endemic problem of *under*compensation in the vast majority of cases (for instance the 80% of products liability actions that are never pursued). The objection also does not consider the possibility that cases like that of silicon-gel implants were built upon discoveries of inadequate testing done by the manufacturers; in this sense the question arises of the degree to which manufacturer negligence should be excused or overlooked simply because of the serendipitous eventuality that no harm occurred.

upon the jury trial in high-stakes litigation – there is persuasive evidence that juries tend to award greater damages in aggregated cases than if the claims were heard individually.[40] This problem is largely unavoidable in the U.S., where a jury trial in many federal cases is constitutionally guaranteed, but it is less of a problem in Canada, where jury trials in complex cases are increasingly rare. Second, non-compensatory damages in the United States are notoriously high,[41] a situation which does not obtain in Canada, where even $1 million punitive damages are considered extreme.[42] Finally, some U.S. jurisdictions require that the defendant post an "appeal bond" in the case of a loss at trial, that in some cases can be even greater than the damages awarded. The intention is to avoid frivolous appeals; practically speaking though, the appeal bond requirement can deny the opportunity to challenge an award that is significant enough to be unpayable without liquidation of the company. In Canada there is no equivalent requirement.

Indeed, in Canada there are strong indications that judicial oversight has been effective in minimising, if not eliminating altogether, the abuse of the class proceeding. There have been no articles written describing any class action settlement as "blackmail," let alone any suggestion that the problem is endemic as has been suggested of the United States. In the one case where a Canadian lawyer launched what was found by the court to be a "strike suit" (which was "settled" by the defendant for the amount of the counsel's fees without prejudice to any absent class members), the Court, obviously incensed at its understanding of the arrangement, approved the dismissal of the action but made an extraordinary order (on the Court's own motion) to deny the payment of fees, also invoking its inherent jurisdiction to make a further order forbidding any transfer of money by any means from the defendant (or its principals) to the plaintiff's counsel.[43]

---

40. For a discussion of the impact of aggregation on jury awards, see Barry F. McNeil & Beth L. Fanscal, "Mass Torts and Class Actions: Facing Increased Scrutiny" (1996) 167 F.R.D. 483 at 491; Kenneth S. Berdens & Irwin A. Horowitz, "Mass Tort Civil Litigation: The Impact of Procedural Changes on Jury Decisions", (1989) 73 Judicature 22.

41. The record appears to be $145 *billion* in a Florida tobacco class action: *Engle et al.* v. *R.J. Reynolds Tobacco Co. et al.*, No. 94-08273 CA-22, (Fla. Cir. Ct., 11th Dist., Miami-Dade County, Nov. 6, 2000).

42. In fact the recent $1 million award in *Whiten* v. *Pilot Insurance Co.* 2002 SCC 18 (representing less than 1/2 of 1% of the defendant's net worth) is the largest punitive claim ever approved by the Supreme Court. For an overview of the Canadian position on punitive damages see generally: Bruce Feldthusen, "Recent Developments in the Canadian Law of Punitive Damages" (1990) 16 Can. Bus. L.J. 241.

43. *Epstein* v. *First Marathon Inc.*, [2000] O.J. No. 452 (Sup. Ct. J.). In fairness to the class counsel involved, the reasons do not offer sufficient detail for the reader to determine whether any bad faith was involved.

One final type of class action "blackmail" should be mentioned: no matter how perfectly any system is designed, defendants who rely especially on the goodwill of consumers could still suffer harm from the publicity surrounding a suit.

Reputational harm is of course not a danger unique to class actions or indeed to litigation; consumer boycotts, for instance, may have similar effect. However, defendants are uniquely vulnerable to allegations made in court documents, which are not subject to the usual constraints of libel law or tort. More to the point, class counsel have a strong pecuniary incentive to threaten the defendant's reputation in a way that boycotting consumers generally do not. It is moreover true that because aggregation will allow, overall, more actions to be brought, and because notice requirements may publicize the alleged wrongdoing more than the filing of individual actions would, class actions may present an additional threat to firms that are particularly sensitive to public opinion. Such defendants are well advised to work closely with counsel and public relations experts to preserve their goodwill, and some firms have developed (or claim to have developed) special expertise in managing public-relations aspects of complex litigation. If courts are ready with appropriate sanctions for cases brought frivolously against such defendants, there is no reason to believe that reputational harm will prove a significant problem for Canadian class action system design.

All allegations of "blackmail" of defendants in the class action process must be weighed against the understanding that whenever the defendant's superior litigation power or high court costs make it uneconomical for a plaintiff to pursue a claim that is legally valid, this too represents a form of "blackmail" – against the plaintiff. The fact that the overwhelming majority of legitimate tort claims are not brought[44] points to a system of "unjust settlements" that is routine. Such "blackmail" does not carry with it the immediacy of the occasional anecdotal case of "blackmail" of defendants only because the claims not brought are unseen, falling beneath the radar of the media and popular consciousness.[45]

(4) Deterrence of Plaintiff Negligence

In basic economic models of negligence law, a tortious event is generally described as "unilateral" or "bilateral," depending on whether the risk of harm was managed by the defendant alone, or by the plaintiff as well. Some mass torts,

---

44. For citations regarding the underutilisation of the tort system by plaintiffs, see footnote 92 in the previous chapter, and below footnotes 6 through 8 and accompanying text, in Chapter 5.

45. This is not entirely so; the success of the book and film *A Civil Action* and widespread awareness of mass torts that have gone largely unaddressed – Bhopal, black lung disease, asbestos and tobacco come to mind – have led to political movements to redress systemic harm, and arguably the Canadian class action regime is a result of frustration with just this kind of "systemic blackmail" of plaintiffs.

such as airplane crashes caused by negligence, might be appropriately described as "unilateral'; the tort victims generally have played no role in their misfortune. However, in most other situations such as many products liability claims, the question of whether the consumer exercised appropriate care may be salient to the determination of liability and the award of damages.

The role of tort law in reducing plaintiff negligence is important, because it may be raised as an objection in cases where aggregation is proposed, in that it might be said that either "fairness" or the efficiency of the tort system demands that such individualistic issues be fully canvassed if tort law is to do its job in regulating behaviour. As such, it stands to reason that if it is asserted (as it is here) that the defendant's scale economy when taking mass-production decisions affects his behaviour in assessing appropriate care, we should also examine whether litigative aggregation affects the level of precautions taken by future plaintiffs.

Even in a regime where the defendant would always be liable for the amount of harm resulting from its negligence regardless of whether the plaintiff too were negligent, the plaintiff would at least take *some* care, because (assuming no punitive damages were possible) his recovery would never match the loss after the costs of litigation were deducted. As the number of potential plaintiffs in the class grows, this incentive to precaution arguably diminishes (but never disappears). In theory, it may diminish to a point where the plaintiff will exercise suboptimal care – be reckless – in expectation that even if he is injured he will recover most of his loss.

Such a calculation leads to the conclusion that some other form of plaintiff disincentive may be required to have the optimal deterrence of plaintiff negligence. There are a number of ways to do this in the context of mass tort litigation. Most obviously, the existing "relative negligence" or "contributory negligence bar" rules might accomplish the task, but would require separate trials on this issue (which raises the possibility that a negligent defendant might escape liability if only a *majority* of plaintiffs had exercised suboptimal care[46]). Some commentators have suggested that the only solution is an aggregated analysis of such defences, so that defendant deterrence is preserved.[47] How and whether the money paid by the defendant is distributed to plaintiffs could be

---

46. For instance, we can imagine an instance where a certain type of car tire fails frequently, but *usually* does so only when the car is being operated over the speed limit (negligently). Assuming no other evidence is available on the speed of the various plaintiffs' vehicles, a court might conclude, in each case, that the failure of the tire was probably caused by the plaintiff's negligence, and deny recovery on that basis in all the cases, even though we know that *some* of the vehicles were not being driven carelessly and the defendant is in fact to blame.

47. See David Rosenberg, "Individual Justice and Collectivizing Risk-Based Claims in Mass-Exposure Cases" (1996) 71 N.Y.U. L. Rev. 210 at 248-52.

decided on insurance principles, which might themselves take plaintiff misadventure into account to deny or reduce claims.

However, it should be recognized that plaintiff disincentives to recklessness exist even outside the present tort regime. Even accidents that result in easily measurable economic loss to the plaintiff provoke secondary losses that may never be the subject of compensation (a securities fraud, even if eventually compensated with interest, will have almost certainly triggered a loss of financial opportunity, for instance, which is generally not compensable; an automobile accident could create numerous "utility" losses in the form of inconvenience that might never be adequately compensated and the risk of which would therefore be avoided).

Where physical injuries are at stake, the disincentives are almost certainly higher still; few people would consent to getting cancer, for instance, no matter how appropriate the scale of pecuniary compensation proposed. Many losses are suffered by more than the risk-taker alone; a father driving his children in a minivan would have incentives to take precautions that went well beyond the financial compensation he would receive if those children were killed or injured in an avoidable accident. To make the point another way, persons may need considerable incentives to avoid harm to complete strangers, but fewer to protect against harm to one's close neighbours, and least of all to guard against harm to oneself or to one's family.[48]

Moreover, structural inefficiencies in the tort system ensure that an injured party can have no expectation of recovering a full measure of her damages.[49] On

---

48. It would appear that the advent of universal automobile insurance has not increased overall driver recklessness, and adoption of "no fault" accident insurance New Zealand has not led to a wave of risk-related injuries in that country, nor apparently to marked "antisocial attitudes toward the legal system": Steven Shavell, "The Fundamental Divergence between the Private and the Social Motive to Use the Legal System" (1997) 26 J. Leg. Stud. 575 at 597. Indeed the studies that indicate that tort might *not* be an effective deterrent tend to focus on the behaviour of individuals: See for instance the authorities cited in Lewis N. Klar, *Tort Law* (2d) (Toronto: Carswell, 1996) at 14–15.

Conversely, evidence is everywhere that the threat of litigation has had significant impact on product design (as in the "child proofing" of cigarette lighters) and the warnings offered to consumers through tickets, labels, instruction booklets, or advertisements. One might conclude, therefore, that the threat of tort litigation might have minimal effect on individuals who bear an equal chance of being tortfeasor or victim, but does exert a powerful influence over the precautions of firms engaged in potentially harmful activities.

49. Michael J. Saks, "Do We Really Know Anything About the Behaviour of the Tort Litigation System – and Why Not?" (1992) 140 Pa. L. Rev. 1147 at 1286–87 (concluding that "[o]nly a small fraction of costs created by actionable injuries will ever be paid by injurers.").

the other hand, to the extent that injuries result when appropriate precautions are not purchased by the defendant, the firm *always* receives the full economic benefit from running the risk.

There are other reasons to believe that deterrence of plaintiff negligence is not as crucial a system design function as deterrence of the negligence of firms, and these reasons are built on the nature of the relationship between the consumer and the mass producer.

First, individuals are notoriously bad at calculating accurately the risk to themselves resulting from a particular activity. If the risk cannot be weighed accurately, then deterrence is, to a large extent, moot, and the activity will inevitably be overdeterred or underdeterred. This effect is only compounded in the aggregate.[50]

Second, in any mass-production activity the defendant will be in a much better position to assess the risk resulting from its activities; it can be taken to have the best knowledge regarding its own products.

Of course, even if the entire cost of mass torts is placed upon defendants and their insurers, it can be expected that consumers in the end will bear the costs as they are passed along the chain of distribution. While this might not provide incentives for individuals to exercise greater care in their use of the product, it does to some extent regulate the amount of the harmful activity by internalising that cost to the activity.

One might conclude, then, that mass tort system design theory need not be so concerned about deterring consumer recklessness and should concentrate instead

---

50. Calabresi, for instance, describes the impact of legislation shifting costs of workplace accidents to employers solely, which he suggests was far more effective than a system which assigned costs to the lowest-cost avoider: Guido Calabresi, *The Costs of Accidents: A Legal and Economic Analysis* (New Haven: Yale University Press, 1970) at 245. The idea is that a worker might see a small risk as so remote as to be not worth taking precautions against. To give a concrete example, an employee at a factory with 200 workers who runs a .05% risk of slipping on a particular staircase on any given workday is unlikely to take precautions as he will probably never slip as long as he works at the firm. Nevertheless, the employer will view the same risks in the aggregate, and weigh the more or less certain harm that every 10 days, one employee will slip on the staircase, and take the appropriate level of care. Much work has been done on the question of whether individuals tend to overestimate or underestimate risks to themselves. The answer seems to be that risks may be systematically under-estimated, unless they are brought to a person's attention in a vivid way, in which case the reverse may be true. See for instance Amos Tversky & Daniel Kahneman, "Judgment under Uncertainty: Heuristics and Biases" (1974) 185 *Science* 1124; W. Kip Viscusi, *Risk by Choice: Regulating Health and Safety in the Workplace* (Cambridge, MA: Harvard University Press, 1983).

on avoiding negligent behaviour by firms. This raises the possibility that courts might consider the idea of calculating such affirmative defences as "contributory negligence" in the aggregate, and sacrificing some plaintiff-deterrent effect for an expedient resolution of the class action.[51]

---

51. Calculation of contributory negligence in the aggregate, like abolishing the defence altogether, will tend to promote plaintiff negligence to the extent that the plaintiff derives some utility from being negligent, and to the extent that compensation for resulting harm will be effective. This is because, as part of a group, he knows that his own negligence will affect him only incrementally, whereas if he is not negligent, he will be subsidizing those who are. It is sort of a variation on the familiar "prisoner's dilemma" in game theory.

CHAPTER FOUR

——

Approaches To "Fairness"

A. INTRODUCTION

This chapter explores one of the most conceptually challenging aspects of class action system design: the idea that, function aside, there are overriding imperatives of "fairness" that must be protected. Sometimes, these objections take the form of concern over the "blackmailing" of defendants, a topic that was discussed in the previous chapter. More often though, objectors express concern that class proceedings, by their very "corporatist" or "collectivist" nature, sacrifice fairness to individual tort victims in favour of expedient wholesale resolution of claims.

B. AUTONOMY VERSUS PEACE

Occasionally, the central controversy in class action system design is described as striking a balance between the plaintiffs' interest in "autonomy" and the defendant's interest in "global peace" with respect to all the classable claims. These ideas, advanced most recently by Professor Nagareda,[1] seem to depend on the belief that it is the *defendant* who is a main beneficiary of claims aggregation, and the tort victims whose interest in pursuing an individual settlement must be sacrificed, to a greater or lesser degree, to satisfy that desire for "peace."

I say that this is curious because neither plaintiff "autonomy" nor defendant's "peace" are defended, by Nagareda or elsewhere in the literature, as independ-

---

1. Richard Nagareda "Autonomy, Peace and Put Options in the Mass Tort Class Action" (2002) 115 Harv. L. Rev. 749 at 751.

ently valid objectives of tort law from the public perspective. In fact the idea raises difficult questions. What interest does the public have in affording a negligent wrongdoer "peace"? What interest does the public have in providing the plaintiff "autonomy," particularly if that autonomy is heavily subsidized, indeed financed, by the taxpayer?

Indeed, it would seem that if either of these objects, "peace" for defendants or "autonomy" for plaintiffs, contrasted sharply with the goal of reducing the overall costs of accidents, then the latter consideration should prevail. Yet as obvious as this might seem, the debate over "autonomy and peace" indicates that acceptance is far from universal.

Unable, then, to wring any substance from assertions that "peace" for defendants is of utility to society or individuals (aside from the negligent wrongdoer), we might turn to other concepts of "fairness" in class proceedings.

C.   INDIVIDUAL VERSUS SOCIAL PREFERENCES AND THE EX ANTE MODEL

Even those who accept the "public law model" of mass tort litigation might labour under the assumption that to do so is to make the choice between the community and the individual in favour of the former, and that acceptance of this position necessarily sacrifices individual rights. Indeed, class proceedings are generally seen as the subversion of individual interests for the good of the whole (i.e. the class) or for the general benefit of society, which will pay less to litigate the claims.

Such a concept is not really accurate. The goal may still be framed in terms of individual interests; the question is really how those interests are viewed. Rosenberg argues that:

> On the rare occasions when commentators, and still rarer occasions when courts, consider the deterrence effects of mass tort litigation, most treat the benefits as accruing to society as a whole rather than to the individuals comprising it. Talk of "individual justice" almost always refers to tort compensation and the benefits to individuals from receiving redress for harm done. When the two goals of deterrence and compensation come into conflict, as they often do in the current system, the sense that doing justice for individuals should count for more than maximizing some abstract social goal of deterrence usually leads to the conclusion that individual interests should prevail over society's. This way of thinking is fundamentally mistaken. The benefits of optimal deterrence necessarily accrue to all individuals – in fact, to everyone who might be exposed to tortious risk – and not merely the relatively small fraction suffering actualized tortious harm. At the most basic level, optimal deterrence benefits every individual because reducing accident costs through reasonable precautions means more welfare to distribute and that makes everyone better off.[2]

---

2.   David Rosenberg, "Mass Tort Class Actions – What the Defendants Have and Plaintiffs Don't" (2000) 37 Harv. J. Legis. 393 at 407-08.

The question is *at what point in time* the individual's interest is considered. In a subsequent article, Rosenberg and the legal philosopher Charles Fried consider that the mass production context provides no opportunity for the individual tailoring of risks and price on a contractual basis. Two brief paragraphs make the issue of state intervention in optimising precautions (and the point at which it must be done) abundantly clear:

> Virtually all business accident risks arise as an intrinsic byproduct of the means of mass production that achieve scale economies by standardizing the design of processes and goods. At the core of those designs is a deliberate decision to strike a balance between expected benefit and corresponding risk of injuring members of some population of potentially affected workers, consumers or others. To exploit scale economies, this benefit-risk decision requires a purely statistical average of an infinite range of outcomes for those who will actually comprise the projected population. A mass producer cannot know or predict and, most importantly, cannot adjust its decision to individual fates — respecting how and in what degree its good will benefit or harm any potential member of the population. In reality, the fixed parameters of that decision incorporate averages of all relevant demographic, legal and other variables, including price. The unitary character of mass production benefit-cost decisions means that the statistical averages dictated by mass production scale economies cannot be disaggregated into individual, one-on-one relationships between the business risk-taker and a potential or actual "victim" without jeopardizing the benefits of those economies as well as lapsing into incoherence.[3]

In other words, the tortious decision (i.e. the decision made with respect to precautions) is inherently an aggregate one, and it is made ex ante. Any attempt to impose state coercion ex post (i.e. through judgment of "reasonableness" at trial) that does not take the ex ante perspective into account is doomed to failure:

> This point, that mass production decisions about precautions (like every other dimension of the undertaking) are probabilistically, indivisibly unitary, is not dependent on transaction costs or imperfect information. It is important to realize that the ex ante choice in favor of mass production precautions is not a creature of market defects [. . .] When maximizing individual expected welfare is the priority of each person behind the veil of ignorance, no one would rationally prefer a legal system that mandated individually bargained, customized arrangements in lieu of the opportunity for scale economy gains from standardized, averaged mass production arrangements. Consequently, a decisionmaker's attempt to disaggregate the synergistically related statistical average estimates of accident risk and optimal precautions is not just an intellectually incoherent exercise and a waste of system resources; it also undermines the fundamental social objective of minimizing the sum of accident costs because brute disaggregation threatens to destroy the standardized means of mass production, to everyone's detriment.[4]

The importance of the above passages is that they introduce us to the concept of the ex ante perspective device and aggregate principles as optimising not only

---

3.   Charles Fried & David Rosenberg, "Making Tort Law: What Should be Done and who Should Do It" (forthcoming 2002: unpublished manuscript on file with the author) at 35.

4.   *Ibid.* at 35-6.

overall social good, but also the good of *every individual* at risk from the defendant's behaviour. Because so many objections to aggregation tend to focus on preserving the interests of individual litigants, it is important to consider this point as we examine the ex ante perspective in more depth.

The root of the law's preference for ex post perspectives might be found in human psychology, and the extent to which we are not purely rational decision-makers. Rather than gather sufficient information, weigh all options and make cold and impartial decisions with a view to probabilistic outcomes, we function instead by extrapolating rules from concrete experiences, generalizations from anecdotes. This is certainly true when we consider "justice" in the tort context; we tend to think of people whom we know who have been injured, and how we can help them, and perhaps how we might feel if we ourselves were in the position of suffering unnecessary harm. We tend to think less about people who have not yet been injured, because, in the negligence setting, we do not know who they will be; their situation has no "availability" for us, and so we disregard the question until real people have real injuries.[5] Fairness and justice, in these contexts, are often malleable terms roughly equated with the provision of reasonable assistance and comfort. But can there be a better, more objective ideal of "fairness" and "justice" in the design of legal procedure?

One method proposed for considering rule design, individual justice and the reasonable preferences of individuals is loosely based on philosopher John Rawls's "original position" thought experiment. Rawls suggested that a rule of conduct could be fairly enforced ("just") if it were designed by individuals before the fact, behind a "veil of ignorance" as to their eventual position in life.[6] The advantages of considering the ex ante perspective are obvious: the device permits a "thought experiment" in which system design decisions are made under circumstances that might be seen as "fair," by persons who are individually attempting to maximise their own self-interests. The resulting rules are socially optimal because they are likely to maximise overall welfare across society. Hay, Rosenberg and other U.S. scholars have applied this idea to mass tort

---

5.   Guido Calabresi, *The Costs of Accidents: A Legal and Economic Analysis* (New Haven: Yale University Press, 1970) at 25 suggested that this phenomenon was in fact evidence of an independent concept of justice, rather than simply irrational and arbitrary system design:

> Our reaction to accidents is not a simple dollars-and-cents one. If it were, I doubt that we would accept railroad crossing accidents because it costs too much to eliminate grade crossings and yet spend "whatever it takes" to save a known individual trapped in a coal mine.

6.   For the classic statement of Rawls's theories see John Rawls, A Theory of Justice (Cambridge, MA: Harvard University Press, 1971). For Rawls's latest reflections on the subject see John Rawls, *Justice as Fairness: A Restatement* (Cambridge, MA: Harvard University Press, 2001).

policy, examining individuals' interests from the ex ante perspective, rather than the ex post perspective traditionally favoured by the courts.[7]

Assuming that rational "rule designers" would prefer the maximization of overall welfare as the guiding principle for products liability law,[8] viewing the tort system from the ex ante perspective demonstrates the effectiveness of maximal aggregation in achieving both optimal deterrence and optimal insurance.

Both for economic and personal reasons, a rational individual ex ante would prefer deterrence to compensation. First, because it costs less to avoid an accident with appropriate precautions than to pay for the harm that results; and secondly, because compensation can never accurately put someone in the position of "restored integrity."[9] A class member's ex ante preference, therefore, will be

---

7. The extensive use of the Rawlsian ex ante perspective is noted in David Rosenberg, "Individual Justice and Collectivizing Risk-Based Claims in Mass-Exposure Cases" (1996) 71 N.Y.U. L. Rev. 210 [Rosenberg, "Risk-Based Claims"] at 238 n. 83. It has had widespread application in a diversity of fields, as described in: Christopher H. Schroeder, "Corrective Justice and Liability for Increasing Risks" (1990) 37 UCLA L. Rev. 439 at 451-60, and has achieved in the past decade broad acceptance in both academia and the judiciary as a tool of fairness in legal system design: see authorities cited in Bruce L. Hay, "Procedural Justice: Ex Ante vs. Ex Post" (1997) 44 U.C.L.A. L. Rev. 1803 at 1846 nn. 118 and 119. Despite its widespread invocation in U.S. cases and articles, the Rawlsian device has not yet been invoked to support or criticize the "fairness" of system design in either Canadian literature or jurisprudence.

8. This was the conclusion of the first application of Rawls" "veil of ignorance" to mass tort system design: Alan Schwartz, "Proposals for Products Liability Reform: A Theoretical Synthesis" (1988) 97 Yale L.J. 353 at 357-61. Schwartz wrote of system design as based upon a modified Rawlsian choice of a "meta-rule" for tort by persons who "should be ignorant of their own wealth and the probability that they will be injured" but who "know [other details, for instance] that states provide workers' compensation and disability insurance, because they might prefer not to adopt a tort solution that would duplicate payment systems now in place." Schwartz concluded that individuals would not design a system based on the worst possible outcome – serious, uncompensated injury – because of social safety nets in place, and so would rather have a system based on utility maximisation: *Ibid.* at 359.

9. David Rosenberg, "Mandatory-Litigation Class Action: The Only Option for Mass Tort Cases" (2001) 115 Harvard L. Rev. 831 [Rosenberg, "The Only Option"] at 864 ("Ex ante, a welfare-maximizing individual rationally prefers avoidance of unreasonable harm to the dubious privilege of bearing such harm and having the opportunity to complain about it."). See also Neil K. Komesar, "Injuries & Institutions: Tort Reform, Tort Theory and Beyond" (1990) 65 N.Y.U. L. Rev. 23 at 58-59 (*inter alia* defending award of non-pecuniary damages on the basis of individuals' ex ante preference for deterrence).

for the threat of immediate and universal claims aggregation upon the commission of a mass tort. In a properly functioning system (all things being equal), that threat alone will ensure that the tort does not occur.

Due to unavoidable accident (reasonable precautions having been taken), informational deficiencies or other market failure, there remains a residual risk of accident. What are the individual's ex ante preferences in such a case?

An individual's strongest preference is for optimal insurance – insurance sufficient to fully compensate for harm suffered. This preference is important, because it contradicts the idea that plaintiffs would want to "overinsure" or "underinsure" – that is, to insure to recover a higher amount or to risk undercompensation for ex ante saving.[10] That an individual would be willing, ex ante, for such insurance to be built into the price of the product seems to indicate a preference for strict liability, rather than negligence-based, regimes[11] to the extent that insurance otherwise purchased (private and public) will not cover the loss.

It follows that these observations must be tempered with considerations of the problem of proof – the notion that some harm suffered ex post will be only uncertainly correlated with the defendant's actions. In such cases, the individual's ex ante preference would tend towards an averaged award,[12] even if she is not fully

---

10. Rosenberg in "The Only Option" above note 9 at 845 says:

    Essentially, full coverage insurance equalizes the individual's marginal utility from wealth between the accident and no-accident states and thus increases expected utility. The individual employs insurance to transfer wealth from the no-accident state to the accident state up to the point at which an additional dollar of wealth yields the same marginal utility in either state. Beyond that point, the individual would follow the reverse course.

11. Assuming that strict liability will provide equal or better deterrence effects, which is still the consumer's ex ante priority. This appears to be the case.

12. To illustrate, consider the case in which, ex ante, the plaintiff knows that, as a result of the defendant's coming tort, she will have a 10% chance of recovering losses amounting to $1000. In such circumstances, the risk-averse plaintiff would prefer the certainty of recovering $100 to "rolling the dice" for the entire amount with a 90% chance of recovering nothing.

    Rosenberg uses the device of the square root to illustrate the impact of risk aversion on overall utility. The square root symbolizes the degree to which persons" "marginal utility" decreases with wealth. Under this paradigm, $100 has a utility to the individual of 10. However, because of decreasing marginal utility, $200 has a utility of its own square root, or about 14.1. The choice of square root (as opposed to a more accurate measure) is arbitrary, but serves well to introduce marginal utility into the calculation. So for instance, in the example here, a certainty of receiving $100 (100% x $\sqrt{100}$ = utility of 10) provides greater utility to a risk-averse individual than a 10% chance of receiving $1000 (10% x $\sqrt{1000}$ = utility of 3.16). Rosenberg persuasively demonstrates that this preference "holds regardless of the

compensated vis-à-vis the discrete accident, because globally, i.e. across claims groups, the insurance effect will be, at least in part, preserved.

Ex post, class members' preferences diverge, with the uninjured having no interest in subsidising the injured, and the injured with the strongest claims unwilling to sacrifice any portion of their recovery to assist those injured with weaker claims.

Because, even in this latter situation, some plaintiffs may benefit from pursuing their claims individually, class members' self interest ex post drives them into the two camps of "lucky" and "unlucky" plaintiffs, and their preferences diverge markedly. "Lucky" plaintiffs (those with strong legal cases) will seek to maximise their own recovery, and will care little for subsidising those "unlucky" ones with weaker claims. This will be so even if the "lucky" plaintiff's disaggregative strategy will, following the analysis undertaken earlier in this book, render the class, as a whole, worse off. This ex post bias is the source of intraclass conflict and will inevitably make mass tort class actions with diverse claim values increasingly less efficient as more members, ex post, withdraw from the class.[13] Members will withdraw even though they would, ex ante, prefer that no one be allowed to withdraw. Systems that discourage opt-outs from the class through some type of "mast-tying" rules will therefore be truer to an individual's ex ante preferences, even as they appear to violate ex post "rights."

The ex ante perspective also assists the case of mass torts increasing the risk of latent disease. Such cases are often discussed from the point of view of "maturity";[14] that is, a claim in which disease can be predicted but the harm has not

---

defendant's solvency and over-rides differences of law uncorrelated with severity of loss [as well as] all factual and other litigation variables": Rosenberg, "The Only Option" above note 9 at 856-57.

Over the course of a lifetime, it might be expected that averaged compensation should "normal out" – that is to say that instances of overcompensation and undercompensation will balance each other. Inevitably, this compensation will not be complete, because only a fraction of harm for which insurance is desired has its cause in actionable activities. This militates in favour of "de-coupling" the insurance and deterrence functions of tort with deterrence pursued on an aggregate basis for the expected value of the wrongdoing's harm, and compensation provided by global first-person insurance, public and private.

13.   This is because settlement structures or intraclass agreements will tend to overcompensate the members of the class with the strongest legal claims to ensure their participation. This is suboptimal from a compensation standpoint, but may not affect deterrence provided that the integrity of the entire class is preserved.

14.   See generally Francis E. McGovern, "Resolving Mature Mass Tort Litigation" (1989) 69 B.U.L. Rev. 659; John C. Coffee, Jr., "Class Wars: The Dilemma of the Mass Tort Class Action" (1995) 95 Colum. L. Rev. 1343 [Coffee, "Class Wars"] at 1359-63 (describing the "mass tort evolutionary cycle," perhaps better described as the "mass tort *life* cycle").

manifest itself is not "mature"; resolution of future claims is rendered correspondingly difficult as scientific information regarding causation and treatment advances through time. As Nagareda notes, "[t]he policy question becomes "not *whether* to aggregate litigation, but *how* and *when*.""[15]

However, when viewed from the ex ante perspective, future development of knowledge is less relevant. From the point of view of "behaviour modification" or general deterrence, it is the level of knowledge that the defendants had, or should have had, at the time the tortious decision was made that is important; the defendant should pay for those damages that could be reasonably foreseen at the time of the decision, not for those which do not become apparent until years or decades later.

So is it more or less just to consider a plaintiff's ex post perspectives when designing a system for redress of tortious harm? Hay concludes that:

> On matters of process design, the preferences a litigant has after a dispute has materialized may easily conflict with the preferences she has before the dispute has materialized. In other words, honoring her "ex post" wishes does violence to her "ex ante" wishes. Yet there is no clear rationale for giving priority to her ex post wishes; on the contrary, there are strong arguments for giving pride of place to her ex ante wishes in such cases of conflict. For this reason, justice to the litigant — respect for her autonomy and welfare — may be offended, not advanced, by implementing her ex post preference regarding process design.[16]

The ex ante perspective is a valuable component of mass tort system design, because it usefully reframes the main debate surrounding the interests of class members. Rather than seeing aggregation as the subordination of individual litigative autonomy and interests to the collective whole, the ex ante/ex post analyst is concerned *only* with fairness to the individual. When the tort system's systematic preference for the ex post perspective is overcome, the interests of society and each individual victim of tort more perfectly align.

The tort system's bias in favour of ex post preferences is a design choice, rather than an inevitability. This leads to the uncomfortable conclusion that while attempting to ameliorate harm in individual cases – i.e. by preserving the "day in court ideal" of litigative autonomy – courts and legislatures are ensuring that, due to suboptimal deterrence, more people will be injured, and that by denying the opportunity for optimal insurance, fewer injuries will be properly compensated. The system designer is, therefore, irrationally choosing to prefer one set of victims over another. This can only be explained by the "availability heuristic" – the tendency to value redress of the harm we see over the harm that could be avoided if we took a more global perspective. This is perhaps a socially safe decision to make – as our fellow citizens too will share those irrational preferences – but it

---

15. Nagareda, above note 1 at 763, citing Hensler et al., *Class Action Dilemmas: Pursuing Public Goals for Private Gain* at 483 (Santa Monica, CA: RAND, 2000).

16. Bruce L. Hay, "Procedural Justice: Ex Ante vs. Ex Post" (1997) 44 U.C.L.A. L. Rev. 1803 at 1804.

is not socially optimal. A system truly concerned with maximising the safety and wealth of its citizenry will prefer the deterrent effects of universal aggregation of classable claims and optimal insurance for the injured.

D. CORPORATISATION OF INDIVIDUAL CLAIMS

The imposition upon plaintiffs of a class action is effectively an attempt to replace the tort litigation system with a more effective administrative compensatory regime by "forcing" the plaintiffs into a kind of corporate form, usually without their explicit consent, and potentially without their knowledge. The similarity of the class action to other methods of corporatisation has been noted. Shapiro writes:

> [A] whole range of voluntary private associations – congregations, trade unions, joint stock companies, corporations – and on a less "voluntary" level, municipalities and other governmental entities, have long been recognized as litigants in their own right – entities whose members may have at best only a limited say in what is litigated, in who represents the organization, and on what terms the controversy is ultimately resolved. Indeed, the rise of those organizations has been noted as one of the reasons for the decline of the class action from the mid-eighteenth to the mid-twentieth century.[17]

The key difference, as Shapiro recognizes, is the right of exit (which in these forms is often practically impossible; a union member for instance, can usually "exit" only at the cost of his job). A class member, reminds Shapiro, "may be dragged kicking and screaming into a lawsuit he does not want, or at least would prefer to conduct on his own."[18]

In fact, some commentators have objected to "lawyer-driven class actions" on this basis — that members "may not even want to be plaintiffs."[19] This is certainly true; there are many reasons to suppose why persons, ex post, would not wish to sue to recover for harm, whether or not their suits were individually viable.[20] But this objection too is stripped away when the ex ante perspective is

---

17. David L. Shapiro, "Class Actions: The Class As Party and Client" (1998) 73 Notre Dame L. Rev. 913 at 921. See also John C. Coffee Jr., "Class Action Accountability: Reconciling Voice, Exit and Loyalty in Representative Litigation" (2000) 100 Col. L. Rev. 370.

18. *Ibid.* This dramatic scenario is possible, but only in a mandatory class action or one in which notice is ineffective.

19. Victor E. Schwartz, Mark A. Behrens & Leah Lorber, "Federal Courts Should Decide Interstate Class Actions: A Call for Federal Class Action Diversity Jurisdiction Reform" (2000) 37 Harv. J. Legis. 483 at 492-493.

20. I have already noted that individuals might have different notions of utility; some would not sacrifice the leisure time that pursuit of a suit might entail; others might find negative value in the associated stress that would outweigh the expected award. There may even be considerable value to some individuals in "putting it all behind" them. But none of these ex post preferences in any way undermines the ex

favoured. To suggest that the individual would not wish aggregation to occur is to argue that, ex ante, they would not have wished for precautions commensurate with optimal deterrence. In other words, it is imposing the supposition that the fictional posited class member would have *preferred a higher level of risk* associated with the defendant's product. It would seem that any person making such an assertion (incompatible with the model of human beings as generally risk-averse welfare maximisers) should at least bear the burden of providing some support for it.

Perhaps a better way of approaching the question is to attempt to measure what is being lost through aggregation. What is the utility of litigative autonomy, divorced from more readily ascertainable preferences such as compensation and deterrence? Can a system which provides optimal deterrence and optimal compensation still be objectionable on some unseen, discrete ground?

E. LITIGATIVE AUTONOMY AND THE "DAY IN COURT IDEAL"

Notwithstanding demonstrable advantages of claims aggregation, and even after plausibly outlining the way in which class actions are "fairer" to individuals within classes as well as to the classes themselves, the system theorist is inevitably confronted with a final "fairness" based assertion: that there is *independent* value in litigative autonomy that is jeopardized through the corporatising process of class certification.

Critics of modern products liability litigation, including class action lawsuits, tend to wax rhapsodic about a magical time, before mass tort litigation, where common law rules "grew over the centuries from slender beginnings to imposing grandeur, like a California redwood,"[21] resulting in a "venerable body of law," "an ancient legacy shrouded in the wisdom of the ages" with which current law is "tampering."[22] A noteworthy feature of this misty recollection is the notion that the law's highest ambition is to provide every aggrieved party her "day in court," a momentous event in which the plaintiff, in complete control of the prosecution of her case, can rally the awesome power of the state in support of her rights, and make the defendant pay fully for the wrongs it has done.

One of the more perplexing assertions made is that the "day in court ideal" – quite apart from its supposed place in our cultural memory[23] – remains a note-

---

ante preference of every individual that their exposure to risk be minimal, assuming that these "litigation averse" members would not need to take an active part in the class proceeding.

21. Peter Huber, *Liability: The Legal Revolution and Its Consequences* (New York: Basic Books, 1988) at 21.

22. *Ibid.* at 17.

23. Robert G. Bone, "Rethinking the "Day in Court" Ideal and Nonparty Preclusion" (1992) 67 N.Y.U. L. Rev. 193 at 288 [Bone, "Rethinking the Day in Court"]("The

worthy feature of the modern individual tort litigation system.[24] At the extreme, Roger Trangsrud describes "the right to control personally the suit" as a "natural right" on par with "the right to practice one's own religion or to think and speak freely."[25]

And yet, there is precious little substance accorded this "right" even by its most prominent proponents. Trangsrud, for instance, suggests that recognition of the "right" requires that courts "adjudicate justly disputes between individuals," or "offer corrective justice in disputes arising between private parties"; yet these are rather nebulous notions, self-justifying and self-referential. Trangsrud offers a characterisation of individual trials in which "plaintiffs enjoy autonomy over the settlement or trial of their particular claim, [obtaining] the outcome best suited to their personal views on the proper disposition" of the case; his argument becomes unrecognisable to anyone who has practiced civil litigation.[26] When the blue-sky account of tort litigation has run its course still without any substantive reason for preferring individual litigation (let alone paying extra for it), Trangsrud attempts to pin the "right" to litigative autonomy to an equivalent right in "property." This effort too crumbles under the weight of the comparison when the assertion is made that "[f]rom a purely economic point of view, our system operates mainly on the assumption that economic decisions are best made by the true owner of property rather than by any other person,"[27] ignoring that the most powerful economic actors in "our system" – corporations, governments, trade unions, managed investment funds – employ specialist managers to make "economic decisions" on behalf of individuals. In fact, the only objective proof offered of the success of the individual tort system is its high rate of settlement;[28]

---

assumption basic to the conventional account of the day in court ideal — that each person has an individual right to control her own lawsuit — is wrong on positive and normative grounds."). See also Robert G. Bone, "Personal and Impersonal Litigative Forms: Reconceiving the History of Adjudicative Representation" (1990) 70 B.U. L. Rev. 213 (reviewing Stephen C. Yeazell, From Medieval Group Litigation to the Modern Class Action (1987))

24. See for instance *Martin* v. *Wilks* 490 U.S. 755 at 762 (1989), quoting Charles A. Wright et. al., *Federal Practice & Procedure* s. 4449 at 417 (1981) for a description of the day in court ideal as a "deep rooted historic tradition."

25. Roger H. Trangsrud, "Mass Trials and Mass Tort Cases: A Dissent", 1989 U. Ill. L. Rev. 69 at 74.

26. And yet it is surprisingly common: See Jerry L. Mashaw, "Bureaucratic Justice: Managing Social Security Disability Claims 95-96 (1983) (suggesting litigative autonomy "increases self-respect") or Laurence H. Tribe, *American Constitutional Law* (2d ed. 1988) (describing the "special concern about being personally *talked to* about the decision rather than simply being *dealt with*"). Both passages cited in Rosenberg, "Risk-Based Claims" above note 7 at 211, n. 3.

27. *Ibid.*

28. Trangsrud cites a RAND Institute study for the proposition that even mass tort

this ignores the central assertion of those advocating aggregation of claims: it is not how many cases settle, *but for how much*. If a system persists where defendants, through their gross advantage in litigation scale economy, can pressure plaintiffs not to file claims or to settle for a fraction of their claim's expected value, of what benefit is that to anybody except defendants?

I have already described the structural features of the litigation system that suggest that many, if not most, individual plaintiffs could never hope to prevail in individual action against a mass tort defendant, and statistics that indicate that in fact only a small percentage even attempt it. There are also structures in place to discourage plaintiffs from insisting on a trial if their cases can settle efficiently beforehand.[29] If there is a "day in court ideal" then, it clearly cannot be a recognized "right" in the ordinary sense, as it is one that a plaintiff can expect to pay dearly for if he insists on it above and beyond whatever pecuniary recovery to which he might be entitled. This is far from the system of "uncompromised due process" that Trangsrud suggests obtains outside the world of class litigation.[30]

If a further argument is needed to demonstrate how foreign to our court system is the "day in court ideal," one might consider how narrowly it is drawn *ab*

---

claims pursued individually will eventually settle "on the basis of recovery patterns projected from relatively few trials" above note 25 at 78 footnote 44. Setting aside the arguments made earlier that these early individualistic judgment amounts will inevitably be depressed due to the defendant's litigation investment incentives, the point actually works against Trangsrud's central thesis in any event, *because the settlement amounts of the individual plaintiffs are being determined in trials over which they have no control.*

29.   For a discussion of the "offer to settle rule" (whereby litigants are penalized for not accepting an offer equivalent to what is eventually obtained at trial) see Kent Roach, "Fundamental Reforms to Civil Litigation" in Ontario Law Reform Commission, *Rethinking Civil Justice: Research Studies for the Civil Justice Review (Vol. 2)* (Toronto, Ontario Law Reform Commission, 1996) at 409-10 (describing the purpose of the rule as to discourage trial, and noting that the rule creates greater trial avoidance incentives for plaintiffs than for defendants).

   Trial avoidance has become the *de facto* policy of the Canadian courts, according to Callaghan A.C.J.H.C. in *Sparling* v. *Southam Inc.* (1988), 66 O.R. (2d) 225 at pp. 230 (H.C.J.):

   . . . the courts consistently favour the settlement of lawsuits in general. To put it another way, there is an *overriding public interest in favour of settlement*. This policy promotes the interests of litigants generally by saving them the expense of trial of disputed issues, and it reduces the strain upon an already overburdened provincial court system. [emphasis added]

   This is especially so with respect to particularly complex cases: *Ontario New Home Warranty Program* v. *Chevron Chemical Co.* (1999), 46 O.R. (3d) 130 at paras. 69-71 (Sup. Ct. J.).

30.   Trangsrud above note note 25 at 74.

initio. There are many aspects of daily life that the ordinary person could find annoying or even intolerable; numerous circumstances that could cause him loss of wealth, that nonetheless would not support even a single day's trial.[31] The point is that one's right to a "day in court" is not as objective as some commentators might suggest; it clearly is the right to a day in court only in those circumstances where it can be said that there is an objective consensus that persons similarly situated should be granted one.[32] Following this argument, if the social benefits of mass tort claim aggregation outweigh the advantages of the individualistic system it replaces, then there is nothing wrong with, nor even particularly unusual in, depriving mass tort claimants the right to an individual day in court.

There is lively discussion about whether such a social consensus should be arrived at strictly through an analysis of "welfare economics," as Kaplow and Shavell suggest,[33] or whether there is a set of principles of "fairness" entirely independent of social utility that demands certain procedural guidelines be followed even if it demonstrably renders everybody involved worse off. This is not to say that innate concepts of "fairness" are irrelevant to the Kaplow/Shavell analysis, indeed those authors propose that such a "taste for fairness" must be factored in when considering individuals' well-being.[34] Their main point is that, when pursuit of conceptual fairness begins to make everyone *worse* off, it is difficult to justify as a matter of policy. Acceptance of this position appears tacit in modern rules of court, mandatory mediation provisions (both in the court process and through judicial enforcement of alternative dispute resolution clauses in con-

---

31. Consider the case of a small shopowner who is crowded out by an encroaching supermarket. The owner may consider the interloper's appearance unfair, given the fact that his small store (and the taxes he's paid) helped to build the community the larger store now wishes to exploit; he might suffer catastrophic financial loss as a result of the intrusion. But does he have the right to a day in court? Assuming his complaint falls outside the very limited number of situations in which competition might be recognized by society (and thus the law) as unduly detrimental, he does not. Mechanisms exist for summary dismissal of his complaint, and (if the complaint were so beyond social recognition as to be considered frivolous or vexatious), possibly sanctions against him as well. This goes well beyond a process for ensuring that baseless claims *do not succeed* in court; rather it purports to prevent some claims from ever being adjudged at all.

32. For a discussion of the normative nature of the distribution of rights of tort action see generally Jules Coleman & Arthur Ripstein, "Mischief and Misfortune" (1995) 41 McGill L.J. 91 and the two articles by Robert G. Bone, above note 23.

33. Louis Kaplow & Steven Shavell, "Fairness vs. Welfare" (2001) 114 Harv. L. Rev. 961.

34. *Ibid.* at 1350-51; Thomas E. Willging, "Mass Tort Problems and Proposals: A Report to the Mass Torts Working Group" (Federal Judicial Center 1999, available at http://www.fjc.gov/public/pdf.nsf/lookup/MassTApC.pdf) at 17.

tracts) and numerous other legal mechanisms designed to discourage – or even bar – litigation that is not cost-effective.

The "right" of access to the courts, then, might be recharacterized as a right of access to another malleable term: "justice." That is to say, there is a legitimate expectation that the legal system will provide a mechanism by which one can advance his legal claim to the extent that social policy considers it valuable that he should be able to, and no further. But what this should mean in the mass tort context is a different question.

In the absence of class proceedings, as already mentioned, mass tort claims tend to be aggregated into "inventories" of claims by plaintiffs' lawyers. In some cases, these claims might number in the tens of thousands. Under such circumstances, it is a fantasy to suggest that the individual plaintiffs retain meaningful litigative autonomy. As Professor Coffee writes:

> [I]ndividual plaintiffs have weak to nonexistent control over their attorneys across the mass tort context for reasons that are inherent to the economics of mass tort litigation. Accordingly, proposals for the return to a traditional system of individual case litigation are apt to be as quixotic as they are costly.[35]

While *ad hoc* aggregation in the individualistic litigation system strips plaintiffs of their individual control, it does not offer the ex post benefits of membership in a fully aggregated class (such as improved average compensation as a result of the greater economy of scale and judicial oversight of settlement terms and attorneys' fees), nor does it offer the ex ante benefits of more effective deterrence.

So any comparison between class actions and individual litigation must be between an almost completely aggregated claim and a very poorly aggregated one, not between a faceless collectivist process on the one hand and a fantastic idealisation of individual justice on the other.

All this being said, there is some persuasive evidence that individuals' satisfaction with the mass tort system is enhanced if they at least have a chance to be heard by a person perceived to be in authority;[36] and perhaps such an opportunity after settlement could be designed in order to provide mass tort victims with

---

35. Coffee, "Class Wars" above note 14 at 1346.

36. Some commentators have even suggested that plaintiffs might prefer *not* to settle in order to have at least a hearing of their grievances. Judge Weinstein discusses some ways in which mass tort litigation can accommodate these preferences, and likely some experiment in the area is needed: Weinstein, *Individual Justice in Mass Tort Litigation* (Evanston, Ill.: Northwestern University Press, 1995) at 10-13. That there is some perceived independent utility simply in the act of "being heard" should not surprise us; it has long been suggested that this is the only explanation for why citizens vote in elections given the poor individual reward they receive from doing so: Amartya Sen, "Collective Choice and Social Welfare" (San Francisco: Holden Day, 1970) at 195-6; Peter C. Ordeschook, "A Theory on the Calculus of Voting" (1968) 62 American Political Science Review 25 at 28.

"catharsis," as Judge Weinstein, for one, suggests[37] On the other hand, the extent to which the tort system should function as a platform for the expression of grievances is debatable; after all, many persons injured by other than tortious acts have no such platform and society seems in no great hurry to provide one.[38] Indeed it might even be suggested that dissatisfaction with a process that denies the right to be heard is only a result of the individual's belief in legal entitlement to do so (i.e. it is an expectation taught by the current tort system itself). Nevertheless, this last, minor aspect of the "day in court ideal" may have sufficient weight to warrant a place in system design or settlement approval, as Weinstein proposes.

F.   SUFFICIENCY OF NOTICE

Considerations of class action system design with respect to notice are inextricably tied with the idea of opt-out rights and the individualistic notion that one should not be bound by a decision of which he had no notice. However, this objection too depends largely on whether a "public law model" or "private law model" of class actions is preferred, and whether the ex ante or ex post perspective is adopted.

In the public law model, the sufficiency of notice is judged, not by its efficacy in alerting every person bound by the pending proceeding to its existence, but rather by its effectiveness in constraining abuse by class counsel. That is to say, the representative plaintiff in any class action is essentially a "self-appointed agent" of the class members; obviously, if there were no notice to the class members, there would be a strong suspicion that the representative might prefer his own interests to those of the class, to the extent that they diverged. In such a case, the public interest in seeing the class claim prosecuted is frustrated, quite apart from any concern over the individual litigative rights of the individual class members. The public law model, then, would consider notice sufficient if it gave enough class members (through a representative sample) an opportunity to object to the representative's appointment or to the class definition. Professor Fiss characterizes the "public law model" of notice thus:

> For the members of this school, the purpose of notice is not to construct a consensual link between the representative and the members of the class, but rather to make certain that the powers of self-appointment are not abused. The notice informs a good portion of the class of what is about to transpire in their name and gives them the opportunity to complain to the court about the adequacy of the self-appointed representative. Notice is not a proxy for consent, but only an instrument

---

37.   Weinstein above note 36 at 13.

38.   For example, someone injured by a manufacturer or polluter's decisions would seem to have the same interest in a "cathartic" exercise whether or not the precautions taken by the defendant turn out to have been "reasonable."

for making certain that the named plaintiff will be a strong and effective advocate for the class.[39]

The U.S. Courts, which appear to prefer private to public law analyses where the two conflict, have unequivocally stated that Rule 23's call for the best possible notice is in fact a requirement for actual notice to all known class members, often an extraordinarily expensive investment.[40] It is uncertain what Canadian statutes require; arguably, provisions that explicitly provide for notice to only a representative sample of class members at the court's discretion[41] evince a legislative endorsement of the "public law" model of notice.

Again, opting for the ex ante perspective over that taken by individuals ex post tends to align more completely the interests of individual class members with the public law model. Ex ante, it would appear that all tort victims would prefer the system that maximises their insurance against harm; this would require optimal aggregation of claims, and indeed to the extent that notice requirements were likely to undermine these ex ante preferences, the individual would sacrifice notice in exchange for fuller compensation.

---

39. Owen M. Fiss, "The Political Theory of the Class Action" (1996) 53 Wash. & Lee L. Rev. 21 at 28.

40. *Eisen* v. *Carlisle & Jacquelin* 417 U.S. 156 (1974). In the *Eisen* case, a random "collective" notice to a class of investors (favoured by the trial court) was estimated at $20,000, while the *actual* notice eventually ordered by the Supreme Court was valued at $225,000.

41. B.C. s. 19(4)(d); Ontario 17(4)(c).

—

CHAPTER FIVE

Managing Structural Costs
of Class Actions

A. INTRODUCTION

As I have attempted to emphasize throughout the previous chapters of this book, the economic market in class actions, if it is to be of more than theoretical interest, must take some account of the distorting effects of the real world. I have already discussed some ways in which individual preferences and biases can distort litigation markets, and how optimal litigation investment can have an impact on outcomes not generally acknowledged. In this chapter I turn to some areas in which much greater market forces can distort the outcomes in aggregate claims. The real world is divided into geographic and political entities that were not, generally speaking, designed for the efficient resolution of litigation. Human behaviour, particularly the self-interested behaviour of the main antagonists – defendants and plaintiffs' counsel – also can have a grossly distorting effect on outcomes. Moreover, the reality of imperfect information, particularly in claims involving indeterminate causation and unknown epidemiology, means that the timing of litigation can have a considerable impact on the global resolution of claims.

B. CONSERVATION OF JUDICIAL RESOURCES

One frequently discussed benefit of class actions is that they can permit the efficient use of judicial resources in resolution of mass claims. However, some objections raised to aggregation, based on anecdotal accounts of rare and chaotic episodes such as asbestos suits in the U.S., suggest that class litigation does not in fact lead to less litigation, but more, and that this is a reason to "rein in" such actions. When considering this claim, we must focus clearly on just what we mean when we say that we should "conserve" judicial resources through class litigation.

An obvious consequence of aggregation is that per-claim litigation costs are reduced. This represents a saving not only to the class members, but also to the court, which can hear thousands of claims simultaneously.[1] There is also persuasive evidence that class actions settle more frequently than individual suits, an effect that is purported to increase as aggregation becomes more complete across the class.[2]

Nevertheless, individual class actions can be very expensive indeed, as Chief Justice Esson warned in *Tiemstra* v. *Insurance Corporation of British Columbia* when he declared that "class actions have the potential for becoming monsters of complexity and cost."[3] However to make this argument in opposition to the idea of aggregation is to miss the point. As Professor Coffee put it:

> Easy as it is to point out that mass tort litigation involves high transaction costs, one must move on to the inevitable next question: "compared to what?"[4]

Courts have historically exploited basic aggregative techniques such as joinder of actions to take advantage of judicial scale economies and avoid wasteful duplication of effort (not to mention the embarrassing possibility of inconsistent results on identical questions). Yet to suggest that the public purse will be spared expense with the blossoming of class action regimes misses a central point of these laws. I have advocated at some length the view that the principal goal of class action suits is to modify behaviour through optimal aggregation and recov-

---

1. Even the notoriously expensive asbestos litigation was made considerably less so through aggregative techniques, even absent class actions. A federal study calculated that each asbestos case cost only 19% of the average litigation, where the average products liability claim was well above average (174%): Thomas E. Willging, "Mass Tort Problems and Proposals: A Report to the Mass Torts Working Group" (Federal Judicial Center 1999, available at http://www.fjc.gov/public/pdf.nsf/lookup/MassTApC.pdf) at 14.

2. One economist who has developed settlement-rate models has found that mandatory aggregation leads to virtual certainty of settlement because, *inter alia*, it eliminates the "signalling" and information uncertainty produced through the opt-out process: Yeon-Koo Che "Equilibrium Formation of Class Suits" (1996) 62 J. Pub. Econ. 339.

3. *Tiemstra* v. *Insurance Corporation of British Columbia* (1996), 22 B.C.L.R. (3d) 49 at 61 (S.C.).

4. John C. Coffee, Jr., "Class Wars: The Dilemma of the Mass Tort Class Action" (1995) 95 Colum. L. Rev. 1343 [Coffee, "Class Wars"] at 1347.

ery. Although I have argued that the advantages of class litigation accrue to all classable claims (not only individually non-viable ones), discussion of the conservation of judicial resources must begin with the recognition that the bringing of aggregate suits which include claims that are not individually viable is one of the purposes of a class litigation system. So while we might seek to employ class actions to reduce consumption of judicial resources *per claim*, we have no right to expect that their employment will reduce consumption *overall*. Class actions seek to move the litigation system towards the optimal level of suit, a level it is at present well below.[5]

This view is not universally accepted. In *Smith* v. *Canadian Tire Acceptance Ltd.* (1995), 22 O.R. (3rd) 433 at 449, Mr. Justice Winkler, in deciding the award of costs, said:

> The *Class Proceedings Act, 1992* was never intended to insulate representative plaintiffs, or class members, from the possible cost consequences of unsuccessful litigation. The goal of the Act is not to encourage the promotion of litigation. Rather it was designed to provide a procedure whereby the courts would be more accessible to groups of plaintiffs.

It is true that Ontario's statute has a different approach to the award of costs from either British Columbia's or Rule 23 in the U.S.[6] Yet it is going too far to say that the goal of the Act is not to promote litigation; at least with respect to low-value, individually non-viable claims, encouraging litigation is *precisely* the goal of the Act, and indeed of any class action regime.

This misconception is pervasive,[7] and may result from the Canadian view of judicial economy as a co-equal goal of class proceedings, on par with access to

---

5.   The optimal level of suit in negligence law would be where every valid action is brought. Judge Willging for instance, above note 1 at 20, reflects that:

> In assessing whether higher claim rates are a problem, one needs to identify potential benefits as well. While higher claiming rates impose burdens on courts, defendants, and other plaintiffs, they may also represent a more complete form of justice.

6.   The award of costs against unsuccessful plaintiffs is discussed in more detail in Chapter 7.

7.   McNeil & Fanscal, for instance, complain that when A.H. Robins (manufacturers of the notorious Dalkon Shield intra-uterine device) filed for bankruptcy and a limited fund class action was certified, "almost 200,000 claimants who had not entered the tort system notwithstanding wide publicity [of earlier individual Dalkon Shield cases] became claimants": Barry F. McNeil & Beth L. Fanscal, "Mass Torts and Class Actions: Facing Increased Scrutiny" (1996) 167 F.R.D. 483 at 494-95.

> The authors argue that "[t]he greater efficiency with which mass tort resolution is dispensed, the greater the number of claimants" (at 493) and later that "it appears that certification may indeed attract new – possibly numerous – claims that would otherwise not be pursued." (at 499) Assuming tort law is being correctly applied (and McNeil & Fanscal do not suggest otherwise – their argument is entirely pro-

justice and behaviour modification. The goal of access for underrepresented plaintiffs is, at least in the case of aggregated low-value suits, frequently at odds with the goal of judicial economy:

> [T]he [Class Proceeding] Act is clearly designed to increase access to justice even if this does entail greater use of judicial resources . . . [the] concern is not so much with too little public law litigation, but with too little."[8]

This observation may lead to the conclusion that the goal of judicial resource conservation means *ipso facto* that Canadian class action legislation is aimed at higher-value suits as well as lower-value ones (a conclusion which might be applauded). Unfortunately, it can also lead to the unrealistic expectation that class aggregation rules will lead to an easing of the burden faced by court systems, and this certainly may not be so.

This is not to say that class litigation can never serve the goal of conserving social resources generally. Indeed a correctly functioning class litigation regime will tend to increase deterrence, reduce the incidence of compensable accidents, promote settlement and ease the associated costs that are currently externalised through formal and informal insurance. Assuming that the secondary benefit of increased compensation for victims is also realised, then these effects will be further enhanced. The money thus saved can be redirected into the judicial system to accommodate these cases.

Furthermore, any additional cost upon the advent of class litigation should reduce over time as market forces respond to the deterrent effect, and standards for typical mass tort claims such as products liability and securities litigation are more clearly defined. At a point of equilibrium, lawsuits will be at the lowest level necessary to diminish uncertainties as to the outcomes in similar suits. In other words, an optimal level of "test cases" will monitor the threshold of tort liability (so that insurance, deterrence and ex post settlement thresholds will in turn be optimised) and track the motion of the standard of care.

---

cedural), it is remarkable that an increase in the number of those who can vindicate their legal rights is seen as problematic.

8.   Kent Roach, "Fundamental Reforms to Civil Litigation" in Ontario Law Reform Commission, *Rethinking Civil Justice: Research Studies for the Civil Justice Review (Vol. 2)* (Toronto, Ontario Law Reform Commission, 1996) at 414. The Ontario Law Reform Commission had also noticed the irony of the "judicial efficiency" objection in its *Report on Class Actions, 3 vols.* (Toronto: Ministry of the Attorney General, 1982) [*Ontario Report (1982)*] at 130:

> Criticisms that condemn class actions aggregating individually nonrecoverable claims – based on the view that they do not contribute to judicial economy, but rather "stir up" unnecessary litigation – implicitly assume that class actions are, in fact, effective in providing access to the courts to a broader range of individuals.

However, the objection that class actions tend to place undue stress on the judiciary, or that "if you build a superhighway there will be a traffic jam"[9] has credibility only to the point that the cases clogging the courts should not, under the law, be brought at all. The answer is that the system incentives must be (and to a large extent are) designed to avoid this. To argue otherwise is to say that it is better to have too little enforcement, that more widespread responsibility of mass tortfeasors is a social harm in itself, presumably because it is economically stifling to hold more defendants to the established standard of care. This argument would perhaps be better directed at actually modifying the standard of care and allowing a higher degree of behaviour now considered "negligent" to be considered "reasonable," or alternately to abandoning a fault/harm–based system altogether in favour of regimes designed around no-fault or risk-based principles.

C.   BARRIERS TO EFFECTIVE AGGREGATION

(1)   Aggregation of Diverse Claims

(a)   *Claim-Value Diversity*

So far, we have looked at simple models to extrapolate the impact of aggregation of claims upon individual recovery and deterrence in low-value claims, or claims that would likely not be brought individually. We have also seen that the value of aggregation (including its deterrent value) extends to higher value claims as well. However, where actions involve both individually viable and non-viable claims, particular problems can arise.

Because aggregation of claims may lead to a relative devaluation of those individual claims having a high probability of high recovery (therefore probabilistically speaking "high-value" claims), private law model theorists often express concern that the right of such persons to "opt out" of the class must be preserved as an essential element of fairness to those plaintiffs.

In actions when opt-out rights are present, the problem is reversed: high-value claimants whose claims are independently viable can use their bargaining power within the class to exact a higher percentage of the settlement in exchange for allowing the class to exploit their superior factual or legal arguments.

This occurs because the exercise of opt-out rights for high-value claimants will diminish the overall welfare of the class. Because, as I demonstrated earlier, both optimal deterrence and optimal compensation rely on the highest possible aggregation, any departure from the class diminishes the per claim recovery for the entire class.

Consider a simplified example in which the class consists of three people harmed by a single defendant. Litigating individually will cost $100 per claim and gain an expected recovery of $1000 ($900 each after expenses). Litigating as

---

9.   Francis E. McGovern, "An Analysis of Mass Torts for Judges" (1995) 73 Tex. L. Rev. 1821 at 1840.

a class will allow either simple elimination of redundancies (increasing each member's recovery to up to $966.67), or increase the overall value of the claim (perhaps investing $200 in litigation will increase expected recovery by an extra $75 per claim) or some combination of the two. In such a case, any plaintiff can exact a "participation premium" from the other by threatening to opt out.

A more realistic example would be to say that the third plaintiff had an unusually strong claim legally, with an expected value of $2000 (but no greater actual harm than the other two). If the class litigates together, recovery will be $4000 and expenses $100 (=$3900); each member would receive $1300 if distribution was averaged, or $975, $975, $1950 (assuming distribution based on strength of legal case). If the high-value claim is pursued separately, the recovery would be $950, $950 and $1900 (=$3800). In this sense, an opt-out class is making everyone worse off. But the larger the role that litigation investment plays in the *chance* of recovery, the greater the consequences of an opt-out, because it is the claims with the strongest law and facts that will tend to opt out.

This disappearance of high-value claims has the further effect of diminishing the overall value of all claims. This problem has led some to the conclusion that only mandatory aggregation can provide truly optimal deterrence, an idea discussed further in Part IV.

(b) Future Claims

Another kind of intraclass problem is that of "futures" claims, i.e. those made by, or on behalf of, persons whose injuries have not yet manifested themselves, and indeed might never do so. Just as claim-value diversity will create conflict within the class, so can future claims, with the compounded problem of agency: the future claimants are not before the court, and cannot be heard on the fairness of the settlement, which may exhaust any fund established, long before the future claimants' injuries are manifest.

The ability of class action suits to provide global resolution for claims not yet manifest has led some defendants in "exposure cases" to aggressively seek resolution of the class claim while only a fraction of the expected harm is apparent. Professor Coffee wrote of this phenomenon:

> [T]his transformation is of historic significance: once a sword for plaintiffs, the modern class action is in some contexts increasingly becoming a shield for defendants . . . the mass tort class action now often provides a means by which unsuspecting future claimants suffer the extinction of their claims even before they learn of their injury.[10]

The problem of future claims is one of compensation, not deterrence, because optimal deterrence can be achieved without knowing the identity of future claimants, or perhaps even the true extent of the harm. This means that the global amount paid by the defendant might, notwithstanding the possibility of future

---

10.   Coffee, "Class Wars" above note 4 at 1350.

claims, be estimated at the time of the lawsuit, and to the extent that it cannot, it would not serve the interests of deterrence to wait further.[11]

However, future claims can be uniquely accommodated by the class action device, because often, though the claimants cannot be known, assessment of risk can determine their injuries and numbers with some degree of precision, at least to the degree to which the defendant could be said to have reasonably foreseen them. In such a case, the problem is one of optimal insurance, rather than deterrence: i.e. how is the aggregate fund to be distributed?

(c) Common Issues Classes

Claim-value diversity within the class, as briefly described above, tends to raise the greatest concerns over fairness in an all-or-nothing aggregation system; the greater the flexibility in the system's accommodation of individual issues while preserving single adjudication of common issues, the less likely are high-value claimants to be concerned – after all, on the common issues, they too enjoy the advantages offered by the scale economy, even if not to the same extent as those with lower-value claims.

All of the arguments that favour aggregation of individual lawsuits into class actions apply with respect to common issues. Since it is precisely with respect to common issues that the defendant enjoys a significant advantage of economic scale, it is these questions which, when heard in a single action, will best allow the plaintiffs to adequately compete. As we have seen, this levelling of the field is important – if not crucial – to the fulfilment of the goals of compensation and deterrence.

There is a residual debate about whether the "private law model" advantages of fragmenting the mass hearing into individual actions for hearing of non-common issues outweigh the "public law model" advantages of considering all claims together to maximise gross recovery and minimise global transaction costs. Many "public law model" scholars, such as Rosenberg, go so far as to suggest that all issues, even inherently individualistic questions such as causation and voluntary assumption of risk, should be considered on a global, statistical basis, and a single compensation figure arrived at. This amount would then be distributed among plaintiffs according to appropriate social priorities.[12]

---

11. This is because deterrence need only "internalise" in the defendant the amount of *foreseeable* damages. If science develops in the future to the point where higher costs can be attributed to the wrong, this amount need not be imposed on the defendant to effect optimal deterrence, which is necessarily based on the defendant's ex ante knowledge of the dangers, either direct or "deemed" as a matter of policy.

12. Rosenberg's proposals are discussed in greater detail below Part IV. The ability of Canadian statutes to support assessment of liability and damages on an aggregate basis is discussed in more detail in Part II below.

Nevertheless, on the central point nearly everyone should agree: except in those rare cases where transaction costs involved in aggregation of common issues outweigh the advantages of a single hearing, or when resolution of the common issues will otherwise not significantly advance the progress of the litigation, aggregation for the purposes of hearing even a single issue will be warranted if it would be burdensome for plaintiffs to litigate that common question individually. This would seem to apply to virtually any question surrounding mass tort *liability*, as opposed to the availability of defences or questions of damages. That is to say, issues concerning the defendant's central decision-making in all cases should generally be amenable to aggregative hearing.

(d) Subclasses

If deterrence and compensation are best served by maximal aggregation, then to what extent do subclasses tend to detract from the effectiveness of the class proceeding?

Obviously, the introduction of a subclass, with independent representation, is a partial disaggregation of the class, and therefore less efficient from the point of view of spreading litigation costs. However, this is not to say that subclassing is equivalent to disaggregation from the point of view of efficiency. In fact, counsel for the various subclasses have strong incentives to pool their resources on all of the common issues at the trial (from the point of view of maximising recovery). This suggests that fee arrangements based on the overall recovery will be more effective at promoting cooperation and efficiency than those which focus on fees or multipliers, which might provide incentives for disagreement and unnecessary duplication of effort.

However, there are certain kinds of subclasses which are unnecessary and unhelpful: those which are drawn without regard for the commonality of issues. The most obvious example is a regime, like British Columbia's, which mandates a separate subclass for out-of-province claimants. There is no good reason for drawing such an arbitrary distinction; certainly, in many cases there will be substantial differences in the law or facts which make nonresident subclasses optimal, but this will not always be so (consider for instance a lawsuit for breach of a federal statute). Efficiency suggests that, where the issues are the same, the class should be one.

(2) Aggregation of Interjurisdictional Claims

All of the principles so far articulated here militate generally in favour of the largest possible class; that is, particularly given the modern state of communication technology, there is no theoretical reason why the class should be restricted geographically. Indeed, this being the case, the most economically efficient aggregate claims would bring together all who had suffered harm from a particular act wherever they live; that is, the tort marketplace should mirror the distributive market of the defendant.[13] Ideally, class actions should consolidate freely.

But, theory aside, we live in a world of geographic jurisdictions, both within Canada and throughout the world, and these jurisdictions do not neatly coincide with the economic marketplace in goods, services and communication.

What is the consequence of this? Some interesting economic observations might be made. It can be stated with some degree of certainty that mass-marketers of products tend to average their prices across the sales territory. That is to say, if a national chain store decides to buy a product for its stores and sell it for $10.99 per unit, it will generally be $10.99 in Winnipeg, Vancouver and Toronto. The store will negotiate a single per-unit price with the manufacturer or distributor, and will either have it shipped to its distribution centre or perhaps directly to each store. While the chain might adjust shipping costs depending on store location (and either average this across the chain or actually sell the product for more in more remote stores), it is unlikely, to say the least, that the retailer will canvass the products-liability regimes in each of the jurisdictions it operates, and adjust the prices for each shipping destination depending on the expected frequency of litigation that is likely to arise from the product's use.[14] Even if the

---

13. Or at least that portion of the marketplace wherein the price of the product (or that component of the price that constitutes the tort insurance premium) is to be the same. It is reasonable to suggest, for instance, that there is a lower tort insurance premium built into an American car when it is sold in Mexico as opposed to Canada: even if liability rules and likelihood of suit are the same, the income differential of victims would lead to damages differential, which might affect the tort premium (in actuality the differential will be averaged to the extent that consumers can offset it through cross-jurisdictional shopping).

14. Price averaging of consumer goods can be easily confirmed. If one visits the websites of national retailers, for instance, the prices offered are, without exception in my experience, valid nationwide. In the United States, for instance, Radio Shack (www.radioshack.com) advertises that the prices listed in its online catalog are valid for all its stores in the 48 contiguous states. I can imagine no one suggesting that higher prices in Hawaii or Alaska are due to higher litigation insurance in those states rather than to higher shipping costs.

   See also Richard Craswell, "Passing on the Costs of Legal Rules: Efficiency and Distribution in Buyer-Seller Relationships" (1991) 43 Stan. L. Rev. 361. Even if a manufacturer were to adopt such a strategy, distributors with business in more than one province would have an incentive to distribute that particular product from the jurisdiction with the lowest tort insurance premiums (assuming that redistribution costs were lower than the amount saved by doing so); yet the market would in turn compensate for this strategy as the manufacturer (who would continue to face tort actions arising from redistributed products sold in the "underinsured" jurisdictions) would respond by building a higher tort insurance premium into products destined for that jurisdiction as well, and price averaging would again result.

store, with knowledge of the relevant points of sale, were to factor in a differential tort premium, could one imagine that the manufacturer, who likely sells his product to distributors in huge quantities with only the remotest ideas about the particular destination jurisdictions, would do so? If that doesn't tax the imagination sufficiently, consider the manufacturer of a *component* of the product who incorporates within his price a nominal litigation insurance rate. Is this rate dependent on the jurisdiction in which any particular product containing the component will be consumed? It would seem not.

It may be that there will be variation in the price based on some factors; local taxes certainly affect pricing in a number of ways beyond the obvious; oversupply in certain markets may lead to discounting if it is cheaper to do so than to move it to an area where demand is higher; similarly, as previously mentioned, transportation costs can affect prices in remote areas. But by and large, these factors too tend to be averaged over the entire market. Price averaging provides additional advantages in that it facilitates national advertising of prices in national magazines, on network television, or on the Internet. Regardless of the causes, the effect seems indisputable.

To my knowledge there has been no serious suggestion that manufacturers of goods adjust their pricing from province to province due to the relative risk of litigation. This is not insignificant in the Canadian context, given the fact that class proceedings have been available prior to 2001 in only three provinces, and that the statutes permitting them were vigorously opposed by various business groups *inter alia* on the ground that they would affect prices and depress economic activity,[15] despite the weight of empirical evidence to the contrary.[16] If

---

15. See for instance the similar objection discussed in the Alberta Law Reform Commission report at 63 that enactment of a class litigation regime would jeopardize the "Alberta advantage" and discourage businesses from locating there. Similar concerns over deterrence of innovation and high product costs as a result of mass tort litigation can be found in Peter Huber, "Safety and the Second Best: The Hazards of Public Risk Management in the Courts", 85 Colum. L. Rev. 277 at 305 – 320; Peter Huber, *Liability: The Legal Revolution and Its Consequences* (New York: Basic Books, 1988) at 11. I do not here consider the impact of mass tort claims on product innovation, as I consider Huber's assertions to be thoroughly refuted by Rosenberg (David Rosenberg, "Class Actions for Mass Torts: Doing Individual Justice by Collective Means" (1987) 62 Ind. L.J. 561 at 577-78) and I am aware of no serious attempt to resurrect them.

16. Objective analysis generally runs counter to repeated suggestions in the popular press that tort liability is either excessive or an economic depressant of any significance, even in the United States: Deborah L. Rhode, "Law, Knowledge and the Academy: Legal Scholarship" (2002) 115 Harv. L. Rev. 1327 at 1347-51 (concluding that the pervasive public belief to the contrary may represent a communication failure on the part of legal scholars). Rhode concludes (*ibid.* at 1350) that

    [R]esearch has painstakingly documented [that] the most serious problem with

they have done so, circumstantial evidence at least seems to indicate that it has taken place quite uniformly across the country, as one would expect with price averaging in a market dominated by goods sold interprovincially.[17]

This leads to the conclusion that, if plaintiffs are more likely to recover in one jurisdiction than in another, then that advantage is being effectively subsidised by consumers in the jurisdictions where recovery is hampered.[18]

Indeed, it would appear, given the increasing parity in consumer goods prices in the U.S. and Canada since the advent of the North American Free Trade Agreement, that price averaging will ignore differences in the legal scheme between the two countries. If products liability lawsuits in the U.S. (where manufacturers are subject to "strict liability" rather than the negligence standard) are indeed driving up the prices of consumer goods[19] then Canadian consumers are subsidising this through higher costs, without enjoying any of the increased potential recovery if they are injured as a result.[20]

---

the American tort system involves undercompensation, not overcompensation. Studies of medical malpractice, unsafe products, and auto and airline accidents consistently find that most victims do not recover the majority of their costs . . . Contemporary debates about frivolous litigation are focusing "on the tip of the iceberg, and probably the wrong iceberg, at that." The relentless focus on "too much" — too much law, litigation, lawyering — deflects attention from issues of "too little": too little access to legal assistance and too little access to legal remedies. [citations omitted]

17. Statistics Canada's "Consumer Price Index" provides a rough and ready comparison of the prices of a standardized "basket" of consumer goods and services across the provinces. Interestingly, in the latest CPI figures released, each of the three class action jurisdictions boasted CPI prices somewhat below the national average, indicating that after years (or in Quebec's case decades) of class litigation, consumer prices, if they have risen as a result of tort insurance premiums, have done so uniformly across the country: Statistics Canada, "Latest Release from the CPI" (Thursday, February 14, 2002) http://www.statcan.ca/english/Subjects/Cpi/cpi-en.htm (accessed March 10, 2002).

18. Although an admittedly crude measure, arguably the fact that the highest CPI jurisdictions are the three prairie provinces (the rural Northwest, Yukon and Nunavut Territories are not included in the CPI release *ibid.*) indicates that transportation and inventory costs, inherently local in nature, are the kinds of costs that will not be averaged by manufacturers on a nationwide basis.

19. Rhode, above note 16 at 1349 (noting that tort liability "premiums" account for perhaps "two percent of the cost of American goods and services, and that liability risks absorb only about twenty-five cents of every $100 in revenue").

20. The "tantalizing but unanswered question" of the implications of diverging negligence law in the NAFTA era is mentioned but not explored by Mr. Justice Linden, in Allen M. Linden, *Canadian Tort Law* (7th ed.) (Toronto: Butterworths, 2001) at 569-70.

(3) Collusion in Settlement

(a) *To the Prejudice of Claimants*

Since the 1982 Ontario Law Reform Commission report, Canadian system designers have struggled to overcome the fear of agency problems between the class members and the representative plaintiff's counsel. The danger is that class proceedings would "produce compromises unfair to class members, either because the representative plaintiff has settled with the defendant for a premium on his or her own claim, thereafter discontinuing the class action, or because the class lawyer has settled in a manner designed to maximize legal fees at the expense of the recovery ..."[21] available to class members.

Professor Coffee draws a distinction between "small claimant" (i.e. not independently viable) and "large claimant" classes. In the former, he suggests, "defendants tend to resist class certification (because plaintiffs have no realistic alternative)," whereas in "large claimant classes, defendants increasingly prefer class certification for a variety of reasons, including . . . their hope to reach a "reasonable" global settlement with cooperative plaintiffs' attorneys."[22] This gives rise to what Coffee calls "structural collusion" where, "even in the absence of bad faith,"

> . . . suspect settlements result in large measure because of the defendants' ability to shop for favorable settlement terms, either by contacting multiple plaintiffs' attorneys or by inducing them to compete against each other. At its worst, this process can develop into a reverse auction, with the low bidder among the plaintiffs' attorneys winning the right to settle with the defendant. Here, it is necessary to confront the comparatively new institution of the "settlement" class action.[23]

Sometimes, settlements can be reached that are of deceptively little utility to the class members. One method which is gaining popularity is known as the "in kind" or "scrip" settlement, involving coupons or some other "benefit" which will accrue to class members who continue to patronise the defendant. These kinds of settlements can be inherently problematic because they come at minimum cost to the defendant (which might even generate a profit from them[24]), and are therefore inadequate or illusory as deterrent. In some cases, they provide class members with only chimeric compensation as well.[25]

---

21. *Ontario Report (1982)* above note 8 at 146.

22. Coffee, "Class Wars" above note 4 at 1353.

23. *Ibid.* at 1354.

24. Consider for instance a movie chain that offers class members free tickets to films in settlement of a class action, knowing that the theatregoers' purchase of snacks will offset losses and possibly more than compensate.

25. To settle the litigation arising from the alleged proclivity of certain General Motors trucks with "side saddle" fuel tanks to explode when struck, the defendant offered $1000 gift certificates – non transferable – against the purchase of a new vehicle, perhaps a 5% discount on the price of the truck: In Re *General Motors Corp. Pick-*

The "in kind" payment strategy sometimes involves "cy pres" payments[26] to charities or other third parties. Describing one such settlement, where a food company agreed to distribute its matzo products to various charities for a period of four years, Coffee observed that the "cynically disposed might see this settlement as an excellent way of simultaneously disposing of both stale matzos and a difficult litigation."[27] But note that cy pres distribution need not sacrifice deterrence; indeed deterrence will be wholly preserved regardless of who gains from the largesse, provided that the defendant *loses* the appropriate amount in real terms, and does not simply give away useless surplus stock as in Coffee's example.

In the United States and now Canada, a process has developed whereby "settlement classes" are certified and settled virtually simultaneously. The putative representative plaintiff and defendant agree to seek the court's approval of a settlement that has been prearranged between the parties; the court then certifies the class and approves the settlement, usually after a single hearing. The key feature of the settlement class is that the defendant's acquiescence to certification is conditional upon the approval of the settlement; if settlement is not approved, the action proceeds as if certification had not been attempted.[28]

The potential for so-called "structural collusion" between plaintiffs' and defendants' counsel is obvious, particularly if several competing actions are vying for class status. Under such circumstances, the various aspiring class representatives are driven into a "reverse auction,"[29] compelling them to settle for less than the class's claim is worth. Even absent such competitive pressure, though, objections to the settlement class might be advanced on the basis that, following the analyses presented earlier in this part, settlement levels will be suboptimal until and unless the defendant is being confronted with a complete

---

up Truck Fuel Tank Prods. Liab. Litig., 55 F.3d 768 at 780-781 (3d Cir. 1995). In such cases, Coffee notes that "[o]ften, the discount is no greater than what an individual plaintiff could receive for a volume purchase, or for a cash sale, or for using a particular credit card . . . " Coffee, "Class Wars" above note 4 at 1367.

26. This term is occasionally spelt "cy-près," "cy-pres" or (mistakenly) "cy-prés." I here adopt the spelling used in the overwhelming majority of Canadian cases, and as it is found in the *New Shorter Oxford English Dictionary*. Cy pres is derived from the Norman French term meaning "near this"; in the class action setting it refers to payment of damages or settlement funds to a person other than a class member.

27. Coffee, "Class Wars" above note 4 at 1368.

28. The history of the settlement class and attempts to alter Rule 23 to explicitly permit it are described in Darren M. Franklin, "The Mass Tort Defendants Strike Back: Are Settlement Class Actions A Collusive Threat or Just a Phantom Menace?" (2000) 53 Stan. L. Rev. 163.

29. John C. Coffee Jr., "The Corruption of the Class Action: The New Technology of Collusion" (1995) 80 Cornell L.Rev. 851 at 851.

aggregation of the claims for which it may be liable as the result of a particular mass tort.

Settlement classes are opposed by "the overwhelming majority of the scholarly community who have expressed a view" on the question,[30] and attempts to formalise their acceptance through legislative reform to Rule 23 have met with a "firestorm of criticism by the academic community."[31]

There is a significant secondary concern that courts, faced with the opportunity to clear troublesome litigation from their dockets, might certify when otherwise they might not, to the detriment of absent plaintiffs (and particularly "futures" claimants).[32] Safeguards against inappropriate "settlement classes" are discussed below in Part II.

(b) To the Prejudice of Non-Settling Defendants

A concern has also been expressed occasionally that an aggressive defendant's counsel may negotiate a settlement with the plaintiff class to the detriment of other defendants. In such circumstances, "bar orders" might be sought to prevent the non-settling defendants from seeking contribution or indemnity from the settling defendants. The objection is most frequently raised by non-settling defendants, concerned that the settlement adversely affects their own rights.

Bar orders to protect settling defendants have been granted in both Ontario[33] and British Columbia[34] as part of the settlement approval process in class action suits.

In jurisdictions where defendants' liability is proportional, bar orders may not present a particular difficulty. For instance, if Defendant A to an action settles its obligations to the plaintiffs for $500,000 and Defendants B and C do not, then the action may continue against B and C. If they are each found to be 20% liable for the plaintiffs' damages of $1 million, then it does not matter that they cannot seek contribution or indemnity from the settling defendant; in such a case, it is the plaintiff who bears the risk.

---

30. Eric D. Green, "What Will We Do When Adjudication Ends? We'll Settle in Bunches: Bringing Rule 23 into the Twenty-First Century" (1997) 44 UCLA L. Rev. 1773 at 1787.

31. Eric D. Green, "Advancing Individual Rights Through Group Justice" (1997) 30 U.C. Davis L. Rev. 791 at 794 (describing the opposition by 120 law professors who organized a steering committee to oppose the reform).

32. Franklin, "Defendants Strike Back", above note 28 at 165 (noting that certifying courts are "sometimes neglecting the superiority requirements of Rule 23(b)(3) of the Federal Rules of Civil Procedure since litigation is not contemplated.").

33. *Ontario New Home Warranty Program* v. *Chevron Chemical Co.* (1999), 46 O.R. (3d) 130 (Sup. Ct. J.) [*ONHWP*]; *Millard* v. *North George Capital Management Ltd.* (2000), 97 A.C.W.S. (3d) 604 (Ont. Sup. Ct. J.).

34. *Sawatzky* v. *Société Chirurgicale Instrumentarium Inc.* (1999), 71 B.C.L.R. (3d) 51 (S.C.).

However, in a jurisdiction with joint and several liability (such as Ontario), each defendant is liable for the full amount of the claim. If A settles for $500,000 when his proportion of liability (carrying on the above example) is actually $600,000, then the plaintiffs might claim the remaining $500,000 from the non-settling defendants (assuming the bar order "credits" the non-settling defendants with the amount of B's settlement) each of whom may be liable in proportion for this portion (i.e., because they were each 20% at fault, they would split the unpaid portion of Defendant A's share at $250,000 each.[35]

If the settlement is the result of a "limited fund" and Defendant A is insolvent, having exhausted its assets paying for the settlement, there is little prejudice to B and C, because the results would be the same had Defendant A not settled first. Where A remains with assets, however, the potential for unfairness is manifest, although of course it is not an unfairness as great as many others that are possible within a system of joint and several liability.

This may create a strong incentive for structural collusion between plaintiffs' counsel and a defendant willing to settle; indeed class counsel may engage his opponents in a "prisoner's dilemma," exacting a substantial (but not full) settlement with the promise to the defendant of escaping a portion of his liability, and content in the knowledge that the plaintiffs are not sacrificing the aggregate total of the award.

One method of evading the problem is for the court to issue the bar order on the condition that the plaintiffs will be able to seek damages from the non-settling defendants only on a several, rather than a joint and several, basis. This method was employed in *Ontario New Home Warranty Program* [*ONHWP*], coupled with a further cap on the liability of non-settling defendants at 35%.[36] Another idea, to similar effect, would be the solution negotiated in *Millard*,[37] with the plaintiffs agreeing that the non-settling defendants would have, as against the plaintiffs, the benefit of any claims for contribution and indemnity which they may have had against the settling defendants. In our earlier example, B and C would be able to claim the contribution amount of $100,000 (the difference between the settlement amount and A's actual proportional liability) from the plaintiff, thus offsetting the difference. In such case, as Farley J. noted in *Millard*, "it is the plaintiffs who have to bear the burden of not getting anything extra from the settling defendants."[38]

Such arrangements may in fact be not only desirable but necessary. Winkler J. in *ONHWP* seems to recognize that the court is *prohibited* from issuing a bar

---

35. The English Court of Appeal has held that the liability of a concurrent wrongdoer who is unable to satisfy its share of liability should be divided between the concurrent wrongdoers in proportion to their respective degree of fault: *Fisher* v. *CHT Ltd. and Others (No. 2)*, [1966] 2 Q.B. 475 (C.A.) at pp. 481 and 483.

36. *ONHWP* above note 33 at 140

37. *Millard* above note 33.

38. *Ibid.* at para. 119.

order that does in fact substantively affect the non-settling defendants' rights, at least as long as the Court continues to consider the *Ontario Act* as strictly procedural in nature.[39] From the point of view of procedural fairness, it may also be appropriate that any "bar order" contain a provision guaranteeing that the settling defendants continue to participate in the proceedings to the extent necessary to provide the non-settling defendants with sufficient information to accurately assess their relative liability.[40]

Courts generally have relied on the broad discretion found within the class proceeding legislation for procedural customisation on orders to stay proceedings to issue bar orders,[41] and no doubt they can be an important tool in softening recalcitrant defendants' bargaining positions. However, because bar orders (if accompanied by conditions like those described above) will usually have the effect of diminishing the overall aggregate claim value, they should be strictly scrutinised by the courts also from the point of view of the interests of the class members.

---

39.   In *ONHWP*, Winkler J. only escapes this substantive/procedural trap by arguing that the rights of contribution and indemnity are actually derivative rights of the plaintiff, and that they are thus unaffected by the court's order. See above note 33 at 142-145.

40.   This was a condition of the agreement in *Millard*, above note 33; it was added as a condition in *ONHWP*, above note 33 at 148-9. In *Millard*, the defendants agreed to continue to participate in the proceedings for the purpose of assessing relative liability. To objections that it would be onerous for the non-settling defendants to have to obtain the court's leave to conduct discoveries, Farley J. replied that "The court in any such leave motion would be able to deal with the request to ensure that [the objecting non-settling defendant] was able to obtain what it reasonably required in the circumstances (prior discussions amongst counsel would likely be very helpful for all concerned) and the court would be able to deal with any actual or likely abuse on any side.": above note 33 at para. 121. It is not clear from the reasons in *Sawatzky*, above note 34 whether the settling defendants agreed as a condition of the bar order to make discovery and evidence available in subsequent proceedings; Brenner J. did not address the problem.

41.   *ONHWP* above note 33 at 141; *Sawatzky*, above note 34 at para. 63.

PART II

—

Class Action Legislation

CHAPTER SIX

—

Canadian Class Action Policy

A. SUMMARY OF THEORETICAL OBSERVATIONS

In the previous part I have demonstrated the three ways in which aggregation increases the internalisation of harm by the defendant: first, claims that otherwise cannot be economically pursued (for both financial reasons and those based on non-pecuniary utility or "psychological factors" can be advanced in the aggregate; second, the "settlement depression effect" inherent in individual litigation of mass claims due to inequalities in plaintiffs' and defendants' litigation investment incentives is reduced, facilitating fuller, more accurate settlements; and third, aggregation permits optimal litigation investment that increases the *chances* that claims will, on average, be successful, and therefore the expected value of all claims is raised closer to the optimal level.

We can then conclude that, in order to maximise deterrence, an aggregate litigation system should (a) promote maximum claims aggregation; (b) promote accuracy in settlements and awards; and (c) provide optimal litigation investment incentives for plaintiffs.

The question of how well, or how poorly, various statutory schemes fit these theoretical imperatives is the subject of this part.

B. FOUNDATIONS OF CANADIAN CLASS ACTION POLICY

(1) Origins of Aggregative Proceedings

(a) *Common Law, Equity and the Rules of Court*

Prior to the advent of the class action provisions of the U.S. *Federal Rules of Civil Procedure* (discussed below), representative suits were not unknown to Anglo-American courts, and had in fact been recognized in various forms for several hundred years.[1] Representative actions developed as an exception to the "necessary parties rule" in equity,[2] and from the "bill of peace," an equitable device for combining multiple suits.[3] Though the cases from this early period are not numerous, the Courts of Equity did demonstrate a remarkable flexibility in their utilization of aggregative actions.[4]

---

1. See generally S.C. Yeazell, *From Medieval Group Litigation to the Modern Class Action* (New Haven, Yale University Press, 1987) [Yeazell, *From Medieval to Modern*]; S.C. Yeazell, "Group Litigation and Social Context: Toward a History of the Class Action" (1977), 77 Colum. L. Rev. 866, at 867 and 872; Marcin, "Searching for the Origin of the Class Action" (1973) 23 Cath. U. L. Rev. 515 at 517-524.

2. The "necessary parties" rule in equity mandated that "all persons materially interested, either as plaintiffs or defendants in the subject matter of the bill ought to be made parties to the suit, however numerous they may be.": *West* v. *Randall*, 29 F. Cas. 718, 721 (CC RI) (1820) (per Story J.). By contrast, an equitable class action could assist where, in the words of an early case, "it would be impracticable to make them all parties by name, and there would be continual abatements by death and otherwise, and no coming at justice, if all were to be parties": *Chancey* v. *May* (1722), Prec. Ch. 592, 24 E.R. 265 at 265. See generally Hazard, Gedid, & Sowle, "An Historical Analysis of the Binding Effect of Class Suits" (1998) 146 U. Pa. L. Rev. 1849, 1859-1860.

3. A "bill of peace" could be maintained where the interested persons were numerous, where they possessed a common interest in the question to be adjudicated, and where the representatives could be expected fairly to advocate the interests of all members of the group: see Charles Alan Wright, Arthur R. Miller, and Mary Kay Kane, *Federal Practice and Procedure*, 2nd ed. (St. Paul, Minn.: West Publishing Co., 1986), at §1751; Zechariah Chafee, Jr. *Some Problems of Equity*. (Ann Arbor: University of Michigan Law School, 1950) at 161-167, 200-203. The bill of peace is discussed more extensively as a consolidation device later in Part III of this book.

4. The Chancery Court in *Wallworth* v. *Holt* (1841), 4 My. & Cr. 619, 41 E.R. 238 at 244, noted that "it [is] the duty of this Court to adapt its practice and course of pro-

With the fusion of the courts of common law and equity in 1873,[5] rules were developed to preserve the equitable aggregate action.[6] English decisions initially continued to view class actions liberally. In 1901 the House of Lords held that:

> The principle on which the rule is based forbids its restriction to cases for which an exact precedent can be found in the reports . . . [it] ought to be applied to the exigencies of modern life as occasion requires.[7]

This changed with the 1910 decision of the English Court of Appeal in *Markt & Co.* v. *Knight Steamship Co.*[8] Although the majority of the Court found no reason to depart from the traditional liberal approach, the lone voice of Fletcher Moulton, L.J. in "sweeping denouncement" of class litigation seemed to have more influence in the years that followed,[9] and this, "combined with the widespread use of limited-liability companies, resulted in fewer class actions being brought."[10]

By the time that *Naken* v. *General Motors*[11] was argued before the Supreme Court of Canada in 1982, the need for a statutory regime for class litigation was widely acknowledged. In *Naken*, the Supreme Court considered whether a U.S.-style class action could be designed within the vestigial "representative action"

---

ceeding to the existing state of society, and not by too strict an adherence to forms and rules . . . to decline to administer justice, and to enforce rights for which there is no other remedy".

5. *Supreme Court of Judicature Act, 1873* (U.K.), 36 & 37 Vict., c. 66.

6. Rule 10 of the *Supreme Court of Judicature Act, 1873* (U.K.), 36 & 37 Vict., c. 66 sched. reads:

> Where there are numerous parties having the same interest in one action, one or more of such parties may sue or be sued, or may be authorised by the Court to defend in such actions, on behalf or for the benefit of all parties so interested.

7. *Taff Vale Ry.* v. *Amalgamated Soc'y of Ry. Servants*, [1901] App. Cas. 426 at 443 (H.L.).

8. [1910] 2 K.B. 1021 (C.A.).

9. W.A. Bogart, "Questioning Litigation's Role – Courts and Class Actions in Canada" (1987) 62 Ind. L.J. 665 at 672. Bogart's article is a good overview of class litigation in the "wilderness years" before statutory reform. To this end see also: Neil J. Williams, "Consumer Class Actions in Canada – Some Proposals for Reform" (1975) 13 Osgoode Hall L.J. 1 and John A. Kazanjian, "Class Actions In Canada" (1973) 11 Osgoode Hall L.J. 397.

10. *Western Canada Shopping Centres, Inc.* v. *Dutton* 2001 SCC 46 [*Dutton*] at para. 24.

11. *Naken* v. *General Motors of Canada Ltd.* (1983), 144 D.L.R. (3d) 385 (S.C.C.) [*Naken*].

preserved as a rule of the Alberta Court. The Court held that it could not, suggesting (if regretfully) that true class litigation could not exist absent a comprehensive statutory regime. Estey J. held at p. 408:

> If the court were now to find that these claims may not be processed under Rule 75 it may mean, in practical terms, the end of many claims which, mathematically at least, may amount to about five million dollars. Furthermore, having regard to the practices in the modern market-place particularly, in national merchandizing of products such as automobiles, it is not an unreasonable risk that the vendor undertakes if he is now found to be exposed to class actions by dissatisfied purchasers . . . . These, of course, are matters of policy more fittingly the subject of scrutiny in the legislative rather than the judicial chamber.

This idea, that class proceedings were designated by, and limited to, the four corners of statute, stalled the development of Canadian jurisprudence for nearly 20 years, despite some lower court decisions which managed to distinguish *Naken*.[12] The recent departure from that posture (indeed the reversal of *Naken*) in *Dutton* is therefore of enormous significance, a theme to which I will return throughout this book.

(b) U.S. Federal Rule 23

Canadian mass tort law, and in particular products liability law, owes at least as much to U.S. jurisprudence as it does to that of the English courts.[13] It is perhaps not surprising, then, that the U.S. example in establishing a class action regime was watched closely in this country, and would eventually provide an example for Canadian legislatures to follow. In order to appreciate the decisions made in the design of the Canadian class action systems, it is necessary to provide some background on the U.S. legislation and its treatment by the courts of that country.

---

12. See for example *Alberta Pork Producers Mktg. Bd.* v. *Swift Can. Col.* (1984), 53 A.R. 284 (C.A.); *Bradley & Forsyth* v. *Saskatchewan Wheat Pool* (1984), 31 Sask. R. 254 (Q.B.).

13. Mr. Justice Linden, for instance, has pointed out that the origins of manufacturer's tort liability in Canada can be traced to an American case, *MacPherson* v. *Buick Motor Co.*, 217 N.Y. Supp. 382 (1916), 111 N.E. 1050 (N.Y.C.A.) and two subsequent Canadian decisions (*Ross* v. *Dunstall* (1921), 62 S.C.R. 393, 63 D.L.R. 63 and *Buckley* v. *Mott* (1920), 50 D.L.R. 408 (N.S.S.C.)), not to the later House of Lords decision in *Donoghue* v. *Stevenson*, [1932] A.C. 562 as is generally assumed (for various expressions of the latter position see Peter Burns ed., *Donoghue* v. *Stevenson and the Modern Law of Negligence: The Paisley Papers* (Vancouver: Continuing Legal Education Society of B.C., 1991)) Allen M. Linden, *Canadian Tort Law* (7th ed.) (Toronto, Butterworths, 2001) at 568.

The modern class action was established in 1966 through amendments to the U.S. *Federal Rules of Civil Procedure*, Rule 23.[14] Because in the United States tort law is generally governed by the state, Rule 23 initially had little application to mass tort claims. However, state laws modeled on Rule 23 and the increasing number of "diversity" cases which, under the U.S. constitution may be heard by the federal courts,[15] led to a body of jurisprudence based upon the wording of that rule. As a result, U.S. class action law, unlike many aspects of tort litigation in the U.S., is somewhat homogeneous, if hardly uniformly so.

Rule 23(a) sets out the basic requirements for a lawsuit to proceed as a class action.

The first prerequisite is "numerosity" of class members: the members of the class must be "so numerous that joinder of all members is impracticable." The second requirement has been referred to as "commonality"; it is the existence of "questions of law or fact common to the class." "Typicality" is a requirement that the claims or defences of the class representatives are "typical of the claims or defenses of the class." This does not mean that all claims must be identical; for example, the fact that individual class members have suffered different damages will not by itself prevent certification. However, typicality might not be present where the very facts establishing a claim of liability differ between the named plaintiffs and class members, as for instance with claims based on detrimental reliance on misrepresentations. Finally, Rule 23(a) requires that class representatives "fairly and adequately protect the interests" of the class.

In addition to meeting all of the Rule 23(a) criteria, a class action may be prosecuted only if it meets at least one of the criteria set forth in Rule 23(b). Suits for money damages under Rule 23 are divided into so-called "(b)(1)" and "(b)(3)" actions.

Most suits are pursued under Rule 23(b)(3), which sets out the basic rules for certification. Under it, a court must consider whether "central" or significant questions of law and fact common to class members "predominate over any questions affecting only individual members,"[16] and must find that the class action device is "superior to other available methods for the fair and efficient adjudication of the controversy." These requirements of predominance and superiority are most frequently involved when class certification is denied, and as we will see were of considerable concern to the Ontario Law Reform Commission

---

14. Fed R. Civ. P. Rule 23 [Rule 23].

15. A "diversity" case is one in which the federal courts have jurisdiction because they involve, *inter alia*, parties from different states.

16. In some cases, the representative plaintiff will seek damages as well as declaratory or injunctive relief and will attempt to certify the class under both Rule 23(b)(2) and (b)(3).

when it formulated its recommendations in 1982, setting the tone for all Canadian systems to follow.

Rule 23(c)(2) requires that members of a class maintained under Rule 23(b)(3) receive "the best notice practicable under the circumstances, including individual notice to all members who can be identified through reasonable effort."

Rule 23(b)(1) permits the certification of a "mandatory class," when separate lawsuits by or against individual class members would create a risk of inconsistent outcomes resulting in "incompatible standards of conduct" for the party adverse to the class or which "would as a practical matter be dispositive of the interests" of non-parties or render it more difficult for them to protect their interests.

In addition, Rule 23(e) requires notice to the members of the class, regardless of whether it is maintained under Rule 23(b)(1), (b)(2) or (b)(3), before the action is dismissed or compromised.

(c) Development of "Mass Tort" Class Action Claims in the U.S. under Rule 23

It is often said that mass tort class actions in the U.S. have developed through several distinct phases.[17] In each phase, American courts have weighed a desire to employ aggregative techniques in mass tort litigation with a respect for individual litigative autonomy and self-determination for injured plaintiffs. Throughout the jurisprudence and commentary, this question of policy has been pivotal: how does one allow group actions for recovery and still preserve individual rights? If it is not possible to satisfy both ambitions, when may individual interests be legitimately suppressed for the greater good of the class as a whole?

Interpretation of Rule 23 has tended to rely heavily on the notes of the Advisory Committee, which is in effect the "legislative" body responsible for

---

17. See John C. Coffee, Jr., "Class Wars: The Dilemma of the Mass Tort Class Action" (1995) 95 Colum. L. Rev. 1343 [Coffee, "Class Wars"] at 1344, 1355-58; Peter Schuck, "Mass Torts: An Institutional Evolutionist Perspective" (1995) 80 Cornell L. Rev. 941 [Schuck, "Institutional Evolutionist Perspective"] at 944. For additional views of the history of mass tort actions, see John C. Coffee, Jr., "The Regulation of Entrepreneurial Litigation: Balancing Fairness and Efficiency in the Large Class Action" (1987) 54 U. Chi. L. Rev. 877; Deborah R. Hensler & Mark A. Peterson, "Understanding Mass Personal Injury Litigation: A Socio-Legal Analysis" (1993) 59 Brook. L. Rev. 961; and Judith Resnik, "Aggregation, Settlement, and Dismay" (1995) 80 Cornell L. Rev. 918.

making changes to the Rules.[18] With respect to class actions, the Advisory Committee notes to Rule 23(b)(3) stated that:

> A "mass accident" resulting in injuries to numerous persons is ordinarily not appropriate for a class action because of the likelihood that significant questions, not only of damages but of liability and defenses of liability, would be present, affecting the individual in different ways. In these circumstances, a class action would degenerate in practice into multiple lawsuits separately tried.[19]

The notes reflect a very incremental approach to mass litigation, and indeed enshrine the traditional position that any system must give priority to the litigative autonomy historically said to inform tort law.[20] In this analysis, tort victims, particularly those who have suffered significant injuries, ought to be able to control their own litigation through to an individual and specific conclusion.[21] As a result, cases from the 1960s and 1970s echoed the views of the Advisory

---

18. By an Act of Congress, the *Federal Rules of Civil Procedure*, developed by standing and advisory committees of the Judicial Council, come into force after a period of time if Congress does not explicitly reject them: 28 U.S.C. 2072. It has been suggested by some that this process does not create binding legislation (because if it did it would be doing so outside the constitutional process of passage and presentment) and does not represent a binding precedent (because the U.S. federal judicial power, unlike that of Canadian courts, is limited to "cases and controversies", excluding the possibility of advisory opinions): See Owen M. Fiss, "The Political Theory of the Class Action" (1996) 53 Wash. & Lee L. Rev. 21 at 29. Nevertheless, the U.S. Supreme Court has routinely decided class action cases as if it was bound by Rule 23: *Eisen* v. *Carlisle & Jacquelin*, 417 U.S. 156 at 166-67 (1974).

19. Rule 23(b)(3) Advisory Committee's note to 1966 amendments (citing *Pennsylvania R.R.* v. *United States*, 111 F. Supp. 80 (D.N.J. 1953).

20. Roger C. Cramton, "Individualized Justice, Mass Torts, and "Settlement Class Actions': An Introduction" (1995) 80 Cornell L. Rev. 811 at 814-15; David Rosenberg, "Class Actions for Mass Torts: Doing Individual Justice by Collective Means" (1987) 62 Ind. L.J. 561 at 566 n.25.

21. See Susan A.T. Koniak, "Feasting While the Widow Weeps: Georgine v. Amchem. Prods., Inc." (1995) 80 Cornell L. Rev. 1045 at 1138-47 (1995); Richard L. Marcus "They Can't Do That, Can They? Tort Reform Via Rule 23" (1995) 80 Cornell L. Rev. 858 at 889-90; David Rosenberg, "Of End Games and Openings in Mass Tort Cases: Lessons from a Special Master" (1989) 69 B.U. L. Rev. 695 at 701; Roger H. Trangsrud "Mass Trials in Mass Tort Cases: A Dissent" 1989 U. Ill. L. Rev. 69 [Trangsrud, "A Dissent"] at 74-76. This "day in court ideal" is discussed earlier.

Committee and generally denied certification of mass tort claims,[22] except in some cases through consolidation or bankruptcy.[23]

In the mid-1980s, however, courts more frequently took a positive view of the aggregative approach, and became increasingly willing to certify classes in mass tort actions.[24] It has been suggested that this acceptance of mass tort certification was driven in part by the siege mentality generated in judges facing an overwhelming array of mass tort litigation, particularly asbestos claims.[25] On the other hand, it appears equally valid to suggest that an increasing judicial recognition of the futility (not to mention costs, both to the parties and society[26]) of repetitive individual litigation also played a significant role in this development. Nevertheless, deference to the goal of litigative autonomy meant that the overwhelming majority of mass tort class actions certified during this period were of the Rule 23(b)(3) "opt-out" variety.[27] Significantly, in 1985 the U.S. Supreme Court suggested for the first time that the right to opt out of a class action to pur-

---

22. See for example, *McDonnell Douglas Corp.* v. *United States Dist. Court*, 523 F.2d 1083, 1085-86 (9th Cir. 1975) (Rule 23 does not "permit certifications of a class whose members have independent tort claims arising out of the same occurrence and whose representatives assert only liability for damages"); *Sanders* v. *Tailored Chem. Corp.*, 570 F. Supp. 1543 (E.D. Pa. 1983); *Marchesi* v. *Eastern Airlines, Inc.*, 68 F.R.D. 500, 501 (E.D.N.Y. 1975); *Harrigan* v. *United States*, 63 F.R.D. 402 (E.D. Pa. 1974); *Hobbs* v. *Northeast Airlines, Inc.*, 50 F.R.D. 76 (E.D. Pa. 1970); for the contrary position see In Re *Gabel*, 350 F. Supp. 624, 630 (C.D. Cal. 1972) which was rejected by the 9th Circuit in *McDonnell Douglas*, above.

23. See Resnik above note 17 at 925-30; Judith Resnik "From "Cases" to "Litigation"", (1991) 54 Law & Contempt. Probs. 5 (1991); Yeazell, *From Medieval to Modern* above note 1 at 64-68.

24. See In Re *School Asbestos Litig.*, 789 F.2d 996, 1009 (3d Cir. 1986) ("the trend has been for courts to be more receptive to use of the class action in mass tort litigation"); See also Scott O. Wright & Joseph A. Colussi, *The Successful Use of the Class Action Device in the Management of Skywalk Tort Litigation*, 52 U.M.K.C.L. Rev. 141 (1984); Note, *Class Certification in Mass Accident Cases Under Rule 23(b)(1)*, 96 Harv. L. Rev. 114 (1983).

25. See Coffee, "Class Wars" above note 17 at 1350 n. 23, 1363-64; see also *Jenkins* v. *Raymark Indus.*, 782 F.2d 468, 470 (5th Cir. 1986). Professor Coffee derides such decisions to grant class certification as a reaction to the "mind-numbing boredom" of presiding over these cases: Coffee, "Class Wars" above note 17 at 1351.

26. One frequently cited figure is from a Rand Corporation study of asbestos litigation which calculates that transaction costs accounted for $0.61 of each asbestos litigation dollar. See Coffee above note 17 at 1348 n.15. The costs of the litigation system are discussed further below.

27. See Rule 23(c)(2). Often, class members have two opportunities to opt out: a so-called "front-end" option under Rule 23(b)(3) at the time of certification, and a "back-end" opt-out if the claimant is unsatisfied with his or her share of the settle-

sue an individualized resolution may be required by the due process protections of the Fourteenth Amendment.[28]

Emphasis on opt-out rights, however, considerably weakened the efficacy of class actions as class members had strong incentives to quarrel and bargain amongst themselves over the terms of their participation. Persons with the strongest factual claims, for instance, could hold out for a larger share of the award than their damages would otherwise admit; in such a case, both the class (and also the defendants, who had an interest in a single resolution to all claims) would give up more than they should to these objectors. This problem was recognized at the time, and as a result class counsel began increasingly to rely upon mandatory classes under Rule 23(b)(1) to achieve global resolution. Because these mandatory classes also represent a much greater move away from the individual rights model, they have proved highly controversial, as I will discuss in greater detail later.

Throughout this period the courts struggled to overcome the focus on individuality in Rule 23(b)(3) and more frequently turned to Rule 23(b)(1) mandatory classes, though their legal justification for doing so was open to question.[29] The efforts to support such a move often led to the employment of the equitable doctrine of the "limited fund," which is discussed together with the mandatory class at some length in Part IV.

The modern era of class actions in the U.S. has seen a remarkable blossoming of innovation in the trial courts in an attempt to preserve mass tort class actions,

---

ment as administered. See Schuck, "Institutional Evolutionist Perspective" above note 17 at 963-64.

28. See *Phillips Petroleum Co.* v. *Shutts*, 472 U.S. 797 (1985) [*Shutts*]. The *Shutts* decision suggests that opt-out rights may be a necessary part of all class actions involving non-resident plaintiffs. See Arthur Miller & David Crump "Jurisdiction and Choice of Law in Multistate Actions After *Phillips Petroleum* v. *Shutts*" (1985) 96 Yale L.J. 1 at 52 ("There is no neat and logical means of resolving the question whether mandatory actions survive *Shutts*"). The question is still unsettled in the wake of the more recent U.S. Supreme Court decision in *Ortiz* v. *Fibreboard Corp.*, below.

29. A number of decisions discuss the issue. See for instance *Jenkins* v. *Raymark Indus.*, 109 F.R.D. 269, 274-77 (E.D. Tex. 1985), *aff'd*, 782 F.2d 468 (5th Cir. 1986); In Re *Asbestos Sch. Litig.*, 104 F.R.D. 422 (E.D. Pa. 1984), *modified*, 107 F.R.D. 215 (E.D. Pa. 1985), *aff'd in part and rev'd in part*, 789 F.2d 996 (3d Cir. 1986); In Re *Federal Skywalk Cases*, 93 F.R.D. 415 (W.D. Mo.), *vacated*, 680 F.2d 1175 (8th Cir. 1982); *Dalkon Shield*, 521 F. Supp. 1188 (N.D. Cal.), *modified*, 526 F. Supp. 887 (N.D. Cal. 1981), *vacated*, 693 F.2d 847 (9th Cir. 1982); *Coburn* v. *4-R Corp.*, 77 F.R.D. 43 (E.D. Ky. 1977), *mandamus denied sub nom. Union Light, Heat & Power Co.* v. *United States Dist. Court*, 588 F.2d 543 (6th Cir. 1978); *Hernandez* v. *Motor Vessel Skyward*, 61 F.R.D. 558 (S.D. Fla. 1973), *aff'd*, 507 F.2d 1279 (5th Cir. 1975).

including the "settlement class action," where the lawsuit, motion for certification, and proposed settlement are filed at the same time. Other courts have struggled with the problem inherent in any tort class action raised by the spectre of future claims; either plaintiffs who are unknown at the time of settlement (having not manifest injury) or those who are identified but the extent of whose injuries is not yet known.

The appellate courts were critical of such innovations, and indeed revived their concerns about the use of class actions to deal with mass tort claims at all. In four cases since 1995, U.S. Circuit Courts have decertified class actions involving HIV-infected blood products,[30] asbestos,[31] penile implants,[32] and cigarettes[33] while wondering anew whether mass tort class actions are ever appropriate.[34] Such objections were generally based on the old "litigative autonomy" objection, but it was occasionally suggested also that class actions create undue pressure on defendants to settle meritless cases, possibly even because of the scale of the action alone.[35]

Most recently, two U.S. Supreme Court decisions have dealt serious blows to the viability of mass tort class actions, at least those involving some claims which would be worth pursuing as individual suits.

In *Amchem Products Inc.* v. *Windsor*,[36] a case concerning claims arising from asbestos exposure, the Court refused certification of a class which included both present and future claimants on the grounds that the two groups' interests were too divergent, and separate representation was required. While the decision's immediate application was fairly narrow, its focus on procedural fairness was thought to signal a general discomfort in the Court with class actions for mass exposure torts. The *Harvard Law Review* suggested that:

> The *Amchem* Court's standard for satisfying the adequacy of representation requirement illustrates how a decision geared toward enhancing procedural fairness may conflict with the efficiency goal of the class action. The *Amchem* decision will make the aggregation and collective litigation of claims more difficult. Courts will

---

30. In Re *Rhône-Poulenc Rorer Inc.*, 51 F.3d 1293 (7th Cir.), *cert. denied*, 116 S. Ct. 184 (1995).

31. *Georgine* v. *Amchem Prods. Inc.*, 83 F.3d 610 (3d Cir.), *cert. granted sub nom. Amchem Prods., Inc.* v. *Windsor*, 117 S. Ct. 379 (1996) (See *Amchem*, below note 36).

32. In Re *American Med. Sys., Inc.*, 75 F.3d 1069 at 1080-82 (6th Cir. 1996).

33. *Castano* v. *American Tobacco Co.*, 84 F.3d 734 (5th Cir. 1996).

34. See *Castano, ibid.* at 741-51; *Georgine*, above note 31 at 626-34; *American Med.*, above note 32 at 1078-82; *Rhône-Poulenc*, above note 30 at 1298-1304. But see In Re *Agent Orange Prods. Liab. Litig.*, 996 F.2d 1425 (2d Cir. 1993) (rejecting claim that class action settlement did not bind future claimants who had lacked an opportunity to opt out from the class).

35. See *Castano*, above note 33 at 746; *Rhône-Poulenc*, above note 30 at 1298-1300.

36. *Amchem Products Inc.* v. *Windsor* 521 U.S. 591 (1997) [*Amchem*].

require more subclasses, the new subclasses will retain additional attorneys, and settlement and adjudication will have to accommodate the separate claims of each subclass. Thus, the Court's decision in *Amchem* not only has undermined the efficiency goal of the class action, but also, instead of ensuring meaningful access to the courts, has created new hurdles for injured plaintiffs.[37]

Ortiz v. *Fibreboard Corp.*[38] is a more recent decision, also concerned with an asbestos claim. In *Ortiz*, the Supreme Court decertified a "mandatory" class on the basis that the limited fund that formed the basis of the settlement was arrived at by stipulation of the parties, and may not have reflected the real ability of the parties to pay. However, the Court also took the opportunity to reiterate its concerns in *Amchem* regarding litigative autonomy and intraclass conflicts, which had not in the Court's view been adequately addressed in the process leading to the settlement for which approval was sought. In so doing, the suggestion was made that mandatory classes might never be permissible, except perhaps in some limited-fund cases. Taken together with *Amchem*, *Ortiz* has been criticized as "likely to leave many injured Americans with no viable legal remedy."[39]

As a result of the U.S. courts' troubled ambivalence, mass tort claims represent only a tiny proportion of class actions in that country.[40] This history makes the Canadian experience, marked by a willingness to certify and deal with even some of the most diverse imaginable mass tort classes, so much more striking.

(2) Canadian Proposals for Reform

Canadian courts have repeatedly referred to class action legislation as advancing the interests of efficiency, access to justice, and the modification of the behaviour of wrongdoers and potential wrongdoers. However, while these three considerations will determine whether a class proceeding is preferable (and thus to an extent whether it will be certified), they do not speak to the desirability of class proceedings *per se*. So what are the conditions which led to such sweeping and powerful legislative reform?

---

37. "Developments – The Paths of Civil Litigation" (2000) 113 Harv. L. Rev. 1752 ["Developments"] at 1815.

38. *Ortiz* v. *Fibreboard Corp.* 527 U.S. 815 (1999); 119 S. Ct. 2295 [*Ortiz*].

39. "Developments" above note 37 at 1816.

40. Deborah Hensler, "Revisiting the Monster: New Myths and Realities of Class Action and Other Large Scale Litigation" (2001) 11 Duke J. of Comparative & Int'l L. 179 at 183-84 (noting that from 1990 to 1997 only one of the 55 U.S. Supreme Court decisions on certified class actions involved a mass tort claim, as did less than ten percent of class action lawsuits decided by U.S. Circuit Courts from 1997). Unfortunately, there are no comprehensive statistics available as to how many of the approximately 15 million civil suits filed in the U.S. annually are class actions; Hensler's research appears to suggest a total of several thousand pending class actions at all court levels: *Ibid.* at 184.

Quebec's class action rules, introduced in 1978, generally followed Rule 23,[41] were met with lukewarm response, and were slow to be used by litigants,[42] an experience which no doubt informed subsequent reforms in other provinces while providing some refutation to critics who feared overutilization if the class proceeding became more widespread.

By the 1980s it had become widely recognized that, without class proceedings statutes, the procedural mechanisms available in common law jurisdictions were inadequate to allow plaintiffs who had the same or a similar interest in the subject matter of the litigation to effectively proceed. Wherever the topic was studied in Commonwealth jurisdictions, recommendations invariably followed for substantive legislative reform.[43] As was said of England:

> As we become an increasingly mass producing and mass consuming society, one product or service with a flaw has the potential to injure or cause other loss to more and more people. Yet our civil justice system has not adapted to mass legal actions. We still largely treat them as a collection of individual cases, with the findings in one case having only limited relevance in law to all of the others.[44]

---

41. Permitting certification, for instance, if provisions providing for individual or other representative actions were "difficult or impracticable": Quebec art. 1003.

42. See footnote 7 in Chapter Two and accompanying text.

43. See for instance, The Alberta Law Reform Commission's *Report on Class Action Legislation* (Final Report #85, 2000) [*Alberta Report*]; The Law Reform Commission, *Grouped Proceedings in the Federal Court, Report No. 46* (Canberra: Commonwealth of Australia, 1988) [*Australia LRC Report*; Ministry of the Attorney General, *Consultation Document: Class Action Legislation for British Columbia* (Victoria: Queen's Printer, May 1994); Canadian Bar Association, *Report of the Task Force on Systems of Civil Justice* (August 1996); Manitoba Law Reform Commission, *Class Proceedings* (Report #100) (Winnipeg: Manitoba Publications Branch, January 1999) [*Manitoba Report*]; Marie Swain, *Class Actions in New South Wales*, NSW Parliamentary Library Briefing Paper No 22/96; Ontario Law Reform Commission, *Report on Class Actions, 3 vols.* (Toronto: Ministry of the Attorney General, 1982) [*Ontario Report (1982)*]; *Report of the Attorney General's Advisory Committee on Class Actions Reform* (Toronto: Attorney General of Ontario, 1990); South African Law Commission, *The Recognition of a Class Action in South African Law* (Report, 1997) / (Working Paper 57, 1995); Scottish Law Commission, *Multi-Party Actions, Report #154* (1996); Ruth Rogers, *A Uniform Class Actions Statute*, 1995 Proceedings of the Uniform Law Conference of Canada, Appendix O [*ULCC Model Act*]; Victorian Attorney-General's Law Reform Advisory Council, *Class Actions in Victoria: Time For A New Approach* (Melbourne: Victorian Attorney-General, 1997) [*Victoria Report*]; Lord Woolf, *Access to Justice* (Final Report, 1996) [*Woolf Report*].

44. *Manitoba Report* above note 43 at 1-2, quoting from the National Consumer Council in its submission to Lord Woolf's inquiry in England.

Lord Woolf agreed, concluding that "[the absence of class proceedings legislation] causes difficulties when actions involving many parties are brought," and that, "[i]n addition to the existing procedures being difficult to use, they have proved disproportionately costly" and that "[i]t is now generally recognised, by judges, practitioners and consumer representatives, that there is a need for a new approach" to multi-party procedures.[45]

The inadequacies of the existing systems were also recognized by the Canadian courts. As I mentioned above, the 1983 *Naken* decision identified "the need for a comprehensive legislative scheme for the institution and conduct of class actions."[46] According to the Supreme Court, the paucity of detail in the then-extant "representative action" rule indicated that it was not intended to facilitate modern multi-party proceedings and was wholly inadequate to support the undertaking of a complex and uncertain action.

By far the most important catalyst for class action reform in Canada was the 1982 Report of the Ontario Law Reform Commission.[47] Indeed, it is not unrealistic to consider the 1982 Report as the foundational document of Canadian class proceedings.[48] Published in three volumes, the report weighed exhaustively the elements of system design and made recommendations that have formed the basis for all class action legislation in Canada that followed.[49] Then, in 1990, a second Ontario Law Reform Commission Report was issued with a proposed Act incorporating many of the features recommended in 1982. That Act became the *Ontario Act* presently in place, and the *B.C. Act* followed, with minor (but as we shall see significant) modifications in 1995.

Today, many of those provinces that have not yet followed the lead of Quebec, Ontario and B.C. seem to be moving in that direction. The Alberta Court

---

45. The *Woolf Report*, above note 43 led to changes in the English procedural rules of 1999 including detailed provisions governing "Group Litigation": United Kingdom, *Civil Procedure Rules 1998*, SI 1998/3132, rr. 19.10-19.15.

46. *Naken*, above note 11 at 410.

47. *Ontario Report (1982)* above note 43.

48. The Supreme Court of Canada in *Hollick* v. *Toronto (City)*, 2001 SCC 68 [*Hollick*] at para. 14 said:

> In my view, it is essential therefore that courts not take an overly restrictive approach to the legislation, but rather interpret the Act in a way that gives full effect to the benefits foreseen by the drafters [of the Ontario Law Reform Commission Reports].

49. Even in British Columbia the *Ontario Report (1982)* above note 43 has taken on some aspects of a legislative history, as Ontario cases that rely upon its recommendations as to the goals of class litigation (access to justice, judicial economy and behaviour modification) have been applied in B.C.: see for instance *Endean* v. *Canadian Red Cross Society* (1997), 148 D.L.R. (4th) 158 at 164 (B.C.S.C.); rev'd on other grounds 157 D.L.R. (4th) 465 (B.C.C.A.), citing the goals as set out in *Adbool* v. *Anaheim Management Ltd.* (1995), 21 O.R. (3rd) 453 at 461 (Div. Ct.).

of Appeal displayed evident frustration with the inadequacy of the vestigial representative proceedings rule recently in *Western Canadian Shopping Centres, Inc.* v. *Dutton*.[50] Speaking of Alberta's Rule 42, the Court commented that "this area of the law is clearly in want of legislative reform to provide a more uniform and efficient way to deal with class action law suits." The Alberta Law Reform Institute undertook a thorough study of the available literature, and it too recommended the establishment of a class proceedings regime.[51] Notwithstanding the hints of legislative change, the Supreme Court overturned the decision in *Dutton*[52] and allowed class proceedings to be imposed absent a statutory regime.

In 1996, the Uniform Law Conference of Canada adopted its Model Class Proceedings Act[53] (*"ULCC Model Act"*). This Act was drafted by delegates from British Columbia,[54] and follows the *B.C. Act* closely. The *ULCC Model Act* has in turn formed the basis for subsequent legislative proposals in Alberta, Saskatchewan, Manitoba and Newfoundland, each of which tracks the Model Act's wording almost verbatim.

As a result, to the extent that the B.C. and Ontario *Acts* diverge on any substantive points (such as the opt-in requirement for non-resident members), "new" class action jurisdictions' jurisprudence can be expected to follow that of British Columbia.[55] This may be of great significance to the future of the national class in Canada, as will be discussed in more detail in Part III below.

(3) Scope of Reform

While the U.S. courts vacillated over the application of Rule 23 to mass tort claims, virtually all of the proposals for legislative reform in Canada have indicated that aggregation could assist the broadest possible variety of tort claims. The Manitoba Law Reform Commission Report gives an indication of the broad types of litigation that might be furthered by class proceedings statutes, a

---

50. *Western Canadian Shopping Centres, Inc.* v. *Dutton* (1998), 228 A.R. 188 (C.A.). Much more recently, the Supreme Court too considered the objectives set out in the Report as correctly identifying the objectives, not only of legislative reform but of class actions generally: see *Dutton*, above note 10 at paras 27-29. See also *Hollick*, above note 48 para. 15.

51. *Alberta Report*, above note 43.

52. *Dutton*, above note 10.

53. Ruth Rogers, *A Uniform Class Actions Statute*, 1995 Proceedings of the Uniform Law Conference of Canada www.law.ualberta.ca/alri/ulc/95pro/395o.htm.

54. Margaret Shone, "Memo re: National Class Actions", (unpublished, March 5, 2001, on file with Alberta Law Reform Institute and with the author).

55. Only the Manitoba Law Reform Commission has rejected B.C.'s opt-in model in favour of Ontario's opt-out national class. See below footnote 58 in Chapter Eight and surrounding text.

description which focuses entirely on torts, an interesting observation in light of the U.S. reluctance:

> Class actions are useful in tort cases for mass disaster claims (claims arising from single incident mass accidents, such as train derailments and environmental disasters) and for creeping disaster claims (claims for bodily injury arising from consumer products, such as tobacco and asbestos, or medical products, such as intra-uterine devices, breast implants, contaminated blood, jaw implants, silver mercury fillings and heart pacemakers). Other uses include "claims of group defamation, nuisance, the principle in *Rylands* v. *Fletcher*, various statutory torts, damages claims for breach of Charter rights, claims arising from illegal strikes, negligent house construction, and negligent misstatement."[56]

Nor was this the only significant departure envisioned from the American model. Rule 23's absolute requirements of numerosity and superiority were roundly rejected, with a strong tendency among Canadian proponents to allow class action suits whenever they can provide, on balance, foreseeable advantages over individual actions.

As a result, it is generally accepted that Canadian class proceedings statutes are much more plaintiff-friendly than the original U.S. model:

> These differences have made class actions arising out of products liability not only viable in Canada, but a more effective remedy than that in the United States. American courts have generally been reluctant to certify actions arising out of products liability claims . . . In the face of . . . individual issues, American courts have been reluctant to find that the common issues predominate, and, therefore, have often refused certification. The differing Canadian legislation has led to a much more liberal approach towards certifying class proceedings in products liability claims.[57]

(4) Objectives of Reform

The general objectives of legislative reform are stated in the recent Alberta Law Reform Institute's report as fairness, certainty, and efficiency.[58] Others, including Michael Cochrane, former Chair of the Attorney General's Advisory Committee on Class Action Reform (the body that oversaw the design of Ontario's *Class Proceedings Act*), are briefer still, describing the "fundamental purpose" of class actions as "one word – efficiency."[59] However, it is useful to remember that any list of goals couched in strictly procedural terms necessarily implies a fourth – the advancement of legitimate legal objectives, whatever they

---

56. *Manitoba Report*, above note 43 at 17-18.
57. Dean F. Edgell, *Product Liability Law in Canada* (Toronto: Butterworths, 2000) at 189.
58. *Alberta Report*, above note 43 at paras 13-16.
59. Michael G. Cochrane, *Class Actions: A Guide to the Class Proceedings Act* (Toronto: Canada Law Book, 1993).

may be. In the case of mass tort class actions, therefore, it is helpful to be mindful, not only of the goals of aggregation, but also of the goals of tort law.

An early (and we shall see persistent) conceptual distinction made was between claims that were individually viable and those which were not.[60] Because considerations of "efficiency" were generally focused on achieving access to justice for plaintiffs, it is not surprising to find that the most frequently cited case in support of class actions is one where the potential recovery for individual claimants is so small as to make resolution impractical, or to discourage risk-averse plaintiffs from proceeding. This conceptual framework has been carried over from the 1982 Ontario Report into the jurisprudence,[61] although more recent efforts have also discussed claims that would not be pursued "for social or psychological reasons."[62]

It is often said by judges that the 1982 Ontario Law Reform Commission Report identified "access to justice, judicial economy and behaviour modification" as three co-equal "goals" of class action system design. In fact, the LRC listed these as "benefits," but emphasized that the choice to permit class actions was to prefer the *goal* of "behaviour modification" over the *goal* of "conflict resolution" in the civil process:

> In order to understand the nature of the controversy surrounding class actions, it is essential to recognize the presence, in many cases, of a fundamental philosophical dispute relating to the functions that may be legitimately served by civil actions, including class actions. On the one hand, it has been argued that the only proper function of civil actions is to achieve the peaceful resolution of conflicts that might otherwise lead injured parties to take the law into their own hands. One commentator has identified this philosophy as the "Conflict Resolution Model." Although

---

60. In fact the Ontario Law Reform Commission, borrowing from the Harvard Law Review, divided claims into three conceptual categories: individually recoverable, individually not recoverable (but "viable" in class proceedings), and "non-viable," the last being those claims where the claimant's costs of asserting his right to his share of the class recovery would be greater than that share: *Ontario Report (1982)*, above note 43 at p. 116, citing Note, "Developments in the Law – Class Actions" (1976) 89 Harv. L. Rev. 1318 at 1325. For the purposes of this book I discuss the distinction more frequently made by courts and commentators between "individually viable" (which the Ontario Report would call "individually recoverable"), and "individually non-viable", which are those claims whose individual litigation costs would be greater than the expected amount of recovery.

61. The Ontario Law Reform Commission described "the goal of permitting the advancement of meritorious claims which have henceforth been uneconomical to pursue because the damages for each individual plaintiff would be too small for each claimant to recover through usual court procedures": *Abdool* v. *Anaheim Management Ltd.* (1993), 15 O.R. (3d) 39 at 45-46 (Gen. Div.), citing *Ontario Report (1982)*, above note 43. Lord Woolf repeated this as a central concern: *Woolf Report*, above note 43 at 223, §2.

62. *Manitoba Report*, above note 43 at 1-2; *Alberta Report*, above note 43 at para. 14.

most persons agree that conflict resolution is an important function of the civil process, many have suggested that civil actions, including class actions, also play an important role in encouraging adherence to social norms by imposing appropriate costs upon wrongdoers and depriving them of the fruits of their misconduct. This philosophy has been identified as the "Behaviour Modification Model."

A general review of the class action literature suggests that most, but not all, critics of class actions subscribe to the Conflict Resolution Model, while many supporters of class actions embrace the Behaviour Modification Model. An awareness of this basic philosophical difference is important in understanding and evaluating various policy arguments for and against class actions, such as the contention that class actions may serve a legitimate function by deterring wrongful conduct, or the condemnation of class actions as a means of stirring up unnecessary litigation.[63]

One must assume that the drafters of the Report, in recommending class proceedings legislation, recognized on some level that they were making a decision in favour of deterrence over other objectives. I emphasize these passages here because I believe, and I attempt to show throughout this book, that important implications flow from the recognition that "behaviour modification" is the principal goal of class actions – it is the method through which most of its other advantages are best conferred. A substantial part of this work is devoted to demonstrating the value of deterrence in the tort system, and the impact of claims aggregation on deterrence.

Viewing "behaviour modification" as the *goal* of class legislation, and other "benefits" such as access to justice, compensation, and so on, as just that – "benefits" – is, as we have seen, supported upon solid – if sometimes surprising – policy grounds. In this respect, the Ontario Law Reform Commission got it precisely right in 1982;[64] since then, Canadian courts have drifted somewhat from these early, perspicacious observations, and are only now beginning to drift back.

There is also a competing interest that is sometimes articulated by those engaged in class action reform: that of "fairness to defendants." As the Alberta Law Reform Institute put it:

> Attention to the principle that defendants should be protected against unreasonable claims will ensure that the procedural balance is not tipped too far on the side of the interests of plaintiffs. The principle embodies the idea that defendants should not have to spend money or face adverse publicity as a result of unfounded claims brought against them. Further, the principle encompasses the idea that, where plaintiffs are able to make out a recognizable cause of action, the civil justice system should provide defendants with an opportunity to make their defence in a proceeding in which the rules are known, and the results can be predicted with a reasonable degree of certainty, obtained within a reasonable length of time and limited in cost[.][65]

---

63. *Ontario Report (1982)*, above note 43 at 114-115.

64. Nevertheless the Commission appreciated the value of deterrence only when the class contained at least some individually non-viable claims: *Ibid.* at 145.

65. *Alberta Report, ibid.* at para. 15.

It is helpful to view this objective too from the point of view of "behaviour modification" or deterrence. That is, it is quite appropriate to say that there should not be such uncertainty in the litigation system that a defendant takes too many precautions, or reduces its potentially dangerous business activity below the socially optimal level.

At this stage of our review we ought to have some regard for the impact of the "efficiencies" of aggregate litigation upon tort law itself. The best litigation system, presumably, is one in which the most legitimate rights may be vindicated, at the lowest cost. In that way, by improving access to justice for tort victims, it is arguable that class actions may go beyond procedure altogether and improve the substantive tort law's ability to meet the challenges presented by a rapidly evolving society, an ability which Professor Linden has described as often constrained by economic reality:

> Lawyers usually work for fees, not for principles; litigants usually sue for money, not for ideals. Investigation of accidents is expensive. Expert witnesses must be paid for their work. In short, tort trials cost money. Lots of it. Unless there is a good chance of winning, litigants are unwise to sue, for losers must pay not only their own legal costs but also those of the winning parties. The allure of a quick settlement dulls the crusading ardour of many a claimant. Because of this, law suits which test the frontiers of tort law are difficult to finance. Only the rare case, the rare litigant and the rare lawyer become involved in such litigation.[66]

---

66.   Linden, above note 13 at 22.

CHAPTER SEVEN

Features and Problems of Canadian Class Action Regimes

A. FEATURES OF CANADIAN CLASS ACTIONS

Canadian class proceedings are patterned on the basic template of Rule 23, although the statutes are of the more linear design favoured here. They foresee mostly opt-out actions launched by a representative plaintiff, and establish formal requirements and processes for certification and notice similar to those in the United States, and similarly provide an active role for the court in overseeing notice and settlement. There are however, some important differences that make a Canadian class action potentially very different from those launched in the U.S. I discuss some of the differences in this chapter, and others in Chapters 8 through 10 in the course of my discussion of options for system design.

(1) Certifying the Class

The most significant step in a Canadian class action is certification, which defines the class and sets the boundaries of the action. The certification hearing is common to all Canadian legislative regimes and the *Dutton*[1] representative

---

1.   *Western Canada Shopping Centres Inc.* v. *Dutton*, 2001 SCC 46.

action, but is not universal.[2] Practically speaking, certification may be dispositive of the action, as the vast majority of certified class actions are settled before
trial.[3] Plaintiffs may seek certification and press their case on to trial; frequently
though, plaintiffs and defendants approach the court together and seek to certify
a class for the purposes of obtaining a court-approved settlement. This latter type
of class is known as a "settlement class," and its associated problems are discussed at some length in Part IV below.

There are three possible types of classes, named for the mechanism of their
imposition upon class members: opt-in,[4] opt-out,[5] and the "mandatory" class. It
is not uncommon for a certification to include more than one type of class, for
instance an "opt-out" class for resident plaintiffs, and an "opt-in" class for non-
resident plaintiffs as provided for under the *B.C. Act*. As I will discuss later, there
has not yet been a true "mandatory" (i.e. no opt-out) class certified in Canada,
though it might be possible to conceive of one under the statutes as they are written.[6]

In Ontario and Quebec, as in the U.S., any person may be part of a class without regard to residency.[7] In British Columbia, only a resident may commence a
class proceeding. So far, only the Ontario courts have certified "opt-out" national
classes involving residents from all provinces.[8] B.C.'s statute, and the *ULCC
Model Act*,[9] provide only for "opt-in" non-resident classes.

---

2.   The federal Australian scheme does not have a certification requirement, based
        upon the recommendations of the Australian Law Reform Commission, which
        found that there is "no value in imposing an additional costly procedure, with a
        strong risk of appeals involving further delay and expense, which will not achieve
        the aims of protecting parties or ensuring efficiency.": The Law Reform
        Commission, *Grouped Proceedings in the Federal Court, Report No. 46*
        (Canberra: Commonwealth of Australia, 1988) at para. 147.

3.   See generally Ward K. Branch and John C. Kleefeld, "Settling a Class Action (or
        How to Wrestle an Octopus)" Presented to the Canadian Institute Conference on
        Litigating Toxic Torts and Other Mass Wrong (Toronto: December 4-5, 2000).

4.   In this most straightforward type of action, only those defendants who formally
        join the lawsuit may benefit and are bound by any decision or settlement in the
        action. In this sense the class action is nothing more than a type of voluntary join-
        der; no non-party is bound by the decisions of the court.

5.   In an "opt–out" action, any potential member of the class who did not formally
        decline to participate in the lawsuit is deemed to be a member of the class and may
        benefit from and be bound by any decision or settlement within the action.

6.   This topic is canvassed more thoroughly in Part IV, below.

7.   Subject to rules governing jurisdiction.

8.   *Nantais* v. *Telectronics Proprietary (Canada) Ltd.* (1995) 127 D.L.R. (4th) 552
        (Ont. Gen. Div.), leave to appeal denied (1995), 129 D.L.R. (4th) 110 (Gen. Div.),
        leave to appeal denied (1996), 28 O.R. (3d) 523n, 7 C.P.C. (4th) 206 (C.A.);
        Bendall v. *McGhan Medical Corp.* (1993), 106 D.L.R. (4th) 339 (Ont. Gen. Div.)

Perhaps the most controversial aspect of the U.S. Rule 23 has been the "mandatory classes," whose members have no right to withdraw.[10] Mandatory actions were designed to assist when allowing opt-outs would jeopardise unacceptably the interests of other class members. While opt-out rights are required in a 23(b)(3) action because it is only those actions in which the interests of the individuals in pursuing their own lawsuits may be so strong as to outweigh the necessity of collective adjudication, mandatory classes are used where it is appropriate to diminish individual control because the collective approach is necessary, even if it may not be universally desired within the class. In either case, it is the interests of the absent potential plaintiff which might be seen to justify the procedure. Because the efficiency of class actions depends on optimal aggregation of classable claims, mandatory classes are of considerable interest to system design theorists, and they are discussed at some length in Part III below.

As described earlier, the U.S. Rule 23 requires that the representative party must demonstrate that the class is not so numerous that joinder of all parties is impractical, that there are questions of law or fact common to the class, that the claims or defences of the representative party are typical of the claims or defences of the class, and that the representative party will fairly and adequately protect the interests of the class. The class must also be defined with sufficient specificity in order to be ascertainable.

The Canadian legislation is somewhat different, requiring that there be an identifiable class of two or more persons that would be represented by the representative plaintiff. The precise numbers or identities of the class members need not be known before certification will be granted. Moreover, there is no explicit "numerosity" requirement such as exists under U.S. Rule 23.[11]

According to the B.C. and Ontario Acts,[12] the determination of whether the plaintiffs have satisfied the requirements for certifying their action as a class proceeding raises the following questions:

- Do the pleadings disclose a cause of action?
- Is there an identifiable class of two or more persons?

---

at 345; *Carom et al.* v. *Bre-X Minerals Ltd. et al* (1999), 44 O.R. (3d) 173 (Sup. Ct. J.); *Webb* v. *K-Mart Canada Ltd.* (1999), 45 O.R. (3d) 389 (Gen. Div.) and *Wilson* v. *Servier* (2000), 50 O.R. (3d) 219 (Sup. Ct. J.). The national class is discussed more thoroughly in Part III, below.

9. Ruth Rogers, *A Uniform Class Actions Statute*, 1995 Proceedings of the Uniform Law Conference of Canada, Appendix O, section 16(2).

10. Rule 23(c)(2) sets out requirements of notice to opt out, but applies only to actions under (b)(3). Thus the combination is read to imply the possibility that where the conditions of a (b)(1) action are met, no right to opt out is required.

11. *Peppiatt* v. *Nicol* (1993), 20 C.P.C. (3d) 272 (Ont. Gen. Div.)

12. B.C. s. 4(1); Ontario s. 5(1).

- Do the claims of the class members raise issues that are common to the class?
- Would a class proceeding be the preferable procedure for the fair and efficient resolution of the common issues?
- Are the plaintiffs "representative plaintiffs" who:
  - would fairly and adequately represent the interests of the class;
  - have produced a plan for the proceeding that sets out a workable method of advancing the proceeding on behalf of a class and of notifying class members of the proceeding; and
  - do not have, on the common issues for the class, an interest in conflict with the interests of other class members.

Significantly, courts in Ontario and B.C. may *not* refuse to certify the action as a class proceeding solely because the class is deficient in any of the following respects: because damages require individual assessment; due to diversity of contractual relationships vis-à-vis different class members; because differing remedies are sought by class members; due to uncertainty in the number or identity of members; and due to the existence of subclasses within the claim.[13]

The Quebec statute, while phrased very differently, has recently been interpreted to similar effect.[14]

Whether the pleadings disclose a cause of action is a low threshold test, familiar to civil litigators as that to be applied in an ordinary application to strike pleadings for disclosing "no reasonable claim." The test to be applied is whether it is "plain and obvious" that the plaintiff cannot succeed.[15]

---

13. Ontario, s. 6; B.C. s. 7.

14. In Quebec, an action will be certified as a class proceeding if (1) the recourses of the class members raise identical, similar, or related questions of law or fact; (2) the alleged facts appear to warrant the conclusions sought; (3) the composition of the group makes joinder impracticable; and (4) the representative is in a position to adequately represent the interests of the class members: see Quebec art. 1003. The similarity of the requirements in all three provinces was discussed by the Supreme Court in *Western Canada Shopping Centres* v. *Dutton*, 2001 SCC 46 [*Dutton*] at para. 38.

15. *Peppiatt* v. *Nicol* (1998), 71 O.T.C. 321 (Gen. Div.). This test was elaborated upon in *Abdool* v. *Anaheim Management Ltd.* (1995), 121 D.L.R. (4th) 496 at 511 (Ont. Div. Ct.):

  (a) All allegations of fact, unless patently ridiculous or incapable of proof, must be accepted as proved;

  (b) The defendant, in order to succeed, must show that it is plain and obvious beyond doubt that the plaintiffs could not succeed;

  (c) The novelty of the cause of action will not militate against the plaintiffs; and

  (d) The statement of claim must be read as generously as possible, with a view

As to the second requirement, this may be broken down into two "subrequirements" of an identifiable class: numerosity and definition. The Canadian Acts require only that a class consist of two or more members. However, it stands to reason that the smaller the class, the less likely that a class action will be found to be the preferable procedure for resolving the issues, and so the absence of an explicit numerosity requirement is perhaps somewhat misleading.

Whether or not the class is "definable" is a more subjective question. In *Bywater* v. *Toronto Transit Commission*, it was said that:

> The purpose of the class definition is threefold: (a) it identifies those persons who have a potential claim for relief against the defendant; (b) it defines the parameters of the lawsuit so as to identify those persons who are bound by its results; and lastly, (c) it describes who is entitled to notice pursuant to the Act. Thus for the mutual benefit of the plaintiff and the defendant, the class definition ought not to be unduly narrow or unduly broad.[16]

Classes and subclasses may be created or deleted as the litigation proceeds.[17] However, in order to obtain certification, at least one class must be identified.

It is questions about common issues and, more particularly, preferability which most often determine the outcome of the certification process in a mass tort claim, and so it is necessary to review each of these in somewhat greater depth.

(2) Common Issues

Recall that Rule 23's "opt-out" scheme set out under 23(b)(3) requires that the "questions of law or fact common to the members of the class predominate" over individual questions. In Canada, the situation was explained thus by Mr. Justice Smith in *Endean* v. *Canadian Red Cross Society*:

> The question of whether individual issues predominate over common issues, which so permeates the American law on this subject, is expressly excluded as a relevant consideration by s. 4(1)(c) of the Act. Further, a common issue need not be dispositive of the litigation. A common issue is sufficient if it is an issue of fact or law common to all claims, and that its resolution in favour of the plaintiffs will advance the interests of the class, leaving individual issues to be litigated later in separate trials, if necessary: *Harrington* v. *Dow Corning Corporation et al.* (1996), 22 B.C.L.R. (3d) 97 at 105, 110 (S.C.).[18]

In numerous proceedings that have been certified, a determination of a common issue clearly advanced the claims of the potential classes to a significant

---

to accommodating any inadequacies in the form of the allegations due to drafting deficiencies.

16. *Bywater* v. *Toronto Transit Commission* (1998), 27 C.P.C. (4th) 172 at para. 10 (Ont. Gen. Div.).

17. *Peppiatt* v. *Royal Bank of Canada* (1993), 16 O.R. (3d) 133 (Gen. Div.).

18. *Endean* v. *Canadian Red Cross Society* (1997), 148 D.L.R. (4th) 158 at 167 (B.C.S.C.).

extent. For example the common issues in both *Campbell* v. *Flexwatt Corporation*[19] and *Chace* v. *Crane Canada*[20] concerned allegedly defective overhead radiant ceiling panels and cracking toilet tanks, respectively. In *Endean*, the common issue related to allegedly contaminated blood products, and in *Harrington* v. *Dow Corning Corp.*[21] the common issue was whether silicon gel breast implants were a dangerous product. Moreover, class proceedings involving a mass tort from a single event have been certified: e.g. *Bywater* v. *Toronto Transit Commission*,[22] where all members of the class were exposed to smoke in a subway tunnel fire.

The common issues do not have to be "at issue" between the parties *per se*: in other words, the defendant cannot escape certification by admitting liability and therefore denying that its culpability is a common issue.[23]

In *Tiemstra* v. *I.C.B.C.*,[24] the plaintiff sought to challenge the Provincial automobile insurance company's policy of "no crash, no cash," which denied certain benefits if there had been no physical damage to the vehicle. The allegation was that I.C.B.C. had breached its statutory, common law and fiduciary duties. The Court rejected the proposed common issue, noting that it was not "dispositive of a significant feature" of the individual claims. The Court contrasted those cases where the resolution of the common issue would advance the claims to an appreciable extent with those where the matter would be likely to dissolve into individual disputes. The Court distinguished the *Tiemstra* class from others which the B.C. courts had previously certified:

> [16] If the common issue pertains to an alleged defective product . . . then it is easy to see that a determination that the product in question is defective or dangerous as alleged will advance the claims to an appreciable extent . . .

> [17] I agree with the statement in the respondent's factum: A class action which will break down into substantial individual trials in any event does not promote judicial economy or improve access to justice, and is not the preferable procedure.[25]

Although the *Tiemstra* decision is arguably sound given the distinctiveness of each cause of action,[26] the reasoning is perhaps awkwardly expressed. The suggestion that the prospect of devolution into individual trials should, *as a rule*, form a basis for the denial of certification is unsupportable, and resort to United

---

19. Campbell v. *Flexwatt Corporation* (1996), 25 B.C.L.R. (3d) 329 at 343 (S.C.).

20. Chace v. *Crane Canada* (1996), 26 B.C.L.R. (3d) 339 (S.C.).

21. *Harrington* v. *Dow Corning Corp.*, 2000 BCCA 605.

22. *Bywater* v. *Toronto Transit Commission* (1998) , 27 C.P.C. (4th) 172 (Ont. Gen. Div.).

23. *Ibid.* at 177-8; *Dalhuison* v. *Maxim's Bakery Ltd.*, 2002 BCSC 528.

24. *Tiemstra* v. *I.C.B.C.* (1997), 38 B.C.L.R. (3d) 377 (C.A.).

25. *Ibid.* at 381-2.

26. However, the authority of *Tiemstra* might be said to be in question since the Supreme Court decision in *Rumley* v. *British Columbia*, discussed below.

States cases is of little assistance given the fact that in that country the common issues must predominate in order for an action to be certified. A court following *Tiemstra* is left trying to deduce whether or not potential individual trials (often required with respect to damages if nothing else[27]) would be "substantial'; a *reductio* not particularly helpful.

However, the B.C. Court of Appeal in *Harrington* has demonstrated how broad the definition of a single common issue can be in a products liability context. The allegations spanned hundreds of models of silicon breast implant from several manufacturers. Citing the apparent common knowledge base of the defendants with respect to risks, the Court determined that whether breast implants were *ever* fit for human use was a sufficient common issue. In the Court's view, if the plaintiffs were content to set the threshold of liability sufficiently high and be prepared to demonstrate that no implant could meet legal standards, the courts might allow an aggregate claim to proceed where it otherwise might not:

> As we have seen, the case management judge recognized that a risk assessment would probably require the respondent "to establish unfitness against the model of silicone gel breast implant which has the strongest claim to fitness" because "only as against that standard could the issue be said to be common to all manufacturers and all models.[28]

While the *Harrington* decision represents an interesting compromise on the "common issue" question, it does raise some concerns with respect to the notice to the class.[29]

(3) Preferability

As might be imagined, the preferability of a class action is largely determined by whether there are sufficient common issues. It may be a technical error to blend the two so closely together (as the B.C. Court of Appeal did in *Tiemstra*, above) but in fact, the interplay between them is considerable.

---

27. Section 7(a) of the *B.C. Act* expressly provides that the Court must not refuse certification merely because damages require individual assessment after determination of the common issues.

28. *Harrington*, above note 21 at para. 35.

29. In such cases, the interests of the absentee class members would be inadequately protected if they were not informed of the strategic decision which had been made by class counsel to set a high bar in order to achieve certification. The spectre of valid individual claims (which do not rely on the allegation that *all* breast implants are unfit) being barred by such a process is very real and should be of concern to the courts. Notification of this decision was apparently possible in *Harrington* as the class members were known. However, in cases where they are not, a court will almost certainly be more reluctant to certify on such a "lowest common denominator" basis.

The proper analysis means that the existence of a common issue is not, on its own, sufficient to render a class action the preferable procedure, though it may in many cases lead to that conclusion. Rather, even an action with a number of common issues might be denied certification if the goals of the legislation, i.e. efficiency, access to the courts, and behaviour modification of wrongdoers, are not met.[30]

Mr. Justice Winkler in *Carom* v. *Bre-X*, summarised the approach to be taken in relation to preferability. He stated:

> The proper approach . . . is to have regard to all of the individual and common issues arising from the claims in the context of the factual matrix. A class proceeding is the preferable procedure where it presents a fair, efficient and manageable method of determining common issues which arise from the claims of multiple plaintiffs and where such determination will advance the proceeding in accordance with the goals of judicial economy, access to justice and the modification of the behaviour of wrongdoers.[31]

Some courts have gone further, holding that the preferability requirement means that, in order to defeat certification once the basic criteria are met, "the party opposing certification must present a concrete alternative to a class proceeding."[32] However, this requirement has not been universally applied.[33]

In 2001, the Supreme Court of Canada pronounced on three certification decisions,[34] and it became apparent that "preferability" is now the principal analytical threshold for class actions.[35]

---

30. See for example *Price* v. *Panasonic Canada Inc.*, [2002] O.J. No. 2362 (Sup. Ct. J.).

31. *Carom* above note 8 at 239.

32. Michael A. Eizenga, Michael J. Peerless & Charles M. Wright, *Class Actions Law and Practice* (Toronto, Butterworths, 1999) at §2.9, citing in example *Bunn* v. *Ribcor* (1998), 38 C.L.R. (2d) 291; supp. reasons unreported (June 19, 1998), Newmarket docket # 354/98, 355/98 (Ont. Gen. Div.).

33. See for instance *Price* v. *Panasonic Canada Inc.*, above note 30 at paras 44-52. The Court in *Price* found that a class proceeding was not preferable, but did not explicitly find that any alternative – either individual actions or some other method of redress – *was* preferable. However, the Court did seem to suggest that, in some cases where the main purpose of the class action was regulatory (i.e. where it did not advance the interests of the plaintiffs *per se*), preferability may be influenced by the existence of a governmental body charged with oversight and prosecution of the wrongs alleged.

34. The third of the "trilogy," *Dutton* v. *Western Canada Stores Inc.*, is discussed in a separate subsection later in this chapter.

35. John C. Kleefeld, "Class Actions in Canada" (2002) 44:3 *For The Defense* 60 at 61 (describing the emergence of preferability as the dominant determinant of certification). See also Shelley M. Feld & Paul J. Martin "Class Actions: Recent Developments of Importance" (Toronto, Fasken Martineau DuMoulin, 2000) www.fasken.com (describing the preferability in the wake of the trilogy as a question of "efficiency versus fairness").

In *Hollick* v. *Toronto (City)*, the Court confirmed that class proceedings statutes "should be construed generously" with a view to their purposes.[36] That case concerned nuisance complaints surrounding a government-operated landfill. Unlike that of British Columbia, Ontario's legislation does not list the policy factors that the court should consider in the "preferability" inquiry; nevertheless, the Court found that they were same: judicial economy, access to justice and behaviour modification. Noting that the Ontario government had set up a claims fund to deal with such complaints and that no claims had yet been made against it, the Court concluded that either the claims were "so small as to be non-existent or so large as to provide sufficient incentive for individual action."[37] As a result, access to justice was not in issue, and the Court otherwise found that judicial economy and behaviour modification were likewise not engaged. The certification was denied.

At perhaps the other extreme, in *Rumley* v. *British Columbia*,[38] the Court did approve certification of a class action in the case of the Jericho Residential School, arising from allegations of sexual and physical abuse of students that spanned five decades. Despite the inherently individualistic nature of such torts, the Court found a common issue in whether there had been systemic negligence at the school and in the government over the periods in question, and that a class action was preferable to other types of procedures.

In both cases, the government had set up compensation funds (in the Jericho School case capped at $60,000, in *Hollick* a "small claims" fund capped at $5,000). Both decisions' consideration of "preferability" seemed based in some part upon a comparison between the class action and the extant claims process; if the latter was found wanting, certification was deemed preferable.

From the deterrence point of view, there is a considerable difficulty in allowing defendants to set up their own compensation scheme as an alternative to class certification. If one of the justifications for class actions is that many victims might not know that they have been harmed or indeed might not sufficiently care to pursue claims from the compensation fund, then the defendant will pay only a fraction of the damages necessary to ensure appropriate deterrence.[39] As an

---

36.   *Hollick* v. *Toronto (City)*, 2001 SCC 68 [*Hollick*] at para. 15.

37.   *Ibid.* at para. 32.

38.   *Rumley* v. *British Columbia*, 2001 SCC 69.

39.   Even after a successful litigation, for instance, many class members do not claim their shares of the aggregate award. The Ontario Law Reform Commission, *Report on Class Actions, 3 vols.* (Toronto: Ministry of the Attorney General, 1982) [*Ontario Report (1982)*] at 133-34, summarising U.S. statistics, noted that, in 15.8% of cases less than half of class members filed claims. The preferability of class proceedings over a pre-emptive defendant-driven compensation scheme derives from the fact that this unspent amount ought not accrue to the defendant if deterrence is to be optimised.

example of the degree to which deterrence is undervalued by Canadian courts, the issue has not yet been fully considered in this light.

So far, the Canadian courts have seen the deterrence factor as a byproduct of "access to justice," in the sense that the more claims are compensated, the greater the deterrent effect. The question of preferability is obvious in a case of numerous, low-value (i.e. non-marketable) claims, where the choice is between a class action and no action at all. However, repeated references to this type of case in the literature and jurisprudence might lead one to conclude that preferability is not as clear at the other end of the claim-value spectrum: in cases of mass tort where each claim *is* individually viable.[40]

(4)   Notice Requirements and Opt-Out Rights

Canadian class proceedings legislation is remarkably flexible on the question of notice. While setting out the factors which the court must consider when determining what notice is required in the circumstances, Ontario and B.C. also allow that the court "may dispense with notice if . . . the court considers it appropriate to do so."[41]

Similarly, while the procedure for permitting "opt-outs" is described, it is not explicitly mandatory in any Canadian legislation except that of Quebec.[42] Despite this flexibility, there has never been a "mandatory" class certified in Canada, nor has any certification occurred where notification of class members was deemed unnecessary. Still the breadth of the discretion is intriguing, and the question of notice in this context is explored in Part IV below.

(5)   Aggregate Assessment of Damages and Non-Restitutionary Distribution

Another remarkable feature of the Canadian class action legislation is its provision for the aggregate assessment of damages. Once liability has been established, the amount of an aggregate award may be calculated on the basis of

---

40.   Without taking exception to the overall holding in *Hollick*, I do question certain aspects of the analysis. In particular, the Court suggests (above note 36 para. at 34), that if claims are individually viable, the defendant "will be forced to internalise the costs of its conduct". This is not quite true: in fact even if every claim is individually viable, a class proceeding will result in a more accurate internalisation of harm than several individual actions due to the litigation investment effect described earlier.

41.   B.C. s. 19(2); Ontario s. 17(2). There is no equivalent in Quebec.

42.   Quebec's law describes the "right ['*droit*'] of a member to request his exclusion," Quebec art. 1007 and the Civil Code state that if this right is exercised the member is not bound: Civil Code s. 2848. A member will be "deemed" to have opted out if he continues an individual action after certification: Quebec art. 1008.

statistical evidence[43] if, *inter alia*, "the aggregate or a part of the defendant's liability to some or all class members can reasonably be determined without proof by individual class members."[44]

I say that this is remarkable because efforts by U.S. courts to perform similar assessments of damages on an aggregate basis[45] have been seen as violation of defendants' rights under the Fifth and Seventh Amendments of the U.S. Constitution, provisions which have no equivalent in Canadian law, where property and civil due process have no such explicit protection.[46]

The Ontario Law Reform Commission Report in 1982 had recommended that aggregate assessment should be the rule, rather than the exception:

> Individual proceedings relating to the assessment of monetary relief should be required only where an aggregate assessment is not feasible or where the amount of monetary relief to which class members are entitled cannot be established by consumer evidence.[47]

---

43. B.C. s. 30, Ontario s. 24.

44. B.C. s. 29(1)(c). See also Ontario s. 24(1)(c).

45. In *Cimino* v. *Raymark* 751 F. Supp. 649 (E. D. Tex. 1990) the trial judge had designed a system whereby the tort victims were divided into groups by disease, and the claimant pool was "sampled" with the damages from these hearings extrapolated across the disease group as a whole.

46. Amendment VII to the U.S. Constitution guarantees a trial by jury in federal civil court. The Appeals Court found that it guaranteed the defendants "to have a jury determine the distinct and separable issues of the actual damages of each of the extrapolation plaintiffs": *Cimino* v. *Raymark* 151 F.3d 297 (5th Cir. 1998) at 320-21. The Court also suggested (at 311) that the procedure employed by the court denied the defendants their Fifth Amendment rights to "due process." Neither a jury trial nor any due process rights are guaranteed in the Canadian constitution (at least with respect to civil trials), so it appears that objections similar to those made in *Cimino* could not succeed against the aggregate damages provisions of the Canadian legislation.

    This analysis is supported by the *Ontario Report (1982)* above note 39 at 536, which explicitly considered the constitutionality question:

    > Most of the American commentary relating to aggregate assessment is of limited usefulness for our purposes, since it has centred on . . . whether this procedure violates the constitutional rights to trial by jury and due process [and] whether aggregate assessment constitutes a change in the substantive law of the United States and is therefore not permitted by the Rules Enabling Act . . .

    > Fortunately, there is no need for the Commission to become enmeshed in the more technical aspects of this debate, as the Rules Enabling Act is obviously inapplicable and there are no similar constitutional rights to trial by jury or due process in civil cases in Ontario.

47. *Ontario Report (1982)* above note 39 at 597. A contemporary commentator noted that this represented a "mirror image of the United States Model": Benjamin S.

The B.C. legislation does permit so-called "back-end" opt-outs from averaged assessment of awards. Plaintiffs who are dissatisfied with an averaged or proportional distribution of an aggregate award may "be given the opportunity to prove that member's claim on an individual basis."[48] This is not, however, a "right" in the sense of constitutional constraints imposed in the U.S., and the B.C. Court may, depending on a variety of factors including the number of such "back-end opt-out" members and the effects of their opting out of the distribution on the viability of the fund, refuse to permit withdrawal.[49]

Canadian legislation further permits cy pres distribution to third parties "in any manner that may reasonably be expected to benefit class or subclass members, even though the order does not provide for monetary relief to individual class or subclass members,"[50] and this applies, apparently, even if doing so requires that persons other than the class members receive "windfalls."[51] The Ontario Law Reform Commission was well aware that this too had been found problematic on "fairness" grounds in the U.S., an objection the Commission rejected.[52]

The cy pres provision is an important one for deterrence purposes, particularly because the Ontario statute requires that undistributed amounts be returned to the defendant after a period of time has elapsed. Cy pres distribution permits the court to order that the money instead go to a third party, thus more fully internalising the costs of harm in the defendant.

(6) The "Common Law Class Action"

The most striking of the "trilogy" of 2001 Supreme Court cases is without a doubt *Western Canada Shopping Centres Inc.* v. *Dutton*.[53] In that case, two

---

Duvall, Jr., "The Importance of Substance to the Study of Class Actions: A Review Essay on the Ontario Law Reform Commission Report on Class Actions" 3 Windsor Yearbook of Access to Justice 411 (Windsor, Ont: University of Windsor, 1983).

48. B.C. s. 31(2).

49. B.C. s. 31(3).

50. B.C. s. 34(1); Ontario 26(4); Quebec arts. 1031-1036; Saskatchewan s. 37; *ULCC Model Act* s. 34.

51. *Ontario Report (1982)*, above note 39 at 577-79.

52. Although the Report only endorsed cy pres distribution as a "last resort" to avoid returning the money to the defendant (which was realized to weaken deterrence) or forfeit to the state. *Ibid.* at 572-81. However, note that subsequent legislation in B.C. and the *ULCC Model Act* permit both cy pres distribution *and* forfeiture to the government (B.C. section 34(5)(b); *ULCC Model Act* s. 34(5)(c)) (but not return to the defendant), rather than requiring, as the *Ontario Act* does, return of undistributed awards. This raises the possibility of cy pres distribution through government welfare services, which I discuss more extensively in Part III below.

53. *Dutton*, above note 14.

debenture holders in a failed company incorporated by the defendant had attempted to file a suit on behalf of themselves and 229 others similarly situated pursuant to Alberta's Rule 42, which was the codification of the previous equitable rules permitting (but not describing in detail) a "representative proceeding."[54]

Reversing its previous decision in *Naken* v. *General Motors*,[55] the Court held that the benefits of class actions had been demonstrated and should be extended to jurisdictions without comprehensive statutory regimes:

> The need to strike a balance between efficiency and fairness . . . belies the suggestion that class actions should be approached restrictively. The defendants argue that *General Motors of Canada Ltd.* v. *Naken*, [1983] 1 S.C.R. 72, precludes a generous approach to class actions. I respectfully disagree. . . . [W]hen *Naken* was decided, the modern class action was very much an untested procedure in Canada. In the intervening years, the importance of the class action as a procedural tool in modern litigation has become manifest. Indeed, the reform that has been effected since *Naken* has been motivated in large part by the recognition of the benefits that class actions can offer the parties, the court system, and society: see, e.g., Ontario Law Reform Commission, above, at pp. 3-4.[56]

The Court thus permitted lower courts to design proceedings along the lines of those available under statutory regimes where four conditions are met:

> (1) the class is capable of clear definition; (2) there are issues of fact or law common to all class members; (3) success for one class member means success for all; and (4) the proposed representative adequately represents the interests of the class.[57]

Upon the satisfaction of those basic conditions, the test becomes one analogous to the "preferability" requirement of statutory certification regimes:

> If these conditions are met the court must also be satisfied, in the exercise of its discretion, that there are no countervailing considerations that outweigh the benefits of allowing the class action to proceed.[58]

However, one possible difference in the "common law class action" defined in *Dutton* is the notice requirements, which might be more stringent than those under the statutes and may even require actual notice with the right to opt out:

> 49 [. . .] A judgment is binding on a class member only if the class member is notified of the suit and is given an opportunity to exclude himself or herself from the proceeding. This case does not raise the issue of what constitutes sufficient notice.

---

54. *Alberta Rules of Court*, Alta. Reg. 390/68 reads in relevant part:
    42. Where numerous persons have a common interest in the subject of an intended action, one or more of those persons may sue or be sued or may be authorized by the Court to defend on behalf of or for the benefit of all.
55. *Naken* v. *General Motors of Canada Ltd.* (1983), 144 D.L.R. (3d) 385 (S.C.C.).
56. *Dutton*, above note 14 at para. 46.
57. *Ibid.* at para. 48
58. *Ibid.*

However, prudence suggests that all potential class members be informed of the existence of the suit, of the common issues that the suit seeks to resolve, and of the right of each class member to opt out, and that this be done before any decision is made that purports to prejudice or otherwise affect the interests of class members.[59]

The full impact of the *Dutton* decision is not yet known, however the philosophy underlying the decision may have several implications for system design. The principal advance of *Dutton* was its recognition that the default position in *Naken* had changed; that class proceedings may exist at common law, and (by implication) that they are modified by statute, but not dependent on it. The idea that class proceedings may be designed by the courts in the interest of fair adjudication of mass torts also leaves the tantalising suggestion that existing legislation might not be exhaustive in its description of the aggregative tools available to judges.

B. SYSTEMIC UNDERDETERRENCE

Throughout this book I have suggested that Canadian courts and commentary recognise deterrence in only two types of class litigation: where the claims involved could not be economically pursued individually; or where the claims, while technically viable, might not be pursued in sufficient numbers due to psychological or other non-economic reasons. Implicit in this reasoning is that the aggregation of individually viable claims absent class litigation will serve no deterrent purpose.[60] It has been one of my main objectives in the first half of this book to demonstrate that this is not so, and that in fact optimal tort deterrence depends on aggregation of any mass tort claim at least to the point of diminishing returns (i.e. to the point where additional investment will not increase the chances of success). Practically speaking, this means that deterrence will improve as aggregation increases, and will suffer each time the class is diminished or split. It also means that deterrence will improve as recovery increases to approximate more closely the harm caused by the defendant's tort.

---

59. *Ibid.* at para. 49.

60. Mary Gardiner Jones & Barry B. Boyer, "Improving the Quality of Justice in the Marketplace: The Need for Better Consumer Remedies" (1971-72), 40 Geo. Wash. L. Rev. 357 at 361 (discussing the value of deterrence only to the extent that defendants would otherwise be "immune" to "some claims"); The *Ontario Report (1982)*, above note 39 at 141-146 also described the value of deterrence as centred upon individually non-viable claims:

> It bears emphasizing that, in the view of the Commission, the justification for endorsing class actions aggregating individually recoverable and individually nonrecoverable claims lies mainly in the ability of these types of class action to achieve either judicial economy or increased access to justice. Behaviour modification is essentially an inevitable, albeit important, by-product of class actions.

Yet there is reason to believe that the true effects of aggregation are not appreciated by the courts. I here briefly examine examples of this undervaluation in three types of decision in class proceedings: at the certification stage, when considering "preferability"; at the settlement stage, when considering approval of a global amount to satisfy the class claim; and in the particular case of the "settlement class," where certification and settlement are sought simultaneously. I then turn to perhaps the trickiest subject, the award of costs against unsuccessful litigants.

(1) Deterrence at Certification

(a) Certification of Individually Viable Claims

There are no other means of redressing mass tort through civil litigation that provide deterrent effects comparable to the fully aggregated litigation class.[61] Yet Canadian courts have been inconsistent in their views on whether class proceedings are appropriate for large, individual claims. The leading case remains *Abdool* v. *Anaheim Management Ltd.*, a decision of the Ontario Divisional Court. Speaking for the Court on this issue, O'Brien J. held that:

> The goal [of the *Class Proceedings Act*] is to permit advancement of small claims where legal costs make it uneconomic to advance them . . .

> [A]s each plaintiff had a very substantial claim the goal of the Act in advancing small claims was not met by the individual plaintiffs.[62]

Abdool and cases like it have led to the belief that non-viability and preferability have a strong correlation, and that cases should only be certified if individually non-viable or, if viable, if the costs of pursuing the claims are otherwise "disproportionate." This idea has gained further support with some of the *dicta* in the Supreme Court of Canada's *Hollick* decision, which likewise noted in its analysis of "preferability" that if individual claims were high enough, this would provide sufficient incentive for them to be pursued individually.[63]

Yet we have seen that, even in individually viable suits, disaggregation of claims will lead to depressed claim value and suboptimal settlements in every case, defendant overinvestment in initial cases, and as a result suboptimal deterrence, and is in effect a tacit endorsement of unreasonable business risks. The rule in *Abdool* would suggest that class actions are appropriate in every case

---

61. There are other techniques, for instance the use of "test cases", which can eliminate common issue litigation redundancies as well as class action suits. However, because these types of actions do not pool claims to obtain optimal litigation investment, their deterrent effect will be inferior to formal aggregation.

62. *Abdool* v. *Anaheim Management Ltd.* (1995), 21 O.R. (3d) 453 at 464 (Ont. Div. Ct.).

63. See above note 39 and accompanying text.

except those where they are most useful – the worst tortfeasors would be allowed to escape full internalisation of their harm simply because the harm is great.

The approach taken by Charbonneau J. in *Isaacs* v. *Nortel Networks Corp.*[64] appears intuitively more realistic, if not reasoned in any more depth than *Abdool*. In *Isaacs*, faced with objections by the defendant in a wrongful mass-dismissal case that each of the claims, if valid, was viable individually, the judge certified the proposed class, noting that:

> The fact that the individual claims may be large is not a bar to certification as a class action. The fundamental test is whether one or more of the three goals of the Act will be promoted. Surely a number of important common issues have been identified. Their collective resolution in one trial in the context of a class action will greatly assist judicial economy. The Act provides for streamlined procedures which will also assist in that regard. It would be naive not to recognise that for any individual to launch and sustain an individual action against a behemoth such as Nortel is a daunting task even when the plaintiff may ultimately be awarded several hundred dollars. Access to justice would certainly be enhanced in a class proceeding.[65]

In *Isaacs*, the court weighed the practical effects that would flow from a denial of certification, and while not describing those effects in explicitly economic terms, came to a decision that would allow recovery where it might otherwise not have been possible. This echoes the words of the Ontario Law Reform Commission in 1982, when that body noted that "effective access to justice is a precondition to the exercise of all other legal rights."[66]

(b) Availability of Alternative Compensation Schemes

Lack of appreciation for the true effects of aggregation is also apparent from the extent to which courts, including the Supreme Court of Canada, consider whether alternative compensation schemes established by defendants are "preferable" to class proceedings. Inevitably in such cases, the "preferability" question focuses on the schemes' administrative efficiency and the extent to which it provides applicants with compensation equivalent to that they might win through collective litigation.

Besides the review of the alternate compensation regimes in *Hollick* and *Rumley*, briefly discussed earlier,[67] courts have weighed such programs as factors

---

64. *Isaacs* v. *Nortel Networks Corp.* 2001 A.C.W.S.J. LEXIS 19244; 2001 A.C.W.S.J. 233890; 110 A.C.W.S. (3d) 246 (Ont. Sup. Ct. J.).

65. *Ibid.* at para. 73.

66. *Ontario Report (1982)* above note 39 at 139.

67. See above notes 36 to 38 and accompanying text.

in the preferability analysis in *Bittner* v. *Louisiana-Pacific Corp.*,[68] *Brimner* v. *Via Rail Canada Inc.*[69] and *Sutherland* v. *Canadian Red Cross Society.*[70]

But since deterrence relies on the defendant paying for the full extent of harm it has caused, then even the fullest compensation through such administrative regimes may fall well short of this goal. Recall that one of the principal justifications for class actions is that, in many cases, victims of tort do not (for whatever reason) pursue compensation. It may be true that more would pursue compensation from a straightforward administrative process than through the courts, but still not everyone would, as indicated by the fact that many class members in successful litigations never actually claim from the administrative fund established through award or settlement to compensate them.[71] Unless the court can be assured that *every* member of the class will in fact be paid, then from the deterrence standpoint such an alternative plan *cannot* be preferable.[72] A court should keep in mind that, barring exigent circumstances (such as severe reputational harm), the only reason that a defendant firm will set up an administrative fund is that it can get away with paying less by doing so.[73]

---

68. *Bittner* v. *Louisiana-Pacific Corp.* (1997), 43 B.C.L.R. (3d) 324 (S.C.) (alternative compensation scheme found preferable).

69. *Brimner* v. *Via Rail Canada Inc.* (2000), 50 O.R. (3d) 114, [2000] O.J. No. 2747 (Sup. Ct. J.), aff'd [2001] O.J. No. 3684 (Div. Ct.) (compensation scheme rejected as not preferable).

70. *Sutherland* v. *Canadian Red Cross Society* (1994), 17 O.R. (3d) 645 at 652-3 (Gen. Div.) (compensation scheme rejected as not preferable).

71. The preferability of class proceedings over a pre-emptive defendant-driven compensation scheme derives from the fact that this unspent amount ought not to accrue to the defendant if deterrence is to be optimised. The *Ontario Report (1982)*, above note 39 at 133-34, summarising U.S. statistics, noted that, in 15.8% of cases less than half of class members filed claims.

72. This is not to say that the incompleteness of the plan could not be so minimal, and the costs and burdens of trial or delay so great, as to make such a plan "preferable" despite its inferior deterrent effect in any given case. The point is that the courts have not shown an inclination to consider the element in their analyses of such alternative compensation plans.

73. An increasingly common corporate strategy is to offer Canadian customers, through newspaper advertisements, the same settlement terms as those won in the United States through litigation. Such a move may be sufficient to lead a court overlooking deterrence to prefer the defendant's compensation scheme. See generally Kleefeld above note 39 at 61 (describing *inter alia* an IBM campaign offering settlements to Canadian customers equivalent to that earned through U.S. class settlement). There is a difficult ethical issue raised when defendant's counsel communicates in this way with potential class members before they are represented (i.e.

Following this reasoning, there is no reason to consider the fact that few or even no claims had been made against the administrative fund as a reason not to certify, unless the court is concerned only with compensation and not with deterrence.[74]

Any compensation regime that does not permit claimants to aggregate – that is to pool their resources and optimise litigation investment – will be suboptimal. Thus the only types of action specifically excluded from the class proceedings acts are those which can be pursued on a representative, rather than an individual basis.[75] Economically, there can be no truly "preferable" alternative process (at least among those established by private defendants) unless two objectives are met: first, the claims process under the regime must be at least as free of transaction costs as claims from a typical class action settlement fund; and second, the court must be convinced that the end result of the compensation process will be an appropriate global loss to the defendant. The fact that courts do not consider the second question when weighing the advantages of direct compensation is indicative of the undervaluation of deterrence as a goal.

Many of the difficulties inherent in the "preferability" analysis are present in the recent dismissal of a class action consisting of cable Internet subscribers who had received service allegedly below the standard represented to them at the time of their subscription. In *Kanitz et al.* v. *Rogers Cable Inc.*,[76] the subscription agreement had contained a clause allowing the provider to unilaterally change any aspect of the contract, without any renegotiation of terms; if the customer didn't like it, she could only cancel her subscription. As it happened, Rogers, the service provider, did make such a unilateral amendment, inserting a mandatory arbitration clause as well as imposing a commitment upon the subscriber not to file a class action (in contract or tort) against Rogers, and indeed to opt out of any class action commenced by others.

In the *Kanitz* case, a typical subscriber's damages were estimated by the plaintiff to amount to perhaps $240, and the case was dismissed in part because the plaintiff had not adduced evidence that no class member would seek individual arbitration for such an amount, i.e. the plaintiffs had not shown that the actions were not individually viable. Moreover, the judge found that the Ontario *Arbitration Act* was worded sufficiently widely to permit an arbitrator to combine individual arbitrations into a single, classwide hearing, and that costs were

---

before certification): see generally Debra Lyn Bassett, "Pre-Certification Communication Ethics in Class Actions" (2002) 36 Ga. L. Rev. 353.

74. Different public policy concerns may obtain where the administrative fund is set up by the government, as in *Hollick*, above note 36 (to the extent that the public interest in deterring the government can be vindicated through the democratic process – this point was not explicitly considered in *Hollick*).

75. B.C. s. 41; Ontario s. 37; to similar effect see the "impracticability" of representative actions provisions of Quebec art. 1003.

76. *Kanitz* v. *Rogers Cable Inc.* 2002 Ont. Sup. C.J. LEXIS 333.

recoverable by successful plaintiffs, in theory offsetting the litigation expense and making even small claims viable. Nordheimer J. expressed the view that if a few class members succeeded individually at arbitration, then the defendant would likely settle the remaining claims for the full amount:

> [I]f their claims were successful, presumably the defendant would then propose some overall resolution rather than face the time and expense of a stream of such arbitrations. If not, then the remaining customers would still be able to arbitrate their claims and recover their costs through the arbitration process.[77]

This view is naïve, except to the extent that the obverse – also noted by Nordheimer J. – is true (i.e. that *defeating* the first few claims will likely allow the defendant to escape all).[78] Let us suppose that the class in *Kanitz* consisted of 100,000 subscribers,[79] each with $240 in damages. The defendants would approach the first arbitration as though there were $24 million at stake;[80] its litigation investment in common issues could easily run into the hundreds of thousands of dollars, if not the millions, an amount it could bring to bear *in each and every arbitration*. An individual plaintiff, though, could not be expected to invest more than a few hundred, even if he or she expected to recover costs.[81]

---

77. *Ibid.* at 30-31.
78. Nordheimer J. is here proposing that the matter might proceed by "test case". Test cases, in theory, provide all of the advantages of claims aggregations offered by class actions except the most important one: the opportunity to maximise litigation investment through cost-spreading across all similar claims. Unless a single counsel managed to sign up as clients each and every one of the potential class members, or unless the numerous competing plaintiffs' counsel could arrange a perfect transaction cost-less cooperation (each for reasons of intraclass competition structurally impossible), test cases cannot produce a result comparable to class actions and therefore are economically inferior to a single, fully aggregated class claim.
79. At the time of filing, Rogers had a customer base of 370,000 (*ibid.* at 1). I choose the smaller number for convenience and because I have no idea how many of these were affected by the alleged service problems.
80. See above footnote 58 in Chapter Two and accompanying text.
81. A plaintiff cannot be expected to invest more than will be recovered; in other words, if the sum total of utility loss from arbitration (costs plus time, stress, etc.) amounts to more than $240 (less a discount for uncertainty of result), the process will be abandoned. Even if (*ad absurdum*) the plaintiff would enjoy a 100% chance of success if she were willing to invest equally with Rogers, and spend perhaps $100,000 on the common issues, she would have to be similarly assured that the arbitrator will not award costs (over and above the damages) of less than $99,760.

> More typically, let us suppose that the a claim had less than a 100% chance of success. A risk-neutral plaintiff would be willing to risk only $480 for a two-to-one (i.e. 66.6%) probability of winning $240, going up to $960 for a four-to-one (i.e. 80%) and peaking at not much higher than $4560 if such an amount guaranteed a 95% chance of success (19-to-one). A typical risk-averse plaintiff (to whom,

The Plaintiffs in *Kanitz* made the expected arguments regarding the contractual terms of the Rogers agreement, based on the "hidden clause" jurisprudence of consumer contract cases.[82] Nordheimer J. rejected this argument:

> In my view, an arbitration clause is not at all the same as an exemption clause. The latter serves to remove one contracting party's liability to the other whereas the former simply requires that the parties seek their relief in a different forum. In that regard, the latter clause can be characterized as substantive and the former as merely procedural.[83]

Again we confront the characterization of class proceedings as a procedural device, simply an alternative forum to that of arbitration. Its denial, therefore, according to the Court, affected no substantive rights.[84] Yet this procedural description of class actions, as I have stressed here throughout, is inadequate; not only might the class members lack incentives or inclination to proceed individually over such small amounts (as the plaintiffs in *Kanitz* argued), but forcing the plaintiffs into a claim-by-claim resolution process means that the value of their

---

because of the diminishing marginal utility of wealth, a loss hurts more than a win helps) will invest still less, further diminishing the probability of success.

Even if doing so earned it only a 5% reduction in aggregate damages (i.e. 5% less per claim or 100% success in 5% of the claims) a risk-neutral defendant facing 100,000 $240 claims would be willing to spend up to $1.2 *million* fighting the same common issues. This amount can all be brought to bear against each plaintiff in arbitration.

82. *Tilden Rent-A-Car* v. *Clendenning* (1978), 18 O.R. (2d) 601 (C.A.), *Toronto Blue Jays Baseball Club* v. *John Doe* (1992), 9 O.R. (3d) 622 (Gen. Div.) and *Badie* v. *Bank of America*, 67 Cal. App. 4th 779 (1998).

83. *Kanitz*, above note 76 at 25-26.

84. Nordheimer J. rejected the idea that barring class actions was in fact denying recourse (*ibid.* at 34):

> [I]t has been held on many occasions by our courts that the *Class Proceedings Act, 1992* is procedural and not substantive. As Mr. Justice Winkler said in *Ontario New Home Warranty Program* v. *Chevron Chemical Co.* (1999), 46 O.R. (3d) 130 (Sup. Ct. J.) at para. 50:
>
> > "Moreover, this court has noted on multiple occasions that there is no jurisdiction conferred by the *Class Proceedings Act* to supplement or derogate from the substantive rights of the parties. It is a procedural statute and, as such, neither its inherent objects nor its explicit provisions can be given effect in a manner which affects the substantive rights of either plaintiffs or defendants."

However, Nordheimer J., like every other Canadian court, examined the availability of recourse only with respect to the viability of each individual claim in an alternate proceeding (in this case arbitration). He did not consider whether, as I argue, denial of class proceedings for common issues will *per se* at least reduce the substantive recovery of each claimant, even if each claim is viable on its own.

claims *will* be diminished, as will the value of the claim of any other member of the class, even if all are individually viable. While the former effect is arguably a question of procedural choice, the latter effect is substantive.

Setting aside the obvious factual questions regarding whether customers knew or ought to have known of the restrictive provisions in the contract (or the possibly better question of whether the unilateral amendment procedure was unconscionable given the consumers' inevitable investment in installing and learning the Rogers system and the costs of switching to a rival broadband provider), there are difficult implications to the invocation of arbitration clauses to escape class proceedings. Most troubling is the fact that mandating opt-out of some customers (perhaps those who "signed on" to the service after the "no class action" clause was introduced) not only defeats the rights of those customers; it also affects the rights of the customers who are *not* bound to opt out, as their smaller class will, according to the analysis in Part II of this work, litigate less efficiently, reducing the expected value of every claim.

A similar impact will be felt by the denial of a national class action through the mandatory arbitration clause. The clause at issue in *Kanitz* would apparently require each province's customers to arbitrate within that province; even if the arbitrator in each province fully consolidated the claims into a "quasi class action," the litigation would still be suboptimal and the defendant would still enjoy a greater litigation scale economy than would the plaintiffs.

As a result of the reasoning in *Kanitz*, a defendant in the position of Rogers, relying on an arbitration clause, can commit many, if not most, breaches of contract or torts with *de facto* legal impunity.[85] This might have been what Rogers' customers agreed to, but then again it might not.

Indeed it should come as no surprise that U.S. courts, state and federal, have viewed clauses that mandate arbitration at the expense of class proceedings dimly, particularly where there are the traditional indicia of power imbalance in the contractual relationship and the use of standardised contracts with no opportunity to bargain. The American views on the unconscionability and public policy subversion of such clauses should in my view set an example for the Canadian judiciary.[86]

---

85. I stress that I am taking no position on the factual or legal validity of the claim against Rogers, which may well have been innocent of all wrongdoing in the case.

86. Arbitration clauses that restrict class proceedings such as that upheld in *Kanitz* have been considered in a number of U.S. cases, with the courts generally refusing to enforce them. See for instance: *Szetela* v. *Discover Bank* 118 Cal. Rptr. 3d 862, 2002 WL 652397 (Cal. C.A. 2002) (holding arbitration clause prohibiting class or representative actions procedurally and substantively unconscionable and void as against public policy of promoting judicial economy and streamlining of litigation through class actions); *Powertel Inc.* v. *C. Bexley*, 763 So. 2d 1044 (Fla. S.C.) (use of arbitration clause to forbid class actions both procedurally and substantially unconscionable); *Johnson* v. *Tele-Cash Inc.* 82 F. Supp. 2d 264 (D. Del. 1999)

Canadian courts must confront in a principled way the interplay between arbitration statutes and the class proceedings legislation. It is submitted that, when they do so, they should take into account more than the economic advantages of aggregation vis-à-vis each claim, and consider the impact of the imposition of arbitration on the global aggregate of claims.[87] If this is done, the courts may find, first, that such procedures are rarely if ever preferable, and second, there are good policy reasons for refusing to enforce such provisions that may overcome the courts' traditional respect for the privity of contract.

(2)   Deterrence and Settlement

The second point at which deterrence should be more prominently considered is where the court is called upon to review a class settlement, and the criteria it applies when doing so. Related questions revolve around whether a "settlement class" – simultaneous settlement and certification – is appropriate. I consider these questions – the terms of settlement generally and the special case of the settlement class – in sequence.

(clause not "so one sided" as to be unconscionable but not enforceable in relation to the class action claims because that would contravene Congress's intent to encourage such actions). *Contra* see *Thompson* v. *Illinois Title Loans, Inc.* (N.D. Illinois, Eastern Division, 2000) WL No. 99 C 3952; *Dunlap* v. *Berger*, [Va. C.A., 2002] West No. 30035 (class proceedings essential to protecting the public interest and effecting just remedies, therefore standardised contract prohibiting class proceedings are generally unconscionable); *Kinney* v. *United HealthCare Service, Inc. et al.* 83 Cal. Rptr. 2d. 348 (Cal. C.A. 1999) (although there is a strong policy reason to favour arbitration, "[t]hat policy is manifestly undermined by provisions in arbitration clauses which seek to make the arbitration process itself an offensive weapon in one party's arsenal." (citing *Saika* v. *Gold* (1996) 49 Cal. App. 4th 1074, 56 Cal. Rptr. 2d 922 at p. 1081); *Baron* v. *Best Buy Co., Inc.* 260 F. 3d 625 (11th Circuit 2001) (arbitration clause which limits or precludes statutory remedies is unenforceable); *Ting* v. *AT&T*, 182 F Supp. 2d 902 (N.D. Cal. 2002) (mandatory arbitration clause prohibiting class proceedings were intended to effectively deter claims, therefore clause unconscionable and unenforceable).

87.   The U.S. Supreme Court has recently considered the conflict between mandatory-arbitration agreements and class action legislation in *Green Tree Fin. Corp.-Ala.* v. *Randolph*, 531 U.S. 79 at 90 (2000) (holding that the existence of large arbitration costs that could prevent a consumer from effectively vindicating her statutory rights might render an arbitration agreement unenforceable). The Court did not consider the special economic effects of aggregation discussed here, but rather considered only the economics of the individual plaintiff's case. For discussion of *Green Tree* see Jason Bradley Kay, "The Post-Green Tree Evidentiary Standard for Invalidating Arbitration Clauses in Consumer Lending Contracts: How Much Justice Can You Afford?" (2000) 6 N.C. Banking Inst. 545.

(a) Settlement Terms Generally

In assessing whether a settlement should be approved, the court will consider a number of factors enumerated in the cases. These include the likelihood of recovery or success, the amount and nature of discovery, evidence and investigation, the settlement terms and conditions, the recommendations and experience of counsel, the future expenses and likely duration of the litigation, the recommendation of any neutrals, the nature of the objections and the force behind such objections, and the presence of arm's length bargaining and the absence of collusion.[88] The court may also consider the extent and nature of communication by counsel for the representative plaintiff with class members during the litigation.[89]

Certainly there is little objectionable in most of these factors from the point of view of optimal deterrence; the strength of the case goes directly to the expected value of the claim, which must be assessed for deterrence to be appropriate. The absence of collusion, as discussed throughout this book, is a necessary condition for optimal recovery and thus deterrence. The level of communication with class members is helpful both from the point of view of minimising the information deficit and assuring the court that all potential objectors would be on notice to appear.

There are, however, factors in the above checklist that might give us some cause for concern, because they illustrate the degree to which compensation and deterrence can be at odds with each other in the settlement approval process.

The list anticipates that the question of litigation costs (both pecuniary and, through the cofactor of "duration," perhaps utilitarian as well) should be given some weight. Of course, litigation costs go to the question of compensation, not deterrence. To the extent that this factor is more heavily weighted than others oriented more towards deterrence, the court must understand that it is sacrificing the deterrent effect.

Similarly, a court may be tempted to consider other factors that, if they influence the settlement-approval decision, also may serve to undermine the goal of "behaviour modification." For instance, in *Millard* v. *North George Capital Management Ltd.*, the Court weighed "the dedication of the defendants to fighting those claims on a variety of issues,"[90] as well as the advanced age of the class

---

88. See *Dabbs* v. *Sun Life Assurance Co. of Canada* (1998), 40 O.R. (3d) 429 (Gen. Div.) at pp. 439-44, affirmed 41 O.R. (3d) 97 (C.A.), leave to appeal to S.C.C. dismissed October 22, 1998; *Parsons* v. *Canadian Red Cross Society* , [1999] O.J. No. 3572 (Sup. Ct. J.) at para. 71; *Ontario New Home Warranty Program* v. *Chevron Chemical Co.* (1989), 46 O.R. (3d) 130 (Sup. Ct. J.).

89. Winkler J. in *Parsons, ibid.* at para. 72.

90. *Millard* v. *North George Capital Management Ltd.* (2000), 97 A.C.W.S. (3d) 604 at para. 136 (Ont. Sup. Ct. J.).

members,[91] in assessing whether the settlement amount was sufficient. I will deal with each of these in turn.

Deterrence principles dictate that whether defendants appear determined to "fight hard" if the settlement is not approved should not be relevant to calculating the proper amount of the settlement. In fact, even to consider the defendant's litigation posture in this way – as a factor which weighs against a fuller settlement – is to invite defendants to adopt an unreasonably harsh strategy, or at least to announce their intention to do so. Such a posture has only limited relevance from a compensation standpoint, in that it requires that the court take the defendant at its word regarding its own litigation strategy, an idea that seems questionable given the defendant's strong incentive under such circumstances to puffery and intimidation.

Turning to the consideration in *Millard* of the claimants' advanced age, one can certainly sympathise with complainants who valued the promise of less cash now above a bigger payout later on, particularly if, as in *Millard*, those claimants were elderly and might lose the utility of an eventual award altogether. For reasons articulated earlier, risk-averse humans of any age value money in hand more highly than the equivalent expected value of an eventual award, and hence will always take less than the "expected value" of their claim up front. One of the purposes of "corporatisation" of class proceedings is, as I have emphasised, the reduction of such behaviouristic factors as this "hyperbolic discounting" in favour of accuracy of settlement. The court that accommodates the risk aversion of individual class members should do so in full awareness that it is *necessarily* providing suboptimal deterrence, and *ipso facto* helping to ensure that more injuries will occur in the future as the result of that decision.[92] That courts will often express this preference (and indeed it is entirely understandable) is a perfect illustration of how we irrationally value the ex post claim before us more highly than the ex ante claim of the future.[93]

A court executing its duties in settlement review should do so with the goals of the class proceeding in mind, and chief among these goals, as I have suggested, must be that of behaviour modification or general deterrence. That is to say, a court ought to weigh all of the pertinent factors while asking itself, "what

---

91. *Ibid.* at 110.

92. And, to the extent that "advanced age" is factored in to further reduce the award, the court is providing a bonus to tortfeasors who prefer to victimise the elderly.

93. This is a problem, like many others, that results entirely from the present tort system's interweaving of compensation and deterrence. It, and many similar problems, would be alleviated if system designers chose to uncouple the insurance and deterrent functions of tort, allowing immediate insurance-based compensation and *subsequent* suit for full deterrence purposes. Some methods of accomplishing this, such as an unrestricted market in subrogated claims, government tort "superfunds", etc., are discussed in Chapter 10, below.

is the likely effect of the settlement amount on the future behaviour of this defendant, and more importantly of all actors in the "tort marketplace?"

Some of these concerns may be ameliorated if the court takes an active interest in the process leading to settlement.[94] In such circumstances, the court might emphasise the public interest in deterrence, and to describe a set of factors that it believes are *not* appropriate to consider when calculating the settlement amount. This way, the problem of a flawed settlement brought before the court on a "take it or leave it" basis can be avoided.

(b) The Problem of the Settlement Class

There are three distinct phases in a class proceeding in which settlements can be made: prior to certification, simultaneous with certification, and after certification. Because of the agency problems described earlier, the timing of the settlement is a crucial component of class action system design.

In the U.S., recent years have seen the emergence of what might be called an "all-or-nothing" settlement-only class; that is, a class which would not proceed as a fully aggregated class action if the settlement were not approved. In some "extreme cases," the settlement is reached before the class action is even filed, let alone certified.[95] It has been criticised as abandoning all the scale-economy advantages of claims aggregation, because as Rosenberg notes, "settlement-only class actions require the defendant's consent, and no defendant would agree to a mode of settlement that increased its total costs above those it would otherwise bear in the standard market process."[96] This type of action, then, "merely reproduces the claim recovery values generated by fractionally aggregated representation."[97] Rosenberg continues:

---

94. In *Dabbs* above note 88 class counsel and counsel for the insurance company reached a settlement after ten months of negotiations and presented it to the court for approval. Fourteen objectors out of a large class were given extensive participation rights. While noting that class action settlements should be "viewed with some suspicion," the Court added that settlements are by their nature "a product of compromise . . . . [f]airness is not a standard of perfection." (*Ibid.* at 440) In *Dabbs*, Sharpe J. himself participated in the settlement process, questioning expert witnesses and counsel for both parties to supervise each stage in the interests of the class members.

95. John C. Coffee, Jr., "Class Wars: The Dilemma of the Mass Tort Class Action" (1995) Colum. L. Rev. 1343 [Coffee, "Class Wars"] at 1379

96. David Rosenberg, "Mandatory-Litigation Class Action: The Only Option for Mass Tort Cases" (2001) 115 Harvard L. Rev. 831 [Rosenberg, "The Only Option"] at 860 n. 63. Professor Coffee concurs, calling this process a "'no lose' proposition" for defendants: Coffee, "Class Wars" above note 95 at 1379.

97. Rosenberg, "The Only Option" above note 96 at 860.

This limitation arises because settlement-only class actions are convened solely to effect classwide settlement. Failure to achieve such settlement – because the parties cannot reach agreement or because they fail to obtain judicial approval – automatically dissolves the class action and disaggregates the claims, relegating plaintiffs to voluntary joinder without affecting the value of their claims. Litigation class action is operationally, and therefore functionally, distinct from settlement-only class action because failure to achieve classwide settlement does not result in dissolution of the litigation. Instead, the case proceeds to trial based on classwide aggregation of all classable claims and with the benefit of the corresponding optimal investment.[98]

Rosenberg allows, however, that the "distinction" he posits between "all–or–nothing" settlement-only and litigation classes is "bound to blur in mass tort cases in which there is some probability that the court will certify a litigation class action [if settlement is not approved]."[99] However, Rosenberg argues that even settlement based on a probabilistic assessment of the likelihood of certification must be (by the magnitude of probability) lower than the correct settlement of a litigation class, and thus inferior.[100]

Because, however, such probabilistic discounting is inevitable in the present Canadian system of opt-out classes, I analyse below the comparative effects of settlement on this second basis.

The model for Canadian settlement class actions has been *Dabbs* v. *Sun Life Assurance Co. of Canada*.[101] In that case, three actions were filed in Quebec, British Columbia and Ontario in an insurance "vanishing premiums" case with an estimated 400,000 class members nationwide. Prior to certification but after the claims were filed, counsel in the three actions undertook settlement negotiations that resulted in a settlement being presented simultaneously with a certification application (with the defendant's consent to certification conditional upon the approval of the settlement). The settlement was challenged by certain class objectors (who argued among other things that the class counsel had a conflict of interest), but the court found it reasonable in all the circumstances. In refusing the objectors' arguments regarding counsel fees, Winkler J. assumed that the fee (between $1.4 million and $6.5 million) had been negotiated simultaneously with the settlement (although in fact the fee structure had been negotiated separately and was subject to a subsequent arbitration process and independent court approval), and held that:

> In the present case, the fee agreement was negotiated at arm's length by experienced plaintiff's counsel from three separate provinces. The payment of class counsel's fee is to be made by the defendant directly, is not from the same fund as the settlement moneys, and will not diminish the recovery of individual class members.

---

98.   *Ibid.* at 860-61.

99.   *Ibid.* at 861, note 64.

100. *Ibid.* at 861.

101. *Dabbs* v. *Sun Life Assurance Co. of Canada* (1998), 35 O.R. (3d) 708 (Gen. Div.) leave to appeal ref'd 36 O.R. (3d) 770 (Gen. Div.).

Further, the fee agreement sets out only the process for arriving at a proper fee, and the range within which the fee shall fall. The minimum fee set out in the agreement is based upon estimates of actual time spent by the class counsel, and is analogous to the base fee contemplated in s. 33 of the *Class Proceedings Act, 1992*. The fee itself will be separately determined once the settlement approval motion has been disposed of, by arbitration before an independent, neutral third party. The arbitrator must do so "having regard to principles drawn from professional conduct standards and the law."

Moreover, the entire fee arbitration process and range of fees as set out in Appendix G, including the minimum fee of $1.4 million, will be subject to the scrutiny of the court by virtue of its inclusion in the terms of the settlement agreement. The arbitration process must receive court approval along with the rest of the settlement, in order to be of any force or effect. As was noted in the Manual for Complex Litigation, above, the ethical concern will be eased where the fee agreement is subject to review by the court. In addition, I have advised counsel for all parties that once the arbitration is concluded, that disposition must be affirmed by this court, thus ensuring scrutiny of the full settlement.[102]

This passage suggests the degree of scrutiny courts will apply when allegations of "sweetheart deals" are made in settlement class proceedings. Moreover, it suggests that the Canadian legislation requiring independent approval of the solicitors' fees can provide an important check on settlement-class abuses as well as so called "strike suits."[103]

Along with the problem of depressed settlement amounts based on inequality of bargaining position, settlement class actions raise the spectre of collusion between the plaintiffs' attorneys and the defendants depressing class recovery even further. Rosenberg describes the objection that arises as follows:

Commentators have viewed the settlement-only class action as being particularly susceptible to the risk of inadequate class recoveries, because in principle the defendant can solicit competing "bids" from different lawyers who seek to act as class counsel, and whose success in this regard depends on their reaching a settlement with the defendant.[104]

Obviously, the plaintiff's counsel in such a case is not necessarily working in the best interests of the class. Indeed, the market incentive for the lawyer (work-

---

102. *Ibid* 35 O.R. (3d) 708 at 715-16. For another example of simultaneous certification/settlement where collusion was rejected see *Ontario New Home Warranty Program* v. *Chevron Chemical Co.* (1999), 46 O.R. (3d) 130 (Sup. Ct. J.) (where settlement was the result of a post-filing mediation process and litigation continued against non-settling defendants).

103. See for instance *Epstein* v. *First Marathon Inc.*, [2000] O.J. No. 452 (Sup. Ct. J.) [*Epstein*] where the Court made a special order to ensure that counsel who had brought what the Court considered a "strike suit" would receive no remuneration – directly or indirectly – from the defendant.

104. Bruce Hay & David Rosenberg, "'Sweetheart" and "Blackmail" Settlements in Class Actions: Reality and Remedy" (2000) 75 Notre Dame L. Rev. 1377 ["'Sweetheart" and "Blackmail" Settlements"] at 1397.

ing perhaps hand in glove with the defendant who may have chosen him out of several "suitors") is to have a settlement as low (and fees as high) as can reasonably be expected to be accepted by members of the class.[105]

Note that this problem is really acute only when there are several competing "overlapping" class claims pending, in which case the defendant might "shop around" among counsel for a "sweetheart" settlement. Such litigation, in which competing counsel build extensive "inventories" of clients as the basis for their application, has so far been virtually absent from the Canadian litigation landscape.[106] Even if such cases were to arise, if the court finds that the course of negotiations indicates that the counsel's interest may be diverging from that of the class, the court has the power, through its supervision of the attorney's fees, to preserve the proper incentive. Rosenberg explains:

> The core task for the court here again is to regulate counsel's fee in such a way as to ensure that his fractional share of a class settlement he negotiates is no greater than his fractional share of what the plaintiffs would recover if he had not negotiated a class settlement. Under such a fee structure, a lawyer acting on behalf of the plaintiffs will not find it in his interest to enter into a class settlement unless the settlement amount is at least as great as the expected value of the plaintiff's claims. Any class settlement he negotiates that gives the plaintiffs less than the value of their claims will leave him worse off than he would be if he did not negotiate the class settlement at all. In this way, the proposed fee regulation approach protects

---

105. In such circumstances, then, notification will go out to the class members who must then decide whether or not to "opt out." Game theory and the general risk-aversion of human beings dictate that, when faced with the alternatives of certain (but inadequate) recovery and a risky recovery, the member will usually prefer the former and not opt out. This is more likely the less serious the injury and the smaller the claim amount. Another insidious effect is a variation on the "prisoner's dilemma." The class member, faced with the suspicion that his fellow members will take the settlement, will be less reluctant to opt out because the opt-outs, taken together, will still have an economy of scale less than the settling class. And even that must be viewed in light of the fact that, in many cases, the defendant may have little left over after the settlement is approved; the more members who do not opt out, the less that will be left over. Faced with such arithmetic, it is fairly certain that members will tend to remain in a settlement that is well below their legitimate expectations.

106. This is probably because hitherto, only one jurisdiction (Ontario) has certified national opt-out classes (and generally though by no means exclusively) does so to the exclusion of members from other class action jurisdictions, reducing the risk that truly competing claims will be filed. Following the universal establishment of a common law class action in the Supreme Court's decision in *Dutton*, above note 14, however, it is more likely that this problem will arise in the future if national classes are attempted.

the class from inadequate settlements while permitting or making possible settlements that give the members the full value of their claims.[107]

Hay & Rosenberg's analysis, however, assumes that the class counsel will retain an interest in their client "inventories" even if certification is granted to a competing representative plaintiff and firm. In Canada, it would appear that "losing" class counsel might simply be left out in the cold as the court selects a single lead counsel and orders all other actions stayed.[108] In such a case, collusive settlement could still be reached for fees well below those which the counsel would receive should settlement not be reached.

To see how the threat of eventual certification affects a claim, consider the case of a thousand claims with a full value of $1 million. Assume that plaintiffs' litigation costs for individuals in small claims court would be $500 each, and litigation costs for the class as a whole (if certified) would be $50,000. For the defendants, we might assign costs of $50,000 to defend against a single class action, or $100,000 to defend against the 100 individual claims. Let us also say that there is a 50% chance that certification would be granted if opposed by the defendant.

If the plaintiffs negotiate with the defendants an "all-or-nothing" settlement-only certification (i.e. a settlement which, if not approved, would result in the disappearance of the class litigation), then the defendant would agree to certification only if it would be cheaper than settling the cases individually (or aggregated through voluntary joinder or some other suboptimal procedure). Assuming that failure to certify would result in complete disaggregation into separate individual claims, this amount would be $800,000, i.e. halfway between the defendants' expected overall loss ($1 million damages + litigation costs = $1.1 million) and the plaintiffs' expected recovery ($1 million – litigation costs of $500,000 = $500,000).[109] This assumes, of course, that we accept Shavell's analysis of settlement outcomes described earlier.

In a completely aggregated class action, the expected settlement amount would be the full $1 million: halfway between the defendant's expected overall loss ($1 million + $50,000 = $1,050,000) and the plaintiff's expected gain ($1 million — $50,000).

If, however, the parties anticipate that the class representative will seek full aggregation even if the settlement/certification is rejected by the court, then the difference between the two amounts determined above (i.e. the "fully aggregated claim" amount of $1 million minus the "settlement-only" amount of $800,000 =

---

107. Hay & Rosenberg, above note 104 at 1398. For a fuller exposition of this fee-limiting proposal, see Bruce L. Hay, "Asymmetric Awards: Why Class Actions (May) Settle for Too Little" (1997) 48 Hastings L. J. 479.

108. See below note 6 in Chapter Nine and accompanying text.

109. In practice in the United States the claims would not disaggregate *completely*, but would rather be reduced to a voluntary joinder of each lawyer's "inventory" of claims.

$200,000) would be discounted according to the probability of certification success (50% x $200,000 = $100,000) and the remainder would be added as a risk premium to the lower amount.[110] In other words, the defendant will offer more if there is a chance that a litigation class will be certified ($900,000) than if the action would be abandoned if settlement fails, but not as much as it would if the claim was already certified ($1 million).

No doubt, a court looking over such an agreement would probably consider it fair compensation for the plaintiffs. Instead of the $500 each would receive in individual actions, here they would receive $850 (assuming litigation costs remain at $50,000 for the class or $50 per claimant – realistically they may be lower because of the early stage of resolution). The court might weigh the $100 uncertainty premium paid by each class member against the costs to the court and society of prolonged litigation, and decide that it was in fact a fair settlement.

Because, however, we are assuming that each of the 1000 plaintiffs is entitled by law to recover $1,000, the defendant is still allowed to escape with total damages less than the harm he has inflicted ($950,000 including litigation costs fixed at $50,000). But again, however, the court may weigh this reduction against the considerable overall costs involved in full litigation, and decide that this level of deterrence is sufficient.

But keep in mind that this is the appropriate level of deterrence only if one accepts that class certification should be a substantive barrier to recovery of otherwise valid claims. Given that the award is discounted only for a factor of legal uncertainty, from the ex ante perspective, such legal uncertainty would be factored in with the "likelihood of litigation success" in the calculations that determine the defendant's level of precautions. Accordingly, the precautions will be lower than the socially optimal level of care that mandatory aggregation would provide.[111] From the point of view of optimal deterrence and optimal compensation, certification and optimal aggregation is preferred except when outweighed by concerns for individual litigative autonomy (as perhaps when very high-value claims are involved) or when distribution of the award would be particularly problematic.

By and large, Canadian courts have been fairly scrupulous in their review of "settlement classes," and to date it does not appear that there has been any "all-or-nothing" class settlement approved (i.e. one where defendant and plaintiff

---

110. Rosenberg, "The Only Option" above note 96 at 861; see also Ward Branch & John Kleefeld, "Settling a Class Action (or How to Wrestle an Octopus)" (Presented to the Canadian Institute Conference on Litigating Toxic Torts and Other Mass Wrongs, Toronto: December 4-5, 2000) at 12: "Other things being equal, a defendant's cost of settling will increase after certification is granted because one risk factor – the risk of certification – has been negated."

111. This scenario assumes the present opt-out certification system. Rosenberg, of course, advocates mandatory certification of all mass tort claims; under such a system, there could be no possibility of a discount for certification uncertainty.

agreed on a settlement amount before the action was filed or where the certification effort appeared likely to be abandoned if settlement failed). Nevertheless the threat may well increase as class actions become more frequent, courts' dockets more congested, and plaintiffs' counsel more competitive.[112]

However, surveys of U.S. cases concluded that a high number of settlements accepted without modification are worrisome;[113] the Canadian experience so far seems to parallel this concern.[114]

What lessons can be taken from the U.S. experience with "settlement classes"? I suggest as a general rule that a court should not accept a settlement/certification unless it concludes that the defendant negotiated under the threat of full aggregation, less only demonstrably appropriate discounts for uncertainty at the certification stage.[115] This does not mean that certification contingent on settlement is necessarily bad, as it does provide judicial efficiencies in most cases,[116] and may in fact replace the litigation process with a more expedi-

---

112. Branch's survey of settlement classes appear to indicate an increase in the device's use: see Ward Branch, *Class Actions in Canada* (Toronto: Canada Law Book, looseleaf) at §§4.1960, 4.1970, but not an excessive one given the increased overall frequency of certifications generally in the same period (1994-2001).

113. Thomas E. Willging et al., *Preliminary Data on Class Action Activity in the Eastern District of Pennsylvania and the Northern District of California in Cases Closed Between July 1, 1992 and June 30, 1994* (Federal Judicial Center, April 1995) at 57-58. The findings suggest "a judicial passivity at the settlement stage": Coffee, "Class Wars" above note 95 at 1348 footnote 14.

114. None of the applications for settlement/certification listed in Branch (15 in Ontario and 9 in B.C.) was rejected by the courts: Branch, above note 112 at §§4.1960, 4.1970.

115. Indeed, the original U.S. judiciary's Manual for Complex Litigation warned of the dangers inherent in settlement class actions. This "per se rule", however, was relaxed in favour of scrupulous judicial oversight of such settlements. The problem is that at such an early stage, perhaps before any hearings or discovery have been conducted, the Court might be in a very weak position to assess the adequacy of such a settlement: Coffee, "Class Wars" above note 95 at 1379-81. Coffee notes (at 1381):

    When courts first accepted settlement class actions, the normal pattern was that parties litigated actively for a period of months or longer, sparring over discovery and related motions – until reaching a tentative agreement on a settlement. In contrast, the newer pattern has involved a settlement reached after little or no active litigation (and sometimes before the complaint is filed).

116. The efficiencies arise from the fact that a second "fairness" hearing is unnecessary, and also because notice of the certification and settlement hearings can be effected simultaneously, in some cases a very significant factor. In *Haney Iron Works Ltd. v. The Manufacturers Life Insurance Company* (1998), 169 D.L.R. (4th) 565 (B.C.S.C.) [*Haney*] at para. 11, an objector argued that the defendant could not

ent administrative one.[117] However, the court should be conscious that settlements approved at certification will necessarily be discounted according to the perceived probability of certification in any event. If it appears to the court that certification is more likely than an offered discount would indicate, it may be appropriate to reject the settlement on that basis alone.[118]

A simple solution would require that settlement submissions be made only at the beginning of a contested certification hearing; if the settlement is rejected, then the hearing devolves immediately into one for certification. This would reduce the danger of structural collusion, and the parties would be in a better position to assess the likelihood of certification and the strength of their cases generally. A drawback, however, is that such a dual-purpose hearing would eliminate any advantage of efficiency gained through the settlement class, because it would force the parties to prepare for the hearing before knowing if preparation were necessary.

---

make certification conditional upon settlement. The court decided that such a view "would require defendants in class actions to decide whether to contest certification prior to any fairness hearing. Instead of opening negotiations when confronted with a proposed class action and trying to achieve an early global settlement, defendants would be forced to contest certification, since on [the objector's] submission, participating in any proposed settlement would foreclose the right to challenge certification."

The Court in *Haney* offered the compromise that, before approving a settlement class certification, the plaintiff must make out a "prima facie" case for certification. While this might avoid some of the problems associated with settlement class actions (in that the requirement to present a "plan" might "shake out" "all–or–nothing" settlements, as described below), it is not otherwise helpful on the central question of collusion. The fear is not that inappropriate classes will be certified, but rather that eminently suitable classes will be short-changed in the settlement.

117. See for instance *MacRae* v. *Mutual of Omaha Insurance Co.* (2001), 98 A.C.W.S. (3d) 282 (Ont. Sup. Ct. J.), which established an arbitrator to assess "vanishing premium" claims arising from insurance policy sales. The settlement/certification approved did not discount or cap damages and permitted opt-outs; the class was therefore seen to be well protected. It bears noting, however, that the presence of opt-out rights is no guarantee of the fairness of the settlement. Many claimants, due to the low value of their claims or their own non-pecuniary utilities, will not opt out of settlements even if they are well below optimal.

118. U.S. courts appear to be very reluctant to take such a step unless "one side is so obviously correct in its assertions of law and fact that it would be clearly unreasonable to require it to compromise to the extent of the settlement, that to approve the settlement would be an abuse of discretion": *Greenspun* v. *Bogan* 492 F. 2d (1st Cir. 1974) 375 at para. 381. Arguably, this threshold is too high, particularly when rejection of the settlement with directions may result in a fairer settlement being offered.

There is another structural safeguard that could be put in place, in the form of a contingent litigation plan. At present, when the "settlement class" is submitted for certification/approval, the putative class counsel is required to make a *prima facie* showing of the suitability of the representative plaintiff.[119] This generally takes the form of affidavits from the plaintiff and counsel. In an ordinary (non-settlement) certification, the "suitability" submission would include a "plan" for advancing the proceedings,[120] a requirement not found in the U.S. regime.[121] In the case of a simultaneous certification/settlement application, courts have not considered the "plan" as particularly important: if the settlement is not approved, certification will no longer be an issue (and thus a *prima facie* showing is not immediately necessary); if the settlement *is* approved, the "plan" is, in effect, the settlement itself.

In fact, though, it may be very useful to require two *alternative* plans; one to be used if settlement is approved (taking the form of the settlement itself), and one if it is rejected. In other words, the plan submitted *should provide for the contingency that the initial settlement offer is not approved*, and offer a timetable, agreed to by both plaintiff's and defendant's counsel, for necessary discovery and the certification hearing itself. It might be coupled with an undertaking from the plaintiff's counsel committing to aggressively pursue the litigation should the settlement be rejected. In other words, a plan that is sketchy or uncertain save its provisions relating to notice and settlement should be rejected by the courts as inadequate in a settlement class action.

If, after presenting such a plan in a certification/settlement motion, the settlement is not approved, then the plaintiff will have committed to the court to pursue the action through an adversarial certification procedure and, if necessary, on

---

119. *Haney*, above note 116

120. See for instance B.C. s. 4(1); Ontario s. 5(1). In theory, the "plan" requirement suggests that a counsel who attempts certification without intending to "advanc[e] the proceeding on behalf of a class" may be abusing the process of the court. For an example of a case that arguably fit that paradigm, see the "strike suit" identified by the Court in *Epstein*, above note 103.

121. In the U.S., the class briefs submitted under Rule 23 need only set out that the plaintiff meets the Rule's requirements: Yvonne W. Rosmarin & Daniel A. Edelman, *Consumer Class Actions – A Litigation Guide*, (Boston: National Consumer Law Center, 1990) at 64-71. There are no statutory factors to be weighed in deciding whether the putative representative plaintiff will "fairly and adequately protect the interests of the class" pursuant to Rule 23(a)(4). However, U.S. courts have read in a commitment to "vigorous prosecution", that includes showing that the representative plaintiff has sufficient financial resources to prosecute the claim on behalf of all members: see generally Aron, Shea, Reaves & Sadowsky, *Class Actions Law and Practice* (NY: Clark, Boardman, Callaghan, 1987), chapter 2. Such a showing is generally required on the motion of the defendant (*Ibid.*, 4.13), which makes the point moot in a settlement class situation.

to trial. The court should then be active in monitoring the progress of this timetable, to ensure that the defendant has not simply switched its negotiating focus to the next putative representative plaintiff in line.[122]

In this way, there can be some assurance that the settlement was negotiated under the threat of fully aggregated litigation, and the court can be to that extent assured that there has been no discounting from the forces of structural collusion.

(3) The Award of Costs

. One of the most difficult questions in class action system design involves whether to award costs against unsuccessful plaintiffs. In the U.S., Rule 23 has no cost-shifting provisions, adopting the *de facto* "own costs" rule that prevails in that country's courts generally. However, the rules for individual suits in Canada are patterned on England's "loser pays" system. The question is, should that system prevail in class action litigation as well?

British Columbia's statute changes the normal rules for the award of costs by adopting the American approach in class proceedings, with each party bearing its own costs regardless of outcome.[123] In exceptional circumstances, however, the court may award costs to punish vexatious or abusive behaviour.[124]

The B.C. model followed the recommendations that had been made by the Ontario Law Reform commission in 1982. Nevertheless, the *Ontario Act* departed from these recommendations and preserved the ordinary rules. These cost-shifting rules apply unless the class proceeding was a "test case, raised a novel point of law or involved a matter of public interest," in which case the Court may exercise discretion to modify the costs award.[125] This is generous wording, as most attempted class actions, broadly speaking, are by necessity "test cases" (in that their outcome will determine the fate of numerous similar claims), and many if not most (at least products liability and toxic tort cases) arguably involve a matter of public interest.

---

122. Should the same defendant attempt to settle a substantially similar claim with a subsequent representative, the original plaintiff's counsel could oppose the matter as *lis pendens* or on *forum non conveniens* grounds. Under such circumstances, the second court must weigh the danger that it is party to a "reverse auction" and decline the settlement/certification if it appears no more suitable than the first attempt rejected by its sister court. The real danger of "reverse auctions" is that simultaneous negotiations will proceed *before* the first certification attempt, not that they will occur strictly sequentially. Forcing the defendant to agree, not to certification in any event, but at least to a *plan* involving certification and litigation might provide a sufficient "mast-tying" device to ward off the worst problems of structural collusion in settlement classes.

123. B.C. s. 37.

124. B.C. s. 37(2).

125. Ontario s. 31.

Awards of costs against unsuccessful representative plaintiffs in class proceedings are necessarily problematic, because the economy of scale is grotesquely reversed. The costs of the defendant's litigation of all classable (i.e. similar) claims can be exacted from a single representative plaintiff whose own interest in the claim might be minimal. Such cost-shifting will systematically deter valid claims from proceeding, routinely permitting defendants to escape the costs of their wrongdoing. While it is conceivable, on the other hand, that "own costs" regimes will encourage illigitimate litigation, the parallel experiences of Ontario and B.C. (the latter where an "own costs" presumption applies) do not seem to bear out such concerns, and no one has suggested that the rate of frivolous litigation is higher in B.C. than Ontario.

Quebec's regime attempts to strike a compromise, by applying the tariff that would apply for claims of between $1000 and $3000, therefore protecting an unsuccessful plaintiff against disproportionate costs awards.[126]

Recently, the British Columbia Attorney General's office announced that that Province's government was considering modifying the cost rules in the *Class Proceeding Act* to discourage unwarranted litigation,[127] though its discussion paper provided no evidence – not even an anecdote – to suggest that *any* frivolous suits were being filed under B.C.'s current regime, let alone at a higher rate than in Ontario or Quebec where "loser pays" systems are available.

Cost-shifting mechanisms could incorporate a simple economic analysis into the equation. We could decide, for instance, that we did not wish to encourage any suit that would have less than a 50% chance of success. In such a case, the award of costs necessary to assure that this threshold was not crossed would be 50% of recovery, i.e. equal to the "expected value" of the suit only if the suit had a 50% chance of success. That is to say, if a representative plaintiff alleges damages of $1000, the potential of a costs award over $500 would discourage that (presumedly risk-neutral) party from proceeding; a cost award of less than $500 would encourage the plaintiff to go ahead. To look at it another way, the threshold of 50% of potential damages means that a suit with little chance of success but equivalent possible value (i.e. 10% chance of recovering the same $1000) would be discouraged by the fact that its expected value ($100) is far less than its expected loss ($500).

But such formulae are much more difficult in practice. To begin with, claims are only rarely easily determined absent a full hearing; therefore, assessing what would have been the representative plaintiff's "upside" if the matter had proceeded to trial is inherently difficult. Moreover, many other members of the class

---

126. Quebec art. 1050.1. The Quebec regime is compared to Ontario's and B.C.'s in John A. Campion and Victoria A. Stewart, "Class Actions: Procedure and Strategy" (1997) 19 *Advocate's Quarterly* 20 at 41-43. See also the discussion in Branch, above note 112, chapter 19.

127. British Columbia Ministry of Attorney General, *Civil Liability Review (#AG02079)* (Victoria, Ministry of Attorney General, April 2002) at 8.

may have much higher or much lower damages; in the case of the former, such a scheme might underdeter representative plaintiffs who had little personally at stake compared to others.

Most of all, though, the problem is that cost-shifting of any type does not account for the fact that the class action is lawyer-driven, not plaintiff-driven. In most class actions, the expenditures by plaintiffs' counsel simply getting to certification (where cost-shifting is available) will heavily outweigh the expected recovery of the representative plaintiff alone. When we speak of deterring frivolous litigation, then, we are speaking of deterring *lawyers*, not individual plaintiffs, and we have moved in a sense around to the problem of "blackmail" suits, discussed in more detail in Chapter Three. Our conclusion might be the same one reached in that discussion: that litigation risks in complex litigation are borne roughly equally by plaintiffs and defendants' counsel; plaintiffs' counsel (with few resources) can expect to be more risk-averse than defendants or their insurers, and frivolous suits will be, in most cases, systemically discouraged by that reality.

Even if it is true, as the B.C. Attorney General suggests (again without citing any evidence), that the defendants' "enormous, and ultimately unrecoverable" costs are "typically not incurred by the plaintiffs,"[128] one might suggest that this phenomenon, if it is significant at all, will result in higher insurance premiums that will be built into the cost of goods sold in the marketplace. Yet no one has been able to point to any evidence that class action regimes, with or without cost-shifting rules, have increased the overall price of consumer goods in any measurable way.

The real risk of frivolous litigation is not that it will prejudice the ability of particular firms to compete in their industry (except in rare, highest-stakes cases), as insurance rates will tend to apply to all businesses within a particular field of endeavour (suits filed against Ford, for instance, whether frivolous or not, will almost certainly raise nominal insurance rates at Daimler-Chrysler).[129] The danger lies not in inordinate expenses for a particular firm, or even an overall reduction in economic activity. Rather, as the costs of suit-prone products rise, consumers can be expected to spend their disposable income on other products or services. If the products targeted for suits are indeed risky, then the resulting reduction in activity is arguably desirable, and the law of tort is fulfilling one of its important regulatory roles in the marketplace. If, however, a particular industry or activity is prone to lawsuits that are baseless, then the disincentive to patronise that industry might be *un*desirable, even if the overall effect on the economy, or the average price of goods, in unaffected. In certain industries crucial to human well-being, such as the pharmaceutical or food industries, the con-

---

128. *Ibid.*
129. I speak here of insurance rates as a conceptual device, whether the firm is self-insured or not.

sequences of this dissuasion of consumers could have an overall adverse impact on health.

Weighing against such considerations, though, is the fact that it is in these very industries where the strictest oversight is necessary because the consequences of error can be particularly tragic. Under such circumstances, absent clear evidence of a higher-than-optimal level of suit overall (regardless of whether any *particular* suit is valid),[130] caution suggests that it is better to err on the side of plaintiff's access to redress over concerns regarding overdeterrence.

---

130. It is important to recall that companies' level of care is in part systemic, rather than specific to any particular product or incident. Therefore, the level of care will be set to a large extent by that companies' *overall* litigation exposure resulting from activities, whether that exposure results from valid or invalid suits. In other words, a company that is only ever sued frivolously will be encouraged to be more meticulous in its precautions (such as product testing) so that such suits can be dealt with quickly and cheaply. More realistically, a company that is occasionally negligent (and usually gets away with it) will be appropriately deterred only if it is also subject to suits which turn out to be unfounded. This is not to suggest that frivolous suits are in themselves a public good – in fact they will tend to overdeter and distort the negligence "marketplace", but only if that marketplace is operating efficiently. To the extent that the level of suit is below the optimal and companies are generally *under* deterred from negligent conduct, a certain level of frivolous suits will not lead to overdeterrence and should be tolerated by system designers.

PART III

—

National Classes In Canada

CHAPTER EIGHT

—

Problems of the National Class

A. INTRODUCTION

At various points throughout my discussion of class action system design, I have suggested that any class whose members are drawn from markets smaller than the one in which all impacts of the tort are felt will be suboptimal from the point of view of both deterrence and compensation. This is especially so within the national borders: where the prices of products are likely to be the same and the substantive law of mass torts is likewise similar, there are strong economic reasons to avoid duplication of class claims and permit a single, market-wide, aggregation.[1]

As Professor Nagareda points out (while discussing the constitutional competence of the U.S. congress to enact compensation legislation), "mass tort claims

---

1.   One marked exception to the efficiency of treatment of mass tort on a national basis is the question of airborne and waterborne pollution or disasters, like Bhopal, caused by subsidiaries of multinational corporations. It certainly is not radical to suggest that these problems, at the least, should be dealt with on an international basis, perhaps through the "joint Canada-United States tribunal" for "non-market" mass tort problems recently proposed by Judge Weinstein: Weinstein, *Individual Justice in Mass Tort Litigation* (Evanston, Ill.: Northwestern University Press, 1995) at 36.

arise from quintessentially commercial activity – the buying and selling of products – that is plainly interstate in scope."[2]

Nevertheless, the Canadian constitution assigns jurisdiction over "property and civil rights" and the "administration of justice" to the provinces, each representing only a fraction of the national market in mass torts. How, then, do we enable mass tort litigation on the scale of the "footprint" of the wrong? How do we "fit the forum to the fuss"?

The answer, clearly, is that the mass tort litigation system must support actions in which claims are aggregated on an interprovincial basis: the "national class."

In general, class action legislation need not set out the rules for the inclusion of foreign defendants or plaintiffs, but rather might leave such questions to be dealt with under the Rules of Court and common law or constitutional principles. Indeed, there is nothing in the Ontario or Quebec legislations which explicitly states that class actions *may* include foreign parties; the B.C. and Saskatchewan Acts, as mentioned previously, provide mechanisms for the inclusion of foreign plaintiffs as an opt-in subclass.[3] As we shall see, the Ontario courts have read their province's legislation permissively, allowing national opt-out classes; British Columbia courts have interpreted their own statutes restrictively, so far allowing non-resident class members *only* on the opt-in basis set out in the statute. Quebec courts seem somewhat ambivalent on the issue.

Obviously, foreign class plaintiffs present some problems of legal theory, particularly opt-out classes which may bind potential plaintiffs if they take no action to remove themselves from the court. If a class action is said to be final with respect to the claims of persons who do not opt out[4], then could this affect the rights of foreign persons who may not even have been aware of the action? And even if they were aware, how are we to view the jurisdiction of the laws of one province over the citizens of another? These are fundamental questions.

Consider the case of a class action begun by Ontario residents, alleging that they had been harmed in Ontario by a product manufactured outside the country. Following *Moran* v. *Pyle*,[5] the tort with respect to those injuries can be said to have happened in Ontario, regardless of where the product was made. However, it may be that others alleging similar injuries from the same products might live

---

2. Richard Nagareda "Autonomy, Peace and Put Options in the Mass Tort Class Action" (2002) 115 Harv. L. Rev. 749 at 769.

3. B.C. s. 8(1)(g), 16(2); Sask. 18(2), 21(1).

4. As is provided for in Quebec Civil Code art. 2848, and as was asserted under the *Ontario Act* in *Carom et al.* v. *Bre-X Minerals Ltd. et al.* (1999), 44 O.R. (3d) 173 (Sup. Ct. J.).

5. *Moran* v. *Pyle National (Canada) Ltd.* (1974), [1975] 1 S.C.R. 393, Dickson J. at 409:

> By tendering his products in the market place directly or through normal distributive channels, a manufacturer ought to assume the burden of defending

outside Ontario. If non-resident class members were allowed to join the suit as part of a "national class," then a foreign defendant might argue that, as to the dispute between it and a non-resident plaintiff, the Ontario court has no jurisdiction and its *Class Proceedings Act* could not apply. This was the case described in *Wilson* v. *Servier Canada Inc.*:

> [89] The defendants state . . . that the subject-matter of claims by the non-Ontario plaintiff has no real and substantial connection with Ontario because (1) the defendants do not reside in Ontario or have any offices in Ontario; (2) the defendants do not have assets in Ontario; (3) the defendants do not operate or carry on business in Ontario; and (4) the defendants do not market, promote or sell Ponderal or Redux in Ontario.[6]

A similar problem was addressed in *Harrington* v. *Dow Corning*.[7] In that case, foreign manufacturers of breast implants were subject to a suit in British Columbia alleging that the implants were unfit. Could non-resident member subclasses be included in the B.C. action? If so, on what constitutional theory of territoriality? What were the implications for the choice of law questions that would necessarily follow?

There are two closely integrated components of the question of provincial superior courts' jurisdiction over class action suits with class members from other jurisdictions. The first, and the one that has generated the lion's share of judicial analysis, is whether the court itself has jurisdiction over the various non-resident claims. This might be viewed as jurisdiction over the non-resident *plaintiffs* (in an opt-out case – obviously in an opt-in case these plaintiffs must attorn and the question of jurisdiction is not an issue), or it might be viewed as jurisdiction over the defendants with respect to non-residents' claims. The second, and more traditional, "extraterritoriality" question is to what extent the provincial *legislatures* might design a system to grant or extinguish rights to parties outside the province's borders. This latter question is premised to an extent on the traditional view of class litigation as a device that does not exist absent legislation, a premise that appears to be moot in the wake of the Supreme Court's decision in *Dutton*.[8] Nevertheless, because both class proceedings statutes and legislation in other provinces with which they might conflict (principally limitations acts as I discuss later) are provincial legislation, and because the provinces do not have the right to legislate extraterritorially, the issue of legislative territoriality cannot be completely evaded.

---

those products wherever they cause harm as long as the forum into which the manufacturer is taken is one that he reasonably ought to have had in his contemplation when he so tendered his goods. This is particularly true of dangerously defective goods placed in the interprovincial flow of commerce.

6. *Wilson* v. *Servier Canada Inc. et al.* (2000), 50 O.R. (3d) 219 at para. 89 (Sup. Ct. J.).
7. *Harrington* v. *Dow Corning Corp.*, 2000 BCCA 605.
8. *Western Canada Shopping Centres, Inc.* v. *Dutton*, 2001 SCC 46 [*Dutton*].

The problem of non-resident class members has thus far been addressed by the Ontario and British Columbia courts from the perspective of the *court's* jurisdiction, not the legislature's. This focus has been largely based upon an adaptation (and arguably an expansion) of the concept of procedural due process established by the Supreme Court of Canada in *Morguard* and *Hunt* as "order and fairness," to which I turn next.

B. PROCEDURAL OR SUBSTANTIVE?

Class proceedings are a means to a remedy, and most provisions in the relevant legislation are not designed to directly affect substantive rights. They do not make conduct that was previously lawful unlawful, they simply permit a different avenue of recourse and, in so doing, engage the economic advantages of aggregation in a way that will substantially (indeed in many cases overwhelmingly) affect recovery.

But separating right from remedy is not a an easy intellectual exercise. In class actions, proceedings that were previously *de minimus* (presumably a substantive objection) are now actionable. The availability of class actions moreover is bound to internalise more costs in defendants, a substantial, if not strictly substantive, effect. Indeed their profound potential to influence the behaviour of defendants across a whole range of previously non-actionable activity is difficult to characterise as simply procedural. When their application is extraterritorial, the difficulties become profound.[9]

The Supreme Court of Canada in *Tolofson* v. *Jensen* noted that "differentiating between what is a part of the court's machinery and what is irrevocably linked to the product is not always easy or straightforward," quoting with approval Walter Cook:

> If we admit that the "substantive" shades off by imperceptible degrees into the "procedural," and that the "line" between them does not "exist," to be discovered merely by logic and analysis, but is rather to be drawn so as best to carry out our purpose, we see that our problem resolves itself substantially into this: How far can the court of the forum go in applying the rules taken from the foreign system of law without unduly hindering or inconveniencing itself?[10]

---

9. The characterisation of class proceeding legislation as solely procedural probably originated in the United States, where the source of class proceedings is Fed R. Civ. P. Rule 23. Because Rule 23 is a rule of court, it cannot have substantive effect without violating the *Rules Enabling Act* which gives it effect (see discussion above note 44 in Chapter Seven). In the United States, limitation periods are not strictly considered substantive law for conflicts analysis, so tolling provisions create no similar problem there.

10. *Tolofson* v. *Jensen*, [1994] 3 S.C.R. 1022 at 1068, quoting Walter W. Cook, *The Logical and Legal Bases of the Conflict of Laws* (Cambridge, MA: Harvard University Press, 1942) at p. 166.

The *Tolofson* Court went on to say:

> This pragmatic approach is illustrated by *Block Bros. Realty Ltd.* v. *Mollard* (1981), 122 D.L.R. (3d) 323 (B.C.C.A.). In that case the issue was whether the requirement of s. 37 of the *Real Estate Act*, R.S.B.C. 1979, c. 356, that a real estate agent be licensed in British Columbia, should be categorized as procedural or substantive. The parties had executed a real estate listing agreement in Alberta for land situated in British Columbia. The plaintiff, an agent licensed in Alberta, sold the land to Alberta residents. The defendant vendor failed or refused to pay the commission. The plaintiff sued in British Columbia. The *lex causae* was Alberta. The defendant pleaded that the British Columbia licensing requirement was procedural. The court, however, ruled that it was substantive, notwithstanding that the section read: "A person shall not maintain an action . . .," language traditionally relied on for a finding that a statute is procedural because it purported to extinguish the remedy, but not the right.

Class proceeding mechanisms go beyond providing a remedy to persons affected by tort. They also toll limitation periods for claimants not before the court (something found in *Tolofson* itself to be substantive) and *ipso facto* defeat the right to sue of, for instance, class members who do not opt out. To these extents at least, class proceedings seem to affect substantive rights and go well beyond what is necessary to simply control what goes on in the courtroom from a procedural perspective.[11]

The difficult question of procedural vs. substantive interpretation permeates the interprovincial application of class action regimes. It is easier to make an argument for the extraterritorial application of class action statutes if they are seen as strictly procedural; on the other hand, their ability to toll limitation periods accruing to defendants in other provinces, or to bind class members on an opt-out basis to decisions, is more aptly characterised as substantive.

It may be, in the end, that the answer is a normative one; the more widespread class actions become, the less unjust it could be to impose them extraterritorially. However, this is a philosophical solution not a legal one, and assists us only conceptually in interpreting the jurisprudence of the national class.

C.   THE "REAL AND SUBSTANTIAL CONNECTION"

By virtue of the "division of powers" provisions of the Canadian constitution, the provinces' rights to enact or enforce laws dealing with "property and civil rights" and the "administration of justice" are limited in application to "within the

---

11.   There are clues in the various statutes that seem to be indicative of substantive law. In Quebec, for instance, the provisions that I suggest are *most* substantive – those affecting limitations and the binding effect on persons not before the court – are enshrined within the Civil Code (ss. 2848, 2897, 2908), not the Code of Civil Procedure where the bulk of the legislation is set out. In B.C. (s. 41(c)) and Ontario (s. 37(c)) the *Act* is explicitly not retroactive to representative proceedings already under way, possibly reflecting concern over retroactive changes to substantive law.

province" itself.[12] Thus the stage is set for the inevitable conflict between a decentralised economy and centralised legal jurisdictions.[13]

(1) *Morguard*

The starting point for an examination of the relevant questions must be *Morguard Investments Ltd.* v. *De Savoye*[14]. In that case, the Supreme Court of Canada was considering the obligations of a court to recognise the judgments and orders of sister courts in other provinces. The plaintiff in *Morguard* had previously obtained a judgment in the Alberta courts against the defendant, a British Columbia resident, who had defaulted on a land mortgage in Alberta. Under Rule 30(g) of the Alberta Rules of Court, the Alberta court could assume jurisdiction over such a dispute even though the defendant had been served outside Alberta territory. The question before the Supreme Court of Canada was the correctness of a subsequent decision by a B.C. judge to enforce the Alberta judgment.

Morguard is noteworthy for two reasons. First, it held that the enforcement of extrajurisdictional *Canadian* judgments was not analogous to the enforcement of judgments that are truly foreign, and that the same rules should not apply. Instead of relying on arcane English rules of private international law, Canadian courts must afford one another's judgments "full faith and credit" providing that the original court indeed had properly taken jurisdiction. LaForest J. held:

As I see it, the courts in one province should give full faith and credit, to use the language of the United States Constitution, to the judgments given by a court in another province or a territory, so long as that court has properly, or appropriately, exercised jurisdiction in the action.[15]

The second question settled in *Morguard* was whether the originating court (Alberta) had properly taken jurisdiction over a matter between parties from outside the province, such that B.C. courts ought to respect the judgment granted.

The Court held that a provincial superior court's jurisdiction is limited by principles of "order and fairness," and that, with respect to a dispute involving parties from other provinces, this principle is satisfied only where there is "a real and substantial connection" between the province assuming jurisdiction and the defendant or the subject-matter of the law suit. Significantly, the Court attributed its departure from the traditional rules to the nature of the federal system and its essentially national marketplace:

---

12. *Constitution Act, 1867*, s. 92.
13. For an overview on "constitutionalization of conflict rules", see Elizabeth Edinger "The Constitutionalization of the Conflict of Laws"(1995) 25 Can.Bus.L.J. 38.
14. *Morguard Investments Ltd.* v. *De Savoye*, [1990] 3 S.C.R. 1077.
15. *Ibid.* at 1102.

In a world where even the most familiar things we buy and sell originate or are manufactured elsewhere, and where people are constantly moving from province to province, it is simply anachronistic to uphold a "power theory" or a single situs for torts or contracts for the proper exercise of jurisdiction.[16]

The *Morguard* decision was one of a series in which the increasingly borderless market played a prominent role in influencing the Court's reasoning. Earlier that same year, La Forest J. said in *Thomson Newspapers Ltd.* v. *Canada*:

... The courts in Canada ... cannot remain oblivious to the concrete social, political and economic realities within which our system of constitutional rights and guarantees must operate ... [A]s the Canadian economy becomes increasingly integrated with the American and, indeed, the global economy, we should be wary of giving an interpretation to the Constitution that shackles the government's capacity to cope with problems that other countries ... are quite able to deal with[.][17]

But *Morguard* has one other striking feature that, while not often commented upon, may bear upon our analysis here. It seems very clearly to suggest that the jurisdiction of courts does not necessarily mirror that of provincial legislatures. That is, while legislatures are territorially limited by the constitution,[18] courts – at least provincial courts of inherent jurisdiction — are not.[19] LaForest J. noted that:

This Court has, in other areas of the law having extraterritorial implications, recognised the need for adapting the law to the exigencies of a federation.[20]

He then cited with approval from the decision of Estey J. in *Aetna Financial Services Ltd.* v. *Feigelman*:

... An initial question, therefore, must be answered, namely, what is meant by "jurisdiction" in a federal context? ... In some ways, "jurisdiction" [of the Manitoba court] extends to the national boundaries, or, in any case, beyond the provincial boundary of Manitoba ... [21]

This idea of the provincial superior courts as – at least in some situations – "national" courts will be more fully explored in the subsequent decision of *Hunt* v. *T&N plc.*, discussed next.

---

16. *Ibid.* at 1108.

17. *Thomson Newspapers Ltd.* v. *Canada*, [1990] 1 S.C.R. 425.

18. It would appear, for instance, that provincial legislatures cannot make laws "aimed at" activities occurring wholly outside the province: *Reference re Upper Churchill Water Rights Reversion Act*, [1984] 1 S.C.R. 297. What remains unclear is whether there is a "real and substantial connection" test applicable to such legislation, mirroring the test for judicial jurisdiction, following *Morguard*.

19. Black, Vaughan. "The Other Side of *Morguard*: New Limits on Judicial Jurisdiction" (1993), 22 *Can. Bus. L.J.* 4.

20. *Morguard*, above note 14 at 1101.

21. *Aetna Financial Services Ltd.* v. *Feigelman*, [1985] 1 S.C.R. 2 at p. 34-35.

(2) *Hunt*

While *Morguard* hinted that the "full faith and credit" and "order and fairness" requirements were constitutional in nature,[22] this was not confirmed until the Court's decision in *Hunt* v. *T&N plc.*,[23] where the Court confirmed that the requirement of "a real and substantial connection" was indeed a "constitutional imperative," such that it "has become the absolute constitutional limit on the power of each province to confer judicial jurisdiction on its courts."[24]

> They are constitutional imperatives, and as such apply to the provincial legislatures as well as to the courts . . . In short, to use the expressions employed in *Morguard* at p.1100, the "integrating character of our constitutional arrangements as they apply to interprovincial mobility" calls for the courts in each province to give "full faith and credit" to the judgments of the courts of sister provinces. This, as also noted in *Morguard*, is inherent in the structure of the Canadian federation, and, as such, is beyond the power of provincial legislatures to override. This does not mean, however, that a province is debarred from enacting any legislation that may have some effect on litigation in other provinces . . . But it does mean that it must respect the minimum standards of order and fairness addressed in *Morguard* . . . One must emphasise that the ideas of "comity" are not an end in themselves, but are grounded in notions of order and fairness to participants in litigation with connections to multiple jurisdictions.[25]

Hunt concerned, *inter alia*, the constitutionality of a Quebec "blocking statute" that prohibited the removal of business records from Quebec to fulfil an out-of-province court's discovery requirements. Following *Morguard*, the British Columbia Supreme Court had held that comity required it to respect the barrier erected by Quebec. However, the Supreme Court of Canada turned the question of "comity" around, and held that the Quebec statute was constitutionally inapplicable to civil proceedings in another province, by virtue of the same *Morguard* principles.

Hunt also appeared to confirm that "the Constitution may itself provide a source of court jurisdiction by prohibiting the ouster of the jurisdiction of the superior courts of a province with a real and substantial connection to the matter."[26] This jurisdiction, once properly exerted, must be respected by all other Canadian courts and, by inference, legislatures.

An objective reader of *Hunt* would realise that the Court was making a subjective value judgment regarding who must show comity to whom. The Court

---

22. See *Morguard*, above note 14 at 1094, per LaForest J.: "For a number of these writers, there are constitutional overtones to this approach . . . It is fair to say that I have found the work of these writers very helpful in my own analysis of the issues."

23. *Hunt* v. *T & N plc.*, [1993] 4 S.C.R. 289.

24. Jean Gabriel Castel, *Canadian Conflict of Laws*, 4th ed. (Toronto: Butterworths, 1997) at 54.

25. *Hunt*, above note 23 at 324-325.

26. Janet Walker, "Interprovincial Sovereign Immunity Revisited" (1997) 35 Osgoode Hall L.J. 379 at 389.

accepted that the Quebec "blocking statute" was valid, as were the B.C. Rules requiring disclosure. Competent courts in each jurisdiction could, with *prima facie* jurisdiction over the matter, enter mutually exclusive orders necessitated by their respective laws – the Supreme Court simply had to choose, in such a case, whose laws would prevail. As a matter of policy, one court's statutory "right" to obtain documents conflicted with another court's statutory "right" to block production.

Once the subjective nature of such a decision is acknowledged, then one might try to peer behind the language of the decision to see what factors the court weighed in deciding the balance of comity. On the one hand, Quebec's interest was to "impede successful litigation" in other provinces; the interest of the B.C. Courts, on the contrary, was to promote interprovincial commerce and the "efficient allocation and conduct of litigation."[27]

This aspect of *Hunt* is rarely considered, yet here it is pivotal. The case in effect affords some degree of *constitutional protection* to the "efficient resolution" of civil disputes, an interest with which another province cannot tamper, at least without a constitutionally sound reason of its own.

(3) National Classes in Ontario

The issue of the propriety of a nationwide opt-out class was first raised in Canada in the 1995 case *Nantais* v. *Telectronics*,[28] a decision of the Ontario Court (General Division). In *Nantais*, Brockenshire J. considered whether a national class made up of the recipients of allegedly faulty heart pacemaker leads was permissible. In the decision, Brockenshire J. identified the issue as fairness to absent plaintiffs (as opposed to fairness to the defendant, as the defendants urged). Considering the American position, he found the Court's reasoning in *Shutts* to be "most persuasive." While questioning to what extent the defendant had standing to raise the rights of absent foreign plaintiffs[29], the analysis adopted appears generally to coincide with that in *Shutts*, with Brockenshire J. noting that part of the litigation plan submitted by the plaintiffs included actual notification of all potential class members across the country. He suggested that although an opt-out class might be permissible, in the case before him "prudence would dictate" that "non-resident" class members be provided the opportunity to opt in.[30]

---

27. *Hunt*, above note 23 at 327.
28. *Nantais* v. *Telectronics Proprietary (Canada) Ltd.* (1995) 127 D.L.R. (4th) 552 (Ont. Gen. Div.) [*Nantais*].
29. This is in contrast to the U.S. Supreme Court's decision in *Phillips Petroleum Co.* v. *Shutts*, 472 U.S. 797 (1985) [*Shutts*] where it was found that the defendants' interest in achieving a global settlement made it appropriate that it should be concerned with whether non-resident plaintiffs would be bound by any settlement or decision.
30. *Nantais*, above note 28 at 567 (D.L.R.).

So, while Brockenshire J. did not explicitly do so, he focused on the two key principles in the U.S. due process analysis – meaningful notice and the appropriateness of opt-out classes for non-resident plaintiffs.

However, in refusing leave to appeal from the *Nantais* decision, Zuber J. of the Divisional Court did not focus on the "due process" elements emphasised by the court below, emphasising instead that the question should be more properly left for subsequent decisions of foreign courts using a *res judicata* analysis:

> Whether the result reached in Ontario court in a class proceeding will bind members of the class in other provinces who remained passive and simply did not opt out, remains to be seen. The law of *res judicata* may have to adapt itself to the class proceeding concept. In my respectful view the order of Brockenshire J. setting out a national class, finds powerful support in the judgment of La Forest J. in *Morguard Investments Ltd.* v. *De Savoye*, [1990] 3 S.C.R. 1077, 76 D.L.R. (4th) 256.[31]

The issue was revisited by Winkler J. in *Carom* v. *Bre-X*.[32] In that case, the plaintiffs argued that Brockenshire J. in *Nantais* did not adequately consider the constitutional question; Winkler J. rejected this idea. While the analysis in *Carom* at times might appear confusing,[33] Winkler J. firmly grounded his answer in the idea of "order and fairness" established by the Supreme Court's decision in *Morguard* and *Hunt*. Unfortunately, though, he approached it from the point of view of the general "order and fairness" of the Ontario *Class Proceedings Act*, not from the circumstances of the individual case before him:

> The CPA is a procedural statute replete with provisions guaranteeing order and fairness. Section 9 permits any member to opt-out of the class proceeding within the time provided . . .
>
> In addition s. 17 requires that proper notice of the certification, in a court approved form, must be provided to all class members. The notice must include the "manner by which and time within which class members may opt out of the proceeding." Additional notices to ensure that the interests of the class members are protected may be ordered by the court under s. 19.[34]

The notice requirements in the Ontario *Act* provide for everything from actual notice to no notice at all; the court has discretion to order notice in whatever form it sees fit or dispense with it altogether. But if, for instance, actual notice is a requirement of "due process" as in the U.S. after *Shutts*, then it behoves the Ontario court to adopt procedures from the more stringent end of the spectrum

---

31. The application for leave to appeal to the Divisional Court was dismissed on October 4, 1995; reasons of Zuber J. are reproduced at the end of *Nantais*, above note 28.

32. *Carom* v. *Bre-X Minerals Ltd.* (1999), 43 O.R. (3d) 441 (Gen. Div.).

33. Winkler J. apparently considered "order and fairness" and "real and substantial connection" as criteria that must be independently satisfied, rather than the latter being an aspect of the former.

34. *Carom*, above note 32 at 451-52.

when foreign members are included in the class. In other words, it is not, as the *Carom* decision suggests, the language of the statute that "guarantees" order and fairness, but rather that the statute is drafted in such a way as to allow the courts to guarantee it in any particular case.

Carom was followed by the decision of Brockenshire J. in *Webb* v. *K-Mart*. That case involved an action launched in Ontario against K-Mart for a mass termination of employees across Canada during an episode of corporate downsizing. In approving the class, Brockenshire J. said:

> Our provincial courts systems are struggling to deal with situations where there is a nation wide impact. So are the state courts in the United States. Obviously, from the points of view of both the national corporation and its employees across the nation, there should not be great disparities in treatment arising solely from an accident of geography. The lack of comparable class action legislation elsewhere in Canada, except for British Columbia and Quebec is a telling argument for extending the reach of the Ontario legislation. We must somehow as Professor Sander says, "fit the forum to the fuss." . . .

> Here, I regard the common interests of the class members, the commercial realities of the situation, and the broad objectives of the Ontario *Act*, as outweighing any concerns expressed over extra territorial involvement of the Ontario Court.[35]

Moreover, the learned Justice relied heavily on the purposes of the Ontario *Act*, one of which was to "modify the behaviour" of potential defendants. The fact that much of the "behaviour" being "modified" was *outside* Ontario in fact may even have encouraged Brockenshire J. to exert jurisdiction over plaintiffs in the other provinces, because he viewed the lack of a class proceedings statute in those provinces as something of an "accident," rather than as a democratic choice of the respective legislatures. This was, prior to *Dutton*, a problematic analysis from the standpoint of legislative territoriality, because it extended the benefits and burdens of class proceedings into provinces where such actions were not possible.

More starkly, in a subsequent decision in the same case,[36] Brockenshire J. directed that lawyers be appointed to conduct hearings in the class members' home provinces and make recommendations as to the quantum owed by K-Mart to particular individuals. Recognising that this represented a significant extraterritorial leap of his Court's authority, the learned Justice cited La Forest J. in *Morguard*,[37] and Winkler J. in *Carom* who had said "*Morguard* and *Hunt* permit the extraterritorial application of legislation where the enacting Province has a real and substantial connection with the subject matter of that action and it

---

35. *Webb* v. *K-Mart Canada Ltd.* (1999), 45 O.R. (3d) 389 at 404 (Gen. Div.).

36. *Webb* v. *K-Mart Canada Ltd.* (1999), 45 O.R. (3d) 425 (Sup Ct. J.).

37. *Morguard* above note 14 at 1095 ("The business community operates in a world economy and we correctly speak of a world community even in the face of decentralised political and legal power. Accommodating the flow of wealth, skills and peoples across state lines has now become imperative.")

accords with order and fairness to assume jurisdiction."[38] The same "full faith and credit" device was rather summarily invoked to overcome objections that such persons were not "officers of the Court" within the meaning of Ontario law.[39]

In denying leave to appeal in *Webb*,[40] MacFarland J. said that:

> Courts must adjust to the realties of modern commercialism which is not only national but international in many instances. Practical solutions to such problems can and must be crafted to respond to modern reality. This is just such a case.

More recently, Cumming J. in *Wilson* clearly confirmed that Ontario's jurisdictional analysis for national opt-out classes was based on *Hunt's* "due process"-based *ratio*. Cumming J. said:

> [84] In determining procedurally whether non-Ontario residents are to be included within an Ontario class action, a court must be guided by the requirements of order and fairness: see *Hunt*, at p. 326.
>
> . . .
>
> [93] This approach is efficacious in extending the policy objectives underlying the CPA for the benefit of non-residents. If there are common issues for all Canadian claimants, this approach facilitates access to justice and judicial efficiency, and tends to inhibit potentially wrongful behaviour. This is to the advantage of all Canadians and to Canada as a federal state. This procedural flexibility serves in the nature of oil in the institutional and jurisdictional machinery of Canadian federalism. Courts in Australia and the United States, both federal states, have addressed similar issues in like manner: see generally *Femcare Ltd* v. *Bright*, [2000] FCA 512 (April 19, 2000) (Australia); *Shutts*, above.[41]

Perhaps unfortunately, Cumming J. did not take this principle to its logical end, because he proposed that his Court's "national jurisdiction" should be truncated by class actions begun in other provinces:

> [94] Mass torts and defective products do not respect provincial boundaries. Complex and costly litigation is not viable for individual claimants. The procedural latitude of the CPA recognises the authority of all provinces and the rights of their individual residents. If a non-resident of Ontario wishes to commence an action in another province, that person can opt out of the Ontario action. If a class action is commenced and certified in either British Columbia or Quebec, that certified class proceeding will take precedence for the residents of that province.[42]

At the time *Wilson* was decided, there were only two other provinces where comparable actions could be begun; thus the "national class" would be preserved, at least for over half of Canada's population. Since Saskatchewan and Newfoundland now have B.C.-pattern statutes, and after the advent of the "com-

---

38. *Webb*, above note 36 at 430 citing *Carom*, above note 32 at 450.
39. *Webb*, above note 36 at 431-432.
40. *Webb* v. *K-Mart Canada Ltd.* [1999], O.J. No. 3286 at para. 10 (C.A.).
41. *Wilson* v. *Servier* (2000), 50 O.R. (3d) 219 at paras. 84, 93 (Sup. Ct. J.).
42. *Ibid.* at para. 94

mon law class action" in *Dutton*, there are nine (or if the territories are included, twelve) other jurisdictions that might host actions that "take precedence" over the national class with respect to those places. In such a way, the national class rather boldly forged by the Ontario courts risks being chipped away – undone, somewhat ironically, precisely because the value of aggregation has become universally recognised and class litigation has spread across the country.

(4) National Classes in Quebec

Like Ontario's, Quebec's statutory regime does not mention the inclusion of non-resident members in class actions. However, unlike those of Ontario or B.C., Quebec's courts have been reluctant to state definitively whether they believe it appropriate to certify an opt-out national class, and indeed have yet to undertake any consideration of the "order and fairness" or "real and substantial connection" tests set out by the Supreme Court of Canada.[43]

Prior to *Morguard* and *Hunt*, the Quebec courts suggested in *obiter* that any class certified should be restricted to claimants who were either residents or who could trace their cause of action to Quebec.[44] More recently the Quebec courts appear to be interpreting the legislation more liberally. In *Masson* v. *Thompson*,[45] the Quebec Court of Appeal refused to overturn certification on the grounds that the opt-out class included members who were resident outside the province. A subsequent decision, *Bourque* v. *Laboratoires Abbott Ltée*[46] also certified a national class. In neither of these decisions did the courts take the opportunity to canvass the issues thoroughly. Moreover, in *Bourque*, it may be that the Court was reasoning along the lines of the old equitable representative actions, reducing the decision's precedential value somewhat.[47]

---

43. Ward Branch, "Chaos or Consistency? The National Class Action Dilemma" (Branch McMaster January 24-25, 2002) www.branmac.com (accessed February 15, 2002).

44. *Werner* v. *Saab-Scania AB*, [1980] C.S. 798 (Que. S.C.), aff'd (unreported, February 19, 1982) Montreal 500-09-001005-800 (C.A.). See also *Bolduc* v. *Compagnie Montreal Trust* (1989), 15 A.C.W.S. (3d) 214 (C.S.C.).

45. *Masson* v. *Thompson*, [1994] R.J.Q. 1032 (S.C.); aff'd [1995] R.J.Q. 329, 67 Q.A.C. 75 (C.A.).

46. Bourque v. *Laboratoires Abbott Ltee* (unreported, April 9, 1998) Montreal 500-06-000023-966 (Que. S.C.).

47. The Court relied in part on the fact that the relief sought – a return of certain funds to a pension plan – would benefit all class members equally. In this sense, the inclusion of the non-resident members was irrelevant unless and until the Quebec action failed and the defendant attempted to bar subsequent actions on the same issue in other jurisdictions.

(5)   National Classes in British Columbia

British Columbia's statute deals explicitly with the issue of extraterritoriality. It provides that foreign class members may benefit from and be bound by a decision on an "opt–in" basis,[48] and the B.C. Court of Appeal, at least in *obiter*, has suggested that this is the only basis on which non-residents might be included.[49] This avoids the worst of the due process conundrums presented by "opt-out" classes with extra-provincial members, but nonetheless it has the ability to affect extraterritorial rights, particularly when the "opting in" foreign class member is trying to take advantage of the host's *Class Proceedings Act* to toll the *Limitations Act* in his own jurisdiction.

What justification do courts provide for extending their reach into other provinces? Certain of the rhetoric in Smith J.'s decision in *Harrington* v. *Dow Corning Corp.*,[50] a breast-implant case, suggests that interprovincial members should be allowed, as "the only practical avenue for relief" for persons, both within and without the province, without otherwise viable claims.[51] This sidesteps the question of whether the availability of a "practical avenue for relief" should depend solely on the presence of one group within the forum with a class action statute. It is ordinarily of no concern to the courts of B.C. that an individual in Manitoba may not pursue an action because he is barred by Manitoba's limitations laws. Should they suddenly be concerned with providing such an avenue of relief simply because there are B.C. residents with similar complaints against the same defendants? This is an unnecessarily shallow argument.

Viewing the *Hunt* requirements broadly, the majority of the B.C. Court of Appeal in *Harrington* expanded Smith J.'s analysis by saying that, with respect to national class certification, "Where the traditional rules are not adequate to ensure fairness and order then other considerations will become relevant . . . By the action of sale, the manufacturer risks an action in any province . . . there can be no injustice in requiring a manufacturer to submit to judgment in any Canadian province."[52]

In her decision for the Court, Huddart J.A. said that certification of a national (opt in) subclass:

> . . . accords with requirements of comity, and with the policy underlying the enactment of legislation enabling class actions to determine the liability of defendants

---

48.   B.C. s. 16(2).

49.   *Harrington* v. *Dow Corning Corp.*, 2000 BCCA 605 at para. 85 ("Section 16(2) *may* preclude the court from certifying a national class on an opting out basis, as was done [by the Ontario Court] in *Nantais*" [emphasis added]). This *obiter* aside, the court probably does retain an inherent jurisdiction to design methods of national resolution of class actions: see footnote 81 below and accompanying text.

50.   *Harrington* v. *Dow Corning Corp.* (1996), 22 B.C.L.R. (3d) 97 (S.C.).

51.   *Ibid.* at para. 56.

52.   *Harrington* v. *Dow Corning Corp.*, 2000 BCCA 605 at para. 92.

for mass injury in one forum to the extent claimants may wish and fairness to the defendants may permit.[53]

The Court emphasised the due process interests of "fairness," but failed to give the idea much substance beyond the rhetorical:

> The fundamental values are fairness to the parties and orderly decision-making ... broad principles of order and fairness must prevail. A decision whether a court has jurisdiction must not depend on a mechanical application of a rigid test.

> Some cases will not require a court to move beyond the traditional rules. If a defendant is within the jurisdiction or has submitted to judgment by agreement or attornment or if a wrong has been committed within the jurisdiction, the test will normally be satisfied. This is the result because no injustice results from a court taking jurisdiction in such cases and orderly decision-making within Canada is respected.[54]

The *Harrington* Court went on to consider the issue of foreseeability as an aspect of procedural fairness or due process, bolstering its arguments with the same "order and fairness" arguments which have influenced the Supreme Court of Canada when considering jurisdiction over individual products liability claims after *Moran* v. *Pyle*:[55]

> Where the traditional rules are not adequate to ensure fairness and order then other considerations will become relevant. One such consideration will be the nature of the subject matter of the action. In this case, the alleged wrongful acts are defective manufacture or failure to warn. When a manufacturer puts a product into the marketplace in any province in Canada, it must be assumed that the manufacturer knows the product may find itself anywhere in Canada if it is capable of being moved. As I suggested earlier in these reasons, it is reasonable to infer that a manufacturer of a breast implant knows that every purchaser will wear that implant wherever she resides, and that if the implant causes injury then the suffering will occur wherever she resides, and require treatment in that location. By the action of sale, the manufacturer risks an action in any province. In these circumstances, there can be no injustice in requiring a manufacturer to submit to judgment in any Canadian province. The concept of *forum non conveniens* is available to deal with any individual case where a different forum is established as more appropriate. As Mr. Justice La Forest remarked in the passage I quoted from *Tolofson*,, above, in some circumstances individuals need not be tied to the courts of the jurisdiction where the right arose, but may choose one to meet their convenience.[56]

The reasoning offers a bridge between the Ontario "national class" decisions and the U.S. "due process" cases. It allows Canadian courts to break away from a slavish devotion to the "real and substantial connection" test, and consider more directly the broader question of "order and fairness."[57] Unfortunately, though, apart from importing elements of the products liability jurisdiction

---

53. *Ibid.* at para. 85.
54. *Ibid.* at paras. 95-96.
55. Above note 5.
56. *Harrington*, above note 52 at para. 97.
57. Peter W. Hogg, *Constitutional Law of Canada* (Toronto: Carswell, Looseleaf) at

jurisprudence going back to *Moran* v. *Pyle*, the decision adds little real help. It is analysed, as one would expect in an opt-in case, from the position of fairness to the defendant, and quite correctly dismisses this concern as irrelevant – a manufacturer cannot claim to be surprised to be haled into court in a single province for wrongs it did in every province. However, the case does not provide any real analysis of the constitutional limits of the legislative reform manifest in the *B.C. Act.*

(6) Analysis

As noted earlier, it seems that at least one motivating factor behind the decision of most provinces to include only "opt-in" nonresident subclasses is a concern over the "fairness," and perhaps even the constitutionality of, binding persons in other jurisdictions who do not "opt out."[58] Now, several years later, the constitutional question is still not definitively settled.

The *Morguard* and *Hunt* decisions have important ramifications for class actions, because in order for a true national class (i.e. an opt-out or even mandatory class) to be successfully prosecuted, the courts of other jurisdictions must recognise the *lis pendens*, or the authority of the forum court at a very early stage (i.e. at certification) if duplication of claims is to be avoided. Unlike in ordinary actions, one could not rely upon the defendant to object to duplicative proceedings, as indeed the defendant may benefit strategically from a fragmented plaintiff class. Moreover, this recognition would need to remain well after the litigation was concluded, through recognition of judgments, and bars to future claims by the class members under the principle of *res judicata*.

In individualistic litigation and in opt-in class actions, the question of jurisdiction arises only with respect to the defendant because the plaintiff, as the initiator of the suit, is attorning to the jurisdiction of the forum court. Opt-out class actions present a somewhat different picture, as it is also the absent *plaintiffs* who will be bound by the decision.

One solution is to hold that judgments are enforceable only with respect to those extraprovincial class members who have sufficient "minimal contacts" or "real and substantial connection" with the forum state, essentially mirroring the

---

13.5(b) says "the [American] due process test . . . could as easily serve as a test of extraterritoriality under the Constitution of Canada."

58. See The Alberta Law Reform Commission's *Report on Class Action Legislation* (Final Report #85, 2000) [*Alberta Report*] at 99 (recommending opt-in for nonresidents "for constitutional reasons"). So far, only the Manitoba Law Reform Commission has recommended following Ontario's lead and permitting opt-out national classes. The Manitoba Law Reform Commission, *Class Proceedings* (Report #100) (Winnipeg: Manitoba Publications Branch, January 1999) at 31, 66 (acknowledging that opt-out national classes are desirable and in fact, following *Morguard* and *Hunt*, binding throughout the country).

test for absent defendants. This solution is less than satisfactory for a number of obvious reasons. First, in a mass tort, there may be hundreds or thousands of class members in other provinces. Clearly the court cannot, in advance, consider the "real and substantial connection" with respect to each *claim*; it can only be assured that, because the claim concerns the same defendant and the same allegations, it is connected with "the subject matter" of the litigation. Nor is it, post-*Morguard* and *Hunt*, any longer legitimate to consider the entire matter only upon enforcement. *Hunt* holds that the initial court either has jurisdiction or it does not; if it does, effect must be given to its pronouncements.[59] There is no basis for imagining a "conditional" existence of individual non-resident claims that comes into being upon certification, with the non-resident claims neither before the court nor absent from it, like Schrödinger's cat, neither alive nor dead until the claims are individually judged in hindsight.[60]

Nor are the problems simply theoretical. Requiring a connection between absent class members and the *forum* would make developing an estimate of the non-resident opt-out class a realistic impossibility. It will disrupt the admission of evidence (if it is done on an aggregate basis through statistical and epidemiological evidence[61]), but most of all it will render settlement vexingly difficult, as neither party will be able to quantify the size of the class or the damages. This

---

59. *Hunt*, above note 23 at 1103 per LaForest J. ("the taking of jurisdiction by a court in one province and its recognition in another must be viewed as correlatives.") and see 1094. This is supported by the analysis of the B.C. Court of Appeal in *Jordan* v. *Schatz* 2000 BCCA 409 at para. 27 ("Jurisdiction simpliciter is not a matter of discretion. Either a court has it or it does not based on the existence of a real and substantial connection between the jurisdiction and the defendant or the cause of action.").

60. Thus the *obiter* of Zuber J. in *Nantais*, above note 28 at 206 that the effect of an order "remains to be seen", and that the "law of *res judicata* may have to adapt itself to the class proceeding concept" should be approached with some caution. Zuber J. did not follow through with an analysis of the operation of *res judicata* and the question has not come before any court since. This cannot mean, however, that individual *res judicata* hearings must be held for absent class members based on individual connections between the members' claim and the class proceeding. Such hearings could not possibly assist the successful and certain resolution of mass tort claims. Also, as noted, such "ex-ex-post" resizing of the class will produce an information deficit that will almost certainly lead to patterns of suboptimal settlement amounts or, worse, higher incidence of claims proceeding to trial: Yeon-Koo Che "Equilibrium Formation of Class Suits" (1996) 62 J. Pub. Econ. 339. *More likely* Zuber J. was proposing a blanket re-conceptualising of the binding *res judicata* effect of interprovincial judgments in the mass tort concept to achieve a binding national class.

61. With the class unknown, how could evidence be introduced on such an aggregate basis? Each statistical analysis of causation or damages would be met by the defen-

"solution" leads inexorably to the conclusion that the only out-of-province participants could be "opt-in" claimants as permitted under the B.C./*ULCC* model.

Another solution is that provided by the United States Supreme Court, which has held that out-of-state plaintiffs may be bound on an opt-out basis, providing actual notice is given. In *Phillips Petroleum Co.* v. *Shutts*,[62] the U.S. Supreme Court had decided that out-of-state plaintiffs could *not* invoke the same due process limits on personal jurisdiction that out-of-state defendants had enjoyed under *International Shoe Co.* v. *Washington*[63] and its progeny.[64] In other words, there was not a constitutional requirement of connection with the jurisdiction before an absent *plaintiff* could be bound. However, the Court did hold that due process required that the member "receive notice plus an opportunity to be heard and participate in the litigation," and said that "at a minimum . . . an absent plaintiff [must] be provided with an opportunity to remove himself from the class."[65]

The *Shutts* principles are important, because the analysis used in the United States – with "minimal contacts" as indicia of "due process" – is essentially identical to the Canadian test outlined in *Hunt*, requiring "real and substantial connection" as an element of "order and fairness."[66] Nevertheless, *Shutts* still suggests that non-resident class members may be entitled to greater due process than those within the forum state.

A third approach is to allow extraterritorial plaintiffs to be bound by the decisions of the forum court on whatever grounds the local plaintiffs might be; in other words, to decide that "sufficiency of notice" or "procedural fairness" need not mean something distinct when the border is crossed. It is this approach that has persuaded the courts of Ontario, which have repeatedly certified opt-out national classes in a series of cases since *Nantais*.[67]

---

dant saying "yes, but we have no idea if the sample is accurate, as we do not know, even in an aggregate sense, who is a member of the class".

62. *Shutts*, above note 29.

63. *International Shoe Co.* v. *Washington*, 326 U. S. 310 (1945).

64. *Shutts*, above note 29 at 806-808. *Shutts* was a state class action for small sums of interest on royalty payments suspended on the authority of a federal regulation. After certification of the class, the named plaintiffs notified each member by first-class mail of the right to opt out of the lawsuit . Out of a class of 33,000, some 3400 exercised that right, and another 1500 were excluded because their notices could not be delivered. *Ibid.*, at 801. After losing at trial, the defendant argued that the state court had no jurisdiction over claims of out-of-state plaintiffs without their affirmative consent.

65. Ibid. at 812.

66. See footnote 57 and accompanying text.

67. *Carom* v. *Bre-X Minerals Ltd.* (1999), 43 O.R. (3d) 441 (Gen. Div.); *McKrow* v. *Manufacturers Life*, [1998] O.J. No. 4692 (Gen. Div.); *Macrae* v. *Mutual of Omaha Insurance Co.* (unreported, July 14, 2000, Court File No. 24257/96

The Ontario experience raises as many questions as it offers answers. First of all, many of these actions were certified as "national classes" with the defendants' consent, which raises considerable conceptual difficulties.[68] Still others appear to have anticipated a sort of national consolidation from the outset, and might prove poor models for cases in which various plaintiffs' counsel are not as cooperative.[69]

The decision of Winkler J. in *Carom* v. *Bre-X* (at p. 450) is typical of the reasoning behind the decision to certify nationally on an opt-out basis:

> *Morguard* and *Hunt* permit the extra territorial application of legislation where the enacting province has a real and substantial connection with the subject matter of the action and it accords with order and fairness to assume jurisdiction.

Note here that "real and substantial connection" is between the jurisdiction and the "subject matter of the action"; this is the way that the Ontario courts have reasoned "bootstrapping" claims which do not, individually, have any independent connection with Ontario.

Nevertheless, as I have described, even the Ontario courts have sometimes shied away from purporting to impose a *truly* national class. Recall that in *Wilson* v. *Servier*, Cumming J. said (at para. 94), after certifying a purportedly national class:

> If a class action is commenced and certified in either British Columbia or Quebec, that certified class proceeding will take precedence for the residents of that province.

(Ont.Sup. Ct. J.)); *Chadha* v. *Bayer Inc.* (1998), 82 C.P.R. (3d) 202; *Webb* v. *K-Mart Canada Ltd.* (1999), 45 O.R. (3d) 389 (Gen. Div.); *Robertson* v. *Thomson Corp.* (1999), 43 O.R. (3d) 161 (Gen. Div.); and *Wilson* v. *Servier* (2000), 50 O.R. (3d) 219 (Sup. Ct. J.).

68. This appears to be the reason that such decisions were not more controversial (the exceptions have produced the only real analyses of the constitutional issues, as in *Nantais*, above note 28, *Carom*, and *Wilson*, both *ibid.*). This raises the issue squarely: if it is truly the litigative rights of out-of-province *plaintiffs* that is of concern, why should it matter that the *defendant* and the local plaintiffs agree that the class should bind them?

69. *Wilson* v. *Servier* is a very interesting example. In *Wilson* (a Phen-Fen diet drug litigation), a national class was certified in Ontario, encompassing all provinces with the exception of Quebec: (2000), 50 O.R. (3d) 219 (Sup. Ct. J.). At the Ontario certification hearing, counsel for the representative plaintiff in a related B.C. action appeared and announced that if the national class were certified, the B.C. plaintiff would apply for inclusion as representative of a B.C. subclass. This is in fact what happened: [2001] O.J. No. 1615 (Sup. Ct. J.), and the B.C. action was not pursued. It would therefore appear that the B.C. action was filed as a "safety"; i.e. in order to "head off" a similar action by competing, non-aligned counsel, and also to have in reserve in case B.C. claims were not accepted by the Ontario Court.

Mr. Justice Cumming offers no support for this idea,[70] and indeed it seems to ignore the spirit, if not the letter, of the rules enunciated by the Supreme Court of Canada. The passage suggests that Ontario courts would, presumably through exercise of "comity," defer to a certification in British Columbia, at least with respect to B.C. class members. However, it does not at all confront the more central question: why should B.C. courts not defer to the initial decision made in Ontario to certify a national class including B.C. residents, and refuse to certify a competing class? Remember, this is not a question of *forum conveniens*; under "full faith and credit," the only ground on which the B.C. court could *refuse* to recognise the Ontario "national class" certification decision would be if Ontario did not have jurisdiction over the claims (and clearly Cumming J. believes it does). This is not a question of which process provides the *most* order, fairness, or due process, it is a simple yes or no: did the original court properly exercise its jurisdiction? If yes, if there is sufficient "order and fairness" in Ontario to justify jurisdiction over B.C. claims, then that is the end of the analysis; following *Morguard*, a B.C. court would simply not have jurisdiction to certify a subsequent,[71] competing claim, and if it did there is no basis for Cumming J.'s assumption that it would "take precedence" over the Ontario action.[72]

---

70.   He does cite the previous decision of Zuber J. of the Ontario Divisional Court in *Nantais*, above note 28 at 114 (D.L.R.):

> It is also argued that other class proceedings may be certified in other provinces relating to the matter which is the subject of this class proceeding. In my respectful view any of these practical difficulties which may develop as the matter proceeds can be met by amending the order in question to adjust the size of the class. If it is shown that the law of another province is so substantially different as to make the trial with respect to class members from that province very difficult, the class can be redefined. Additionally, if a class is certified in another province that group can be deleted from the Ontario class.

> Again, the suggestion in *Nantais* above note 28, that the forum court could "pare down" its national class if a competing class is certified ignores the question of whether an overlapping class *can* be certified given the original certificiation. Perhaps, if the originally-certifying court does in fact qualify its certification with a commitment to reduce the national class if other jurisdictions certify (as arguably Zuber and Cumming JJ. did), then subsequent certifications may be constitutionally permissible even under a "full faith and credit" paradigm. But if no such qualification is made, there seems to be no theoretical basis upon which a subsequent certification will "take precedence" over the original national class .

71.   The problem would not arise, of course, if the B.C. case was certified *first* on a province-wide basis; a subsequent certification in Ontario should then acknowledge the B.C. jurisdiction over such cases.

72.   This raises the question again: upon whose motion would certification be refused? In this case, the defendant might wish a separate B.C. class, because its economy of scale advantage is more pronounced if the plaintiffs are split into two camps. Nor

Moreover, in the wake of the "common law class action" designed by the Supreme Court of Canada in *Dutton*, there are now *nine* other provinces and three territories in which competing claims might be filed. In Cumming J.'s paradigm, each subsequent certification would be valid, and the original "national class" would be pared down, province by province. Each subsequent action would mean a reduction in the economy of litigation scale, and each would mean a marked disincentive for the original plaintiffs' counsel to maximally invest, as its potential recovery would be constantly shrinking.

This flaw is not necessarily fatal. Just as cooperative agreements are made in individualistic mass tort litigation, we might expect class counsel in the various provinces to cooperate to various extents, as they appear to have done to good effect in *Wilson* v. *Servier*.[73] It may even be the case that a single, national law firm will emerge to file simultaneously in each province. However, far preferable would be a uniform system of consolidation for class proceedings in particular. Consider that if a firm wished to prepare for consolidation of a national class along the lines of that achieved in *Wilson* v. *Servier*, it would have to file in nine or ten jurisdictions and then apply (presumably in Ontario) for an opt-out national class anticipating the inclusion of the eight or nine individual non-resident subclasses. Once consolidated, the challenge would then be for the consolidating court to issue orders preventing competing actions as they emerged in other jurisdictions. Analytically, the problem turns full circle; if a court can issue such orders *after* consolidating, it should have been able to issue them concomitant to originally certifying a national class.

Another problem that follows from the "provincial classes" model is the problem of "free riders." Once discrete opt-out classes are certified in the respective jurisdictions (and assuming that there are no prior cooperation agreements in place among class counsel), then there will be a strong incentive to wait until a claim is pursued elsewhere, in order to gain the benefit of the work product.[74] In such circumstances, class members in the leading jurisdiction can expect a lower percentage of the aggregate award than those in "following" jurisdictions, assuming that the lawyers' fees are set with some relationship to effort expended.[75] Worse still is the potential for agency problems: assuming that fees

---

would counsel for the representative plaintiff wish to see his action barred through operation of comity. In such a case, and without a national consolidation mechanism in place, the only proper route would be for the court to hear an application for the original national class.

73. See above note 69 and accompanying text.

74. This is particularly so if counsel for a "following" class can obtain a court order for the full sharing of the fruits of discovery.

75. If, on the other hand, the awards are made entirely on a percentage of recovery basis, then the leading province's class counsel will be undercompensated, the free riding counsel will be overcompensated, and the class members will still recover less than they would have through a single national class.

are calculated, at least partially, on the basis of class recovery, the class counsel's incentive is to proceed slowly, against the interests of the class. This phenomenon might lead class counsel in competing jurisdictions to negotiate with one another, not in the interests of maximising aggregate recovery, but in the interests of maximising their respective fees, again to the detriment of overall aggregate recovery.

To their credit, Ontario courts have resisted arguments based on the alleged interests of some fictitious non-resident plaintiff whose "rights" are being offended. Sharpe J. (as he then was) in *Robertson* v. *Thomson Corp.*, dealing with the possibility of foreign nationals being included in a class said, "In my view the possibility that such questions might arise elsewhere with respect to an atypical class member cannot be sufficient to defeat this claim from proceeding in Ontario."[76] Yet we ought to be cautious not to draw the line solely on demographics; there is no reason that a class action ought not to be commenced in Ontario even if the *majority* of those affected are outside the province.

There is support for this idea in the Supreme Court, which has acknowledged that we are not, in Twenty-first-century Canada, dealing with the vast disparity of legal systems against which the original English rules of "private international law" were meant to guard. As La Forest J. noted in *Morguard*, "fair process is not an issue within the Canadian federation."[77] His Lordship had earlier expanded on those aspects of Canadian federation that made Canadian court systems well integrated and homogenous:

> The Canadian judicial structure is so arranged that any concerns about differential quality of justice among the provinces can have no real foundation. All superior court judges — who also have superintending control over other provincial courts and tribunals — are appointed and paid by the federal authorities. And all are subject to final review by the Supreme Court of Canada, which can determine when the courts of one province have appropriately exercised jurisdiction in an action and the circumstances under which the courts of another province should recognise such judgments. Any danger resulting from unfair procedure is further avoided by sub-constitutional factors, such as for example the fact that Canadian lawyers adhere to the same code of ethics throughout Canada. In fact, since *Black* v. *Law Society of Alberta*,, above, we have seen a proliferation of interprovincial law firms.[78]

---

76. *Robertson* v. *Thomson Corp.*, [1999] O.J. No. 280 at para. 45 (Gen. Div.).

77. *Morguard*, above note 14 at 1103.

78. *Ibid.* at 1100. Unfortunately, the *Morguard* Court did not deal directly the problem of what would happen if the legislature of one province imposes through statute a procedural scheme that *is* unfair. Would the legislature be barred from doing so in order to preserve the "fair process" within the "Canadian federation" as a whole? Or would the courts then be instead in a position to judge whether another province's legislation constitutes "fair process"? This question was not addressed until *Hunt*, above note 23.

I have already remarked on *Morguard's* apparent dismissal of the notion that the courts of each province are limited by the jurisdiction granted them by their respective provincial legislatures. A lively debate exists in the United States over whether courts' adjudicative jurisdiction over multi-state classes is restricted by the ability of the sovereign – i.e. the individual state – to grant jurisdiction to its courts. But here, the Supreme Court appears to be emphasising that, with respect to the superior courts of the various provinces, the sovereign is the same: it is the Crown, and to a large extent it is the federal Crown.[79] This observation would appear to preclude any suggestion that jurisdiction must be viewed as arising from two sources – private "due process" and legislative "sovereignty" – as some in the United States have argued,[80] and instead a Canadian court considering the limits of its jurisdiction over non-resident class members might consider only the former.

Importantly for some of the analysis that follows, the superior courts of the various provinces retain the inherent powers to impose national classes that they had prior to the class proceeding acts' advent.[81]

Some compromise of plaintiff autonomy inheres to class litigation; it is recognised that this trade-off is necessary in order to preserve the considerable advan-

---

79.   Especially in cases of "horizontal" disputes between the provinces, rather than "vertical" disputes between a province and the federal government. See Jason Herbert, "The Conflict of Laws and Judicial Perspectives on Federalism: A Principled Defence of *Tolofson* v. *Jensen*" (1998) 56 U.T. Fac. L. Rev. 3 (referring throughout (apparently without irony) to the courts' role as "horizontal umpires").

80.   Diane A.T. Wood, "Adjudicatory Jurisdiction and Class Actions" 62 Ind. L.J. 597 (1986) at 623.

81.   Provincial superior courts, like U.S. state courts, are courts of inherent jurisdiction: *C.H.R.C.* v. *Canadian Liberty Net*, [1998] 1 S.C.R. 626 at para. 35. This provides a "residual source of powers, which the court may draw upon as necessary whenever it is just and equitable to do so, in particular, to ensure the observance of the due process of law, to prevent improper vexation or oppression, to do justice between the parties and to secure a fair trial between them": *Halsbury's Laws of England*, vol. 37, 4th ed. (London: Butterworths, 1982) at para. 14. The Supreme Court of Canada has accorded inherent jurisdiction both a substantive and a procedural meaning: *Société des Acadiens du Nouveau-Brunswick* v. *Association of Parents for Fairness in Education*, [1986] 1 S.C.R. 549 at paras. 94 – 95.

In the latter case, the Court held that a court may exercise its inherent jurisdiction in respect of matters regulated by statute as long as it does so without contravening or conflicting with a statutory provision. In fact, even in the face of comprehensive statutory provisions, courts retain a residual discretionary power to grant relief unless they have been *explicitly* denied this through legislation (*Liberty Net*, above at paras. 10, 32) provided that (a) the subject matter is within the jurisdiction of the court, and (b) that the court has taken into consideration all the relevant factors: *Société des Acadiens, ibid.* at para. 123.

tages arising from claims integration. No effective class action system could insist that the court's jurisdiction over each *plaintiff* is as "solid" as that over each defendant. If so, there would have to be formal notice to each class member as there must be to each defendant; in such a case, a class proceeding would be reduced to a simple voluntary joinder of action. When considering whether it is "unfair" to non-resident plaintiffs to be included in an action without their explicit consent (and perhaps without their knowledge), one must weigh the dangers against the advantages of optimal claims aggregation. Requiring actual notice for non-resident claims will severely limit the size of many, if not most classes. It will also make the number of claimants involved *less*, rather than more, certain.[82] Under such circumstances, it would be impossible for an aggregation of claims to achieve optimal deterrence, optimal compensation, or accurate settlement. The national class is thus important in the interests, not only of tort objectives generally, but also of each class member, when viewed from the ex ante perspective emphasised throughout this book.

The Ontario courts have never openly confronted the true issue underlying the national class: that is to say, they have never acknowledged that the defendants' litigation scale economy is national, and therefore so must be the plaintiffs'. As a result, Ontario decisions are inconsistent in their defence of the opt-out national class. In *Webb* v. *K-Mart*, for instance, the Court said that "[t]he lack of comparable class action legislation elsewhere in Canada, except for British Columbia and Quebec, is a telling argument for extending the reach of the Ontario legislation."[83] This somewhat imperialist view echoed one U.S. court's binding of Canadian class members to its own decision, excepting only those who lived in class action provinces.[84] In *Carom*, the statute was simply being described as

---

82. That is to say, while the number in the class will be more certain as an absolute number, the defendant would not know how many additional claims it might face outside the class, and therefore what proportion of all claims relating to its mass tort it is confronting.

83. *Webb* v. *K-Mart* above note 67 at 404. The Court found at para. 58:

    In my view, we have here a single corporate decision by a corporation carrying on business across the country that is alleged to have adversely affected people who are working for it from coast to coast. Our provincial court systems are struggling to deal with situations where there is a nation wide impact. So are the state courts in the United States. Obviously, from the points of view of both the national corporation and its employees across the nation, there should not be great disparities in treatment arising solely from an accident of geography . . .
    We must somehow as Professor Sander says, "fit the forum to the fuss."

84. This decision was additionally distasteful in that the Canadian members bound by the court received a lower level of compensation than their American counterparts. In Re *Silicone Gel Breast Implant Products Liability Litigation* (1994) U.S. Dist. LEXIS 12521 (N.D. Al. 1 Set 1994). Contra: *Bersch* v. *Drexel Firestone Inc.* 519 F.2d 974 at 986 (2d Cir. 1975).

"replete with provisions guaranteeing order and fairness."[85] These are defensive arguments, and unconvincing ones at that. An approach based on more than deontological assertions of "justice" is needed to support a robust national class action regime. Closer to the truth might be Professor Sander's remarks that we must "fit the forum to the fuss";[86] however, the best explanation offered in *Webb* as to *why* we must do so is to avoid a disparity of treatment across the provinces, an assertion with no more real substance than those that have come before. There are many variations among provinces on matters of substantive law, particularly tort law. Why should the recovery in *Webb* be uniform when the recovery in any "ordinary" actions should not? These questions were left unanswered, because they have never been actually asked. I suggest here that the Ontario approach is *correct*, but I acknowledge that it has never been adequately *explained*.

Nor, given the benefits of optimal (i.e. maximal) aggregation, is it desirable for courts or legislatures to simply throw up their hands and allow extraprovincial subclasses on an "opt-in" basis alone. In fact, even if viewed entirely from the point of view of the rights of extraterritorial class members, there is no reason to suppose that constitutional interests in "fairness" and "justice" militate in favour of this "province-by-province" litigation model. If it is accepted that individual ex ante preferences favour maximal aggregation, then it might be argued that British Columbia, or any other single province for that matter, *cannot* constitutionally require that non-residents may only participate on an "opt-in" basis.

This assertion would appear counterintuitive or bizarre until it is considered in a functionalist paradigm, based on the simple assertion that no single province has the constitutional authority to enact legislation that will reduce the recovery of class members in other jurisdictions. Constitutional objections to the national class generally focus on the possibility that it might deprive non-resident class members of their right to pursue an individualistic resolution of their respective claims. So, the argument goes, a provincial court or legislature cannot deprive persons of rights held outside its borders.

But consider if the matter were framed the other way. If it is accepted that only full aggregation of all claims will allow the type of litigation investment that will maximise potential recovery, and if the claimants reside in more than one province, then a legislature that insists that non-resident members "opt-in" to a subclass may be denying all class members the opportunity to maximise their recovery.[87] They may have the right to restrict their own citizens' recovery in this way (though significantly none has), but why does that right extend to the citi-

---

85. See footnote 34 and accompanying text.

86. Cited in *Webb*, above note 83.

87. Throughout this analysis I am assuming that "opt-out" actions will generally produce a larger and more universal class than "opt-in" actions. This seems to be uncontroversial in most foreseeable cases. See *Alberta Report*, above note 58 at 93 ("An opt in regime tends to produce a smaller class and is therefore preferred by those with defendant interests.")

zens of other provinces? In other words, by certifying an opt-out class effectively restricted to the province, a court is *de facto* denying residents of all other provinces the fullest recovery to which they are entitled, *even if they are allowed to pursue a similar action in their own jurisdiction on an opt-out basis.*[88] This is affecting "property and civil rights" in other provinces, and could therefore be impermissibly extraterritorial, at least with respect to mass torts with demonstrably interprovincial impact.

D. "FAIRNESS" TO THE DEFENDANT: THE PROBLEM OF LIMITATION PERIODS

(1) Substantive or Procedural Law?

Whenever the courts have considered the question, class action legislation has been regarded as procedural, and not substantive, law.[89] It is accepted that the procedural law of the forum, the *lex fori*, will always guide the court hearing a matter. However, it has also recently been held that it is the *lex loci delicti*, the law of the place of the tort, which is the substantive law to be applied. This is where the problem begins.

Tolofson v. *Jensen*[90] was a case involving a British Columbian child who was injured while riding in a car driven by his father in Saskatchewan. The defendant was resident in Saskatchewan. The plaintiff brought action in British Columbia because Saskatchewan law barred him there.[91] The defendants brought an application by consent to determine whether the B.C. court was *forum non conveniens* or whether Saskatchewan law applied.

For present purposes, the Supreme Court in *Tolofson* made two important holdings based upon its belief that the rules of "order and fairness" set out in *Morguard* and *Hunt* gave preeminence to "order":

> While, no doubt, as was observed in *Morguard*, the underlying principles of private international law are order and fairness, order comes first. Order is a precondition to justice.[92]

According to the Court, "order" required hard and fast rules respecting choice of law with respect to limitation periods. The first rule set out in *Tolofson* was

---

88. This is because, even if the non-resident members begin a class action in their own jurisdiction on an opt-out basis, the national class is still bifurcated and optimal litigation investment is denied. One might view the legislature's act as one essentially pulling its citizens out of a potential national class, to the detriment of all.

89. See note 24 in Chapter Two and accompanying text.

90. *Tolofson* v. *Jensen*, [1994] 3 S.C.R. 1022.

91. The limitation period had run; moreover, Saskatchewan law, unlike that of British Columbia, did not permit a gratuitous passenger to recover, absent wilful or wanton misconduct of the driver of the car in which he or she was traveling.

92. *Tolofson*, above note 90 at 1058.

that limitation periods gave rise to substantive rights of repose, and were therefore substantive law, as going to the "right" rather than the "remedy." This represented a significant departure from the common law tradition. The corollary rule established in *Tolofson* was that the substantive law to be applied was (at least with respect to choice of law problems between domestic jurisdictions[93]) always the law of the place of the tort, or the *lex loci*.

(2) The *Tolofson* Dilemma

If limitation periods are substantive law, then by the same token, statutes which extend limitation periods are regarded as substantive as well.[94] They grant the right to sue where it would not otherwise exist, and moreover they serve to defeat the right of the defendant to be free from suit, a right which vests upon the expiry of the limitation period.

Canadian class action legislation provides that limitation periods will be suspended while certification is decided.[95] This device is to assist plaintiffs who, absent the provision, may find that their limitation period has run by the time that the certification is denied, and that they have thus lost the right to sue individually.

But the problem, by now, should be clear: if a court is faced by a "national class" that purports to include members from each of the provinces, and if those members suffered the harm (and thus the tort was committed) in their respective home provinces, then those extraprovincial plaintiffs are restricted by (and the defendants are assisted by) the limitation periods in each "foreign" province following the new "choice of law" rules established by the Supreme Court of Canada.

The possibility exists, therefore, that a plaintiff might exhaust his limitation period in, say, Alberta while he is waiting for the B.C. class action to be certified. Moreover, the defendants in B.C. could argue that the extraprovincial limitation period actually continues to run until the trial is concluded. If such an

---

93. LaForest, for the majority, held that no exception to the *lex loci delicti* rule would be permitted within Canada, but that one might be justified in international choice of law cases. The minority would have allowed the possibility for exceptions even within Canada (*ibid.* at 1078 per Sopinka J.):

> . . . I doubt the need in disposing of these appeals to establish an absolute rule admitting of no exceptions. La Forest J. has recognised the ability of the parties by agreement to choose to be governed by the *lex fori* and a discretion to depart from the absolute rule in international litigation in circumstances in which the *lex loci delicti* rule would work an injustice. I would not foreclose the possibility of recognising a similar exception in interprovincial litigation.

94. *Stewart v. Stewart* (1997), 145 D.L.R. (4th) 228 (B.C.C.A.).

95. B.C. s. 39; Ontario s. 28; Quebec Civil Code ss. 2897, 2908.

argument were accepted, it would virtually bar plaintiffs in other provinces from tort-based class actions. A "national class" would be a practical impossibility.

The question of the conflict between class proceeding legislation and limitations statutes applicable in non-resident class members' jurisdictions has not yet been fully explored by a Canadian court. Nevertheless the conclusion that plaintiffs who are statute-barred in their home jurisdictions might not be included in a class action suit afforded some justification to deny certification in *Bittner* v. *Louisiana-Pacific Corp.*:

> [These problems] create different interests between class members and the various jurisdictions. The provincial distinctions increase management difficulties by requiring the court to consider multiple legal regimes, and will result in the creation of individual trial processes that are sensitive to choice of law issues. In my view, those are problems which . . . cumulatively constitute a bar to certification.[96]

In Ontario, Winkler J. in *Carom* considered the issue of limitations and came to the opposite conclusion:

> The defendants also argue that s. 28 of the *CPA*, which provides for the suspension of limitation periods upon commencement of a class proceeding, cannot apply to residents outside the province. I disagree. If the *CPA* applies it applies in its entirety, subject to a determination on the question, should it arise, in the other jurisdiction. Further, no prejudice to the defendants results. A non-resident plaintiff could not avoid the binding effect of s. 27(3) [binding effect of judgments] while at the same time claiming the benefit of s. 28 [limitations tolling]. Either both sections will have effect or neither will have effect.[97]

This argument essentially sidesteps the question of provincial territoriality raised by the defendant, and focuses squarely on the procedural fairness to the defendant vis-à-vis class members both within and without the jurisdiction. In other words, it did not address the underlying question of an Ontario action, facilitated through statute, binding non-resident members who do not opt out. The defendant in *Carom* may have felt that if it could shift the Court's analysis to one of *legislative* territoriality and away from "fairness," it would prevail on the limitations question. At the time *Carom* was decided, this may have been persuasive; however, as I will argue below, it is less so today since the Supreme Court of Canada's decision in *Dutton*.

(3) Analysis

(a) A Fairness-Centred Approach

In essence, the rights which accrue upon the expiry of a limitation period are said to be the defendant's. The policy reasons behind the accrual of these rights are many and varied, but they essentially depend on the assumption that a defendant should not be surprised, years down the road, by a lawsuit which he is not adequately able to defend because of the passage of time.

---

96. *Bittner* v. *Louisiana-Pacific Corp.* (1997), 43 B.C.L.R. (3d) 324 at 338-39 (S.C.).
97. *Carom* v. *Bre-X Minerals* (1999), 43 O.R. (3d) 441 (Gen. Div.).

But how does such a right accrue to a defendant in a national class action? Clearly, a defendant who has notice of a class action suit proceeding on a particular issue in B.C., and also has notice that the action may include plaintiffs from the foreign jurisdiction, can be said to have notice that the suit is being filed, and suffers no prejudice, as Winkler J. suggested in the passage from *Carom* v. *Bre-X* reproduced above. Why should such a defendant be able to stand on his rights with respect to those foreign claims?

On the other hand, Winkler J. is perhaps incorrect when he suggests that, once it is established that the Ontario court has jurisdiction over the defendant, the Ontario legislation must be applied in its entirety, including its substantive provisions, to torts committed entirely in other jurisdictions. Certainly Winkler J. offered no support for this proposition that a statute must be considered either "procedural" or "substantive" as a whole (indeed the idea seems counterintuitive as many statutes contained both types of provisions). Nor is it adequate to suggest, as Winkler J. did, that the question is more properly decided by subsequent actions in foreign jurisdictions; a non-resident class member should know, in advance, whether he is relinquishing his right to sue should certification be denied after his limitation period has run.

Although there is no decision regarding the ultimate effect of the expiry of limitations periods in other jurisdictions, The *Harrington* Court, confronted with the defendants' argument that the limitations problem should bar certification, possibly missed the gist of the objection[98] when it stressed the question of "fairness" and the defendants' reasonable expectations in a mass tort case:

> [98] The appellants are manufacturers of an allegedly defective product for personal use which they market throughout Canada. Such a person must anticipate the possibility of being haled into any Canadian court. The issue of that product's fitness is common to all purchasers wherever they reside. The Supreme Court has properly accepted jurisdiction over all claims by purchasers resident in British Columbia. The appellants are defending those claims. The Supreme Court has certified an issue common to all purchasers for resolution in a class proceeding. These are compelling reasons for British Columbia courts to accept jurisdiction. British Columbia has more than a little interest in accommodating a national resolution of this dispute.

> [99] New types of proceedings require reconsideration of old rules if the fundamental principles of order and fairness are to be respected. To permit what the appellants call "piggy backing" in a class proceeding is not to gut the foundation of conflict of laws principles. Rather, as I have tried to explain, it is to accommodate the values underlying those principles. To exclude those respondents who do not reside in British Columbia from this action because they have not used the product

---

98. Mr. Justice Finch, writing for the majority, appears to be perplexed that the limitations issue is raised at all at the certification stage. He apparently considered the issue to be simply another defence that would be evaluated in the fullness of time, not a question of a "ticking clock" that could lead to the expiry of non-resident class members' rights of action even while the B.C. courts proceeded with the trial: *Harrington*, above note 52.

in British Columbia would, in these circumstances, contradict the principles of order and fairness that underlie the jurisdictional rules. By opting-in the non-resident class members are accepting that their claims are essentially the same as those of the resident class members. To the extent the appellants can establish they are not, they can be excluded by order of the case management or trial judge upon application . . .[99]

Unfortunately, following *Tolofson*, it is not easy to adopt a more flexible rule from U.S. mass tort jurisprudence: that substantive law of the forum may apply if such an application is not violative of the defendant's due process rights. In *Shutts*, the U.S. Supreme Court found that applying the law of the forum (Kansas) to all the claims (97% of which arose in other jurisdictions) was unjust *if the laws of those fora were substantially different so that applying the forum law would violate the expectations of the parties* .[100]

Recently, the Canadian Supreme Court analysed the nature of limitation laws in *Novak* v. *Bond*, [1999] 1 S.C.R. 808. Madam Justice MacLachlin (as she then was) said for the majority at para. 64:

> In *Peixeiro* v. *Haberman*, [1997] 3 S.C.R. 549, this Court affirmed its earlier iden-tification of the traditional rationales of limitations statutes in *M. (K.)* v. *M. (H.)*, [1992] 3 S.C.R. 6, at pp. 29-30. Limitations statutes were held, at p. 29, to rest on "certainty, evidentiary, and diligence rationales." In *M. (K.)*, above, this Court noted at pp. 29-30:
>
>> Statutes of limitations have long been said to be statutes of repose . . . . The rea-soning is straightforward enough. There comes a time, it is said, when *a poten-tial defendant should be secure in his reasonable expectation* that he will not be held to account for ancient obligations . . . .
>> The second rationale is evidentiary and concerns the desire to foreclose claims based on stale evidence. Once the limitation period has lapsed, the potential defendant should no longer be concerned about the preservation of evidence rel-evant to the claim . . . .
>> Finally, plaintiffs are expected to act diligently and not "sleep on their rights"; statutes of limitation are an incentive for plaintiffs to bring suit in a timely fash-ion.
>
> It is apparent that these rationales generally reflect the interests of the potential defendant. *Murphy* v. *Welsh*, [1993] 2 S.C.R. 1069, at pp. 1079-80, *per* Major J. *They rest on the view that a potential defendant should not have to defend a stale claim brought by a plaintiff who has chosen not to assert his or her rights diligently* [emphasis added].

Moreover, as the dissenting Justices in *Novak* v. *Bond* remind us at para. 8, the "discoverability" doctrine developed as an equitable exception to limitations statutes:

This equitable doctrine constitutes an incursion on the limitations period to account for the fact that it would be unfair to require a plaintiff to bring a law-suit "before he could reasonably have discovered that he had a cause of action."

---

99.   *Ibid*. paras. 98-99.
100.   *Shutts*, above note 29 at 814-823.

Novak and the cases it cites might tend to support the conclusion that the class proceedings legislations' limitation-tolling provisions may indeed prevent a defendant from relying upon a limitation period running in a foreign jurisdiction, if it is in the interest of "order and fairness" in all the circumstances of the case to do so. Possibly, Canadian courts might reintroduce the questions asked by the U.S. Supreme Court in *Shutts,*, above: (a) what proportion of the plaintiffs' claims are governed by the foreign limitation periods; (b) to what extent are the limitation laws in the foreign jurisdiction materially different; and therefore (c) would the defendant suffer significant prejudice from the application of the forum's limitation laws?[101]

The adoption of "order and fairness" as the standard for determining the extraprovincial reach of legislation might also assist courts in avoiding unjust results, as when, for instance, slavish devotion to the private choice of law principles is unsatisfactory. The B.C. Court of Appeal in *Stewart* v. *Stewart* considered itself bound to apply the *Tolofson* rule, even when the resulting dismissal of an action would be unfair:

> If I were free . . . to apply British Columbia limitation law, I would do so. The application of the limitation law of Saskatchewan to this case will not produce a "more just result." Indeed, it will produce a patently unjust result.[102]

The "fairness" argument against the applicability of other provinces' limitation periods may have received a substantial boost from the Supreme Court of Canada's decision in *Dutton*,[103] where the Court determined that citizens of provinces without class proceeding legislation nonetheless might exploit the vestigial "representative action" rule to similar effect.

Remember that, in *Hunt*, the expectations of the defendant in the context of nationally marketed products weighed significantly in the Court's decision to reject the application of the Quebec "blocking statute." In the end, questions of territoriality were reduced to questions of jurisdiction:

> The problem in the end, then, involves issues of jurisdiction and whether that jurisdiction should be exercised. The British Columbia courts . . . dismissed a challenge to jurisdiction, and leave to this Court was refused. That is scarcely surprising. The case would appear to be similar to *Moran* v. *Pyle National (Canada) Ltd.*, [1975] 1 S.C.R. 393, where a corporation that had in one province manufactured goods that were defective was sued in a province where the plaintiff suffered damage as a result. As here, the manufacturer must be taken to have known that the goods would be used outside the province of manufacture in the manner they were. Given the significant connection with the province where the injury took place, it is difficult to see how it could be said to offend the principles of order and fairness for the British Columbia courts to take jurisdiction. A court might, I suppose, also be

---

101. It could certainly be argued, for instance, that the prejudice is less with respect to jurisdictions who also have class proceedings statutes with limitation-tolling provisions.

102. *Stewart*, above note 94 at 232.

103. 2001 SCC 46.

asked to consider whether it should decline jurisdiction on the basis of the doctrine of *forum non conveniens*. Indeed the court in *Hunt* v. *T&N*, above, was asked to decline jurisdiction. But in my view the court was right to refuse to do so. The additional factor that the case involved the British Columbia court in considering the interpretation and constitutional validity of the Quebec statute is not, given the considerations that weigh in favour of the British Columbia court's exercising jurisdiction, sufficient to make a court of that province a *forum non conveniens*.[104]

Later in *Hunt* there is an interesting passage suggesting that "order and fairness" might guarantee that an "accident of geography" did not defeat a plaintiff's litigation rights:

> The lack of order and fairness in the present situation is evident in a further incongruity. It is that full rights of discovery are available to parties in the civil procedure of Ontario and Quebec. It is not as if these jurisdictions have a totally different tradition of civil procedure. If the litigation was proceeding in either of those provinces there would be full discovery. And if both parties to the action had been from British Columbia there would be discovery. But somehow, because of the fortuitous combination of litigation in British Columbia involving a defendant from Quebec or Ontario, the discovery process is barred.[105]

This argument is directly applicable to the question of limitations. Following *Dutton*, class claimants in *both* B.C. and Alberta would have a right to redress through class litigation (and presumably associated rights of limitations tolling) if they pursued the matter within their own province. The "fortuitous combination" of simultaneous harm in several jurisdictions should not be able to defeat these rights.

Nevertheless, applying "order and fairness" as the operating principle will still probably require that the court employ one of two devices to "overcome" the *Tolofson* dilemma in order to accommodate mass torts. First, the courts might draw a limited exception to the *lex loci delicti* in domestic mass tort cases, as the minority would perhaps have allowed; alternatively, they might decide that limitations periods are not *always* substantive. In either case, the result would be to allow the limitations rules of the forum to prevail, including the limitations tolling provision. Either method is arguably consistent with *Morguard, Hunt*, and the notion of "order and fairness." However, it is regretably not consistent with the absolutist language of *Tolofson* itself. *Tolofson* must, if such an argument were to succeed, yield, and "order and fairness" must be reintroduced as a factor in determining choice of law questions, at least regarding limitation periods, at least in cases of mass tort.

For now, the courts have been able to sidestep the problem, perhaps content in the knowledge that the cases before them will almost certainly settle without the question of limitations periods ever being decided. From a system design point of view, this is unfortunate, as it will lead to a distortion of the settlement amount to the extent that plaintiffs' otherwise valid claims are cast into doubt by

---

104. *Hunt*, above note 23 at 315-16.
105. *Ibid*. at 330-31.

uncertainty over applicable limitation bars, something which should be, in theory, a fairly straightforward question.

(b) A Legislative Territoriality Approach

A second method of dealing with the *Tolofson* dilemma in national classes is to employ principles of legislative territoriality to hold provincial limitation periods inapplicable to cases in other provinces whose courts have taken jurisdiction properly.

One of the seldom-discussed aspects of the *Hunt* decision was its holding that the courts of one province may pass judgment on the constitutionality of the laws of another. Mr. Justice LaForest said:

> [P]rovincial superior courts . . . are the ordinary courts of the land having inherent jurisdiction over all matters, both federal and provincial, unless a different forum is specified; see *Ontario (Attorney General)* v. *Pembina Exploration Canada Ltd.*, [1989] 1 S.C.R. 206, at pp. 217-18.

He went on to cite the decision of Estey J. in *Attorney General of Canada* v. *Law Society of British Columbia* (the *Jabour* case):

> . . . The provincial superior courts have always occupied a position of prime importance in the constitutional pattern of this country. They are the descendants of the Royal Courts of Justice as courts of general jurisdiction. They cross the dividing line, as it were, in the federal-provincial scheme of division of jurisdiction, being organized by the provinces under s. 92(14) of the *Constitution Act* and are presided over by judges appointed and paid by the federal government (sections 96 and 100 of the *Constitution Act*).[106]

LaForest J. in *Hunt* continued:

> This approach . . . is supported by previous cases from as early as *Valin* v. *Langlois* (1879), 3 S.C.R. 1, where Ritchie C.J. emphasised that these courts "are not mere *local* courts for the administration of the local laws" (p. 19) but "are the Queen's Courts, bound to take cognizance of and execute all laws, whether enacted by the Dominion Parliament or the Local Legislatures" (p. 20) (emphasis added). See also Pigeon J. in *R.* v. *Thomas Fuller Construction Co. (1958) Ltd.*, [1980] 1 S.C.R. 695, at p. 713.

> This jurisdiction must include a determination of whether the laws sought to be applied are constitutionally valid. In Laskin J.'s words in *Thorson* v. *Attorney General of Canada*, [1975] 1 S.C.R. 138, at p. 151: "The question of the constitutionality of legislation has in this country always been a justiciable question." This was also referred to in *Northern Telecom*, above, where Estey J. stated, at pp. 741-42:

> > It is inherent in a federal system such as that established under the *Constitution Act*, that the courts will be the authority in the community to control the limits of the respective sovereignties of the two plenary governments, as well as to police agencies within each of these spheres to ensure their operations remain

---

106. *Attorney General of Canada* v. *Law Society of British Columbia*, [1982] 2 S.C.R. 307 at 326-27.

within their statutory boundaries. Both duties of course fall upon the courts when acting within their own proper jurisdiction. The *Jabour* case, above, was concerned with the superior courts of general jurisdiction in the provinces, but the same principles apply to courts of subordinate jurisdiction when they are acting within their limited jurisdiction as described by their constituting statute. Such courts must, in the application of the laws of the land whether they be federal or provincial statutes, determine, whenever the issue arises, the constitutional integrity of the measure in question. Such a court of limited jurisdiction must, of course, be responding to a cause properly before it under its statute.

That is scarcely cause for surprise.

Later, Mr. Justice LaForest said:

> This approach is even more persuasive where, as here, the issue relates to the constitutionality of the legislation of a province that has extraprovincial effects in another province . . . [I]t is simply not just to place the onus on the party affected to undertake costly constitutional litigation in another jurisdiction.

In *Hunt*, the Court would find that a Quebec "blocking statute" that barred the release of documents for out-of-province discovery, while not invalid on its face, was constitutionally inapplicable to discovery conducted in other provinces. Recall LaForest J.'s hostility to the Quebec "blocking statute" in *Hunt*, *inter alia*, because its purpose was to "impede successful litigation" in other provinces, with the effect of discouraging interprovincial commerce and "efficient allocation and conduct of litigation."[107] Earlier I suggested that this decision represented a value judgment, favouring B.C.'s discovery laws over Quebec's.

Consider this aspect of *Hunt* when applied to limitation periods. *Hunt* provides a convenient analytical device for an Ontario court confronted by a defendant which says that it intends to rely upon the limitation periods in force in non-resident jurisdictions to bar the claims of non-resident class members from those jurisdictions. The court need not accomplish its objective (the ignoring of the expiry of the out-of-jurisdiction limitations periods) by holding that the limitations-tolling provision in the Ontario *Act* is "procedural" (which it clearly is not if limitation rights themselves are substantive, as the Supreme Court held in *Tolofson*). Rather, the Ontario court can simply hold that "order and fairness" require that the other provinces' (otherwise valid) limitation periods are *inapplicable*[108] to a case over which the Ontario court properly has jurisdiction. Like the "blocking provision" in *Hunt*, a limitations act from outside Ontario cannot operate to defeat relief granted in Ontario, providing the Ontario court has jurisdiction. This serves *Hunt*'s objectives of "efficient allocation and conduct of litigation," which, absent some valid competing constitutional interest,[109] appear

---

107. *Hunt*, above note 23 at 327.

108. Note that this is different from finding that a statute is invalid due to extraterritoriality, as in *Churchill Falls*, above note 18.

109. And what could the competing constitutional interest be? As mentioned, the only reason generally offered in support of limitations periods is to prevent the defen-

to form a sufficient basis for preferring the law of the class's forum over the law of the province seeking to enforce its "blocking" limitations period.

E. "FAIRNESS" TO THE PLAINTIFF: THE PROBLEM OF NOTICE AND THE NATIONAL CLASS

The question of whether an "opt-out" national class should be allowed is generally viewed as a question of fairness to the prospective plaintiffs, and it is usually framed this way: under what conditions would it be fair to bind persons in other jurisdictions to the decision of the forum court? Once the questions of legislative and judicial territoriality are answered in general terms by saying that it is not *per se* unjust to bind non-residents, attention will focus on the sufficiency of notice to them. The question has received, over the years, substantial consideration in the United States under Federal Rule 23 and similar state legislation, and more recently in Australia under the "representative action" provisions of the *Federal Court of Australia Act*[110] and equivalent state legislation.

The leading U.S. case, mentioned in the previous section, is *Phillips Petroleum Co.* v. *Shutts*.[111] In that case, the Supreme Court held that a Kansas state court could not bind absent plaintiff members of the class in a "common question" class action (brought under a state rule virtually identical to Federal Rule 23(b)(3)) unless the plaintiffs were provided with "minimal procedural due process protection," including the right to opt out.[112] Rehnquist J, speaking for the Court, said this (at 811-12):

> If the forum State wishes to bind an absent plaintiff concerning a claim for money damages or similar relief at law, it must provide minimal procedural due process protection. The plaintiff must receive notice plus an opportunity to be heard and participate in the litigation, whether in person or through counsel. The notice must be the best practicable, "reasonably calculated, under all the circumstances, to apprise interested parties of the pendency of the action and afford them an opportunity to present their objections..'.. Additionally, we hold that due process requires at a minimum that an absent plaintiff be provided with an opportunity to remove himself from the class by executing and returning an "opt out" or "request for exclusion" form to the court.[Citations omitted.]

The decision of the Court was specifically restricted to class actions which seek to bind *known* plaintiffs concerning claims wholly or predominantly for money judgments.[113]

---

dant from being surprised by suit, an interest that is preserved equally well by the filing of a national class action in another province as it is by filing it locally.

110. *Federal Court of Australia Act 1976* (Cth), Pt IVA.

111. 472 U.S. 797, 105 S.Ct. 2965, 86 L.Ed.2d 628 (1985).

112. Id. at 811-12, 105 S.Ct. at 2974.

113. There is a question whether this decision has application to types of class actions such as those seeking equitable relief. *Shutts*, above note 29 at 811 n. 3, 105 S.Ct. at 2974 n. 3.

In the *DES Cases* Weinstein J. noted that the Supreme Court decision in *Shutts*, "suggest[s] the need for modified jurisdictional analysis in the special context of mass litigation."[114] The Eastern District Court found that, because national class actions are necessary to provide relief where it might otherwise be unattainable, *Shutts* adopted a lower standard of "minimal procedural due process" – i.e. to replace the "minimal contacts" standard with sufficiency of notice and opportunity to opt out.[115]

This position can be seen as essentially analogous to those of the Ontario courts since *Nantais*: provided that the imposition of a national class did not offend a minimal due process requirement, the interests of justice required the Court to engage in the "time-honored jurisdiction stretching technique of implied consent to cope with the special problem of jurisdiction in mass class actions. . . ."[116] Yet *Nantais* did not impose additional requirements of notice for extraprovincial plaintiffs, nor examine the sufficiency of notice differently for out-of-province claims.

As mentioned, though, in *Shutts*, the class members were known and it was possible to contact most individually to apprise them of the lawsuit and their right to opt out.[117]

In Australia too, the High Court has rejected the notion that an opt-out national class is barred from certification, provided that sufficient notice is given to nonresidents. The standard of notice was recently described in *Femcare Ltd.* v. *Bright*[118] as follows:

> In determining what is "*reasonably*" practicable and not "*unduly*" expensive for the purposes of s 33Y(5), the Court is bound in our view, to take account of the possible adverse consequences to a group member of the representative proceeding as well as any possible benefits. A value judgment is required. Plainly the Court would be more likely to be satisfied that personal notice **is** reasonably practicable and **not** unduly expensive if an adverse determination will have significant consequences for a group member. Moreover, s 33Y(5) must be understood in its statutory context. This includes s 33ZF, which empowers the Court to make any order it thinks appropriate to ensure that justice is done in the proceeding.

---

114. In Re *DES Cases*, 789 F. Supp. 552, 576 (E.D.N.Y. 1992) *appeal dismissed*, 7 F.3d 20 (2d Cir. 1993).

115. *Ibid*. 789 F. Supp. at 576.

116. *Ibid*. at 577.

117. It is interesting that in *Shutts*, the final class as certified contained 28,100 members; 3400 had "opted out" of the class by returning the request for exclusion, and notice could not be delivered to another 1500 members, who were also excluded. The Supreme Court did not explicitly discuss, though, whether excluding those who did not receive the notice would be constitutionally required, an important question if notice was by less certain means than registered mail, if it was effected for instance through advertisements: *Shutts*, above note 29.

118. *Femcare Ltd.* v. *Bright*, [2000] FCA 512 (H.C.A.).

In assessing the requirements of the judicial process it is also important to bear in mind the objects underlying s 33Y(5). As the extract from the [Law Reform Commission's] *Grouped Proceedings* report . . . shows, the objective is to find the most economical means of ensuring that the group members are informed of the proceeding and their rights. The LRC considered that *"the more at stake for each person, the more effective the notice should be."* It also took the view that the procedures adopted should not shut out the very cases for which the representative procedure is most appropriate — claims involving small individual claims which are large in aggregate. [emphases in original].[119]

However, it is somewhat inapt to cite *Femcare*, as did Cumming J. in *Wilson v. Servier*, as directly analogous to the U.S. Supreme Court's decision in *Shutts* and the Ontario decisions of *Nantais* and *Bre-X* simply on the basis that Australia too is a federal system. While the High Court in *Femcare* was indeed seeking to define a procedure that would meet due process standards, it was doing so within the confines of a valid *federal* act, as opposed to the provincial legislation in the Ontario cases. In other words, the Australian Court was not considering the extraterritorial competence of the certifying court or enabling legislation. While the decision, and its reasoning, are helpful on the issue of appropriate notice, it is not unreasonable to argue that notice requirements for non-resident class members ought to be somewhat more stringent than those appropriate for persons within the jurisdiction.[120] A more useful Australian example might be that of the State of Victoria's group proceedings provisions. There, the legislation allows the Court to decline class members where "the person does not have sufficient connection with Australia to justify inclusion as a group member."[121] This distinction, wherein even though the legislation is based in the state, the minimal contacts are considered with respect to the entire nation, is similar to that which I propose here. The constitutionality of the Victoria Act's extraterritorial reach has recently been upheld by the High Court of Australia in *Mobil Oil Australia Pty Ltd.* v. *State of Victoria & Anor.*[122]

This is not to say that any of the "national classes" certified in Ontario would not have been certified had this analysis been applied. In fact, they very likely

---

119. *Ibid.* at paras. 73-4.

120. This is so for a number of reasons: a non-resident member, unlike a resident, is not presumed to know the forum's law, and would not ordinarily expect to be bound by an order of the forum's court. Such a distant non-resident will also be less likely to hear of the claim but for the notice.

121. *Victoria Supreme Court Act 1986* Part IVA ("Group Proceedings") (as amended by *Courts and Tribunals Legislation (Miscellaneous Amendments) Act 2000*) [*Victoria Act*], s. 33KA(2)(a).

122. *Mobil Oil Australia Pty Ltd.* v. *State of Victoria & Anor*, [2002] HCA 27.

would have been.[123] No case in Ontario has determined whether, as implied in *Shutts*, there ought to be more stringent notice requirements for non-resident members of an opt-out class.

There is a further complicating factor in the wake of the *Dutton* decision, which sets out the rules for class actions in provinces without comprehensive legislation, and which might be read as requiring that there be *actual notice and opportunity to opt out* in such cases.[124] Recall that, in *Dutton* the S.C.C. held:

> [35] Absent comprehensive codes of class action procedure, provincial rules based on Rule 10, Schedule, of the English Supreme Court of Judicature Act , 1873 govern. This is the case in Alberta, where class action practice is governed by Rule 42 of the Alberta Rules of Court :
>
> > 42 Where numerous persons have a common interest in the subject of an intended action, one or more of those persons may sue or be sued or may be authorized by the Court to defend on behalf of or for the benefit of all.
>
> [36] The intention of the Alberta legislature is clear. Class actions may be brought. Details of class action practice, however, are largely left to the courts.

Note that there is nothing in the *Dutton* decision that suggests that the "common law class" must be restricted to provincial residents. In fact, the "class" that was eventually certified as a representative action in *Dutton* consisted of "231 foreign investors who lost money through investments under an immigration investment regime created by the Federal Government."[125] Moreover, the Supreme Court

---

123. For instance *Nantais*, above note 28 dealt with the wiring on heart pacemakers where the class members were notifiable, and the value of each claim relatively high; similarly, *Webb* v. *K-Mart*, above note 67 involved mass dismissals of employees by the defendant who can be taken to have known at least recent personal details of the class members; and *Carom* v. *Bre-X*, above note 67, a securities fraud case, had a class which was known and was in any event likely to be a "limited fund" case.

    Only the notice in *Servier*, above note 67 could be viewed as inadequate to a high U.S. style "due process" standard; apart from letters to "known" plaintiffs, the court required only a single publication in two newspapers, two magazines, and a medical journal [at paras. 150-1]. *Quaere* whether such notice is sufficient to defeat the rights of persons who had taken a popular diet drug and who may not know that they are ill. However, while Cumming J. in *Servier* did consider *Shutts* in certifying the "national class" before him, he did not explicitly address whether he felt himself bound to meet the higher standard of notice alluded to in that case and others since.

124. *Dutton*, above note 8 at para. 49.

125. *Western Canadian Shopping Centres Inc.* v. *Bennett Jones Verchere*, 1998 ABCA 392, 73 Alta. L.R. (3d) 227, 30 C.P.C. (4th) 1, 84 A.C.W.S. (3d) 838, 1998 A.C.W.S.J. LEXIS 56623, 228 A.R. 188, 188 W.A.C. 188 (C.A.). The non-resident status of the class members is not apparent in the Supreme Court decision that followed.

brushed aside concerns over the application of foreign laws, clearly signalling that it understood that this was a class originating in diverse jurisdictions.[126]

The Court discussed the question of notice as an aside because it was not at issue in *Dutton* (as all the investors were known and had apparently consented to participate in the action). Nevertheless, the Court seems to suggest that, if they hadn't, they would still be bound if they had been provided notice and the opportunity to opt out:

> A judgment is binding on a class member only if the class member is notified of the suit and is given an opportunity to exclude himself or herself from the proceeding. This case does not raise the issue of what constitutes sufficient notice. However, prudence suggests that all potential class members be informed of the existence of the suit, of the common issues that the suit seeks to resolve, and of the right of each class member to opt out, and that this be done before any decision is made that purports to prejudice or otherwise affect the interests of class members.[127]

There is persuasive reason to believe that the framework set out in *Dutton* for class actions absent statute permits interjurisdictional actions, either on an opt-in basis, as in *Dutton* itself, or following an opt-out pattern provided that adequate notice is given. This makes perfect sense. The Rules of Court, under which the decision is made, are just that – the rules applicable whenever the court has appropriately taken jurisdiction over a matter. They mirror the powers of a court in equity and are as binding upon non-resident parties as they are on resident parties. No one, for instance, would suggest that a court's power to issue injunctions pursuant to equity and its own rules was restricted to the province's borders; why should a modern "Bill of Peace" be so constrained? And yet, the question of differential notice remains unsettled.

Ironically, the "opt-in" requirement for foreign residents in the B.C. *Act* and *ULCC Model Act* was developed out of concern for the principles of territoriality and, by extension, out of concern for the rights and interests of residents in other jurisdictions. It is ironic because, as more provinces adopt the *ULCC Model Act*, class members both within *and* without each jurisdiction can expect to pay more for a class action, and receive less. This is because, upon universal acceptance of the opt-in non-resident model, Canada will be reduced (with the possible ongoing exception of Ontario) to a series of provincial opt-out classes. Consider the simplified example that follows.

---

126. The Court held, *Dutton*, above note 8 at para. 54:

    Different investors invested at different times, in different jurisdictions, on the basis of different offering memoranda, through different agents, in different series of debentures, and learned about the underlying events through different disclosure documents. Some investors may possess rescissionary rights that others do not. The fact remains, however, that the investors raise essentially the same claims requiring resolution of the same facts.

127. *Dutton*, above note 8 at para. 49.

Imagine a mass tort has occurred that has caused $1 million in damage across the country, and that this loss is equally spread among 10 provinces ($100,000 per province). Let us say that the class members are not known, so notice must be effected through advertising. The cost of using local media within the province is $10,000; the cost of taking advantage of the national media is $50,000.

Under the Ontario "national opt-out class" model, the representative plaintiff could spend $10,000 in each province for local media and another $50,000 in national media to be assured of the best possible notice in the circumstances. In such a case, the total cost spread across the entire class would be $150,000, consuming 15% of each class member's claim value.

To accomplish *exactly the same* notice under the competing ULCC model of several provincial actions, the representative plaintiff in each province would have to pay $10,000 to have only provincial coverage, and a further $50,000 for national coverage, the bulk of which would be "wasted" on other provinces. Each provincial class representative would therefore pay $60,000, or 60% of each class member's recovery.

Consider also that there is no reason to believe that notice is better handled locally, i.e. that it will be *more* effective simply because it is generated from within a class member's own province. In an age of increasingly national (and international) media, this model implies that it may even be less so.[128]

This example considers only the cost of notice. Duplication of litigation expense with each partitioning of the national class will serve to diminish further each member's recovery and moreover will reduce the bargaining position of the aggregate and thus depress settlement values. In other words, preferring provincial over national classes will mean that each member can expect not only a smaller piece of the pie, but also a smaller piece of a *smaller* pie.

This example emphasises the simple fact that obsession with territoriality in class actions does not come cheaply; the price is in fact paid, not only by non-resident class members, but also by those within the jurisdiction. In trying to preserve everybody's rights, the opt-in non-resident model renders everybody worse off, and possibly by a considerable margin.

In reality most losses will be more heavily concentrated in some provinces than in others. Depending on the expected per-member recovery, restricting opt-

---

128. For instance, doubling the investment in local media may be far less efficient than a small investment on a national scale. Consider a class member who resides in Manitoba and reads the *Globe & Mail* and watches CBC national television exclusively. It may not be cost-effective for a Manitoba-only class to advertise in these national sources as well as the purely local ones. On the other hand, this model demonstrates that a national class would *always* be able to avail itself of the most efficient combination of national and local media across the country.

out classes to provincial borders would also tend to reduce the number of valid suits brought as the smaller provinces are deprived of the economy of litigation scale. This would tend to reduce optimal deterrence, as the absolute number of claims brought throughout the country for a single tortious action would be reduced.

As suggested in the previous section on certification of national classes generally, there appears to be no persuasive argument to support the idea that notice requirements for a national opt-out class should be more stringent than those for a purely provincial class. All the same arguments made earlier, and particularly those dealing with the unitary nature of the Canadian judiciary, apply with at least the same force.

One can also consider how much more effective notice is likely to be in a national class compared to a multiplicity of provincial opt-out proceedings. It is difficult to argue, as those favouring territorial subdivision of opt-out rights must, that they are serving the interests of class members while making notice less effective and simultaneously more expensive. As such, the exercise provides another level of criticism of the ULCC "opt-in" model.

Still, there may be some who favour the U.S. *Shutts* approach as a reasonable compromise. In fact it too may be problematic in its overemphasis on the litigative autonomy of individual class members. Consider a case in which actual notice is, for one reason or another, impossible. *Shutts* requires the best possible notice under the circumstances, but it appears clear that the constitutionally-imperative notice for non-resident plaintiffs is a higher standard than that which might otherwise prevail in state courts.[129] Certainly in "numerous low value claims" situations, notice is irrelevant from a private law point of view. No one could pursue the issue in court on his own in any event, so there is no harm done by allowing the class to proceed as representative with only token notice.

In considering the notice requirements of a national opt-out class, therefore, some conclusions might be reached:

- It is not necessary to afford a higher level of notice to non-resident members, but it is not necessarily bad to do so, and indeed an opt-out national class will make notice more effective and/or cheaper on a per-claim basis.
- When considering adequacy of notice, a court might consider whether the per-member potential recovery justifies extraordinary steps to provide notice.
- In cases where, due to a low potential recovery amount, notice requirements may be sacrificed, it will often be better to provide excellent notice to only

---

129. See John C. Coffee Jr. "Mass Torts After 'Georgine' and 'Castano'" *The New York Law Journal* May 30, 1996: "The problem for defendants is, however, that *Phillips Petroleum* v. *Shutts* may impose higher and more costly notice requirements on such nationwide settlements in state court . . ."

part of the class than poor notice to the class as a whole (to allow greater assessment of the degree and tenor of the objections from those class members notified).

The key point, though, is that there is no reason to accept that notice that is sufficient within the forum province is not also sufficient in other Canadian jurisdictions.

CHAPTER NINE

—

Interprovincial Consolidations

A. INTRODUCTION

The purpose of consolidating proceedings is to save expense, avoid a multiplicity of pleadings and proceedings and avoid inconsistent judicial findings.[1] As such, the purposes of consolidation parallel closely those of class proceedings, particularly because mass torts that form the basis for class actions are frequently committed in several jurisdictions. However, the structure of the federal system might allow concurrent, and even overlapping, class claims to proceed simultaneously in situations where individual claims would almost certainly not.[2]

When viewed with the purpose of maximum aggregation, I have suggested that national opt-out classes appear to be the optimal method of adjudicating mass torts which have an impact across provincial borders. This requires that we consider the question of interprovincial consolidations, whether they involve numerous province-wide actions or several overlapping "national class" actions.

I canvass below several options available to courts and legislatures to facilitate consolidations of several smaller or overlapping actions into national classes,

---

1.   *Pilon* v. *Janveaux*, [2000] O.J. No. 4743 (Sup. Ct. J.); *The City of Toronto* v. *British American Oil Company Limited*, [1946] O.W.N. 398 (Master); *Goldhar* v. *J.M. Publications Inc.*, [2000] O.J. No. 843 (Sup. Ct. J.).

2.   In an ordinary individualistic litigation, the defendant has a strong motive to block a plaintiff from proceeding in two different fora. With class claims, this is not necessarily the case, as the defendant may benefit substantially from allowing the plaintiff class to be split into two or more.

and I divide my approach along the same lines, considering first methods that might be available to courts and parties under the current legislative and jurisprudential system; and second, methods that will require legislative intervention to be effective.

B. NATIONAL CONSOLIDATION UNDER EXISTING LAW

(1) Class Counsel-Driven Consolidations

One method of consolidation available under existing law would be for the class counsel to file opt-out claims in all affected provinces simultaneously, relying on the "common law class action" of *Dutton*[3] in those jurisdictions without a class proceeding statute. Once that is done, counsel could appear in one jurisdiction to request a consolidation order of those actions pursuant to its rules of court,[4] or alternatively to "roll them in" as subclasses in a single national opt-out class in Ontario. In theory, the claims could be filed and application made on the same day, and the matter settled in short order. It would remain to be seen how principles of *res judicata* might bar certification attempts in other jurisdictions should that in the forum fail.

This solution sidesteps the *Tolofson* dilemma by preserving limitation rights in each jurisdiction. Principles of comity would require that, once consolidation in the forum jurisdiction has been granted, the process of the forum court would be respected and further proceedings would be barred.[5]

---

3.   *Western Canada Shopping Centres Inc.* v. *Dutton*, 2001 SCC 46.

4.   In Alberta, for instance, the *Judicature Act*, R.S.A. 1980, c. J-1 gives the Court of Queen's Bench broad powers to avoid multiplicity of proceedings. Section 8 provides:

   > The Court in the exercise of its jurisdiction in every proceeding pending before it has power to grant and shall grant, either absolutely or on any reasonable terms and conditions that seem just to the Court, all remedies whatsoever to which any of the parties thereto may appear to be entitled in respect of any and every legal or equitable claim properly brought forward by them in the proceeding, so that as far as possible all matters in controversy between the parties can be completely determined and all multiplicity of legal proceedings concerning those matters avoided.

5.   In the United States, the Supreme Court has barred a shareholder's class from litigating claims in Federal Court that were not advanced at the time that the class settled an earlier state claim, invoking the terms of the settlement agreement (which barred future claims based on the impugned tender offer) and the requirement that the Federal Court must give the decisions of the State courts "full faith and credit": *Matsushita Electrical Industrial Co.* v. *Epstein* 516 U.S. 367 (1996).

(2) Certifying a National Opt-Out Class Outside Class Proceedings Legislation

In B.C., Saskatchewan or any other province using the "non-resident opt-in" model, a second option would be to apply for a national opt-*out* class, arguing that it is not explicitly forbidden by the legislation and is therefore permissible. Certainly the jurisprudence at present would not provide any explicit support for such an option, but there is a strong suggestion that the Supreme Court of Canada might look upon it sympathetically.

In all of the provinces which provide for inclusion of non-resident subclasses on an "opt-in" basis, the language is permissive, not mandatory. While the Acts say that a national class *must* be divided into resident and non-resident sub-classes, they describe only the terms on which non-resident plaintiffs "may" opt in to the action. They do not, in short, specifically preclude a national opt-out subclass. Certainly, B.C. courts have tended to read the provision as restrictive. However, when the Supreme Court of Canada set out the terms for certification *absent* class proceeding legislation in *Dutton*, arguably the rules of the game changed.

That is because the underlying constitutional concern that had been restraining the B.C. courts was whether they could justify affecting the litigative rights of a person in, say, Alberta. But this analysis depended entirely on the assumption that the right to affect litigative autonomy through inclusion in an opt-out class action was based in statute. In designing class litigation (and in particular opt-out class litigation) for jurisdictions without statutes, the Supreme Court of Canada removed that concern. After *Dutton*, an Alberta court does not need legislative authority to bind Albertans who are not before it on an opt-out basis. There is no reason to believe then, that a B.C. court would need legislative authority before it could bind those same Alberta residents, provided at least that *Dutton*'s notice requirements were observed.

In fact, a B.C. court's ability to bind Albertans is not constrained by legislative territoriality, but rather only by the principles of "comity" and "order and fairness" set out in *Morguard* and constitutionalized in *Hunt*. Following this line of reasoning, if it is not a violation of these principles for a court to impose an opt-out proceeding on plaintiffs *within* the territorial jurisdiction of the province (and clearly the Supreme Court of Canada would not have designed a common law rule that was, by its very nature, violative of order and fairness), then it cannot be violative of the same principles to do so with respect to residents of another province. Unless, that is, there is something inherent about the provincial border that renders something "unfair" on one side and not the other. In light of the fact that no province has attempted to overcome *Dutton* with "anti class action legislation," and indeed with more and more provinces enacting class proceedings statutes, such an argument would be difficult to make.

(3) Consolidation Through Injunction

It is not immediately clear why the problem of competing class representatives has been so successfully avoided in Canada. To date, there has only been one case in which the court has sought to choose between competing class plaintiffs; in all other cases, it would appear that, where competition was looming, accommodation was reached among counsel (as between Ontario – i.e. "national class" – counsel and those for the B.C. class in *Wilson* v. *Servier*[6]).

In the case that did consider the question, *Vitapharm Canada Ltd.* v. *F. Hoffman LaRoche Ltd.*,[7] the court was confronted with ten separate actions (all in Ontario) vying for class certification regarding alleged vitamin price-fixing conspiracies across Canada. The plaintiffs were various retail and wholesale firms, as well as some individuals. After considering the various options available, a single counsel group (which had been advancing five of the claims) was appointed lead counsel for carriage of all vitamins class actions. The remaining pending litigations that were entirely duplicative were stayed until further order of the court. Finally, there was a prohibition upon the commencement of new class actions related to the same subject matter without leave of the court save and except any class action commenced by the favoured counsel group. The Court held that:

> Factors to consider in determining who should be appointed as solicitor of record in a class action include: the nature and scope of the causes of action advanced, the theories advanced by counsel as being supportive of the claims advanced; the state of each class action, including preparation; the number, size and extent of involvement of the proposed representative plaintiffs; the relative priority of commencing the class actions; and the resources and experience of counsel. See generally *Newberg on Class Actions* (West Group, 1992), 3d ed, s. 9.35, pp. 9-96 and 9-97.

> . . . There is nothing in the record to suggest that any putative representative plaintiff(s) for the retail purchasers might be a preferable choice in representing class members.

> The record indicates both competing counsel groups have given considerable thought to the action(s) on behalf of the retail purchasers. The record also establishes that the Strosberg/Siskind counsel group has done more extensive research to this point in time into the alleged complex web of conspiracies and the appropriate approach for an economic analysis as to damages.

> Which counsel group should be given carriage and appointed solicitors of record in the circumstances of the class action vitamin litigation in Ontario?

> The approach offered by the Borden group of having one action for the retail purchasers that proceeds in tandem with the reconstituted actions pursuing the claims of all persons other than retail purchasers introduces many disadvantages. First, it multiplies the global assessments two-fold from a probable five to ten, since it is

---

6. See footnote 69 in Chapter Eight and accompanying text.
7. *Vitapharm Canada Ltd.* v. *F. Hoffman LaRoche Ltd.* (2000), 4 C.P.C. (5th) 169, 2001 A.C.W.S.J. LEXIS 22101 (Ont. Ct. Gen. Div.).

agreed there must be a global assessment. Moreover, this must be done on a product by product basis. This means there would have to be at least five global assessments (assuming only five different products) for the reconstituted actions and five more for the Horvath action as retail purchasers were involved in respect of each product.

Thus, the approach of the actions continuing to proceed in tandem multiplies the expense significantly. It would also leave open the possibility of different, and conflicting global assessments for a given product. As well, the global assessment for a given product would be in itself meaningless without discounting, and removing, the assessment by the loss attributable to the retail purchasers in the reconstituted actions. At the same time it would be necessary to discount the global assessments in the Horvath action by the amount of the loss attributable to all claimants other than the retail purchasers, to leave remaining the isolated amount of the damages suffered by the retail purchasers. This complex determination would have to be done on a product by product basis, that is, probably at least ten times.

In my view, and I so find, the least expensive method of determining the common issues requires that all actions except the Strosberg/Siskind counsel group actions be stayed. This approach avoids needless complexities and confusion through trying to deal with the retail purchaser claimants for all products in a single class proceeding, being the Horvath action. It is preferable to have the reconstituted actions which isolate in separate actions the divergent interests that may well result from different products used by the retail purchasers. Moreover, as I have said above, there are different groups of defendants from product to product.

At the same time, having the same counsel for all the reconstituted actions allows for efficiencies in determining matters and issues of commonality that run across the different products. The reconstituted actions of the Strosberg/Siskind counsel group reflect the advice of economists that there must be a global assessment of damages on a product by product basis. The reconstituted actions are the most comprehensive of all the Ontario actions. In my view, they represent the best opportunity to meet the interests of all the class member claimants.

In my view, while the approach suggested by the Strosberg/Siskind counsel group is in the best interests of all claimants, it also is in the best interests of the defendants as it reduces unnecessary costs to them.[8]

Courts might also make orders facilitating "virtual" consolidation through motions for access, which might be termed "court-ordered freeloading." In a subsequent decision of *Vitapharm Canada Ltd. et al.* v. *F. Hoffman-Laroche Ltd.*, the Ontario plaintiffs had sought an order in a U.S. court for access to discoveries of the same defendants being conducted in a concurrent class action there. The defendants attempted to have the Ontario court issue an injunction to prevent the U.S. court from allowing the motion. In dismissing the application for the injunction, Cumming J. said:

The plaintiffs' U.S. Motion *prima facie* has the purpose of saving considerable time and money in the Canadian proceedings. If successful in gaining access to U.S. discovery in the U.S. Litigation, the plaintiffs can determine earlier and with greater certainty the nature and extent of the precise evidence available that is relevant to

8.   *Ibid.* at 35-36 (A.C.W.S.J.).

the Canadian proceedings. To deny access to the present U. S. discovery could conceivably mean that the plaintiffs over time would have to pursue separately s. 1782 orders in respect of the corporate Niacin defendants in the U.S. Litigation. At the least, success in obtaining access to the present U.S. discovery means that the plaintiffs can much more easily determine and discard what is *not relevant* for the purpose of the Canadian proceedings.

The plaintiffs' action in seeking access to the U.S. discovery is not oppressive or unfair to the defendants in the Canadian proceedings. To the contrary. Such access is consistent with the three policy objectives underlying the *CPA* — facilitating access to justice, judicial efficiency and behaviour modification. In particular, there will be significant savings in litigation costs through such access.[9]

(4) Equitable Consolidation Through the Bill of Peace

The use of the equitable Bill of Peace dates to at least the seventeenth century,[10] when the Courts of Equity in England decided that they could take control over a "multiplicity" of actions where there was a commonality of interest. An early case summarises the concept:

> So where a bill was brought by some few tenants of Greystock Manor against the lord, to settle the customs of the manor as to fines upon death and alienations; and an issue was directed to be tried at law . . . ; and it was insisted upon, that there being but some of the tenants parties to this bill, the rest would not be bound by this trial: But my Lord Keeper (Sir Nathan Wright) held they would; and he said he remembered the case of Nether Wiersdale, between Lord Gerrard and some few tenants, and Lord Nottingham's case in the Dutchy, concerning the customs of Daintree Manor, for grinding and baking at the lord's mill and bake-house, and said in these and 100 others, all were bound, tho" only a few tenants parties; else where are such numbers, no right could be done, if all must be parties, for there would be perpetual abatements.[11]

Professor Chafee, who in 1932 undertook a systematic review of Bills of Peace as consolidative devices and vehicles for class actions, summarised the application as follows:

> Each such separate suit sought or would have sought the recovery of money and nothing else – no injunction, specific performance, or other relief outside the competence of a jury and judge sitting at law. No equitable right or title was involved. The only reason for coming into equity was that it could settle in a single suit the common question: — was the maintenance and use of the dam a legal wrong to a lower riparian owner? Was a subscriber to the new stock a shareholder? The alternative to a bill of peace was a large number of actions at law, in each of which this common question might be disputed over and over again by the adversary and the particular member of the multitude concerned. The same witnesses would be repeatedly called, the same arguments repeatedly made, and each successive case

---

9. In *Vitapharm Canada Ltd. et al.* v. *F. Hoffman-LaRoche Ltd.*, 2001 Ont. Sup. C.J. LEXIS 111 at 20-21.
10. *How* v. *Tenants of Bromsgrove* (1681), 1 Vern. 22.
11. *Brown* v. *Howard* (1701), 1 Eq. Cas. Abr. 163, pl. 4.

must receive fresh consideration by court and jury. The doctrine of res judicata would not apply to make the first judgment binding in the later suits.[12]

Unlike the consolidation rule of Lord Mansfield, the Bill of Peace did not require the consent of the parties to be bound by the single "test case."[13] Also, the record reveals that although Bills of Peace were generally sought by defendants in order to settle multiple actions (or potential actions) against them, they could also be employed by "the multitude" – i.e the numerous plaintiffs. Chafee explains that:

> [I]t is sometimes urged that the multitiude [i.e. plaintiffs] can not bring a bill of peace . . . This argument is fallacious . . . the expense and vexation to each member of the multitude will be greatly reduced if he can join with the others in prosecuting or defending one suit in equity, and furthermore, a bill of peace does not lie solely for the benefit of the parties, but also to prevent the waste of judicial time and public money and the delay of other litigation.[14]

There were two prerequisites for the Bill to be granted. The first required numerosity; that a multitude of suits against a defendant be either "pending" or "possible"[15] and the second that a "commonality of interest" existed across the class. The main controversy over the application of Bills of Peace as they began to be used in the United States in mass tort cases at the end of the nineteenth century concerned the latter.

Chafee, citing Pomeroy and numerous cases, concludes that *some* degree of commonality was always required, but that this requirement could be satisfied through the existence of "common question," perhaps coupled with "the kind of relief":[16]

> There is no advantage to justice in a requirement that the adversary in an ordinary bill of peace must have a property right. *Multiplicity with respect to common question makes the remedy at law sufficiently inadequate to support equitable jurisdic-*

---

12. Zechariah Chafee Jr. "Bills of Peace with Multiple Parties" (1932) 45 Harv. L. Rev. 1297 at 1299.
13. *Ibid.* at 1300.
14. *Ibid.* at 1303.
15. *Ibid.* at 1299-1300.
16. Pomeroy, *Treatise on Equity Jurisprudence* (1881) s. 269., cited in Chafee, *ibid.* at 1313. Pomeroy decries decisions which purported a more restrictive rule:

    This objection has been repeated as though it were conclusive; but like so much of the so-called "legal reasoning" traditional in the courts, it is a mere empty formula of words without any real meaning, because it has no foundation of fact, it is simply untrue; one arbitrary rule is contrived and insisted upon as the reason for another equally arbitrary rule . . . The jurisdiction *has* been exercised in a great variety of cases where the individual claimants were completely separate and distinct . . . and the single decree *has* without any difficulty settled the entire controversy and determined the separate rights and obligations of each individual claimant.

tion. Any attempt to require a general right of the nature of property is bound to raise difficult questions as to the meaning of the phrase. [emphasis added][17]

Perhaps the most useful thing about the Bill of Peace was that it not only provided a remedy, but also jurisdiction, including that over absent parties who could be bound without their consent. This aspect of its use made it controversial in the U.S., because it allowed a judge exercising equitable jurisdiction to circumvent the constitutional requirement for a jury trial in high-value civil litigation, in theory to the advantage of defendants.[18]

Chafee's analysis of the Bill also provides the first justification for the limited fund doctrine:

> Joinder in a single suit is especially desirable when the multitude are seeking to divide a fund or a limited liability. Here the usual disadvantages of multiplicity of suits are greatly aggravated. The objection to many separate suits is not merely the vexation and expense to the adversary of trying the same question over and over. In addition there is danger that the aggregate of the separate jury verdicts might exceed the limit of liability, and also it is impossible to make a fair distribution of the fund or limited liability to all members of the multitude except in a single proceeding where the claim of each can be adjudicated with due reference to the claims of the rest. The fund or limited liability is like a mince pie, which can not be satisfactorily divided until the carver counts the number of persons at the table.[19]

While it is still occasionally invoked in the U.S.,[20] the Bill of Peace has remained virtually unused in contemporary Canadian legal practice since the fusion of law and equity began toward the close of the nineteenth century.[21] Nevertheless, it is still available, as was confirmed in the very recent decision of *Dykun* v. *Odishaw*, where the Alberta Court of Appeal invoked the doctrine to

---

17.   Chafee, *ibid.* at 1309.

18.   *Ibid.* at 1320: "Behind all this insistence on the formula of "community of interest" lurks the fear that large corporate defendants will readily escape jury trials after widespread disasters." In fact, as we have seen, the availability of more universal aggregation can be expected to have the opposite effect, and moreover is irrelevant in the Canadian context where no such right exists.

19.   *Ibid.* at 1311.

20.   See for instance *Yuba Consol. Gold Fields* v. *Kilkeary*, 206 F.2d 884 (9th Cir. 1953); *Leaf River Forest Prod., Inc.* v. *Deakle*, 661 So. 2d 188 at 192 (Miss. 1995) (The defendant applied for a bill of peace to consolidate several toxic tort cases. The court said that it might be possible: "while the label "bill of peace" may not have survived the adoption of the [class action rules], the chancery court's authority to grant substantive relief through equity remains viable and available") See also Thomas D. Rowe, Jr., "A Distant Mirror: The Bill of Peace in Early American Mass Torts and Its Implications for Modern Class Actions" (1997) 39 Ariz. L. Rev. 711.

21.   See generally Paul M. Perell, *The Fusion of Law and Equity* (Toronto: Butterworths, 1990).

frustrate a frivolous litigant who "insist[ed] on the use of public forums to indulge oblique motives."[22]

If we combine the superior courts' inherent and equitable jurisdiction over related claims and the principles of *Morguard* and *Hunt*, we might conclude that, where jurisdiction is properly taken by a superior court over the "subject matter" of a national class action, that court may combine all similar actions (or potential actions) into one. Present practice permits the issuance of anti-suit injunctions to block competing foreign proceedings (where the interests of comity allow), and it is not so great a leap to the idea of equitable consolidation, at least with respect to actions within Canada.

(5) Consolidation Through National Central Case Management

Finally, a course that might facilitate consolidation even if the national opt-out class is eventually rejected would be for the establishment of a central case-management system for mass tort claims, perhaps established through the auspices of the Canadian Judicial Council. Such a body would make recommendations regarding the consolidation of similar actions from several jurisdictions to be heard in a single provincial superior court. In many respects, such a system might resemble the U.S. Judicial Panel on Multidistrict Litigation.[23]

It is unclear whether the mandate (or funding) of the CJC is broad enough to support such an initiative, but the CJC's enabling legislation appears to present

---

22. *Dykun* v. *Odishaw*, 2001 ABCA 204, 286 A.R. 392, 253 W.A.C. 392 at para. 11. The Court directed that the Alberta courts refuse the issuance of any new pleadings by the plaintiff "of any new action that derives from his dispute with Canada Post or with his first lawyer . . . " The Court reflected at para. 8 (footnote 1):

    At equity a perpetual injunction may issue to restrain all further and repetitious proceedings at law by litigating parties where the question has been satisfactorily settled. The remedy was known as a "Bill of Peace". It issued when the Court of Chancery reached the conclusion that "a matter had been litigated enough". *Earl of Bath* v. *Sherwin* (1709), 4 Bro Parl Cas 373, 2 E.R. 253 (H.L.). Patently, it should only issue in the rarest of cases but it is available when justified.

23. The Judicial Panel on Multidistrict Litigation has the authority to transfer "civil actions involving one or more common questions of fact . . . pending in different districts . . . to any district for coordinated or consolidated pretrial proceedings . . . for the convenience of parties and witnesses and [to] promote the just and efficient conduct of such actions.": 28 U.S.C. 1407(a) (1993). Even though the transferee court is not empowered to conduct a trial of the transferred actions, it "ultimately disposes of most MDL cases, either by way of dispositive motion, settlement, or trial": Rhonda Wasserman, "Duelling Class Actions" (2000) B.U. L. Rev. 461 at 510.

no impediment to such a scheme.[24] Funding would require a political commitment at the federal level, perhaps in coordination with the provinces. Unfortunately, the history of the United States' Judicial Panel, which was a response to a perceived crisis in multidistrict complex litigation, suggests that reform might have to await an emergency in provincial dockets.

Unlike the U.S. district courts, though, Canadian superior courts of inherent jurisdiction are not organized on the national level, and the cases before them in mass tort cases are not "federal cases." Even if a committee of the Council could be established to organize the consolidations, the ultimate success of the procedure in any given case, absent statutory reform, would depend on the inherent power of the courts (transferor and transferee) for enforcement, either through injunction, Bill of Peace, the rules of court of the various provinces, or some similar device. Challenges to the authority to consolidate might still arise, perhaps from a class counsel in one of the combined actions who finds his role in representing the larger, national class either reduced or eliminated.

C.   STATUTORY REFORM

It is also possible to coordinate legislation to facilitate case management of class actions on a national scale. There are many potential avenues for accomplishing this, only a few of which are discussed here.

In 1994, the Uniform Law Conference of Canada adopted a *Court Jurisdiction and Proceedings Transfer Act*[25] to facilitate consolidations through uniform statutory jurisdiction rules that would articulate guidelines compatible with the Supreme Court of Canada jurisprudence as it then existed. Though designed principally for individual actions, its transfer and convenient forum rules could, as the Alberta Law Reform Commission has pointed out,[26] also assist in avoiding forum shopping problems that might occur with national consolidations.[27]

---

24.   Section 60 of the *Judges Act* permits the Council to "establish conferences of chief justices, associate chief justices, chief judges and associate chief judges" "to promote efficiency and uniformity, and to improve the quality of judicial service, in superior and county courts . . ."; section 61 gives the council broad powers to set up committees in furtherance of its goals, and section 62 permits it to "engage the services of such persons as it deems necessary for carrying out its objects and duties": *Judges Act*, R.S.C. 1985, c. J-1.

25.   *Proceedings of the Uniform Law Conference of Canada (1994)* at 48 (http://www.ulcc.ca/en/us/).

26.   The Alberta Law Reform Commission, *Report on Class Action Legislation* (Final Report #85, 2000) at 63.

27.   Note also though that, unlike in the United States, the common law rules regarding choice of law, liability and damages are not set out at the local level, but rather are coordinated through the operation of Canada's unitary court system in the form of

It would also be possible to amend the non-resident provisions of the various class proceedings acts to provide for a national opt-out class. This could be done either by eliminating the opt-in provision altogether (in effect adopting the Ontario model), or by augmenting it with a consolidation section.

This section could be framed to allow opt-out subclasses from those provinces where opt-out classes are already certified. For instance, if three discrete opt-out certifications have been granted in B.C., Alberta and Saskatchewan, then class counsel for Alberta and Saskatchewan could apply in B.C. to be joined in that province as non-resident subclasses, but preserving their opt-out nature. This essentially mirrors the process used in Ontario when the B.C. subclass was certified in *Wilson* v. *Servier*; unfortunately it is a technique not easily adaptable to the ULCC-model CPAs in force in B.C. and Saskatchewan, and pending in other provinces.

A drawback to this approach is that it requires class counsel being motivated to combine with their counterparts in other provinces, and, absent the kind of *a priori* agreement in place between Ontario and B.C. counsel in *Wilson* v. *Servier*, this will not often be the case.

Another legislative route would be a change in substantive federal law facilitating class actions in any jurisdiction for claims arising out of products sold or moved interprovincially, or which are alleged to have caused harm in more than one jurisdiction. While there does not seem to be any constitutional impediment to such an action, discussions of class actions at the federal level have so far apparently been restricted to facilitating class litigation in Federal Court.[28]

Supreme Court of Canada decisions. This means that, while forum shopping might still occur for procedural advantages, it is less likely to make a difference with respect to substantive rules, particularly as the forum court will apply the law of the place of the tort to the extent that it is different from the forum's own.

28. Federal Court of Canada, The Rules Committee, *Class Proceedings in the Federal Court of Canada, A Discussion Paper* (June 9, 2000). A Federal Court class action regime would assist only those actions which are subject to the limited, statutory jurisdiction of that Court (cases dealing with maritime law, tax cases, copyright, or other matters within federal legislative jurisdiction). This is in marked contrast to the Federal Court system in the United States, which can hear mass tort claims on the constitutional basis of "diversity of citizenship."

Nevertheless, the federal government could establish a *federal cause of action* with respect to products liability or securities law, where the tort committed had interprovincial implications. In fact, if a federal class action regime is approved, it may be possible to certify a national class based on, for instance, the "misleading advertising" cause of action contained within the federal *Competition Act*, R.S.C. 1985 c. C-34 s. 36; however, this would require that the plaintiffs elect not to pursue possibly more fruitful torts based in the common law. Moreover, it remains to be seen what "comity" would be extended by provincial superior courts to certifications of national classes in Federal Court.

PART IV

—

Refining Class Action System Design

CHAPTER TEN

—

Proposals For Reform

A. INTRODUCTION

This chapter looks to the future to see whether and how Canada's emerging class action regime can more fully accommodate the pursuit of optimally aggregated claims, and overcome some of the endemic problems of mass tort litigation. I focus here on some of the ideas gaining currency in the United States, such as mandatory class actions and a system that might provide economic advantages of aggregation by combining classes, as it were, *across* claims rather than only within them. Such an idea raises the possibility that mass torts might be pursued through a "superfund" idea, combining the universally recognised advantages of insurance-based compensation with tort-based deterrence.

B. THE "MANDATORY CLASS"

As mentioned earlier in this book, U.S. courts have, from time to time, designed so-called "mandatory classes" – certifications which preclude potential class members from opting out, and bind all to the decisions of the court.

Mandatory classification has several obvious advantages. Most notably, it automatically maximises the aggregation of claims, thereby optimising litigation scale efficiencies for plaintiffs. It also eliminates the innate problems of intra-class conflict as members with higher value claims (i.e. claims with either a larger recovery or stronger evidentiary or legal basis improving the chances of that recovery) bargain with the remainder of the class over the terms of their participation. As such, it has gained substantial support from scholars like Rosenberg, who has recently proposed the mandatory aggregation of *all* mass tort claims.[1]

On the face of it, Rule 23(b)(1) mandatory classes can be employed whenever allowing opt-outs would create the risk of systematic unfairness to other class members, outweighing the interests in litigative autonomy of individual plaintiffs. In practice, however, the broad wording of Rule 23(b)(1) has been read quite restrictively, and U.S. courts' flirtation with the mandatory class has been limited to a single type of case: that in which the judgment must be realised from a defendant with finite available resources; this is known as the problem of the limited fund. In other words, a mandatory class has been seen to be appropriate in cases where, if the absentee potential plaintiffs were *not* entitled to share in the settlement or judgment, there would be nothing left for them when they had their day in court.

(1) The "Limited Fund" Doctrine

A limited fund has been defined as a readily identifiable, specific, limited sum of money upon which numerous claims existed, when those claims exceeded the amount of the fund.[2] It is thought that mandatory classes might prevent a "race

---

1. David Rosenberg, "Mandatory-Litigation Class Action: The Only Option for Mass Tort Cases" (2001) 115 Harvard L. Rev. 831 [Rosenberg, "The Only Option"].

2. See *e.g., Phillips Petroleum Co.* v. *Shutts*, 472 U.S. 797 [*Shutts*]; In Re *Dennis Greenman Sec. Litig.*, 829 F.2d 1539, 1546 (11th Cir. 1987); In Re *Bendectin Prods. Liab. Litig.*, 749 F.2d 300, 305-06 (6th Cir. 1984); *Green* v. *Occidental Petroleum Corp.*, 541 F.2d 1335, 1340 n.9 (9th Cir. 1976); *County of Suffolk* v. *Long Island Lighting Co.*, 710 F. Supp. 1407, 1417 (E.D.N.Y. 1989); *Alexander Grant & Co.* v. *McAlister*, 116 F.R.D. 583, 590 (S.D. Ohio 1987); *Bower* v. *Bunker Hill Co.*, 114 F.R.D. 587, 595-96 (E.D. Wash. 1986). A mandatory class under subdivision (b)(1)(B) is appropriate in such cases because:

    > an adjudication as to one or more members of the class will necessarily or probably have an adverse practical effect on the interests of other members who should therefore be represented in the lawsuit. This is plainly the case when claims are made by numerous persons against a fund insufficient to satisfy all claims. A class action by or against representative members to settle the validity of the claims as a whole, or in groups, followed by separate proof of the amount of each valid claim and proportionate distribution of the fund, meets the problem.

    Fed. R. Civ. P. at 23(b)(1)(B) (Advisory Committee's note).

to the courthouse" in which the first claimants could recover while later claimants received only empty judgments.[3]

In *Ortiz* v. *Fibreboard Corp et al.* (1999), the U.S. Supreme Court summarised the three necessary characteristics of a "limited fund" mandatory class: first, that the fund be limited and definitely ascertained; second, that all the claims upon the fund must be based on a common theory of liability; and third, that all of the fund must be distributed to satisfy all those with such claims on an equitable, pro rata basis.

The mandatory class received a lukewarm reception in the U.S. appeal courts, with many certifications being reversed,[4] even though some appellate courts appeared to sympathise with the reasoning of the judges below.[5] Some did per-

---

3. Occasionally, courts seeking to create a mandatory class attempted to certify punitive damages for a single, mandatory treatment under the "punitive damages overkill" theory (The phrase was coined in Judge Friendly's opinion in *Roginsky* v. *Richardson-Merrell, Inc.*, 378 F.2d 832, 839 n.11 (2d Cir. 1967)). In these cases, punitive damages are considered akin to a limited fund because state law or constitutional due process requires that such damages be paid only once.

4. See In Re *School Asbestos Litig.*, 789 F.2d 996 (3d Cir. 1986); In Re *Bendectin Prods. Liab. Litig.*, 749 F.2d 300 (6th Cir. 1984); *Dalkon Shield*, 693 F.2d 847 (9th Cir. 1982); In Re *Federal Skywalk Cases*, 680 F.2d 1175 (8th Cir. 1982). See also *Payton* v. *Abbott Labs.*, 83 F.R.D. 382, 389 (D. Mass. 1979) (absent evidence of likely insolvency, "numerous plaintiffs and a large *ad damnum* clause should [not] guarantee (b)(1)(B) certification").

   Courts reversing Rule 23(b)(1) certifications also expressed concern over the *Anti-Injunction Act*, which prohibits a federal court from enjoining state court proceedings "except as expressly authorized by Act of Congress, or where necessary in aid of its jurisdiction or to protect or effectuate its judgment." 28 U.S.C. §2283 (1994). When state cases were already pending, the certification of the federal action could be seen as an injunction of those state court proceedings. See In Re *School Asbestos Litig. ibid.* at 1002; In Re *Federal Skywalk, ibid.* at 1181-83. Courts also noted that in diversity actions "certification of a mandatory class raises serious questions of personal jurisdiction and intrusion into the autonomous operation of state judicial systems." *School Asbestos Litig. Ibid.* at 1002. Concerns about personal jurisdiction reflect questions about the scope of the Supreme Court's decision in *Shutts*, above note 2.

5. See In Re *Bendectin, ibid.* at 307 ("[o]n pure policy grounds, the district judge's decision may be commendable"); In Re *Federal Skywalk, ibid.* at 1177 n.4, 1183 (noting the district court's "legitimate concern for the efficient management of mass tort litigation" and commending the court for its "creative efforts in attempting to achieve a fair, efficient and economical trial for victims"); *Dalkon Shield, ibid.* at 851 (recognising that mandatory classes might be appropriate in some mass tort cases).

mit mandatory classes but employed stringent definitions of the "limited fund,"[6] sharply limiting their application. In a few, exceptional cases, mandatory Rule 23(b)(1) classes were not reversed, most notably in "Agent Orange"[7] and Dalkon Shield litigation.[8]

The *Ortiz* Court emphasised that the fund cannot be limited by agreement between the parties and the class counsel, raising the question of whether a mandatory class can ever be certified without the bankruptcy and liquidation of the defendant:

> Assuming arguendo that a mandatory, limited fund rationale could under some circumstances be applied to a settlement class of tort claimants, it would be essential that the fund be shown to be limited independently of the agreement of the parties to the action, and equally essential under Rule 23(a) and (b)(1)(B) that the class include all those with claims unsatisfied at the time of the settlement negotiations, with intraclass conflicts addressed by recognising independently represented subclasses. In this case, the limit of the fund was determined by treating the settlement agreement as dispositive, an error magnified by the representation of class members by counsel also representing excluded plaintiffs, whose settlements would be funded fully upon settlement of the class action on any terms that could survive final fairness review. Those separate settlements, together with other exclusions from the claimant class, precluded adequate structural protection by subclass treatment, which was not even afforded to the conflicting elements within the class as certified.[9]

In fact, in *Ortiz*, the U.S. Supreme Court, while setting out some guidelines for when a mandatory class is *not* appropriate in a "mass accident" tort case, declined to rule on whether one *ever* was:

> It is simply implausible that the Advisory Committee, so concerned about the potential difficulties posed by dealing with mass tort cases under Rule 23(b)(3), with its provisions for notice and the right to opt out, see Rule 23(c)(2), would have uncritically assumed that mandatory versions of such class actions, lacking such protections, could be certified under Rule 23(b)(1)(B). We do not, it is true, decide the ultimate question whether Rule 23(b)(1)(B) may ever be used to aggregate individual tort claims, cf. *Ticor Title Ins. Co.* v. *Brown*, 511 U.S. 117, 121 (1994) (per curiam) . But we do recognise that the Committee would have thought such an

---

6. See, e.g., *Dalkon Shield, ibid.* at 851-52 (mandatory class only permitted where "separate damages awards inescapably will affect later awards").

7. In Re *"Agent Orange" Products Liability Litigation* 100 F.R.D. 718 (E.D.N.Y. 1983), *mandamus denied sub nom.* In Re *Diamond Shamrock Chems. Co.*, 725 F.2d 858 (2d Cir. 1984), *and aff'd*, 818 F.2d 145 (2d Cir. 1987).

8. In Re *A.H. Robins Co.* 85 B.R. 373 (E.D. Va. 1988), *aff'd*, 880 F.2d 709 (4th Cir. 1989); see also *Coburn* v. *4-R Corp.*, 77 F.R.D. 43 (E.D. Ky. 1977), *mandamus* denied sub nom. See also *Union Light, Heat & Power Co.* v. *United States Dist. Court*, 588 F.2d 543 (6th Cir. 1978); *Hernandez* v. *Motor Vessel Skyward*, 61 F.R.D. 558 (S.D. Fla. 1973), *aff'd*, 507 F.2d 1278 (5th Cir.), *and aff'd*, 507 F.2d 1279 (5th Cir. 1975).

9. *Ortiz* v. *Fibreboard Corp.* 527 U.S. 815 (1999); 119 S. Ct. 2295 [*Ortiz*] at U.S. 864.

application of the Rule surprising, and take this as a good reason to limit any surprise by presuming that the Rule's historical antecedents identify requirements. [footnotes omitted][10]

(2)   The Mandatory Class in Canada

Despite the fact that no Canadian court has certified – or even considered – a "mandatory class," one can not necessarily conclude that they will share the U.S. courts' reluctance to impose a broad, mandatory class in this country. Many of the U.S. decisions in which mandatory classes are rejected, such as the class in *Amchem*[11] which purported to preclude future actions by everyone who had been exposed to the defendants' asbestos products (whether or not they had yet manifested any illness), failed largely because such a definition could not satisfy the predominance test in Rule 23, a test which, as described earlier, is explicitly absent from Canadian class action cases. In denying the certification for settlement on those grounds, the Court also recognised the grave question of whether "class action notice sufficient under the Constitution and Rule 23 could *ever* be given to legions so unselfconscious and amorphous."

The *Amchem* Court intimated that the mandatory class, while perhaps appropriate where the individual plaintiff's interest was small and the advantages of collective action large, would be inappropriate in cases of catastrophic personal injury where individual rights of recovery must prevail.

There is no corresponding provision in Canada to that in Rule 23(b)(1) which might explicitly deny a potential plaintiff the right to "opt out"; however, this is not to say that "mandatory classes" are not possible in Canada. The U.S. Supreme Court in *Ortiz* noted that mandatory classes were permissible at equity long before the advent of Rule 23(b):

> Equity, of course, recognised the same necessity to bind absent claimants to a limited fund when no formal imposition of a constructive trust was entailed. In *Guffanti* v. *National Surety Co.*, 196 N. Y. 452, 458, 90 N. E. 174, 176 (1909), for example, the defendant received money to supply steamship tickets and had posted a $15,000 bond as required by state law. He converted to personal use funds collected from more than 150 ticket purchasers, was then adjudged bankrupt, and absconded. One of the defrauded ticket purchasers sued the surety in equity on behalf of himself and all others like him. Over the defendant's objection, the New York Court of Appeals sustained the equitable class suit, citing among other considerations the fact that all recovery had to come from a "limited fund out of which the aggregate recoveries must be sought" that was inadequate to pay all claims, and subject to pro rata distribution. Id., at 458, 90 N. E., at 176. See Hazard, Gedid, & Sowle 1915 ("[Guffanti] explained that when a debtor's assets were less than the total of the creditors' claims, a binding class action was not only permitted but was required; otherwise some creditors (the parties) would be paid and others (the absentees) would not"). See also Morrison v. Warren 174 Misc. 233, 234, 20 N. Y. S. 2d 26, 27 (Sup. Ct. N. Y. Cty. 1940) (suit on behalf of more than 400 benefici-

---

10.   *Ibid.* at U.S. 844.

11.   *Amchem Products Inc.* v. *Windsor*, 521 U.S. 591 (1997).

aries of an insurance policy following a fire appropriate where "the amount of the claims . . . greatly exceeds the amount of the insurance"); National Surety Co. v. Graves, 211 Ala. 533, 534, 101 So. 190 (1924) (suit against a surety company by stockholders "for the benefit of themselves and all others similarly situate who will join the suit" where it was alleged that individual suits were being filed on surety bonds that "would result in the exhaustion of the penalties of the bonds, leaving many stockholders without remedy").

As previously noted, Canadian courts retain an inherent jurisdiction to "ensure the observance of the due process of law, to prevent improper vexation or oppression, to do justice between the parties and to secure a fair trial between them" unless this ability has been explicitly removed by the statute they are interpreting.[12]

Perhaps the closest thing Canada has yet seen to a "mandatory class" was the global settlement agreement reached as a result of simultaneous class actions commenced in British Columbia, Quebec and Ontario over the tragic contamination of the nation's blood supply.[13] The classes in the former two provinces were restricted to plaintiffs in those jurisdictions, and in Ontario, as is often the case, to everyone else in the country, all on an opt-out basis. The defendants established a "fund" of about $1.5 billion to settle all three actions, with the proviso that any subsequent individual judgments from individual plaintiffs who "opted out" would be deducted from the fund, thus providing a single, global, "cap" on damages. The chambers judge required that this provision be altered, so that any deduction made from the fund for the damages awarded to the opt-out plaintiff would be no greater than that to which the opt-out plaintiff would have been entitled had he or she remained a member of the class[14], and thus that the defendants were still liable to "top up" the settlement amount to match the individual damage awards.

Although plaintiffs in the tainted blood cases could still "opt out" of the settlement and try their luck in court, there was a strong disincentive for them to do so. The only certain fund from which to draw was that established in the settlement, and their recovery from that fund could not exceed that of those who decided against opting out. Certainly, the defendants *could* be called upon to "top up" the amount provided by the fund for individual litigants, but the Canadian Red Cross Society was effectively bankrupt and the vicarious liability of the fed-

---

12. See footnote 81 in Chapter Eight and accompanying text.

13. The terms of the settlement and the reasons for approval are described in the decisions of Smith J. in *Endean* v. *Canadian Red Cross Society* (1999), [2000] 1 W.W.R. 688, 68 B.C.L.R. (3d) 350, the decision of Winkler J. in *Parsons* v. *Canadian Red Cross Society*, [1999] O.J. No. 3572 (Sup. Ct. J.), and the decision of Morneau J. in *Honhon c. Canada (Procureur général)*, [1999] J.Q. no 4370 (S.C.).

14. *Parsons* v. *Canadian Red Cross Society*, above per Winkler J. This aspect of the decision was also endorsed by Smith J. in B.C.: *Endean* v. *Canadian Red Cross Society*, above.

eral and provincial governments was far from certain. Practically speaking then, the decision of Mr. Justice Winkler to "cap" individual recovery from the fund might have kept the overwhelming majority of plaintiffs within the class.

Another interesting example of a "limited fund" case is *Sawatzky*, one of three classes certified for the benefit of hundreds of recipients of defective surgical jaw implants. The defendant manufacturer was bankrupt, and it was accepted by all parties that its insurer's liability for the whole period in question was $7.5 million, creating a "limited fund" (including interest by the projected time of payouts) of just over $10 million. The settlement approved by the Court involved setting aside a fixed amount ($1 million) to pay any individual claims from members who had exercised their right to opt-out. However, this fund would not last indefinitely:

> The reserve fund will provide payments to individuals who would otherwise be eligible to make claims under the settlement agreement but who continue to assert claims against Instrumentarium. Subject to claim payouts the reserve fund will be maintained for three years at which time $500,000 plus interest will be transferred to the settlement fund for distribution to class members. After an additional three years any remaining funds will be transferred to the settlement fund for distribution to class members.[15]

In this way, the court creates a strong disincentive to opting out, or at least sharply limits the number of people who may opt out. Any plaintiff considering "going it alone" would face the prospect of the "race to the courthouse," and finding an empty judgment upon arrival. While not true "mandatory classes," such cases do indicate the courts' willingness to consider methods of restricting or discouraging opt-outs less directly.

(3) The Rosenberg Proposals

The leading advocate of mandatory classes in mass tort actions is Harvard professor David Rosenberg. Rosenberg's work in the area has been described by Nagareda — himself an occasional critic of Rosenberg — as "canonical,"[16] and Coffee has referred to his writing as the "fullest and best" exposition of "the public law vision" of mass tort litigation.[17] His views on class action system design are persuasive; indeed no discussion of class action reform in the United States can ignore them.[18]

---

15. *Sawatzky* v. *Société Chirurgicale Instrumentarium Inc.* (1999), 71 B.C.L.R. (3d) 51 at para. 18 (S.C.).

16. Richard Nagareda, "Autonomy, Peace and Put Options in the Mass Tort Class Action" (2002 115 Harv. L. Rev. 749 [Nagareda] at 749 (note).

17. John C. Coffee, Jr., "Class Wars: The Dilemma of the Mass Tort Class Action" (1995) 95 Colum. L. Rev. 1343 [Coffee, "Class Wars"] at 1346, citing David Rosenberg, "Class Actions for Mass Torts: Doing Individual Justice by Collective Means" (1987) 62 Ind. L.J. 561 at 569-74.

18. See for instance the dominant position of Rosenberg's proposals — and the defer-

But there are other reasons to give Rosenberg's views particular weight in the Canadian context. Peter Schuck, himself a leading commentator, has offered that:

> The most striking feature of [Rosenberg's] model is the extent to which common-law courts have already incorporated its main elements — class actions, proportional liability, damage scheduling, averaged judgements, insurance-fund judgments, fee- and cost-shifting arrangements — into the mass tort system.[19]

Rosenberg's analyses of the benefits of aggregation have been employed throughout this book. However, until this point, I have not discussed in any detail the most controversial position he advocates – mandatory litigation class actions for mass tort.

In short, Rosenberg suggests that all mass tort claims should be subject to immediate and universal aggregation to the fullest possible extent on all common issues, so that the disparity of scale economies between plaintiff and defendant are minimised and optimal tort deterrence will be achieved. He argues that the fund generated from judgment or settlement should be paid out to the claimants through an administrative process based on insurance (i.e. need-based) principles, which he supports as optimally fair to plaintiffs from the ex ante perspective. A key component of his proposal is that no claimant be allowed to opt out of the aggregate class and pursue individual litigation. Moreover, Rosenberg advocates the aggregation of both present and future claims in the same action, using techniques of sampling, averaging and projection to determine at the earliest practical stage the overall measure of harm done by the tortfeasor.

Rosenberg's critics generally focus, not on any fundamental flaws in his argument, but instead upon the incompatibility of Rosenberg's model with present American jurisprudence surrounding Rule 23.[20] While Rosenberg has recently addressed these criticisms,[21] he does not make any sustained attempt to render his

---

ence shown to them — in Thomas E. Willging, "Mass Tort Problems and Proposals: A Report to the Mass Torts Working Group," (Federal Judicial Center 1999, available at http://www.fjc.gov/public/pdf.nsf/lookup/MassTApC.pdf) at 39-42.

19. Peter Schuck, "Mass Torts: An Institutional Evolutionist Perspective" (1995) 80 Cornell L. Rev. 941 at 981. To this list I would add aggregate awards based on statistical evidence and cy pres distribution schemes (including distribution via government health services), features of Canadian class action statutes that are, as I will argue below, very consistent with Rosenberg's proposals.

20. See for instance Nagareda, above note 16 at 749 n.: "[D]isagreements . . . stem principally from my commitment to an analysis of mass tort class actions that takes as given the content of existing tort doctrine . . . Rosenberg does not accept these premises."

21. Most recently in David Rosenberg, "The Regulatory Advantage of Mass Tort Class Action" in *Regulation by Litigation* W. Kip Viscusi ed., (forthcoming 2002), and Rosenberg, "The Only Option", above note 1.

ideas compatible with the jurisprudence, as he apparently believes that the cases are wrongly decided, or if correctly decided, are nonetheless fundamentally wrongheaded.[22]

The reason for examining the possibility of universal mandatory aggregation in Canada is that the Canadian courts and legislatures are unconstrained by the very considerations that have led the U.S. Supreme Court to a conservative application of class actions in mass tort cases. The Canadian constitution does not contain formalistic due process protections for civil trials, nor can any argument be found for a constitutionally-based right to trial on individual issues, for plaintiffs or defendants. Further, the strictures of Rule 23(b)(1) "mandatory classes," to which the Supreme Court declares itself bound, have no equivalent in Canadian law. So the question presents itself: to what extent could the Rosenberg proposals be adopted in Canada?

(4) Analysis

The question of opt-out rights may be the most challenging philosophical issue facing the development of mass tort litigation. There is the very real likelihood that the greater the opt-out rights, the less effective the class will be in achieving social goals of deterrence and compensation overall. On the other hand, opt-out rights preserve the notion (if not the reality) of litigative autonomy, and some commentators have also suggested that the number of class members who "opt out" is a barometer of confidence in the class counsel or the settlement reached.[23]

U.S. figures indicate that in three quarters of certifications, fewer than 1.2% opt out;[24] from that one might conclude that the problem is not of serious concern. However, such statistics are misleading, as most of the class actions studied are for claims not viable individually.[25] Obviously, mandatory classes are moot in such situations; the "hard cases" are the large claims involving catastrophic injuries and significant damages, where presumably the opt-out rate is much higher. Moreover, most mass tort class actions could not even be certified in the United States due to restrictive interpretations of Rule 23.

---

22. Rosenberg refers to the individualistic notions of fairness extrapolated from *Ortiz* and *Martin* v. *Wilks*, 490 U.S. 755 (1989) as "simply incoherent": "The Only Option" above note 1 at 865.

23. Coffee, "Class Wars" above note 17 at 1382-83: "[T]he existence of substantial opt outs may be the best evidence that the original settlement was inadequate (and possibly collusive)."

24. Thomas. E. Willging *et al.*, *Empirical Study of Class Actions in Four Federal District Courts: Final Report to Advisory Committee on Civil Rules 1996*, cited in Manitoba Law Reform Commission, *Class Proceedings* (Report #100) (Winnipeg: Manitoba Publications Branch, January 1999) at 27-28.

25. *Ibid.* at 23, citing the same study for the proposition that median recoveries were between $315 and $528 per claim.

In examining under what circumstances the "corporatisation" of class members is desirable, it might assist to examine the member's role within the class in a way analogous to a member's role in other corporate bodies, as Professor Coffee has done,[26] discussing the relative values of "exit," "loyalty" and "voice." The suggestion is that as any one of these features is reduced within the class, more scrupulous protection of the others is required.

The point is that reduction, or even elimination, of any one of those features is not necessarily fatal to the efficacy of the action. Procedures for overseeing the representative counsel's loyalty to the class are less important if the class members either have a direct voice in the direction of the proceeding and/or the right to exit if they do not approve of the way the litigation is proceeding. Similarly, control of "voice" is less important to the extent that both exit and loyalty are maximised.

We accept similar arrangements in many other aspects of the law. Union membership, for instance, may be mandatory, but the fairness of this is seen to depend on legislation requiring the union to act in its members' interests, and to provide members with a voice in governance. In a more pertinent example, one could discuss the "fairness" of legislative compensation schemes, such as workers' compensation or the Black Lung statutes, in similar terms. While the individual's participation is mandatory (i.e. no "exit"), provided that there are sufficient safeguards to avoid conflicts of interest between the administrative body and the claimant (i.e. no problems of "loyalty"), then the system might be considered "fair," even though any "voice" the claimant has in system design is largely symbolic (in the form of the democratic process).

In the administrative systems established by class action regimes, though, bound members effectively have no individual "democratic" voice in the system's design, except to the limited extent that they can appear as "objectors" at settlement fairness hearings.[27] To the extent that exit is eliminated *and* voice is limited, concern over agency problems is heightened, in the sense that both class counsel and the supervising court must be acutely aware of, and deferential to, the interests of the absent class members.

So called "cram down" provisions of bankruptcy reorganisation laws follow a different standard of "fairness," binding objecting creditors to a restructuring plan if equality and non-discrimination criteria are observed. The courts assume that the debtors endorsing the plan are acting in their own interest, and they overcome objections by ensuring that absent class members receive comparable

---

26. John C. Coffee Jr., "Class Action Accountability: Reconciling Voice, Exit and Loyalty in Representative Litigation" 100 Col. L. Rev. 370 (2000).

27. Nagareda, above note 16 at 795 ("The question at the heart of the mass tort class action is how to legitimate transactions . . . that lie in the uncharted territory between the actual consent found in aggregate settlements and the political consent thought to legitimate public legislation.").

treatment.[28] Similar arguments can be made that sufficient judicial oversight and principles of equality and non-discrimination might also be sufficient philosophical bases for the binding of absent class members in a mandatory class action lawsuit, providing that commonality of interest is preserved.[29]

There is also the question of whether and to what extent courts should be designing binding compensatory schemes, traditionally the purview of the legislatures.[30] One could argue that the legislatures have, through the enactment of class proceedings statutes, delegated that responsibility to the courts (assuming of course, that the legislation can be read to allow classes without opt-outs). The natural riposte is that if they have not delegated explicitly then they cannot be seen to have intended to provide schemes in which participation could be made mandatory.

While class action legislation in Canada makes no explicit allowance for "mandatory classes," it is possible to read various acts as permitting them in theory. For instance, the B.C. *Act* explicitly permits opting out, but only "in the manner and within the time specified in the certification order."[31] At the same time, the Act provides that the "court may at any time stay any proceeding related to the class proceeding on the terms the court considers appropriate,"[32] a power that would appear to extend to bar actions by opt-out class members. In the section describing notice of certification, the B.C. *Act* notes that the "court may dispense with notice if . . . the court considers it appropriate to do so."[33] One of the factors that the court must consider in deciding whether notice is appropriate is "*whether* some or all of the class members may opt out of the class pro-

---

28. See for instance Peter E. Hamilton & George J. Wade, "Restructuring Under the CCAA: An Examination of Principles and Solutions in Light of the Experience in the U.S." in Queen's Annual Business Law Symposium, *Issues and Perspectives 1995* (Toronto: Carswell, 1995) at 73 (describing protection against "unfair discrimination" and "disparate treatment" in the interpretation of the Bankruptcy Code's "non-consensual restructuring plans" 11 U.S.C. s. 1129).

29. Robert G. Bone, "Rethinking the 'Day in Court' Ideal and Nonparty Preclusion" (1992) 67 N.Y.U. L. Rev. 193 (describing the history and theoretical basis of "interest representation").

30. Nagareda, above note 16 at 795 ("The job of choosing between different settlement regimes while behind the "veil of ignorance" and imposing one preferred choice to serve greater instrumental goals is quintessentially the job of legislatures, not litigants"). This position receives some support from the Supreme Court of Canada's determination in *Western Canada Shopping Centres, Inc.* v. *Dutton*, 2001 SCC 46 [*Dutton*] that, absent a class action statute, "prudence" requires that plaintiffs retain the right to opt out.

31. B.C. s. 16(1).

32. B.C. s. 13.

33. B.C. s. 19(2).

ceeding" [emphasis added].[34] While not explicit, these passages might be interpreted to permit a court to certify a class without notice or opt-out rights.[35]

Ontario's *Act* has the same features,[36] but has no equivalent of B.C.'s section 19(3)(f), which compels the court to consider "whether . . . class members may opt out." Both B.C.'s and Ontario's *Acts*, however, permit either no notice, or notice to only a "sample group within the class."[37] This provides some support for the idea that the legislators considered situations in which notice would be required, not to facilitate opt-outs, but only to ensure that valid objections would be heard and the class is protected against exploitation by the representative plaintiff's counsel.

Certainly the Ontario Law Reform Commission had originally preferred that mandatory classes should be available to the courts. Section 20(1) of the draft bill provided:

> The court shall determine whether some or all of the members of the class should be permitted to exclude themselves from the class action.[38]

There followed a number of criteria that the court "shall consider" when imposing a mandatory class; taken together, they seem designed to deal mainly with claims that would probably not be pursued individually. Nevertheless, the discussion within the 1982 report itself appeared to provide a broader endorsement.[39] At any rate, the mandatory class provision did not survive into final leg-

---

34. B.C. s. 19(3)(f). In context, it is not clear if "whether" class members "may opt out" is a reference to such members' *ability* to remove themselves, or simply the likelihood that they might choose to do so. The use of "may" rather than "might" seems to favour the former interpretation, but one could also argue that "some or all" favours the more conservative reading (as there are no immediately imaginable circumstances where a court would bar only certain members from opting out but not others).

35. Statistical estimation of aggregate awards, as permitted by the statutes, may also at times be at odds with opt-out rights. Because, presumably, it will be legally stronger and economically larger claims that opt out, the aggregate award to the remaining members will be difficult to calculate (because the defendant will argue – correctly – that those who have opted out are likely to be those at law entitled to higher recoveries.

36. Ontario ss. 9, 13 and 17.

37. Ontario s. 17(4)(c); B.C. s. 19(4)(d). See also Saskatchewan s. 21(4)(d) and ULCC 19(4)(d), Newfoundland s. 19(4)(d). Quebec's legislation, however, appears to permit opt-out as a matter of right: Quebec arts. 1007, 1009.

38. Ontario Law Reform Commission, *Report on Class Actions, 3 vols.* (Toronto: Ministry of the Attorney General, 1982) [*Ontario Report (1982)*] at 867.

39. *Ibid.* at 471: "To the extent that class members exercised their right to exclude themselves from the class for the purpose of prosecuting their individual suits, the desired economies would suffer and the possibility of inconsistent judicial holdings would increase."

islation, perhaps because it was thought that flexible notice requirements would fulfill this same limited purpose.[40] While the mandatory class has enjoyed occasional rediscovery among system designers in other countries,[41] it has not yet been embraced outside its limited application in the U.S.

In light of the ambiguity on the question of opt-out rights in class proceedings in Canada, courts here will need to decide in future whether to "fill in the gaps" by designing mandatory classes.[42] If they do so, they might rely on a generous and purposive interpretation of the *Class Proceedings Acts* of British Columbia and Ontario. The power to stay any proceeding "relating" to the class action underway[43] has been interpreted to allow so-called "bar orders" to prevent settling defendants from being subsequently sued for contribution by non-settling defendants.[44] It might be suggested that the same provisions, perhaps combined with the court's power under the legislation to "make any order . . . to ensure [the proceeding's] fair and expeditious determination" or "impose . . . terms" on any

---

40. Cochrane suggests that notice is optional to accommodate two situations: first, if the "members of the class were known and were aware of the claim", or alternatively "if notice of certification would be for all intents and purposes impractical and would not increase the participation of class members in the proceeding". Michael G. Cochrane, *Class Actions: A Guide to the Class Proceedings Act* (Toronto: Canada Law Book, 1993) at 33.

41. The Victorian Attorney-General's Law Reform Advisory Council, in *Class Actions in Victoria: Time For A New Approach* (Melbourne: Victorian Attorney-General, 1997) at 48-49 (recommending in 1997 an "opt out scheme pursuant to which the right to opt out is subject to judicial approval.") found that "[a]n unregulated and unrestricted right to opt out, such as the one provided by s. 33J, can have a number of undesirable consequences such as reducing the opportunities for settlement by reducing the willingness of defendants to settle, and increasing the possibility of inconsistent judicial holdings." The subsequent legislation, however, appears to require opt-out as a matter of "right": *Victoria Supreme Court Act 1986* Part IVA ("Group Proceedings") (as amended by *Courts and Tribunals Legislation (Miscellaneous Amendments) Act 2000*) ss. 33A, 33X.

42. The idea of "filling in the gaps" would have seemed less likely before the decision of the Supreme Court in *Dutton*, above note 30, where a very vague rule of court was "filled out" with policy-driven procedural detail Moreover, the instruction in paragraph 15 of *Hollick* v. *Toronto (City)*, 2001 SCC 68 that courts should apply the statutes "generously" and with a view to their central purposes might also encourage mandatory certification should the court be convinced that opt-out rights operated to the detriment of access to justice, judicial economy and behaviour modification, which, I have argued here, they often do.

43. Ontario s. 13; B.C. s. 13.

44. See *Sawatzky*, above note 15 and *Ontario New Home Warranty Program* v. *Chevron Chemical Co.* (1999), 46 O.R. (3d) 130 (Sup. Ct. J.).

party[45] might be interpreted so as to permit a "mandatory class" (except, as mentioned, in Quebec) and bind even those plaintiffs who attempt to "opt out."[46] Such an interpretation, though, is hampered by the present characterisation of class proceedings acts as purely procedural.

In cases where the per-member amount is small, there appears to be less need for concern over the individual litigative rights of class members, particularly in cases of a limited fund. Consider that, pursuant to the federal *Bankruptcy and Insolvency Act*, the superior court of each province has broad powers to order the consolidation of actions, without the consent of plaintiffs (and in some cases without even a hearing before a judge), if the amounts are less than $1000. While a plaintiff to such a proceeding may advance certain objections throughout, there is no right to "opt out" of such a proceeding.[47]

But what about mandatory aggregation of catastrophic mass tort claims, particularly those where the harm suffered may take years, or even decades, to "mature"? *Sawatzky*[48] introduced us to this other conundrum of mass tort litigation, the problem of so-called "future" or "futures" claims resulting from "immature torts" – in other words, an uncertainty regarding the harm suffered by each class member. In *Sawatzky*, the class was known (recipients of jaw implants), as were initial damages (costs of removing implants, etc.). However, each patient could expect to suffer varying degrees of complications as a result of Teflon left in the body by the implants, and it was expected that future surgeries would be required. In establishing a central fund to be distributed according to a "point system," the *Sawatzky* settlement relied entirely upon assessment of the plaintiffs' present condition in order to estimate future needs. This is consistent with traditional tort damage models,[49] but is not necessarily appropriate in mass tort cases.

Another aspect of "future claims," of course, occurs when the class itself is indeterminate. This would occur, for instance, when a broad class of persons has been exposed to a substance or product that is known to cause disease, but it is not known which of the exposed persons will actually become sick. So far, no Canadian court has tackled this problem head-on.

---

45. B.C. s. 13; Ontario s. 12.

46. For a discussion of "bar orders" see above notes 32 through 40 in Chapter Five and accompanying text. There seems to be little principled difference between barring a suit by an absent defendant (through a bar order), and barring a suit by an absent plaintiff (through a mandatory class).

47. *Bankruptcy and Insolvency Act*, R.S.C. 1985, c. B-3, ss. 219-226.

48. Above note 15.

49. See for instance *Krangle (Guardian ad litem of)* v. *Brisco*, 2002 SCC 9 at para. 21: "[T]he rule that damages must be assessed once and for all at the time of trial (subject to modification on appeal) requires courts to peer into the future and fix the damages for future care as best they can."

However, if an insurance-fund model is indeed adopted to resolve the problem of future claims, it is difficult to see how it would not require a "mandatory" class.

Moreover, from a deterrence point of view it is irrelevant whether scientific estimates of harm arising from the product prove to be mistaken; the court at trial, with all the evidence before it (principally the evidence of risk that was either known or ought to have been known by the defendant at the time of the tortious decision) is in at least as good a position to predict the probable consequences of the tortious decision as the manufacturer was at the time the decision was made. Since the purpose of deterrence is to internalise the costs of that decision, it should be made on the same probabilistic terms as the defendant would use in considering the appropriate level of precautions to take. Certainly aggregate decision-making can avoid many of the traditional expenses of individual trial, which turn on questions of particularistic causation that, in the aggregate, make no difference at all.[50] There is also reason to suggest, as does Resnik, that

---

50. Probabilistic causation is another troublesome area of the law in which tort "moralists" oppose "functionalists," with the former suggesting that the Aristotelian idea of "corrective justice" requires, *on a moral level*, a connection between the wrongdoer and the damage. In other words, it is contrary to natural justice to force a wrongdoer to pay for harm he did not factually cause. This objection loses much of its sting when it is considered in the mass tort setting, because in such cases we generally know that the wrongdoer did factually cause harm, we just don't know *to whom*. Moreover, tort moralists generally ignore the fact that "traditional" rules of liability work on the balance of probabilities, so when a court says it has found the requisite causation, it is really saying that it has found that there is *probably* a causal relationship; in the aggregate of all such claims, in only the *majority* of cases will "causation-in-fact" actually have occurred.. The House of Lords recently came down heavily on the side of the functionalists in *Fairchild et al.* v. *Glenhaven Funeral Services Ltd. et. al.*, [2002] UKHL 22, dispensing with the requirement to show "causation in fact" and imposing risk-based liability in an asbestos case without resort to the "traditional" fictions of burden-shifting, inferences, or presumptions.

For articulation of the moralist position on causation, see: Richard Epstein, "A Theory of Strict Liability" (1973) 2 J. Legal. Stud. 151; Richard Epstein, "Causation – In Context: an Afterword" (1987) 63 Chi.-Kent L. Rev. 653; Ernest J. Weinrib, "Causation and Wrongdoing" (1987) 63 Chi.-Kent L. Rev. 407. The functionalist case has been made in Guido Calabresi, "Concerning Cause and the Law of Torts" (1975-76), 43 U. Chi. L. Rev. 69; Richard A Posner, "A Theory of Negligence" (1972) 1 J. Legal. Stud. 29; "The Concept of Corrective Justice in Recent Theories of Tort Law" (1981) 10 J. Legal. Stud. 187; "Epstein's Tort Theory: A Critique" (1979) 8 J. Legal. Stud. 457; Rosenberg, "The Causal Connection in Mass Exposure Cases: A 'Public Law' Vision of the Tort System" (1984) 97 Harvard L.R. 851; Troyen A. Brennan, "Causal Chains and Statistical Links: The Role of Scientific Uncertainty in Hazardous-Substance Litigation" (1987-88), 73 Cornell L. Rev. 469.

even taking into account the margin of uncertainty in probabilistic projection, compensation for those eventually suffering injury will be more complete with mandatory aggregation than through individual claims.[51]

C. REGULATORY CLASS ACTIONS FOR "FUTURES" CLAIMS

(1) Problems of Causation

Even the most farsighted proponents of class actions struggle with the related questions of indeterminate causation and the treatment of future claims. These two issues present problems that can likely never be addressed outside a comprehensive, regulatory, class litigation regime facilitating either a public or private aggregation by insurers across claims groups.

Consider the classic case of a mass exposure tort in which drug A is alleged to cause disease X in a small number of its many users, some of whom will also suffer from X even had they not taken the drug. Assuming also that there was some negligence that "caused" the statistical increase in illness (perhaps inadequate testing), then a properly aggregated class action should succeed. Given the level of scientific proof available at time of trial, it may also be possible to quantify damages and assess the likelihood of future claims. We might know with some certainty, for instance, that of 100,000 exposed to drug A, 1000 will develop disease X, and of those, 100 cases were actually caused by the drug (i.e. would not have arisen but for the exposure). In such a case the appropriate level of damages should be that sufficient to compensate for the harm in those 100 per-

---

For further discussion of the problem of causation in the modern tort context see: John G. Fleming, "Probabilistic Causation in Tort Law" (1989) 68 Can. Bar. Rev. 661; McLachlin, J., "Negligence Law — Proving the Connection", in Mullany and Linden, eds. *Torts Tomorrow, A Tribute to John Fleming*, LBC Information Services 1998 at 16; Richard Delgado, "Beyond Sindell: Relaxation of Cause-in-Fact Rules for Indeterminate Plaintiffs" (1982); Glen O. Robinson, "Multiple Causation in Tort Law: Reflections on the DES Cases" (1982) 68 VA. L. Rev. 713; Glen O. Robinson, "Probabilistic Causation and Compensation for Tortious Risk" (1985) 14 J. Legal Stud.; 779; in J.D. Fraser and D.R. Horwarth, "More Concern for Cause" (1984) 4 Leg. St. 131; H.L.A. Hart & Tony Honore, *Causation in the Law* (2d) (London: Oxford, 1985); Michael S. Moore, "Thomson's Preliminaries About Causation and Rights" (1987) 63 Chi.-Kent L. Rev. 497; Richard M. Wright "Causation in Tort Law" (1985) 73 Calif. L. Rev. 1735; Ginsberg & Weiss, "Common Law Liability for Toxic Torts: A Phantom Remedy" (1981) 9 Hofstra L. Rev. 859.

51. Judith Resnik, "Litigating and Settling Class Actions: The Prerequisites of Entry and Exit", (1997) 30 U.C. Davis L. Rev. 835 at 843-44.

sons. Any foreseeable model based on traditional tort causation principles will almost certainly result in either overdeterrence or underdeterrence.[52]

Canadian class action law has sensibly evolved to permit certification of classes based on exposure alone.[53] However, once the certification hurdle is overcome and the claim either settles or succeeds on an aggregate basis, the problem of distribution remains.

Under such circumstances, though we can assess aggregate damages with some degree of accuracy, and even predict how many future claims will arise as a result of latent disease processes, the benefit of our knowledge is limited to calculating the gross amount that the defendant should pay to achieve optimal deterrence. When we turn to the question of optimal compensation, the problem remains that we do not know which of the class members became sick because of the product, and we don't know which ones will in the future, or whether their sickness will be causally attributable to the negligence.

Presumably, from the Rawlsian ex ante perspective, individuals would prefer to receive compensation for their illnesses whether they turn out to be caused by particular negligence or not. High rates of first-person insurance sales in the United States, and the system of socialised medicine that obtains in Canada seem to bear this out. But this is not just a problem of "who becomes sick and who does not," which can be dealt with entirely through the application of insurance principles to the available compensation fund. The problem – at least at this ini-

---

52. For instance, assuming the causal mechanism cannot be traced but only inferred statistically (as, for instance, with most cancers), then a claim such as that described, in which there is a one in ten chance that a user of drug A with disease X contracted the disease as a result of the drug, would under traditional tort rules (balance of probability) result in no recoveries and therefore no deterrence. On the other hand, judicial attempts to redress this imbalance through burden-shifting devices are almost equally ineffective and provide no accurate remedy in the aggregate, and thus either overdeterrence or underdeterrence. As a result, some courts and commentators have flirted with the idea of discounted aggregated damages (in this case, the 1000 users of drug A with disease X would together receive 10% recovery to reflect the probability of causation). See generally David Rosenberg, "The Causal Connection in Mass Exposure Cases: a 'Public Law' Vision of the Tort System", (1984) 97 Harv. L. Rev. 851.

53. Indeed to do otherwise would force the court to inquire into a person's injury before even deciding whether they were members of the class. In *Bywater* v. *T.T.C.* (1998), 27 C.P.C. (4th) 172 (Ont. Gen. Div.), Winkler J. rejected an argument by the defendant that the class should be restricted to the passengers during a train fire who had actually suffered injury resulting from smoke inhalation. Winkler J. felt that this would run counter to the three purposes of a class definition, which are (a) to identify those persons who have a potential claim for relief against the defendant; (b) to define the parameters of the lawsuit so as to identify those persons who are bound by its result, and (c) to describe who is entitled to notice.

tial stage – is rather "whose sickness is attributable to the plaintiff?" This is a vexing question not only because it is difficult to answer, but also because it is difficult to justify the question; to put it another way, why should it matter?[54]

It clearly doesn't matter from a deterrence point of view; notwithstanding some insurance-based arguments to the contrary, it is best to ensure that it is the wrongdoer who bears the cost of his wrongdoing,[55] but it doesn't matter at all which of the persons the defendant put at risk became sick as a result. On the other hand, it might matter from the point of view of deterring *plaintiff* recklessness, and this concern can be addressed through contributory negligence defences, considered in the aggregate along with other aspects of liability. The suggestion, then, is that we might consider ways of disconnecting the deterrence role of class action suits with their concomitant aspirations to compensate, and think of deterrence and compensation as independent objectives.

So what of compensation in this paradigm? Assuming that "immature torts" are prosecuted via a class action based on the best scientific data available at the time of trial (or more accurately for deterrence purposes, at the time of the tortious decision), inevitably the resulting aggregate award is only an approximation. In some cases, subsequent data undermining the causal link between the tort and injury might reveal the fund as excessive. More often, as further details of harm related to the product become known, it will be too small.

There are two answers to this objection. The first is simply to say that such inadequacies are not likely to be any worse than those that accrue if the courts wait until the tort is "mature," when the defendant may be unable to pay or is no

---

54.   For a thought-provoking overview of the irrationality of the present tort system's selective compensation mechanisms from a "fairness" perspective, see: Jon O. Newman, "Rethinking Fairness: Perspectives on the Litigation Process" (1985) 94 Yale L. J. 1643.

55.   Craig Brown, for instance, argues that making the wrongdoer bear the costs does not have the promised deterrence effect because the wrongdoer is, in all likelihood, insured himself. In such circumstances, argues Brown, it "is just a question of which insurer is going to pay." Craig Brown, *Insurance Law in Canada* (Toronto: Carswell, 2001) at 13-21 et seq.

      While this reasoning may pertain vis-à-vis the behaviour of individuals, it is not as persuasive in the case of firms engaged in activities which carry a constant threat of liability. In many cases, the firms may be self-insured, in which case the deterrent effect is fully preserved. Even if this is not the case, the increasing cost of premiums and deductibles for careless firms prompted by correctly-set damages awards will pressure a firm (and arguably other similarly risky ventures) to adopt appropriate precautions. Moreover, there is at least anecdotal evidence to suggest that insurance companies can and do bring pressure to bear on their corporate clients to operate more safely. See Allen M. Linden, *Canadian Tort Law* (7th ed.) (Toronto: Butterworths, 2001) at 10-11.

longer extant, or when prophylactic measures available to the plaintiff (frequent testing, preventive medicine) are no longer effective.

The second answer is to design a way in which all the funds from actions are themselves aggregated, averaged, and paid out on insurance principles. Inevitably, such a fund is going to be suboptimal, as attributing causation to harm in every case will not be possible. But such inadequacies will be supplemented, as they are now, by the government through social insurance and by private insurers, essentially topping up the mass tort "superfund," whether the fund itself is privately or publicly administered.

(2) Aggregation Across Claims

While regulatory class actions for "immature" claims may solve one causation-related problem (that of "futures" claims), they do not address the second problem, which is the indeterminate cause of disease *across claimant groups.*

Consider a case in which the incidence of a particular disease X is elevated above the "background level" (the level at which X exists in non-exposed persons) by either drug A, drug B, or environmental pollutant C. Lawsuits are successful against the manufacturers of drugs A and B, and against the environmental polluter. However, it may never be known, even years later, whether a particular patient's case of X was caused by A, B, or C, or was part of the background risk.[56] In such a case, it stands to reason that the proceeds of the funds of A, B, and C should be combined so that compensation will be more complete. It is also arguable that A, B, and C should be combined with government universal health care programs so that adequate coverage can be provided.

In other words, just as maximum aggregation across individual claims maximises deterrence, in order to optimise compensation, aggregation of judgment or settlement funds is desirable. This idea "disentangles" compensation from deterrence, but its realisation is very difficult to imagine without government intervention or a massive system redesign to allow large private insurers to "own" – i.e. prosecute and compensate – diverse portfolios of claims.

It may be possible, at least where subrogation of health care costs is allowed,[57] for a government to bring today a representative action including "futures"

---

56. This is so even if it can be shown that the patient took Drug A to the exclusion of B or of exposure to pollutant C. Provided, as in most cases, that the disease could possibly have another cause, any individual case cannot be attributed with any certainty to a particular defendant.

57. The claim could not presently proceed by way of subrogation in British Columbia, but the Attorney General might well be able to file a class action lawsuit in that jurisdiction, which unlike Ontario permits a non-member to represent the class, but "only if it is necessary to do so in order to avoid a substantial injustice to the class": B.C. s. 2(4). The idea that a government or public-interest body might prosecute class actions without actually being a member of the class is explored in Vince Moribato, "Ideological Plaintiffs and Class Actions – an Australian Perspective"

claims similar to that described in the previous section. In such a case, if an aggregate award is made but cannot be distributed because of causal indeterminacy, the various *Acts* provide for cy pres distribution for the benefit of the class members.[58]

Practically speaking, in the vast majority of Canadian personal injury accidents many costs arising from the wrongdoing are borne by the state. The plaintiff cannot himself recover the costs of hospitalisation, treatment and therapy that are covered by the social safety net. Similarly, in cases involving a risk of future disease, the costs of necessary "medical monitoring" are financed by the government through its medicare programs.

Recently the Supreme Court has clarified that, where government care programs are available to ease care expenses, claims will not succeed for the costs of that care.[59] In other words, state-provided medical benefits will be deducted from any award made to an individual, except where recovery and subrogation rights are explicitly provided for by statute.

Yet in Canada, subrogated claims brought by government medical plans on behalf of mass tort victims have been rare,[60] although it appears that this may be

---

(2001) 34 U.B.C. L. Rev. 459. Moribato describes cases in which non-member plaintiffs have been permitted in Australian cases, notwithstanding that the applicable statutes do not seem to foresee it.

58. Ontario s. 26(4); B.C. s. 34(1); Saskatchewan s. 37(1); *ULCC Model Act* s. 34(1)

59. *Krangle (Guardian ad litem of)* v. *Brisco*, above note 49. Subject, however, to a contingency award representing the likelihood that the benefits will not be continued by the government in the future. In *Krangle*, the Court discounted the cost of future care that would be incurred by the parents when the infant plaintiff reached the age of 19, as at that time he could be placed in a group home, subject to a 5% probability that the program would be reduced or eliminated by the government in the future. Some commentators and courts have suggested that these contingencies might become larger and more common as the pressure upon social programs increases: Jamie Cassels, *Remedies: The Law of Damages* (Toronto: Irwin Law, 2000) at 403-04.

As an aside, *Krangle* is a good example of how the present tort system overvalues compensation and undervalues deterrence. Here, the negligent doctor is allowed to "offload" or externalise the cost of his wrongdoing on to society as a whole. While the compensation for the victim may be adequate, as long as the full harm is not being paid by the tortfeasor the deterrence effect is suboptimal. Inexplicably, the court found that payment of these costs would represent *unfairness* to the defendant as well as representing a "windfall" to the plaintiffs: *Krangle*, at paras. 22-23.

60. The claim has been advanced in the Phen-Fen diet pill litigation, where provincial health plans are claiming as subrogees for the cost of medical monitoring. The hearing judge refused to dismiss the claim, and on appeal it was noted that medical monitoring claims have been advanced previously in Canada: *Wilson* v. *Servier*

changing.[61] There are several reasons for the rarity. Aside from the uncertainty of medical monitoring claims,[62] not all Canadian provinces even have statutes permitting subrogation for the recovery of such expenses,[63] in part because such clauses have proven cumbersome and inefficient in individual actions. Also, it is not certain whether such statutes are sufficient to grant full control of the proceedings to the government insurer (a problem that sometimes plagues private insurers as well).[64] Multijurisdictional class proceedings complicate this matter further. As a result, a large component of the costs of accidents "falls through the cracks" in the courthouse, and can therefore be expected to be systemically externalised, with deterrence accordingly reduced and overall costs correspondingly increased.

Because of the significant role of government insurance in offsetting the harm caused by mass torts, any fundamental comprehensive reform of mass tort liability might consider ways to separate the compensation from the deterrence function. There are many ways of accomplishing this.

The most straightforward proposal is simply to abolish the negligence system altogether and rely on insurance, social or private, to compensate tort victims. Judge Weinstein, for instance, has advocated taking advantage of the (then)

Canada Inc. (2000), 50 O.R. (3d) 219 (Sup. Ct. J.). Cumming J. found the question of whether a subrogated claim can be maintained for the cost of medical monitoring was a common issue. *Ibid.* para. 133, leave to appeal dismissed: (2000), 52 O.R. (3d) 20 (Sup. Ct. J. Div. Ct.). The court of appeal found (at para. 18) that the "issue is arguable and should not be excluded at this stage of the proceeding." Medical monitoring pleadings had been allowed to proceed in *Nantais* v. *Telectronics Proprietary (Canada) Ltd.* (1995), 127 D.L.R. (4th) 552 (Ont. Gen. Div.) and *Anderson* v. *Wilson* (1999), 44 O.R. (3d) 673 at 675-76, 175 D.L.R. (4th) 409 (C.A.). Neither case offered resolution of the legal question.

61.   Apart from *Wilson* v. *Servier,* and the earlier case of *Nantais,* both *ibid,* plaintiff's counsel has confirmed with the author that he expects government subrogation claims to be advanced in two lawsuits (in Ontario and B.C.) recently filed against Medtronics over the replacement and monitoring of allegedly faulty heart pacemaker components.

62.   See *Ibid.* American courts have disagreed about whether a plaintiff can recover medical monitoring costs where the monitoring confirms that the disease is not present. Some cases regard the test as being whether the exposure to a toxic substance is the "proximate cause" of a "significantly increased risk" of contracting a serious latent disease: see *Barnes* v. *American Tobacco Co.,* 161 F.3d 127 at 138-39 (Pa. C.A. 1998); *Ayres* v. *Jackson,* 525 A.2d 287 (N.J. 1987) at 298 at 311. Some aspects of the issue are discussed by the United States Supreme Court in *Metro-North Commuter Railroad Co.* v. *Buckley,* 521 U.S. 424 (1997) at 441-44.

63.   Ontario has such a plan (*Health Insurance Act,* R.S.O. 1990, c. H.6 ss. 30-36), but B.C. as yet does not.

64.   Craig Brown, *Insurance Law in Canada* (Toronto: Carswell, 2001) at 13-21 et seq.

pending U.S. national health care program to do away with tort liability, as New Zealand has done,[65] and simply compensating victims directly on a need-driven basis. In Weinstein's idea, the regulatory (deterrence) function of mass tort law would then be provided by criminal sanction in the form of an immediate fine.[66]

Although it is true that insurance can provide much better compensation than the existing tort system, there are difficulties with the second element of Weinstein's plan. First, regulatory bodies have proven themselves to be largely ineffective in everything except setting the most basic standards of safety or conduct; the bureaucracies necessary to police all aspects of industry currently subject to negligence liability would almost certainly be bloated and inefficient compared to the self-interested plaintiffs' bar.[67] Second, the criminal system would need to rely on fines, which would either be arbitrarily set (and thus generally overdeter or underdeter) or would be based on calculations of the actual harm caused (in which case a trial would be required in any event).[68] Alternative proposals to levy a tax on dangerous industries (presumably to a higher degree than is already done) do have the effect of internalising harm (though, again, crudely), but would have very little deterrent effect.[69]

---

65. New Zealand's plan, instituted in 1974, provides compensation for personal injury, defined as physical injury and any mental injury arising from covered physical injuries. Benefits include: weekly compensation, an independence allowance, cover for medical costs, and rehabilitation assistance. The benefits available in fatal claims include: surviving spouse weekly compensation, compensation for children, a survivor's grant and a funeral grant. The scheme has replaced workers' compensation and the common law action for damages. The funding comes from a transfer of the now-redundant insurance premiums that were previously being paid to various insurance companies into the Accident Compensation Corporation (ACC), the only organisation involved in distributing compensation. See generally Lewis H. Klar, "New Zealand's Accident Compensation Scheme: A Tort Lawyer's Perspective" (1983) 33 Toronto L.J. 80; Colleen M. Flood, "New Zealand's No-Fault Accident Compensation Scheme: Paradise or Panacea?" (1999/2000) 8 Health L. Rev. 3.

66. Weinstein, *Individual Justice in Mass Tort Litigation* (Evanston, Ill.: Northwestern University Press, 1995) at 170.

67. Weinstein provides no support for his contention that "The many federal regulatory agencies can deter more effectively than a tort system" except anecdotal evidence that a fine might be imposed "promptly while the responsible management is still in control": *Ibid.* at 170.

68. Weinstein offers only the vaguest guidelines for how fines might be calculated, based on a valuation of human life amounting to $3 to $5 million: *Ibid.*

69. Unless the tax were closely related to standards, as for instance workers' compensation plans might strive to be, rates would be set or adjusted only as quickly as political will and legislative agendas permitted, hardly a recipe for accurate calculation of deterrent effect. Indeed the taxation model provides disincentives to pre-

Instead, an optimal system design might take the best aspects of the two existing systems and allow each of them to do what it does best. Insurance, including
a New Zealand-style comprehensive social insurance, is a far better compensator
than is tort. Conversely, for all its failures as an insurer, tort litigation may be a
far better deterrent than is any pressure from insurers or tax advisors.

A government-based initiative could create a mass tort "superfund" into
which aggregate tort damages would be deposited to "top up" tax dollars and
medicare premiums to provide appropriate redress for harm resulting from systemic negligence.[70] This would permit persons who wish only basic coverage to
eschew additional insurance, although experience indicates that most would have
it in any event. Lawsuits would be still be filed by entrepreneurial lawyers on
behalf of the class; the key difference would be that distribution to class members would be unnecessary – the money could be split between the lawyer pursuing the action and the "superfund."

Some approximation of this system might be possible within the existing legislative framework. While the cy pres distribution provisions of the various *Acts*,
described above, appear to foresee distribution only of those parts of the awards
that are not otherwise distributed to class members, there is strong suggestion in
the 1982 Report that these passages were intended to allow the benefit to accrue
to the welfare state for the general good.[71]

---

cautions; in order to gain a competitive edge, industries will be pressured to cut corners on safety to lower costs, safe in the knowledge that the penalties for doing so
will not be immediate and will be spread throughout the industry. This would likely
produce a "prisoner's dilemma" — a "race to the bottom" among competing firms.

70. See for instance the proposals and discussion in Troyen A. Brennan, "Causal
Chains and Statistical Links: The Role of Scientific Uncertainty in Hazardous-
Substance Litigation" (1987-88), 73 Cornell L. Rev. 469 (proposing a mass tort
"superfund," overseen through a national "science panel").

71. The *Ontario Report (1982)* above note 38 says at 575:

An example of a "benefit" distribution in the class action context is the first
antibiotics settlement, *State of West Virgina* v. *Chas. Pfizer & Co., Inc.* In that
case, the Court of Appeals for the Second Circuit approved a settlement in
which the class members were notified that a failure on their part to file an individual claim would constitute an authorization to the state Attorneys General
representing the class to apply any unclaimed moneys for the benefit of the citizens of the state in such a manner as the court might direct. [citations omitted]

The report continued (*ibid.* at 575 n. 261):

The unclaimed residue was ultimately applied to a number of public health proj-
ects, such as drug abuse programs, lead poisoning and sickle-cell anemia
research, and community health clinics.

It is also apparent that the authors of the report included provisions that cy pres settlements may be made even if third parties benefited from them in order to clarify
that such "windfalls" to third parties should not provide a basis for rejecting cy pres

However, the various governments have shown comparatively little enthusiasm for recovering their health care expenditures from tortfeasors through the courts. Recently, Ontario amended its *Health Insurance Act* to allow a direct right of action against a wrongdoer for health care costs.[72] To date no actions have been taken in Canada based on this provision. As I mentioned earlier, British Columbia and Newfoundland have passed specific legislation to recover tobacco-related health care costs only.[73] Yet these remain isolated examples.

Another proposal that has been made in the United States is to permit a free market in subrogated claims, separating compensation – which would then be provided by insurers on a first-party basis – from deterrence, which would be provided by aggregate suits by insurers on behalf of efficiently aggregated claims. This would create a market-based system that is roughly the equivalent of the government-sponsored "superfund" that I moot above. Fried and Rosenberg explain:

> One far-reaching, indeed potentially transformative device entails a relatively small change in the law governing the assignment of tort claims. In particular, courts could promote coordination and other goals simply by lifting restrictions on first-party insurance subrogation that limit the insurers to recovering the amount or value of benefits paid or promised under the policy or plan. This change would immediately create an ex ante market in which insurers — commercial and governmental — could purchase the entire, generally undifferentiated portfolio of *potential* claims in tort that might arise from an insured loss. Thus, insurers could acquire complete ownership interest in the prosecution and proceeds of their insureds' tort claims regardless of limitations on the insurance coverage. Notably, in personal injury actions insurers could recover tort damages far exceeding their normal economic loss coverage, including awards for non-pecuniary harm which under optimal insurance theory are unnecessary for compensation of individual insureds. Insureds will greatly benefit from this arrangement: transferring ownership of their potential tort claims to insurers will enhance the deterrence benefits of litigation because of the increased coordination in information investment and also because insurers can exploit unique advantages of risk-neutrality and additional advantages of scale. The exchange also increases insureds' welfare by providing them with optimal insurance coverage plus immediate payment of financial consideration in the form of reduced premiums or taxes or direct rebate equal to the

---

distribution. (*ibid.* at 577-78. See for example B.C. 34(2), allowing cy pres distribution even if it "would result in unreasonable benefits to persons who are not members of the class or subclass").

72. *Health Insurance Act*, R.S.O. 1990, c. H.6 s. 36.0.1 provides that
   (1) If the Plan has paid for insured services as a result of the negligence or other wrongful act or omission of a person, the Plan has a right, independent of its subrogated right under subsections 30 (1) and 46 (5), to recover, directly against that person, the costs for insured services that have been incurred in the past and that will probably be incurred in the future as a result of the negligence or the wrongful act or omission.

73. Above notes 68 and 69 in Chapter Two and accompanying text.

expected value of the insurers' aggregate net tort recovery. Unlimited insurance subrogation thus negates the inefficient and negative distributive effects of "tort premiums and insurance" for non-pecuniary harm, converting the expected recovery of such tort damages into immediate certain premium and tax reductions and other financial benefits. At the same time, unlimited insurance subrogation would press claims for full tort recovery in order to provide optimal deterrence, including price-effects that disadvantage riskier activities in competitive markets.[74]

This is another method of achieving aggregation across claims, because each major insurance company would be holding a diverse portfolio of claims at any given time. Claims against particular defendants could then be traded among the insurance companies ending up with those who could pursue them with greatest efficiency.

Nevertheless, such dramatic change is unlikely in the foreseeable future. This does not mean, however, that aggregate litigation cannot better address mass torts creating risk-based harm. It might even be possible to reproduce many of the benefits of a truly comprehensive system with the existing tools and jurisprudence.

(3) Class Actions for "Immature" Claims

Because direct action by the government for mass tort or nuisance is often a process as cumbersome and expensive as large criminal or regulatory prosecutions, proposals have been developed to allow the market to operate in the bringing of public-interest suits. Many statutes in the U.S. and Canada permit individuals to bring claims for breach of a particular statutory provision, but these almost always require that the plaintiff suffer some harm as a result of the wrongdoing, for which that plaintiff is allowed to recover. Under some U.S. laws, "treble damages" awards are possible to encourage a greater deterrence effect from these "private attorneys-general." But, however effective against "crimes," these are crude devices with which to confront the regulation of precautions against accident.

However, it is possible to envisage a scheme empowering a group of individuals to sue any mass tort defendant for *increased risk* arising in the populace from exposure.[75] Using the best statistical and epidemiological evidence avail-

---

74. Charles Fried & David Rosenberg, "Making Tort Law: What Should be Done and who Should Do It" (forthcoming 2002: unpublished manuscript on file with the author). Rosenberg had sketched out such systems before: see David Rosenberg "The Uncertainties of Assigned Shares Tort Compensation: What We Don't Know Can Hurt Us" (1986) 6 Risk Analysis 363; David Rosenberg, "Of End Games and Openings in Mass Tort Cases: Lessons from a Special Master" (1989) 69 B.U. L. Rev. 695.

75. The academic support for the idea is described in Alan Schwartz, "Causation in Private Tort Law: A Comment on *Kelman*" (1987) 63 Chi. Kent. L. Rev. 639 at 646. Some of the articles exploring the idea of risk-based claims include: David

able, an assessment of damages could be made entirely in the abstract. The proceeds from this action, were it to succeed, would be paid into a central fund that would be used for medical and court costs, or into an insurance fund to protect the future health of class members.[76] Such an idea has the advantage of simultaneously addressing the opposite problem of immature claims pursued on an individual basis – overcompensation and overdeterrence based on erroneous assessments of causation – because as risk-averse humans we would prefer the defendant to act on the best information reasonably available to it, and not to take the risk that scientific indications of disease causation might later turn out to be erroneous.

Should the defendant's liability be established, an aggregate award might be calculated on the basis of statistical evidence[77] if, *inter alia*, "the aggregate or a part of the defendant's liability to some or all class members can reasonably be determined without proof by individual class members."[78] The cy pres provisions allow the court to order that undistributed moneys "be applied in any manner that

---

Rosenberg, "Causal Connection" above note 52; Glen O. Robinson, "Probabilistic Causation and Compensation for Tortious Risk" 14 J. Legal. Stud. 779 (1985); and Christopher H. Schroeder, "Corrective Justice and Liability for Increasing Risks" 37 UCLA L. R. 439 (1990). U.S. scholars have suggested a range of solutions: Wendy E. Wagner, "Choosing Ignorance in the Manufacture of Toxic Products" (1997) 82 Cornell L. Rev. 773 (suggesting a presumption of causation when manufacturers cannot show that they have performed minimal safety testing); Margaret A. Berger, "Eliminating General Causation: Notes Towards a New Theory of Justice and Toxic Torts" (1997) 97 Colum. L. Rev. 2117 at 2122 (suggesting a legal duty to adequately research and warn, fulfillment of which by defendants would constitute a complete defense to liability); Andrew R. Klein, "A Model for Enhanced Risk Recovery in Tort" (1999) 56 Wash. & Lee L. Rev. 1173 (proposing recovery for enhanced risk when plaintiff can show that exposure to the product has at least doubled plaintiff's risk of injury).

76. The relationship of the risk-based claim with insurance is discussed in David Rosenberg, "Individual Justice and Collectivizing Risk-Based Claims in Mass-Exposure Cases" (1996) 71 N.Y.U. L. Rev. 210 at 220.

77. B.C. s. 30.

78. B.C. s. 29(1)(c). It will be apparent by now that there are numerous advantages to early and complete aggregation of all possible claims. One further advantage bears mentioning here: among the factors that might give rise to "blackmail settlements" (and thus overdeterrence) is the concern that juries tend to award greater punitive damages to less severely injured plaintiffs when their claims are presented alongside those of more severely injured persons.": Irwin A. Horowitz & Kenneth S. Bordens, "The Effects of Outlier Presence, Plaintiff Population Size, and Aggregation of Plaintiffs on Simulated Civil Jury Decisions" (1988) 12 Law & Hum. Behav. 209 at 225. If this is indeed the case, then more accurate settlements may be reached with *less* evidence of individual damages.

may reasonably be expected to benefit class or subclass members, even though the order does not provide for monetary relief to individual class or subclass members."[79] Similar rules obtain in Quebec[80] and Ontario.[81]

These passages would appear to allow, for instance, for the moneys to be applied to the provision of long-term extended health or disability insurance (through government or private carriers) to those who have been exposed to the harm. Such an award would also remove an obstacle sometimes voiced with respect to "windfalls" for plaintiffs; in such an action, no class members gain any net financial benefit from the scheme, except to the extent that the resulting insurance provides them with treatment or disability payments to which they might not otherwise have been legally entitled.

There remain legal hurdles to the success of such a claim. A defendant might argue that the action should be barred as "no damages" have been suffered by any identifiable person, and that economic loss is recoverable only to the extent that it has arisen from personal injury.[82] These are as yet unsettled questions of substantive tort law,[83] and the courts' repeated description of class action legis-

---

79. B.C. s. 34(1). Identical provisions are found in the *Saskatchewan Act* (s. 37) and the *ULCC Model Act* (s. 34).

80. Quebec arts. 1028, 1031-1036, 1044.

81. Ontario s. 26(4).

82. It is a dichotomy of the common law of remedies that a plaintiff's damages may be *reduced* in accordance with the likelihood of contingencies (everything from pre-existing illness to propensity to suicide), but not *increased* in the same way. For instance, if an asbestos worker or coal miner is injured in a car accident, his recovery from the negligent driver might be reduced on the basis that working life expectancy (and hence future earnings) for a worker in his industry was less than average. This is so whether or not he has manifested any symptoms of disability; it is an actuarial figure arrived at through probabilistic analysis. However, he cannot recover from his employer for the probabilistic reduction of life expectancy without proof on the balance of probability that some harm has occurred. For a discussion of contingencies see Linda D. Rainaldi, ed., *Damages and Remedies in Tort* (Toronto: Carswell, 1995) at §§76-78.

83. As mentioned, Canadian courts have allowed class claims based on "nervous shock" and "medical monitoring" to proceed in certain cases where plaintiffs have not yet manifested otherwise actionable injuries (see above note 59 and accompanying text). If one considers that nervous shock at learning of exposure can be compensable even in a nominal way (as the Court of Appeal in *Anderson* v. *Wilson*, above note 60, allowed may be the case even where subsequent testing revealed that disease did not result from the exposure), then it is not unreasonable to suggest that economic loss that foreseeably flows from the shock of exposure (such as the costs of appropriate health and disability insurance) should be recoverable as well. Only in this way would the wrongdoer bear the full cost of its negligence and optimal deterrence be achieved.

lation as strictly procedural may hinder application of the statutes to change any of these rules, though they appear intended to do so.[84] Another barrier is the question of opt-out rights,[85] although, as mentioned in the discussion of the "mandatory class," the Acts may be read to permit suits where no opt-out is permissible.

There is a strong argument that, from a regulatory point of view, such suits are desirable and necessary. It is only from the purely ex post compensatory point of reference that the adequacy of such an aggregate judgement can be questioned, and in the case of diseases that might take years or decades to become manifest, a strong presumption might favour early action based on the best evidence, rather than waiting for the wrongs to "mature," at which point the defendant may have disappeared as a legal entity.

D. APPROPRIATE LITIGATION INCENTIVES: THE UNPOPULAR QUESTION OF COUNSEL FEES

As difficult as it may be to accept, any discussion of counsel fees must begin with the recognition of a simple fact: any assessment of fees that amounts to less than the class recovery risks being, from a deterrence point of view, suboptimal. This is because the defendant will make a litigation investment appropriate to his prospective loss, which is the amount awarded in damages plus his own litigation costs. The class counsel, on the other hand, is going to invest only that amount which is reasonably assured of an appropriate investment return.

This leads us rather abruptly to the conclusion that, if deterrence is to be truly optimised, the investor in the class litigation must be in the position to recover the entire amount at stake. While some commentators indeed have suggested such an idea, it would be impermissible in a system that holds compensation to be a primary goal of mass tort litigation. Nevertheless, it is salient to adopt this principle as a starting point to emphasise that, while the idea of lawyers enjoying windfall profits is politically difficult, any sharp restriction on the amount of fees recoverable by class counsel will not only mean that fewer plaintiffs will be compensated, but also that more persons will be injured as a result of suboptimal deterrence. It is thus unhelpful to examine the appropriateness of counsel's fees in any isolated case without weighing the public regulatory value of class actions.

---

84. It is difficult to read the various Acts' anticipation of calculating "the aggregate . . . of the defendant's liability" "without proof by individual class members' otherwise.

85. Class members with the strongest claim could opt out of the central action, but still take advantage of the socialised medicine supported, in part, by the class action. In this way the class members would be subsidising the opt-outs. This would be only inefficiently remedied through subrogation of the medicare portion of the recovery (I say inefficiently because individualistic recovery, for the reasons outlined earlier in this book, will be less than that obtainable through optimal aggregation).

Any proposal that counsel fees should, in general, be increased is bound to be greeted with suspicion, and indeed it is difficult to consider the topic rationally. The benefits of high counsel fees – increased deterrence and thus fewer accidents – are invisible; we do not have the opportunity to see the suffering and harm that the deterrence has alleviated; we can only imagine it. On the other hand, the sheer magnitude of some class counsels' fees – and (in the U.S. at least) some class counsels' ostentatious lifestyles, are visceral and strike many hard-working people as obscene. Such a dichotomy may be at the heart of courts' reluctance to set fees high enough, even when it is pointed out that jet-setting lawyers are no wealthier nor more ostentatious than other types of successful market investors (in fact on average, it would seem, far less so), and indeed have become wealthy (if the substantive law is operating correctly) by doing a positive public good rather than by simply speculating in a neutral market.

In Canada, counsel fees may be negotiated prior to the commencement of the action, but this is largely *pro forma*; actual court approval of the fees generally occurs when the matter has been resolved, raising the risk that hindsight will skew the court's view of the risks undertaken by counsel in pursuing the action.

Canadian courts frequently adopt a "multiplier" or "lodestar" approach to counsel fees, and then assess their reasonableness by comparing the gross figure arrived at with a percentage of the total recovery to determine the fees" overall "reasonableness." The Ontario Court of Appeal, in the leading case of *Gagné* v. *Silcorp* said that:

> One yardstick by which [the multiplier] can be tested is the percentage of gross recovery that would be represented by the multiplied base fee. If the base fee as multiplied constitutes an excessive proportion of the total recovery, the multiplier might well be too high.[86]

Yet this approach is not without pronounced difficulties. It is not possible, for instance, to know the amount of recovery (or the eventual figure for the "base fee") in advance, i.e. at the time the investment risk is being assessed, except in cases of so-called "settlement class actions," where certification and settlement occur simultaneously. More importantly, though, from the point of view of max-imising litigation investment (and therefore settlement incentive and general deterrence) it is preferable to avoid reducing the fee simply because the recovery will be small. That is to say, if optimal deterrence is to be achieved, fees must be set with a view to promoting the optimal litigation investment, *even if this amount approaches the amount of damages.*

It is worthwhile to emphasise this point because of the argument that certifi-cation should not be granted in cases where the counsel fees are likely to con-sume the entire settlement amount, or "in kind" settlements where the plaintiffs are paid through gift certificates, etc. and only the class counsel receives direct pecuniary benefit. Whatever the problems with such "scrip" settlements (they will not, generally speaking, promote optimal deterrence), the reluctance demon-

---

86.   *Gagné* v. *Silcorp* (1998), 41 O.R. (3d) 417 at 425 (C.A.).

strates a further underappreciation of the role of deterrence, and that of class counsel as "private attorneys-general." Moreover, it is worth remembering that in such cases compensation is hardly enhanced by the denial of certification; true, if the lawyers' fees consume the entire judgment there will be no recovery, but in such cases there would almost certainly be none in any event.[87]

While we are discussing the topic of the impact of fee structures on settlement incentives, it may be worthwhile to point out that there is an argument against any multiplier-based system in that it tends to reward overinvestment in litigation, i.e. time spent well in excess of that which would provide the optimal investment and optimal deterrent effects. There have also been objections raised on the basis that calculating the base fee is an unnecessarily cumbersome task that might be spared a court, with one dismissing such calculations as "so much Mumbo Jumbo."[88]

Perhaps the strongest endorsement that can be made of contingency fees calculated on a straight percentage basis is that they add a welcome degree of certainty to the calculations of risk undertaken by class counsel at the outset of litigation. Quite often, substantial outlay is required to investigate the factual and legal basis for the claim, to gather together representative members of classes and subclasses, and so on. Coalitions are frequently built by collaborating counsel across the continent, and arrangements made for division of eventual fees.

Nevertheless, the sometimes very large awards that percentage-based calculations can generate is bound to be controversial. Indeed, at least one court has suggested that "a percentage fee should generally be lower where the recovery is higher."[89]

It may be that such a rule of thumb can generate appropriate results, but it certainly will not always be so. Indeed, it is important to remember that, the more that is at stake in the litigation, the more incentive a defendant has to maximise his litigation investment. In other words, it may be more important to have higher fees in cases where the recovery is highest, particularly in cases that are likely to be "investment sensitive."[90]

Some types of settlements, particularly those involving structured payment plans, "in kind," or "scrip" settlements, discussed earlier, provide attitional prob-

---

87. Assuming counsel's fees reflect work done to further the litigation, then clearly if a class proceeding is not economically viable no individual claim is likely to be either.

88. In Re *Union Carbide Corp.* v. *Consumer Products Business Securities Litigation*, 724 F. Supp. 160 at 170 (S.D.N.Y., 1989).

89. *Harrington* v. *Dow Corning Corporation*, unreported (January 29, 1999) Vancouver C954330 at para. 6 (B.C.S.C.).

90. A case is investment sensitive if its outcome is more likely to be influenced by the amount of money spent on litigation. Thus factors such as complexity of legal or factual issues, number and calibre of experts, document management issues, and so on, all contribute to the investment-sensitivity of a case.

lems of agency because the class counsel's incentives to oversee fair distribution diminish upon the payment of fees. In the case of "in kind" and "scrip" settlements, as noted, both the recovery by class members and the deterrent effect may be minimal, and I have proposed that such settlements should be discouraged on those grounds. Manipulation of counsel fees is one way to accomplish this, and indeed the RAND Institute has suggested that in "coupon" cases, for instance, the class counsel's fees should be based upon the number of coupons *redeemed*, rather than the number *issued*.[91] Such schedules, of course, anticipate that attorney's fees would be paid in instalments; such an idea would provide further incentives for the class counsel to ensure the widest distribution of the award.

Such observations militate against any "one size fits all" calculation of fee schedules, but further reinforce the powerful, perhaps all-powerful, role of counsel fees in fulfilling the public policy objectives of class litigation.

Another factor to consider is the type of lawsuit; courts and commentators recognise that plaintiffs' counsel have a preference for high-return investments, particularly in the securities field. Moeller writes:

> Although class actions encourage optimal investment in mass injury litigation by making valuable economies of scale available to plaintiffs, they also create the possibility of overlitigation and overdeterrence. Like other investors, profit-maximizing plaintiffs' attorneys actively seek out the highest return on the dollar. In the class action context, this strategy leads them to favour such low-cost, high-value claims as securities fraud. Securities litigation often involves the use of "boilerplate allegations" and "generally follow[s] a recognisable pattern based on federal securities statutes and case precedent," all of which lowers the costs of litigation . . . It is crucial, however, that the potential excesses and abuses of securities class actions not blind policymakers to the no less harmful problem of underinvestment in litigation. An intelligent reform of class action attorneys' fees must seek to provide practical assurance that attorneys will invest at the optimal level.[92]

One way to compensate for the inexactness of calculating plaintiffs' fees is to consider the litigation investment made by the defendants, and base a multiplier in consideration of that amount. This would avoid the problem of overspending (as the defendant has no incentive to do so) and would also emphasise the goal of "levelling the playing field." In such a system, class counsel would be more likely to optimise investment, the issues are more likely to be thoroughly aired, and investment predictability arguably enhanced. This is not to say that class counsel's fees should simply be based on the defendant's expenditures, but rather

---

91. Deborah R. Hensler & Thomas D. Rowe, "Beyond 'It Just Ain't Worth It': Alternative Strategies for Damage Class Action Reform" (2001) 64 *Law & Contemporary Problems* 137 at 151. This makes sense from both the deterrence and compensation viewpoints. RAND also recommended that judges award lower fees when cy pres distribution is employed unnecessarily in settlements to the detriment of claimants.

92. Sally Moeller, "Class Auctions: Market Models for Attorney's Fees in Class Action Litigation" (2000) 113 Harv. L. Rev. 1827 [Moeller] at 1837.

that the latter should be taken into account when calculating the base amount to which the multiplier should be applied. It should be noted, however, that to take full advantage of this idea would likely require either the voluntary cooperation of the defendant in disclosing its own expenditures (though this could be done in the most general fashion[93]), or testimony from experienced expert witnesses on what the defendant would likely have spent in such a case. How the defendant's expenditures are calculated is less important than the fact of consideration of this factor in setting the plaintiff's base fee.

In the U.S., there have been several attempts to design systems which exploit market incentives to arrive at the correct attorney fees. Two of the most unusual and provocative are "lead counsel auctions" and "claim auctions."[94]

A lead counsel auction is a process for dealing with situations in which several claims seek certification to represent the same class. Generally, these simultaneous applications are consolidated to a single court within the jurisdiction. At that point, the court must decide which investor will be allowed to proceed. In the United States District Court for the Northern District of California, Judge Walker has repeatedly employed a technique whereby each firm "bids" on its representation of the class.[95] Because the firms bidding were essentially equivalent in "background, experience, and legal abilities,"[96] Judge Walker felt that the market should operate on the basis of price competition; in other words, the firm that would accept the lowest amount (generally expressed as a percentage of overall recovery, often on a sliding scale) would win the right to prosecute the claim.

There are obvious flaws in this idea. Some have pointed out that it is hardly self-evident that the best lawyer is also the cheapest.[97] Moreover, from the point of view of optimum litigation investment, the lead counsel auction creates the opposite incentives from those that a system designer would desire. In other words, in seeking to offer the lowest price, a firm would be calculating on maximising its own recovery by minimising its investment, regardless of whether such a level of investment was sufficient to maximise the class's recovery. With lead counsel auctions, not only would the lawyers receive less, but probably so would the class; in such a system, only the defendant benefits.

---

93. At least one court has embraced the idea of such a general disclosure of fees, ordering class counsel to provide "more general information summarised from their time records" to assist the court in calculating the appropriate fee: *Murphy* v. *Mutual of Omaha Insurance Co.*, [2000] B.C.J. No. 2046 at para. 43 (S.C.).

94. For an overview of market models for attorneys' fees in class actions, see Moeller, above note 92.

95. The first employment of the technique can be seen in In Re *Oracle Securities Litigation* 131 F.R.D. 688 (N.D. Cal. 1990).

96. In Re *Oracle Securities Litigation* 132 F.R.D. 538 at 542 (N.D. Cal. 1990).

97. Nanette L. Stasko, "Comment, Competitive Bidding in the Courthouse: In Re *Oracle Securities Litigation*" (1994) 59 Brook. L. Rev. 1667 at 1696.

A more rational – if radical – solution is the *claims* auction. In this proposal, "investors" would bid on the value of the claim as a whole. If for instance, a products liability action had a probabilistic recovery of $1 million with an optimum litigation investment of $200,000, then a risk-neutral investor could be expected to bid up to $800,000 for the claim. That money would be paid into the court "up front," to form a compensation fund for the class members, offset court costs, pay for social insurance programs, etc. The "investor" would then prosecute the action to realise the maximum return on the investment. Numerous modifications of this system have been proposed, including a "staged" bidding process that allowed the market to intervene at several stages of the litigation process.[98]

Realistically, though, "claims auctions" rely upon investors with resources nearly equivalent to those of corporate defendants and their insurers. In Canada, the class action plaintiffs' bar is still dominated by a handful of small firms and there is no indication that first-party insurers are clamouring to take over prosecution of such cases. While investment in class actions has been permitted,[99] it has been sharply limited,[100] and restrictions based on champerty and maintenance

98. See generally Moeller, above note 92, "Developments – The Paths of Civil Litigation" (2000) 113 Harv. L. Rev. 1752 at 1845-50. Claim auctions have been most thoroughly explored in three leading articles by Cornell professor Jonathan Macey and N.Y.U.'s Geoffrey Miller: Jonathan R. Macey & Geoffrey P. Miller, "The Plaintiffs" Attorney's Role in Class Action and Derivative Litigation: Economic Analysis and Recommendations for Reform" (1991) 58 U. Chi. L. Rev. 1; Jonathan R. Macey & Geoffrey P. Miller, "Auctioning Class Actions and Derivative Suits: A Rejoinder" (1993) Nw. U.L. Rev. 458; Jonathan R. Macey & Geoffrey P. Miller, "A Market Approach to Tort Reform Via Rule 23" (1995) 80 Cornell L. Rev. 909.

99. Eizenga et al. cite *Nantais* v. *Telectronics Proprietary (Canada) Ltd.* (1996), 28 O.R. (3d) 523 (Gen. Div.), one occasion where a non-lawyer investor has been permitted to lend the representative plaintiff's counsel $300,000, repayable in the event of success at a rate of 20% per annum. Eizenga notes that the arrangement "would appear to have been carefully designed to not be characterised as champerty or maintenance": Michael A. Eizenga, Michael J. Peerless & Charles M. Wright, *Class Actions Law and Practice* (Toronto, Butterworths, 1999) at §11.17.

100. In *Smith* v. *Canadian Tire Acceptance Ltd.* (costs motion) (1995), 22 O.R. (3d) 433 (Gen. Div.), aff'd (1995) 26 O.R. (3d) 94 (C.A.), Winkler J. ordered solicitor-and-client costs against non-party organizers of an early credit card interest rate litigation. The organizers had solicited members of the class to invest $100 each in the litigation, promising them a share of contingent fee over and above any damages they would have collected should their lawsuit alleging overcharge of interest succeed. The rather crass nature of the investment scheme in *Smith* (advertised nationally under the headline "Collect Your Share of a Billion Dollar Award") and the

will likely prevent a true market in claims from developing at any time in the foreseeable future, however desirable that may be.[101]

In truth, the present system of court supervision of fee schedules for class actions may be the best at present available, provided that the court takes into account the role of fee-setting in optimising litigation investment. Without appropriate fees, it is simply impossible for the class action to realise its potential in deterring wrongdoing and reducing the overall costs of mass accidents. A true appreciation of the importance of the deterrent function will lead courts to prefer avoidance to compensation, and to err on the side of providing too many incentives to class counsel rather than too few.

Court's thinly disguised disgust with it may have dampened indefinitely enthusiasm for litigation investment.

101. For an excellent discussion of the prospects for investor financing of litigation, particularly aggregate litigation, in Canada see Poonam Puri, "Financing of Litigation by Third-Party Investors: A Share of Justice" (1998) 36 Osgoode Hall L.J. 515 at 565 (arguing for a regulated market in claims, and asserting that "the existing rules and exceptions are fairly incoherent, and that the justifications are ancient and anachronistic and hold little force in contemporary society."). Puri describes the more extensive experience in U.S. with investor financing *ibid.* at 540-41.

CHAPTER ELEVEN

—

Conclusion

The past two decades have seen the most comprehensive rethinking of tort litigation in Canada since the emergence of negligence law itself. This same period has been marked by broad jurisprudential experimentation in Constitutional law driven by a new appreciation of the increasingly global marketplace in which many areas of law – most notably laws involving transjurisdictional business – operate.

The juxtaposition of these two movements – complex litigation and economic "superterritoriality" – leads naturally to the idea that we might want to change the way we approach the systemic and diffuse harms that arise as a matter of course from centralised business activity. Continued fiscal pressure on governments over mounting health care expenses, some of which is the result of tortious harm, supports the idea of fundamental reform.

Throughout this book I have attempted to provide support for the view that this "rethinking" should involve a move towards increased aggregation of mass tort claims, with the exploitation of all the tools – national classes on an opt-out or even a mandatory basis, aggregation across claims through insurance-based judgements, increased counsel fee structures, and so on – that such an ambition implies.

My goal in this book has been to suggest ways in which the class action lawsuit might be used as a vehicle for rationalizing the tort system to address mass accidents. Relying principally on the work of American legal theorists, lawyers and judges, I have attempted to demonstrate ways in which the aggregation of mass tort claims can lead to an efficient system of controlling undesirable risks and the resulting costs. I have also tried to anticipate and refute the objections of those who would reject a more aggressive use of claims aggregation on the basis that such claims are somehow "unfair" or strip litigants of the "rights" they supposedly enjoy under an individualistic tort regime.

Finally, I have attempted to compare the theoretical models of optimal aggregation against the backdrop of complex litigation regimes currently in existence, and have found that the various provinces' systems are sufficiently flexible to accommodate the essential characteristics of the systems proposed.

Nevertheless, substantial challenges confront many of these ideas. The Canadian tort system, even more so than the American (at least in the products liability context), remains wedded to notions of "corrective justice," retribution and fault which linger as vestiges of the emergence of the civil law system as a method of dealing with intentional wrongs. Ideas of "fairness" and "rights" in the civil context focus narrowly on bilateral relationships which bear little resemblance to the systemic problems of large-scale negligence faced today, and on corrective measures that are self-limited to the ex post perspective. As a result, our tort system is too expensive, compensates only marginally if at all, and has at best a limited impact on the level of risk experienced by victims. Class actions have helped, but they could do more. We should re-examine the way we think of individual "rights" and "fairness" in the aggregate context if we wish to exploit the full advantages of class litigation.

There are also sharp economic and social constraints on the scope of reform. It is possible, for instance, that providing every citizen meaningful access to justice to redress all harm from negligence as currently defined would lead, at least initially, to a level of suit that threatened to become unsustainable. In reaction, the system would be faced with adjusting the threshold standard of care to reclassify activity that is currently considered to be unreasonable (when only a fraction of unreasonable harm is addressed through tort) as reasonable. If such a visible relaxation of standards is not feasible (and it may not be – people may generally be loath to consciously relax established standards of safety), then the choice might be between an overall depression of certain business activities on the one hand (as "tort insurance" premiums in dangerous industries price them out of competition for consumer dollars) and the maintenance of something like the current system on the other, where the majority of tortious business harm is externalized through the population in a way that is not immediately visible.

How these essentially political questions are resolved in the mass tort era will not be decided by any single person or set of ideas, and probably will not even be consciously decided at all. I have attempted to make the case for achieving the socially optimal level of acceptable harm through internalisation of business risks because I find persuasive indication that this will be, overall, the most cost-effective way of minimising the social impact of systemic wrongdoing. Class litigation is well placed to play an important role in such an effort.

Table of Cases

Index